# Enhancing Student Learning Outcomes in Higher Education

# Enhancing Student Learning Outcomes in Higher Education

Kayoko Enomoto, Richard Warner and Claus Nygaard (Eds.)
Foreword by Professor Curtis J. Bonk

THE LEARNING IN HIGHER EDUCATION SERIES

First published in 2023 by Libri Publishing

Copyright © Libri Publishing

Authors retain copyright of individual chapters.

The right of Kayoko Enomoto, Richard Warner and Claus Nygaard to be identified as the editors of this work has been asserted in accordance with the Copyright, Designs and Patents Act, 1988.

ISBN 978-1-911451-20-4

All rights reserved. No part of this publication may be reproduced, stored in any retrieval system or transmitted in any form or by any means, electronic, mechanical, photocopying, recording or otherwise, without the prior written permission of the copyright holder for which application should be addressed in the first instance to the publishers. No liability shall be attached to the author, the copyright holder or the publishers for loss or damage of any nature suffered as a result of reliance on the reproduction of any of the contents of this publication or any errors or omissions in its contents.

A CIP catalogue record for this book is available from The British Library

Cover design by Helen Taylor

Design by Carnegie Book Production

Libri Publishing
Brunel House
Volunteer Way
Faringdon
Oxfordshire
SN7 7YR

Tel: +44 (0)845 873 3837

www.libripublishing.co.uk

# Contents

**Foreword**
*Curtis J. Bonk* — vii

**Chapter 1:** How to Enhance Student Learning Outcomes in Higher Education: *The ESLO Model*
*Kayoko Enomoto, Richard Warner and Claus Nygaard* — 1

**Chapter 2:** Physician, Heal Thyself: Enhancing Student Learning Outcomes through Reflective Practice
*John D Branch* — 33

**Chapter 3:** Enablers of Student Learning Outcomes Based on Eight Cases of Second Language Learning and Teaching in Higher Education
*Kayoko Enomoto and Richard Warner* — 57

**Chapter 4:** Developing STEM Doctoral Students' Collaboration Skills as Learning Outcomes
*Janet De Wilde and Elena Forasacco* — 91

**Chapter 5:** Enhancing Student Learning Outcomes through Contextualised Learning Activities
*Claus Nygaard* — 117

**Chapter 6:** Interactive Practices in a Library Makerspace Using Technology to Deliver Positive Student Outcomes
*Henriette van Rensburg* — 147

**Chapter 7:** Enhancing Student Learning through Hidden Motivational Learning Outcomes
*András Margitay-Becht and Udayan Das* — 171

**Chapter 8:** Enhancing Learning Outcomes for STEM Doctoral Students through Perspective Taking in Safe Spaces
*Janet De Wilde and Elena Forasacco* — 205

## Foreword

to travel to Bangkok for an educational conference due primarily to safety reasons. So Ta was wondering if I would be interested in taking his place and give the conference keynote at Ramkhamhaeng University. After more than an hour on the phone with him, I finally agreed. Fortunately, it was the right choice. I was delighted by the hospitality and highly respectful nature of everyone in Bangkok as well as Chiang Mai and Maha Sarakham with whom I encountered during my week in Thailand. I even got to celebrate my birthday there into the wee hours of the night on December 16, 2006.

Fast forward to February 2014, and the anti-government protest movement was growing much louder in the Land of Smiles (BBC News, 2014). Once again, I was warned to be cautious if I was to go there. Demonstrations and military responses had been front-page news the month before. By some reports, on some days, more than 150,000 people had massed in the streets of Bangkok, along with approximately 20,000 security personnel (BC News, 2014). I had also read that eight people had already died in the violence and hundreds more were injured (Olarn et al., 2014). The New York Times even named the university in which I was supposed to speak at, Chulalongkorn University, as one of the key institutions which was divided (Fuller, 2014). To my surprise, some of my Chula friends that I talked to were involved in the protests.

What was evident was that thousands of people were marching, demonstrating, and protesting against the government of Prime Minister Yingluck Shinawatra's as well as the former Prime Minister Thaksin Shinawatra, who was her older brother. The marchers wanted the prime minister replaced for corruption, ineptitude, and an assortment of other reasons, among which included being a puppet of her billionaire older brother (Fuller, 2014). Of course, her attempts at getting an amnesty bill passed for her brother certainly did not help matters (Olarn et al., 2014).

A few weeks earlier, Ta once again assured me not to be scared out of coming to Thailand. I told him that I had survived an incident three years prior in Riyadh, Saudi Arabia after the Second International Conference on e-Learning and Distance Learning in which I thought I was being kidnapped by my taxi driver. Fortunately, the power window still worked after he locked me inside and went out to yell at someone on his mobile phone late that night. Later, it was determined that this crazed taxi driver was only attempting to scare the bejesus out of me, and, thereby, extort some money before delivering me to the airport for my journey home. The extortion part did not work; the other part definitely did. This situation in Thailand sounded mild in comparison.

The email that I received from Ta that day concerned another matter. In that February 14, 2014 email, he told me that: *"Folks at Chula [Chulalongkorn University] would like to ask if they could modify the name of the topic of your talk to 'Education 3.0: This is the Next Generation.' Education 3.0 has been their key performance indicator. Would you be willing to do that?"* I thought for a moment and responded, *"If I could travel to Thailand during a military coup on my previous trip, speaking on Education 3.0 would be a breeze."* In effect, I had survived much worse; for instance, back in the first six months of 2011, I had a series of a dozen straight travels with incidents such as ice in the engines, flat tires on the runways, canceled flights, people being bumped off flights just as we were about to take off, pilots who could not find the airport runway due to fog, pilots who could not land the plane due to extreme weather, and so on. Kidnappings, extortions, military coups, etc., I had seen it all (Bonk, 2011). So, naturally, I said yes when he asked me to return to Bangkok to speak on Education 3.0 during yet another military cue. How difficult or stressful could it be?

Now, I started to scratch my head. *"What is Education 3.0?"*, I asked Ta. He really did not know and said that they wanted me to speak on it anyway. Thailand wanted to push their educational system and economy ahead and this was one of the key mechanisms for doing so. It was for me to figure it out and create a presentation.

What I did know, just like the title of this book implies, is that Education 3.0 was another way of saying that they wanted to enhance student learning outcomes in these fast-changing economic and educational times. Instruction in the 21st century must prepare learners in higher education settings for vastly different careers than they would have experienced in the previous one. I am a product of 20th-century skill training to be an accountant, and, so, therefore, I fully realize that such drill-and-kill curriculum approaches are no longer sufficient. We need to enhance student learning outcomes, not in the coming decade, but today. Right here, right now. Given climate change and the transformation of learning and work settings, we need to immediately enhance, extend, elevate, and transform student learning outcomes (Bonk & Zhu, 2022; Khoo & Bonk, 2022). The world needs problem finders as much as it needs problem solvers. It also requires workers to increasingly have global collaboration skills to negotiate and build ideas as well as the communication skills to present them. People need innovation and idea-generation mindsets as well as analytical skills to properly evaluate novel designs and artifacts.

## The Search for Education 3.0

So, as most people do when asked to present something new halfway around the world, I went on a fact-finding mission. My initial search through the literature yielded minimal results. But I did eventually stumble upon a couple of writings. As I informed Ta less than an hour later, "*There are many definitions of it. Some are more mobile-focused; some are thinking skill-focused; some are K-12 focused; and some are eclectic. I tend to be more eclectic.*" Then I asked him what he thought I might do.

In that same email chain, I mentioned that I had already discovered one highly informative and quite unexpected source related to Education 3.0. It was an intriguing article found in a 2007 issue of *First Monday* describing the emergence of Education 3.0 and its potential utility in Africa. Authored by Derek Keats and J. Phillip Schmidt of the University of the Western Cape in Cape Town, South Africa, that article reflected on three educational generations in higher education (Keats & Schmidt, 2007). Across these three generations, Education 1.0, Education 2.0, and Education 3.0, there is increasing access to information and greater control over the creation and use of it.

In Education 1.0, the teacher or professor is the key source of content knowledge; most of which is covered by traditional copyright. Learners are given tests to assess their understanding of that knowledge. These courses and exams are offered by an accredited institution. As we all know, such teaching to the test system is largely passive. It is a one-way transmission system from an instructor to awaiting students. If technology is involved, it is mainly in the service of the storage of that course content to which the learner clicks his way through. In the early days of e-learning, such a system was referred to as 'shovelware' (Bonk & Dennen, 1999; Oliver & McLoughlin, 1999). Fellow educational psychologists deemed this approach as a continuation of behavioral theories of learning. Such objectively based approaches have been dominant in education for more than a century with prominent psychologists such as Ivan Pavlov, John Watson, B. F. Skinner, and a host of others.

For Keats and Schmidt (2007), Education 2.0 changes the role of the instructor from a deliverer or source of information to that of a guide as well as a source of knowledge. This is a hybrid type of approach which might entail lectures and traditional copyrighted materials one minute and active and collaborative learning approaches using free and open educational resources in the next. There is a gradual sense of increasing ownership over learning on the part of the learner. What one sees in Education 2.0 is a learning approach more in tune with cognitive psychology and notions of a cognitive apprenticeship (Collins et al., 1991).

According to Keats and Schmidt (2007), Education 3.0 dramatically changes the learning situation into one that is highly open, flexible, and filled with learner choice. In an Education 3.0 world, learners are allowed more opportunities for personal expression and creativity as well as the co-creation of content with others. In terms of fostering pure learning innovation, there might be global or cross-institutional collaboration and interaction and the free and open sharing of these products or artifacts such as Wikibooks (Bonk et al., 2009, 2010), podcast shows, and recorded and reusable content in YouTube channels. Any materials produced can be repackaged, remixed, reused, and shared in alternative ways. Importantly, learning becomes increasingly personalized and the results of that learning are recorded in individual as well as group portfolios. In terms of the institution, the learners begin to seriously network with others outside their discipline, institution, country, and region of the world.

It is clear that Keats and Schmidt (2007) as well as Salmon (2019) view an Education 3.0 environment as heavily reliant on digital technologies that provide learners open access to a goldmine of useful learning tools, resources, and activities. And, in it, students find themselves in a more learner-centered age and the focus is on impactful and positive learning outcomes as is described in the assembly of chapters in this particular book. Not just open access by a single person to a single learning resource, but also massive open online course (MOOC) access of tens of thousands of people with their open communities of knowledge sharing and collaboration as well as open peer review of any content generated and shared (Kop et al., 2011; Zhang et al., 2020). The accelerating development and deployment of learning technologies make this vision of the future of education increasingly possible.

From a learning theory standpoint, a learning environment based on Education 3.0 ideas is effectively an eclectic mix of them all—behavioral, social learning, cognitive, constructivist, connectivist, and other theories and approaches. As such, it recognizes that no one theory or perspective is omnipotent. Each has a purpose depending on the situation and prevailing cultural tools, norms, and needs. When properly understood and employed, each of these distinct views of the learner and the learning process can play a vital role in transforming educational settings.

So what does Education 3.0 signal from the point of view of Keats and Schmidt? Principles of openness, creative expression, informal collaboration, and ownership of learning and the learning process are the essential pillars for the powerful learning environments in this century. Learning should be active and learner-centered. Those pillars effectively push the instructor from being the source code for all ideas, actions, and information items to someone who nurtures the access, use, and negotiation of content and ideas.

Keep in mind that this article was published in 2007. Much of what Keats and Schmidt anticipated is more widely possible today. Unfortunately, the all-too-prevalent 'teach to the test' system found in schools around the globe forces educators, educational administrators, politicians, and the general public to severely constrain or limit the time and resources devoted to such learning learner-centered Education 3.0 principles and ideas.

As I continued my search, I was relieved to come across the writings of Jeff Borden, who, at the time, was the Vice President of Instruction and Academic Strategy and Lead of the Center for Online Learning at Pearson. Borden, who became the Chief Innovation Officer at Saint Leo University, argued that Education 3.0 is a complex concept since it revolves around three key elements: (1) cognitive neuroscience, (2) the psychology of learning and cognition, and (3) educational or instructional technology (Borden, 2017a, 2017b). Importantly, Borden also makes a strong case that no one theory or perspective can capture it all.

For Borden, Education 3.0 is only possible when attempts are made to transform education as we know it. From his perspective, framing instruction from the standpoint of Education 3.0 helps to better prepare learners for careers of the future (e.g., data scientists, cloud architects, environmental specialists, artificial intelligence engineers, robot technicians, fitness consultants, etc.). In fact, Borden boldly claims that *"the role of ed tech in Education 3.0 is far more important than anything Hollywood has produced"* (Borden, 2017a). He assumes that the most valuable classrooms of tomorrow will be Web-based, social, digitally rich, mobile, competency-based, social, instantaneous, and complex. Such predictions certainly came to fruition during the recent COVID-19 pandemic (Bonk, 2020).

According to Borden, now Dean of the School of Leadership Studies at Gonzaga University, Education 3.0 requires that educators understand the principles of how people learn and then actually use these principles in their instruction. Deeper forms of learning require an amalgamation of learning perspectives and experiences. Borden insightfully argues that one might synthesize the writings of Ed Catmull (Catmull & Wallace, 2014), Elizabeth Gilbert (2015), and Sir Ken Robinson (2015) on creativity with Tony Wagner (2012) on innovation and Daniel Pink (2009) on motivation as well as Lev Vygotsky (1986) on scaffolded learning and zones of proximal development. Such a synthesis would reveal that the principles underlying the gamification of learning, inquiry learning, flipped classrooms, problem-based learning, the maker movement, collaborative learning, Bloom's taxonomy, multiple intelligences, and much more could be combined into this notion of Education 3.0. Such complexity and conceptual fuzziness likely contribute to the tepid reception Education 3.0 has received to date.

It is a concept that is difficult to pin down. Unfortunately, Borden was not specific about the set of guiding principles that instructors should turn to in creating Education 3.0 learning environments. So, my search for Education 3.0 continued.

## Education 4.0…Say What?

As I searched for material related to Education 3.0, I attempted to detail what a few scholars directly or, more often, indirectly have detailed about it. What I express here is admittedly just a faint starting point. It is not a conclusion. It is a rough amalgamation of ideas from some of the world's best thinkers about education.

## Foreword

These searches through the literature revealed that Education 3.0 entails notions of learner empowerment, autonomy, choice, and self-direction as well as opportunities to take risks and fail and iteratively learn from those mistakes and try again. Learners will be more motivated to make a series of attempts when the task or situation is personally relevant and meaningful. Above all, in such times, there is typically a spirit of exploration and discovery that tends toward self-initiation; or, as Carl Rogers (1969, 1983) argued, a freedom to learn. As with the recent movement toward participatory forms of learning with social media, Education 3.0 also attempts to make the generation and sharing of products and ideas as important as the consumption of them and accountability for them. These are some of the core learning principles my quest had revealed, many of which were also embedded in my TEC-VARIETY framework for fostering online motivation and innovative pedagogical practices (Chen et al., 2023); importantly, that framework now has two free and open books with hundreds of activities outlined to operationalize it (Bonk & Khoo, 2014; Bonk & Zhu, 2022). As far as I could tell, Education 3.0 did not.

For an instructional setting to fully utilize or embrace this suite of learning-related principles, axioms, and approaches, ideas about the emerging roles of the instructor and learner must be better understood and in sync. If one were to compare a course syllabus today with one from the same course two or three decades ago, it would be clear that the present-day instructor orchestrates masses more free and open resources, wherein myriad learner-centered activities are now possible. As a result, she must be comfortable with learning environments that foster greater learner control and autonomy as well as greater ambiguity and creative expression, at least at times, for the intended learning outcomes.

The instructor or trainer must also be adept at fostering collaboration and teaming on projects. Equally important is finding and indexing the resources that her learners will need to successfully navigate such learner-centered projects. These projects might be local, multi-institutional, or cross-national. As part of such efforts, she must be able to train learners in information search, filtering, and synthesis. And when success is not immediately found, the learning environment must not only accept the assorted failures or temporary stumbles but encourage all stakeholders to view them as part of a normal problem-solving process. As I continued to dig deeper, some clarity about Education 3.0 seemed to be emerging.

After my search through the literature, I flew to Bangkok in early March 2014 with confidence to speak about Education 3.0 for the first time. It went better than I expected. Little did I realize that many other organizations around the world would be interested in this topic in the next couple of years resulting in visits to Seoul, Singapore, Shanghai, Madrid, Hong Kong, Helsinki, London, Cambridge, Beijing, and myriad places in the United States. Maybe there was something to this Education 3.0 idea.

Not so fast. Just when I thought that I was finally coming to some kind of understanding of what this concept meant so that I could pass it on to others, something new was tossed into the air and bounced those misconceptions from my brain. What happened? Well, in the fall of 2016, I sent an email to my former student, Dr. Suthiporn Sajjapanroj, who, at that time, was Assistant Dean for Quality Development and International Affairs at Thammasat University. I informed Suthiporn that I would be in Singapore for a problem-based learning conference in March 2017 and that I planned to stop in Thailand on the way. She quickly and enthusiastically helped arrange a tentative schedule.

Among the pending stops were Srinakharinwirot University (SWU) as well as Chulalongkorn University and Thammasat University in Bangkok. *"Would I be interested in speaking about my research on MOOCs and future trends in education?"* Suthiporn politely and calmly asked. "Sure" I replied. Then things got interesting. *"Could you speak about Education 4.0"*, she quickly inserted. *"Wait a minute. What?"* I thought to myself. Was there a typo in their email to me? "Education 4.0?" I replied. Certainly, she was joking. I had difficulty enough coming to grips with Education 3.0. I asked Suthiporn, *"Has the Thai government created effective educational training and teacher professional development programs for Education 3.0?"* Could it be that Thailand was the only country on this planet that had succeeded in mastering Education 3.0 and it was now ready to advance to some higher-order state of learning for the entire country? Not likely.

This created a conundrum for me; would I need to go on another fact-finding mission or would someone in Thailand be able to define Education 4.0 for me? As with before, I received incomplete explanations. Still, I thought why not. I knew that the military was still in charge of the government, but at least I would not be kidnapped, and money would not likely be extorted from me. The conference would be called the Thai National Seminar: Future Trends and Insights for Education 4.0 Revolution and would be held on March 9-10, 2017, at SWU in Bangkok. That fit my schedule perfectly.

So how is 4.0 different from 3.0. It is difficult to tell in Thailand, given the seemingly interchangeable use of Thailand 4.0, Education 4.0, Research 4.0, and so on. At first glance, it appears that Education 4.0 is more reliant on the organization or institution to define, discuss, and ultimately determine. Stated another way, it seems to be whatever a department and entire university targets or intends to target. In fact, the only available information about Education 4.0 at the time came from Chulalongkorn University itself; their initial ideas related to the creation of an 'Innovation Society'. In such a society, the educational organizations and institutions would be innovation producing as opposed to reliant on reception and consumption of that which is created by outside others, be they textbook writers, instructional designers, learning experience designers, or graphic artists.

More recently, others have begun writing about Education 4.0 (Salmon, 2017) operating in parallel with the fourth industrial age brought about by the Internet of Things (IOT), artificial intelligence, and advances in digital technologies for learning. If anything, the use of this term Education 4.0 helps to focus educators and learners on the skills, competencies, and knowledge needed in the coming decade or two. Notably, in the June 18, 2017, issue of The Hindu, it was argued that 20$^{th}$ century methodologies will no longer suffice for 21st century jobs (Krishnan, 2017). In that article, Abhaya Kumar, Founding Executive Chairman of Auronya College in India contended, *"As the barriers between man, machine and technology dissolve, we need to define education for the next generation by keeping intact elements, values, beliefs and insights that makes us 'human.' This is the essence of Education 4.0"* (Krishnan, 2017). Within such a symbiotic relationship, Generative AI becomes a tool to augment and supplement human knowledge (Cao & Dede, 2023; Dede & Lidwell, 2023).

Auronya College might be the first institution of higher learning in the world with the stated goal of designing for Education 4.0 (Auronya College, 2017); well, at least the first such organization outside of Thailand. Auronya founders recognize that the world of work demands transformative and disruptive approaches to education. There is a need to adopt pedagogical practices for smartphone classrooms, virtual and augmented reality technologies, open education, 3D printing and making, robotics, and more. Auronya's Founding Chairperson, Dr. Indira Parekh predicts that the education programs and principles that they have put in place *"will prepare students to understand transformations in the global context…The education of tomorrow, teaching pedagogies and the content of education have to be redesigned"* (Krishnan, 2017). Parekh further contends that, *"What worked yesterday may be sufficient today, but may be inadequate or irrelevant in the future"* (Krishnan, 2017). Of course, for more institutions of higher learning to follow in Auronya's footsteps, everything as we know it — content, pedagogy, ideas about assessment, etc. — needs to be rethought and redesigned.

Global thought leader and author, Peter Fisk (2017), discusses the pending age of Education 4.0. He, too, notes that the rise in global connectivity, artificial intelligence, and interactive forms of media have brought about a new age of work and learning. His predictions for the world of learning include the need for inferencing and data interpretation over calculation skills and mechanical abilities. Additionally, he suggests educational programs and curricula include more opportunities for real world field-based or internship experiences as well as collaborative projects that include timely mentoring. Mentors and instructors will help these teams of learners wade through and grapple with the reams of information coming in from all directions. Fisk also views students as more empowered in this Education 4.0 world. Accordingly, they will work through personally chosen topics and projects using the technologies and resources of their choice. Feedback will be customized and adapted to student capabilities and progress.

Fisk has several more predictions. I mention the ones above to show that these are really not much different from Education 3.0. I am sure that in a decade or two some educational leaders and researchers housed in think tanks will be discussing Education 6.0 or perhaps even Education 10.0. No doubt, such jargon will become increasingly meaningless. In response, in the paragraphs below, I describe a framework that I designed involving 20 new roles for instructors and 20 principles of instruction, under the moniker of Education 20/20. My hope is for it to not just be easier to remember but for it to stand for something of lasting value. If you prefer to call Education 3.0 or Education 4.0 that is fine. I will use these terms interchangeably since that all connote some sort of educational progress or movement forward.

## Instructor Roles in the Education 20/20 World

Back in Education 1.0, the primary role of the instructor was that of a content creator who generates and delivers lesson plans. He was also a court room judge assessing student tasks and examinations, and, of course, a credit manager giving out grades at the end of the course or learning experience.

As we move to Education 20/20, there is a shift of instructor roles with whole new set of 'C' words for the instructor in the 21$^{st}$ century; in fact, there are 20 of them, including instructor as a concierge, cultivator, curator, counselor, consultant, course ambassador, community organizer, care giver, orchestra conductor, camping trip guide, and much more. Those are 10 distinct roles for the instructor today, each opening up educational possibilities for learners, rather than closing them off. When combined, they shift the role of instructor to be more of a guide and assister of learning (Tharp & Gallimore, 1988). I include 10 more roles in Education 20/20 including instructor as a coach, chemist, cook, captain, change catalyst, comedian, course expedition leader, consumer advocate, creator of a cognitive apprenticeship, and, perhaps most importantly, as a co-constructor of meaning. Effective instructors move in and out of these various roles and responsibilities in a fluid and dynamic manner. They are resource providers, thought supporters, and community builders. As indicated, across these roles, instructors guide and mentor the learner and assist in the learning process. In Education 20/20, instructors challenge learners and provide content, tools, and artifacts, often open educational resources (OER), to supplement or aid learners to meet those challenged.

What is clear is that humankind has entered the dawn of a new learning age (Dede & Lidwell, 2023; Salmon, 2019). Learning is changing in dozens of ways (Bonk, 2016). It is more problem-based, inquiry-driven, self-directed, informal, collaborative, global, open, and online (Bonk, 2009). It is also more immersive, visual, digitally rich, hands-on, blended, massive, game-like, direct, mobile, and on demand (Bonk, 2016). In such transformational times, the role of the instructor or teacher is no longer as firmly cemented in the direct instructional and authoritarian past. Today, savvy instructors are at times a coach and cultivator of talents, and, at other times, a concierge, orchestra conductor, or curator finding the golden nuggets from the open educational world and offering learners a diverse and exciting array of learning paths and opportunities. Still other times, the instructor offers timely scaffolds and sage guidance as an on-demand consultant or counsellor. There is also the increasingly vital role of course ambassador who excites the world into an emerging idea, event, or concept, or perhaps an entire course, program, or discipline through a massive open online course or 'MOOC' (Bonk et al., 2015; Zhang et al., 2020). These are exciting, enriching, and, at times, quite daunting times to be an instructor in higher education.

These Education 20/20 roles place greater emphasis on finding and assembling course materials as well as providing experiences as opposed to using prepackaged materials and offering lectures and lessons on them. Education 20/20 instructors organize inspiring events involving a local and often global audience and community, instead of mundanely preparing lecture notes to deliver to a captive, and at times, a seemingly time-incarcerated, audience. As Dede and Lidwell's (2023) review of post pandemic reports from MIT, Stanford, and Harvard makes evident, these three prestigious institutions detect a permanent shift from direct forms of instruction and associated testing and grading to fostering self-directed forms of learning and greater flexibility in the curriculum and grading systems. Dede and Lidwell also astutely mention that these three reports also place a greater focus on such curricula fostering psychological well-being, a sense of comfort and belongingness, and the building of engaging learning communities.

Suffice to say that learning environments in all educational sectors around the world are in a state of flux. There is a struggle to not overteach and overreach. I am reminded of a quote in Parker Palmer's (2007:135) book, *The Courage to Teach: Exploring the Inner Landscape of a Teacher's Life*. As Palmer states,

> "Like most professionals, I was taught to occupy space, not open it: after all, we are the ones who know, so we have an obligation to tell others about it! Even though I have rejected that nonsensical norm, I still feel guilty when I defy it. A not-so-small voice within me insists that if I

*am not filling all the available space with my own knowledge, I am not earning my keep".*

Changing the foundational principles of our learning environments is difficult and requires much experimentation, testing and retesting, and repeated refinement. Famed adult learning expert, Steven Brookfield (1990, 2012, 2013), offers us glimpses of an evolving and dynamic learning environment for adult learners. His writings include eye-opening simulations, real-life case studies, specific examples, metaphors, scenarios, checklists of assumptions, and evaluations. Stepping back from his wide array of structures, tools, and techniques allows one to begin visioning the complexities of teaching; especially as it entails creating structures to foster self-directed learning (Brookfield, 2013).

And so it is today; we educators are faced with a mounting dilemma and series of choices—should we rely on our knowledge banks to inform our learning participants or should we allow them to seek out the knowledge that interests them and is pervasively available without much need of an instructor or learning guide? Palmer warns that there will be much initial resistance to opening spaces for our learners; any change in the teacher-learner relationship or the instructional situation is inherently complex and difficult. Such transitions take time, reflection, and experimentation to successfully navigate to a more open teaching and learning space. He further cautions that, when in transition, there may be some highly unsuccessful and psychologically rough days. We humans make mistakes; especially, when implementing new strategies or approaches. Self-doubt and feelings of guilt may pop up time and again when we are not the most effective or successful. This is normal; such dips and turns will also confront those looking to implement Education 20/20 activities, pedagogical principles, and philosophies.

Similar to what Parker argues, instead of filling space, Education 20/20 instructors open up spaces to learn. There are many principles of Education 20/20 which have been directly and indirectly stated above. I have been researching and writing about the following 20 key principles for more than a decade. Unfortunately, I do not have space here to fully describe each one.

*Key Learning Principles of in the 20/20 World*

1. The Principle of Flexibility
2. The Principle of Convenience
3. The Principle of Collegiality
4. The Principle of Cheerfulness and Optimism
5. The Principle of High Expectations
6. The Principle of Choice and Options
7. The Principle of Empowerment and Autonomy
8. The Principle of Support and Feedback
9. The Principle of Spontaneity
10. The Principle of Organization
11. The Principle of Sharing
12. The Principle of Nontraditional Learning
13. The Principle of Passion and Inspiration.
14. The Principle of Relevance and Meaningfulness.
15. The Principle of Trial and Error (i.e., it is ok to fail)
16. The Principle of Expanded Resources
17. The Principle of Human Connectedness
18. The Principle of Cognitive Apprenticeship
19. The Principle of Purpose and Vision
20. The Principle of Openness

The above learning principles can be modified as situations dictate, and cultural norms and values change. However, this list provides a base for educators to discuss their instructional intentions and designs for innovative learning environments. The Education 20/20 framework offers a safe harbor or base from which those discussions can unfold. These discussions might take place at strategic planning meetings for an entire institution or just as easily in an introductory course in a teacher education program. As base level, Education 20/20 is a means for a researcher to describe an innovative classroom or school. More than a talking point with parents, principals, or professionals of practice, Education 20/20 is a way of life for any educator, trainer, or learning technologist. It is what you do to provoke to life new learning skills and competencies.

Whatever the purpose, Education 20/20 is a vision of the possible. It is a guiding philosophy or framework to ground one's instructional decision making and actions. Without a doubt, there have been many attempts to research and describe the next steps for education. There is much overlap in what progressive educators and scholars are finding and advocating. Now is the time to find your place in this movement. Now is the time for you to reflect on your instructional environments and approaches and make some adjustments. It is time to make your Education 20/20 visions come to fruition.

True pioneers will not only engage in conversations with others about Education 20/20 and Education 3.0 and 4.0 that help establish new teaching and learning benchmarks but they will find unique ways to soar far beyond them. They will fashion unique learning environments that, as the chapters of this book detail, enhance student learning outcomes. Naturally, their constant movement toward unchartered educational ends brings with it healthy doses of excitement, trepidation, curiosity, fulfillment, and learning success.

## No Going Back

There is no going back, however. Some of you may recall the 1980s, when cable TV and VCRs put content consumption in the hands of the consumer to determine when, where, what, and even how one watched television programs. Two or three decades later, people were producing and sharing such content in YouTube, TikTok, WeChat, Vimeo, Facebook, LinkedIn, and Instagram. The same trends are occurring in education. The last century as well as the nine preceding it were based on learner consumption of limited content. Now the learning faucets are turned on with free and open podcasts of that content as well open textbooks, digital books, infographics, video primers and demonstrations, online test preparation banks, simulations and animations enhanced by augmented or virtual reality, and online communities to share and discuss that content. That is just a short list of what is available to learn from. And that was prior to the recent emergence of Generative AI (Cao & Dede, 2023; Dede & Lidwell, 2023; Huang et al., 2023), which has quickly impacted many disciplines; especially, online language learning (Gally, 2022; Kohnke et al., 2023; Li et al, 2023a, 2023b). As with cable TV several decades ago, the learner of today has more control over the content scheduling and programming. More choice. More on-demand and informal avenues to learning.

There are endless channels today from which to learn. As this happens, new questions about student learning outcomes are front and center. For instance, are informal learning outcomes as important and powerful as formal ones? Who assesses or accounts for those informal and self-directed forms of learning. How does one represent such informal and nontraditional learning events and results on a resume or CV? Much is still to be determined.

The thunderstorms of change are no longer out on the distant learning horizon to impact us at some point in a far future forecast. Look up, they have already arrived in full force. There are vast quantities of resources and tools to draw upon as an instructor; countless channels for one's educational programming. Such transitionary educational times beg for rethinking every aspect of education. Clearly, the role of the instructor as well as that of the instructional assistant, related support personnel, and instructional design staff are all now drenched in storms of change. These new roles are apparent in books like this one. To that end, I hope that this foreword and this book might inspire reflection and experimentation that eventually results in wholly new forms of instruction. Learners of Education 20/20 deserve nothing less.

As I write this in the fall of 2023, I am waiting for my mobile phone to ring and someone on the other end asking me to travel to Thailand and speak on Education 5.0 or Education 6.0. This time I would have a simple answer; namely to forget about flying me there, and, instead, buy copies of this book and many others previously mentioned and discuss and debate them. Find ways to enhance student learning outcomes here in the early reaches of the 21st century; and when you do, you will have realized Education 5.0 and beyond. Those exploring this new learning age realize that effective and successful learning now entails learner empowerment, autonomy, choice, freedom, flexibility, meaningfulness, collaboration, engagement, interactivity, and so much more.

Dipping into the pages of this book in any order will serve to help you ponder where the ESLO model has begun to make a significant impact in different educational settings and learning environments. Like my Education 20/20 model, ESLO highlights the dramatically changing roles and responsibilities for instructors and learners here in the third decade of the 21$^{st}$ century. Perhaps this book will also inspire the rethinking or redesign or your own curricula and educational programs as well as usher in the emergence of new learning programs. As Parker Palmer argued, let's open up spaces for learning rather than being perpetually transfixed on filling them in.

Professor Curtis J. Bonk<br>Indiana University

## Bibliography

Auronya College (2017, May 17). Sridhar Sunkad: Vision of Education 4.0. *YouTube*. https://www.youtube.com/watch?v=FBCdoIlyUxo

BBC News (2014, March 29). Thailand protests: Anti-government march in Bangkok. *BBC News*. http://www.bbc.com/news/world-asia-26798407

Bonk, C. J. (2009). *The world is open: How Web technology is revolutionizing education*. Jossey-Bass.

Bonk, C. J. (2011, June 20). Who wants to fly with TravelinEdMan?: A dozen consecutive examples of why not… *TravelinEdMan*. http://travelinedman.blogspot.com/2011/06/who-wants-to-fly-with-travelinedman.html

Bonk, C. J. (2016). What is the state of e-learning?: Reflections on 30 ways learning is changing. *Journal of Open, Flexible and Distance Learning, 20*(2), 6-20. http://jofdl.nz/index.php/JOFDL/article/viewFile/300/205

Bonk, C. J. (2020). Pandemic ponderings, 30 years to today: Synchronous signals, saviors, or survivors? *Distance Education, 41*(4), 589-599. https://doi.org/10.1080/01587919.2020.1821610

Bonk, C. J., & Dennen, V. P. (1999). Teaching on the Web: With a little help from my pedagogical friends. *Journal of Computing in Higher Education, 11*(1), 3-28.

Bonk, C. J., & Khoo, E. (2014). *Adding Some TEC-VARIETY: 100+ activities for motivating and retaining learners online*. OpenWorldBooks.com and Amazon CreateSpace. http://tec-variety.com/; DOI 10.59668/698

Bonk, C. J., Lee, M. M., Kim, N., & Lin, M.-F. (2009, December). The tensions of transformation in three cross-institutional wikibook projects. *The Internet and Higher Education, 12*(3-4), 126-135.

Bonk, C. J., Lee, M. M., Kim, N., & Lin, M.-F. (2010). Wikibook transformations and disruptions: Looking back twenty years to today. In H. H. Yang, & S. C-Y. Yuen (Eds.), *Collective intelligence and e-learning 2.0: Implications of Web-Based communities and networking* (pp. 127-146). Information Science Reference.

Bonk, C. J., Lee, M. M., Reeves, T. C., & Reynolds, T. H. (Eds.). (2015). *MOOCs and open education around the world*. Routledge. DOI: https://doi.org/10.4324/9781315751108

Bonk, C. J., & Zhu, M. (Eds.). (2022). *Transformative teaching around the world: Stories of cultural impact, technology integration, and innovative pedagogy*. Routledge. https://doi.org/10.4324/9781003213840

Borden, J. (2013, September). Education 3.0: Embracing Technology to 'Jump the Curve'. *Wired*. https://www.wired.com/insights/2013/09/education-3-0-embracing-technology-to-jump-the-curve/

Borden, J. (2013, October). Education 3.0: 'Learning psychology' – Embracing better ways to teach. *Wired*. (October 2013). https://www.wired.com/insights/2013/10/education-3-0-learning-psychology-embracing-better-ways-to-teach/

Brookfield, S. D. (1990). *The skillful teacher*. Jossey-Bass.

Brookfield, S. D. (2012). *Teaching for critical thinking: Tools and techniques to help students question their assumptions*. Jossey-Bass.

Brookfield, S. D. (2013). *Powerful techniques for teaching adults*. Jossey-Bass.

Cao, L., & Dede, C. (2023). *Navigating a world of Generative AI: Suggestions for educators*. The Next Level Lab at Harvard Graduate School of Education. President and Fellows of Harvard College: Cambridge, MA. https://bpb-us-e1.wpmucdn.com/websites.harvard.edu/dist/a/108/files/2023/08/Cao_Dede_final_8.4.23.pdf

Catmull, E., & Wallace, A., (2014). *Creativity, Inc.: Overcoming unseen forces that stand in the way of true inspiration*. Random House.

Chen, W., Bonk, C. J., & Sanders, J. (2023). Applying TEC-VARIETY to motivate students for online learning success. *Journal of Continuing Education in the Health Professions* (JCEHP). DOI: 10.1097/CEH.0000000000000495. Available: https://tinyurl.com/bdz3absz

Collins, A., Brown, J. S., & Holum, A. (1991). Cognitive apprenticeship: Making thinking visible. *American Educator.* http://citeseerx.ist.psu.edu/viewdoc/download?doi=10.1.1.124.8616&rep=rep1&type=pdf

Dede, C., & Lidwell, W. (2023). Developing a next-generation model for massive digital learning. *Education Sciences* 13, no. 8: 845. https://doi.org/10.3390/educsci13080845

Fisk, P. (2017, July 31). Education 4.0...the future of learning will be dramatically different. *Gamechanger.* http://www.thegeniusworks.com/2017/01/future-education-young-everyone-taught-together/

Fuller, T. (2014, January 2) Anti-government protesters try to shut down Bangkok. *The New York Times.* https://www.nytimes.com/2014/01/13/world/asia/protests-thailand.html

Gally, T. (2022, December 7). *Using ChatGPT for language learning.* YouTube. https://www.youtube.com/watch?v=l41hZLRsDos&t=9s

Gilbert, E. (2015). *Big magic: Creative living beyond fear.* Riverhead Books.

Huang, X., Zou, D., Cheng, G., Chen, X., & Xie, H. (2023). Trends, research issues and applications of artificial intelligence in language education. *Educational Technology & Society,* 26(1), 112-131. https://doi.org/10.30191/ETS.202301_26(1).0009

Keats, D, & Schmidt, J. P. (2007, March). The genesis and emergence of Education 3.0 in higher education and its potential for Africa, *First Monday* 12, no. 3-5, http://journals.uic.edu/ojs/index.php/fm/article/view/1625/1540

Khoo, E., & Bonk, C. J. (2022). *Motivating and supporting online learners.* Burnaby, BC, Canada. Commonwealth of Learning. http://hdl.handle.net/11599/4481

Kohnke, L., Moorhouse, B. L., & Zou, D. (2023). ChatGPT for language teaching and learning. *RELC Journal,* 00336882231162868:

Kop, R., Fournier, H., & Mak, J. S. F. (2011, November). A pedagogy of abundance or a pedagogy to support human beings? Participant support on massive open online courses. *International Review of Research on Open and Distance Learning,* 12(7). Retrieved from http://www.irrodl.org/index.php/irrodl/article/view/1041/2025

Krishnan, M. S. (2017, June 17). Education 4.0 is here, *The Hindu.* http://www.thehindu.com/education/education-40-is-here/article19093549.ece

Li, B., Bonk, C. J., & Kou, X. (2023). Exploring the multilingual applications of ChatGPT: Uncovering language learning affordances in YouTuber videos. *International Journal of Computer-Assisted Language Learning and Teaching (IJCALLT),* 13(1), 1-22. http://doi.org/10.4018/IJCALLT.326135

Li, B., Kou, X., & Bonk, C. J. (2023). Embracing the disrupted language teaching and learning field: Analyzing YouTube content creation related to ChatGPT. *Languages, 8*, 197. https://doi.org/10.3390/languages8030197

Olarn K., Mohsin, S., & Mullen, J. (2014, January 16). Pockets of violence amid Thai anti-government protests in Bangkok. CNN. http://www.cnn.com/2014/01/14/world/asia/thailand-protests/index.html

Oliver, R., & McLoughlin, C. (1999). Curriculum and learning-resources issues arising from the use of web-based course support systems. *International Journal of Educational Telecommunications, 5*(4), 419-436.

Palmer, P. J. (2007). *The courage to teach: Exploring the inner landscape of a teacher's life.* Jossey-Bass.

Pink, D. H. (2009). *Drive: The surprising truth about what motivates us.* Riverhead Books.

Robinson, K. (2015). *Creative schools: The grassroots revolution that's transforming education.* Viking.

Rogers, C. R. (1969). *Freedom to learn: A view of what education might become.* Charles Merrill.

Rogers, C. R. (1983). *Freedom to learn for the 80s.* Charles E. Merrill Publishing Company.

Salmon, G. (2019, July 18). May 4 be with you: Creating Education 4.0. *Journal of Learning for Development, 6*(2), https://jl4d.org/index.php/ejl4d/article/view/352/404

Tharp, R. G., & Gallimore, R. (1988). *Rousing minds to life: Teaching, learning, and schooling in social context.* Cambridge University Press.

Vygotsky, L. (1986). *Thought and language* (rev. ed.). The MIT Press.

Wagner, T., (2012). *Creating innovators: The making of young people who will change the world.* Scribner.

Zhang, K., Bonk, C. J., Reeves, T. C., & Reynolds, T. H. (Eds.). (2020). *MOOCs and open education in the Global South: Challenges, successes, and opportunities.* Routledge. DOI: https://doi.org/10.4324/9780429398919

Chapter 1

# How to Enhance Student Learning Outcomes in Higher Education: *The ESLO Model*

Kayoko Enomoto, Richard Warner and Claus Nygaard

## Introduction

As university educators, we have always been passionate about empowering our students to reach their full potential and succeed academically and professionally. To us, learning outcomes are an essential component of higher education that can help students realise their highest capabilities and prepare them for their future careers. Over the last three decades, we have witnessed the transformative power of incorporating learning outcomes into our teaching practice.

Yet, as to what constitutes a learning outcome, there is no one universally accepted definition. Indeed, the rich learning outcome-related literature is characterised by robust debate — to which we will return later. Learning outcomes in higher education have been defined in many ways, from the almost tongue-in-cheek: *"[learning] outcomes describe what the student actually achieves, as opposed to what the institution intends to teach"* (Allan 1996, in Nusche, 2008:7) to something broader and institutionally focused: *"learning outcomes… should be seen as a device for teaching, learning and assessment but also as a governance and management tool, since their introduction entails a move to a results orientation"* (Casperson & Frølich, 2017:3). Our definition of learning outcomes, however, has student-centredness as a focus. That is, with learning outcomes, we mean the knowledge, understanding, and skills students are expected to attain following a specific learning experience (Biggs & Tang, 2011).

Working with learning outcomes has allowed us to provide a clear and measurable framework for designing, delivering, and assessing our courses and communicating our expectations to students. By focusing on learning outcomes, we have seen that we can enhance the quality and relevance of our teaching practices and contribute to the success of our students. Through our collective experiences as university educators at five universities (University of Edinburgh, Scotland; University of Adelaide, Australia; Copenhagen Business School, Denmark; Aarhus University, Denmark; and Stockholm School of Economics, Latvia), we have seen first-hand how, by focusing on learning outcomes, we have been able to improve the quality and relevance of our educational practices, leading to the success of our students. We explain that in more detail in our chapters elsewhere in this book (Enomoto & Warner, 2023 in this book; Nygaard, 2023 in this book).

In this introductory chapter to the book, *Enhancing Student Learning Outcomes in Higher Education*, we have joined forces to provide fellow university educators with a comprehensive and practical guide to enhancing students' learning outcomes in higher education. We present a central model — ESLO (Enhancing Student Learning Outcomes) that can guide you to transform your teaching approach, shifting focus away from an input-based curriculum towards an output-based learning experience. As you read through the book, you will find that each subsequent chapter focuses on various aspects of ESLO, providing diverse perspectives and strategies to help you refine your educational practices to enhance student learning outcomes. At the end of this chapter, we will briefly introduce all the chapters in the book. As you embark on this journey with us, we hope that our experiences and the experiences of the authors in the following chapters will inspire you and provide you with the essential tools to thrive in your pursuit of enhancing your students' learning outcomes.

## Chapter overview and key takeaways

Section 1 interrogates understandings of learning outcomes by discussing types, issues and values of learning outcomes in higher education contexts. In Section 2, we introduce our ESLO model, explaining how the model theoretically relates to and is underpinned by certain conceptual paradigms. Following the introduction of the ESLO as a theoretical model, we then describe each of the three phases of the ESLO model: designing, doing and diagnosing phases. In Section 3, we give a brief precis of each chapter contained in this book.

Reading this chapter, you will gain an understanding of:
1. Types, issues and values of learning outcomes informed by relevant literature;
2. The three-phased ESLO model and its theoretical underpinnings; and
3. What and how each of the remaining 14 chapters contributes to this book.

## Section 1: Understanding learning outcomes

To optimise student learning outcomes, it is essential to grasp what learning outcomes entail and how they align with our teaching activities and assessment methods. As we alluded to, in the above introduction, our student-centred learning outcomes refer to the knowledge, understanding, and skills students are expected to acquire as the result of a specific learning experience (Biggs & Tang, 2011). These outcomes provide a clear structure for designing courses and assessments and communicating expectations to students and other stakeholders (Suskie, 2018). Learning outcomes can be categorised based on various levels of cognitive complexity, such as Bloom's taxonomy (Bloom et al., 1956), and can be utilised and adapted to specific course learning activities and assessment tasks. By defining well-designed learning outcomes, we can assist our students in achieving more profound learning and higher-order thinking skills. We have observed that learning outcomes enable students to navigate their learning journey efficiently by focusing on their specific learning goals that closely align with course/program expectations. Moreover, by providing our students with well-designed learning outcomes, we can not only maximise students' success in achieving their learning goals, but also increase and enrich their career aspirations; they can effectively communicate their knowledge and skills to potential employers (Zimmerman, 2002; Jenkins, 2004), utilising the framework of course/program learning outcomes.

## Types of learning outcomes

Learning outcomes serve as a roadmap with clear signposts for both teachers and students by clarifying the goals of the learning process and describing the expected abilities and knowledge that students should acquire upon successful completion of a course/program (Biggs & Tang, 2011; Suskie, 2018). They have often been categorised into three types based on their focus (Simpson, 1972; Krathwohl et al., 1964; Anderson & Krathwohl, 2001):

1. Cognitive outcomes: These learning outcomes emphasise students' intellectual skills, such as knowledge acquisition, critical thinking, problem-solving, and decision-making. For example, a cognitive learning outcome could be:
   o 'Students can analyse the historical and political contexts of events in international relations'.

2. Affective outcomes: These learning outcomes focus on students' emotions, values, and attitudes. Affective outcomes might include statements such as:
   o 'Students will appreciate the diversity of cultural perspectives'.

3. Psychomotor outcomes: These learning outcomes refer to physical and motor skills, such as technical skills in a laboratory, artistic performance, or sports abilities. An example of a psychomotor outcome would be:
   o 'Students can perform basic laboratory techniques safely and accurately'.

With this understanding, we can now delve into the complexities and issues surrounding these learning outcomes in the subsequent section.

## Issues around learning outcomes

To develop learning outcomes, it is crucial that these outcomes are concise, clear, and measurable (Biggs & Tang, 2011). When learning outcomes are appropriately set and communicated, students can then use them as guides to focus their study efforts and self-assess their progress throughout the course (Nicol & Macfarlane-Dick, 2006). Yet, the literature surrounding both the types and values of learning outcomes is one of great debate, which we do need to touch upon briefly. Learning outcomes themselves may be steered — in the increasingly managerial, business-model-driven landscape of higher education that many of us now work within — towards partially functioning so as to fit a systemic 'tick box' role, as opposed to being solely an educational tool. Havnes and Prøitz (2016:213) express this significant issue thus: *"...as the policy perspective is applied to transforming education... conceptualisations of learning outcomes, in the context of educational practice, may be pushed to align with the policy purposes of learning outcomes".* Indeed, as Hadjianastasis (2017) points out, learning outcomes are also positioned at the heart of an intense nationwide push, for both quality assurance and accountability, in organisations such as the UK Quality Assurance Agency and the Australian Tertiary Education Quality Standards Agency, where metrics control processes. This 'cart before the horse' (product over process) approach appears to be diametrically opposite to constructivist approaches to learning (Biggs, 1996), whereby learning outcomes function as student learning support through the process of constructive alignment (Hadjianastasis, 2017). For example, Eisner (1979), in support of the process-orientated learning outcomes, sees learning outcomes as the result of, and not necessarily the aim of, some type of pedagogical engagement. Likewise, Hussey and Smith (2003; 2008) who question whether learning outcomes can be exactly specified or utilised for auditing purposes, firmly prioritises the educational dimension of learning outcomes.

Thus, whilst the debate on what learning outcomes actually represent remains vigorous and unresolved, we, as university educators, need to push forward to generate learning outcomes that satisfy a range of different stakeholders concerned, including students, academic teaching staff, curriculum designers and regulatory organisations. The problem is, as Hadjianastasis (2017:2263) succinctly states: *"How can learning outcomes be precise enough to be measurable on the one hand but also flexible enough to allow the student to construct their own knowledge, to explore, discover, grapple with, dismiss and adopt – and ultimately create – knowledge?"* Yet, as we have seen, higher education sectors, national and international, are increasingly ridden with (and perhaps, hidebound by) quality-assurance and accreditation concerns, which involve learning outcomes and the assessments thereof.

Perhaps, the ideals of quality enhancement, posited by Nygaard et al. (2013), can point us in an appropriate direction in learning outcome development, with their focus on quality enhancement. Quality enhancement, whilst situated at an institutional point of reference, does involve the institution anchoring safeguards around the educational quality of learning outcomes. Crucially, quality enhancement shifts the focus from compliance (Nygaard et al., 2013) towards enhancing the institution-specific learning environment (including learning outcomes); giving voice and power to academic teaching staff, curriculum designers and students, amongst other institutional stakeholders. The resultant learning outcomes are then pertinent to the particular higher education institution, rather than being systemically and quality-assurance driven; this *"opens the door for approaches that value and effective practices and disseminate these where appropriate"* (Nygaard et al., 2013:5).

Such a quality enhancement perspective is what we are building upon in this book, where we showcase 14 examples of student-centred innovation in the learning outcome space. We trust that the examples presented, which follow our own ESLO model (to be presented in Section 2), indicate that enhancing vital and relevant learning outcomes, from a 'bottom up' perspective, can still operate and flourish in a wide range of contemporary higher education contexts.

## *Value of learning outcomes — why they are essential to students*

It is our observation, that specifying learning outcomes can help students understand the expectations of a course and guide their learning process. We have seen that through our teaching practices, as we report elsewhere in this book (Enomoto & Warner, 2023; Nygaard, 2023) and have written about in previous books (Enomoto & Warner, 2022; Nygaard et al., 2013; Nygaard et al., 2009). Navigating the complex world of educational experiences can be daunting for students; this journey can become even more challenging without clearly understanding the expected learning outcomes. Learning outcomes function as signposts illuminating the path ahead, giving students a sense of direction and purpose in their academic pursuits (Biggs & Tang, 2011). However, when these guiding lights are not included or obscured, students may be 'adrift in a sea of uncertainty', hindering their progress and diminishing their motivation to learn (Nicol & MacFarlane-Dick, 2006).

Thus, students can use the intended learning outcomes to monitor their progress, reflect on their understanding, and identify areas where they may need additional support or resources (Zimmerman, 2002). Learning outcomes also help students communicate their knowledge and skills to potential employers or graduate programs by providing a clear framework for their learning achievements (Jenkins, 2004). Students unaware of the intended learning outcomes may need help connecting the dots between the imparted knowledge, personal goals, and real-world applications (Ambrose et al., 2010). Moreover, without well-delineated learning outcomes, students may become overwhelmed by many topics, failing to discern core concepts from peripheral details (Wiggins & McTighe, 2005). This lack of clarity can hinder their ability to focus on the course material's most salient aspects or develop a holistic understanding of the subject matter (Hattie & Donoghue, 2016).

It is important to note that the absence of clear learning outcomes can adversely affect students' ability to manage their time and effort effectively. Without specific benchmarks to measure their progress, students may deviate excessive energy to unimportant concepts, while neglecting more critical aspects of their curriculum (Pintrich, 2004). This misalignment can decrease performance and negatively impact their performance and final grades (Biggs, 2003). Moreover, in cases where students, without learning outcomes to serve as a guide, struggle to understand the relevance, value, or purpose of their education, they may experience disengagement and a decreased sense of responsibility for their learning (Jenkins, 2004; Kuh et al., 2006). This can create an environment that deprives them of opportunities for growth, reflection and a deeper understanding of their learning processes (Zull, 2004).

When students lack a clear understanding of intended learning outcomes, their learning journey can be plagued with uncertainty and frustration. As a result, it can undermine their intrinsic motivation and self-regulation (Zimmerman, 2002). In addition, when learning outcomes are not explicitly communicated or understood, the assessment process can become a source of anxiety and confusion for students (Suskie, 2018). They may need help determining what aspects of their learning will be evaluated and may need help deciding how to best prepare for examinations or other assessment forms. This can lead to unnecessary stress and a diminished ability to perform optimally during assessments, ultimately detracting from their learning experience (Zeidner & Saklofske, 1996).

Therefore, it is imperative to provide students with clear learning outcomes and expectations for their course/program. This enables them to prioritise their efforts and take ownership of their learning experience, leading to a more rewarding learning journey and better outcomes. Therefore, it is crucial for educators to communicate learning outcomes effectively and support students in comprehending the goals of their educational pursuits (Ewell, 2001). By doing so, educators can help students navigate their learning journey with purpose and confidence, ultimately enabling their growth and success in achieving their full potential.

In this section, we introduced our definition of and understanding of what we mean by learning outcomes. We discussed learning outcomes in terms of types, we examined contemporary issues around learning outcomes and looked at their value — particularly the benefits of understanding learning outcomes — through examining the related literature. Having done so, we now move forward to present our ESLO model.

## Section 2: The ESLO model

This model aims to guide you in transforming your teaching approach, transitioning from an input-based curriculum to an output-based learning experience. Nygaard (2023 in this book) thoroughly debates the need to transform HE from input-based to output-based; therefore, we will not repeat it here. Before presenting the ESLO model, though, we will briefly expand upon the conceptual paradigms of constructive alignment (Biggs, 1996, 2003) and output-based education (Biggs & Tang, 2011). This is because the ESLO model draws heavily on these two conceptual paradigms as its theoretical underpinnings.

### *Paradigms of constructive alignment and output-based education*

Constructive alignment emphasises the significance of aligning teaching activities and assessment tasks to ensure students achieve the desired learning outcomes. This approach is based on the understanding that effective teaching and learning occur when there is a clear alignment between intended learning outcomes (ILOs), teaching and learning activities (TLAs), and assessment tasks (ATs) (Biggs, 1996). This alignment guarantees that students know what they are expected to learn, how they will learn, and how their learning will be assessed. Consequently, constructive alignment supports the development of deep learning strategies, as opposed to surface learning strategies which are often associated with rote memorisation and lack of understanding (Biggs, 1996, 2003). Constructive alignment is a critical component in successfully implementing output-based education (Biggs & Tang, 2011).

By ensuring that the ILOs align closely with TLAs and ATs, constructive alignment contributes to creating an effective learning environment — where students are more likely to achieve the desired learning 'outputs' (Biggs, 2003). Past research has shown that constructive alignment leads to improved student learning and performance. For instance, a study by Baeten et al. (2013) revealed that students attained higher levels of understanding when a curriculum was designed following these principles and could more effectively apply their knowledge in new situations. Likewise, Gijbels et al. (2008) found that students in an output-based learning environment, where this alignment was present, demonstrated higher levels of deeper learning strategies and improved performance. Moreover, Boud and Falchikov's research (2006) suggests that when ATs closely align with the ILOs, students engage in deep learning strategies and show higher competence.

Indeed, much research has examined the implementation, effectiveness, and challenges of output-based education, resulting in invaluable insights into potential benefits and areas for improvement. A key aspect of output-based education is aligning the curriculum, instruction, and assessment with the ILOs. Research on constructive alignment by Biggs (2003) underscores the importance of coherence between ILOs, TLAs, and ATs in promoting deep learning strategies and enhancing student performance. Similarly, studies by Baeten et al. (2013) and Gijbels et al. (2008) demonstrate that when a curriculum is designed to follow the principles of constructive alignment, within an output-based education paradigm, students achieve higher levels of understanding and are more adept at applying their knowledge in new situations.

In addition, research on output-based education has also explored its impact on student motivation and engagement. This impact is exemplified in a study by Kember et al. (2008) who revealed that an output-based approach to teaching heightened students' intrinsic motivation and fostered a deep learning approach. In a similar vein, Langan et al. (2015) found that implementing output-based learning experience in higher education, improved student satisfaction and engagement. However, to do so effectively demands clearly defining the knowledge, skills, and competencies that students should acquire by the end of a learning experience.

Consequently, the implementation of output-based education also has its challenges. Lizzio et al. (2002) raised concerns about the potential for output-based education to narrow the curriculum, focus on easily measurable outcomes, and overemphasise assessment at the expense of meaningful learning experiences. Furthermore, Fullan's research (2007) suggests the need for comprehensive change management strategies when implementing output-based education, as it requires significant shifts in institutional culture, teaching practices, and assessment processes. Fullan's findings (2007) 'piggyback' on problems raised in the afore-mentioned work of Hadjianastasis (2017). To reiterate, the latter outlined tensions between learning outcome measurability and allowing sufficient flexibility for students' ability to fashion their own knowledge — through their explorations, interactions and adoptions — eventually creating knowledge. Output-based education could be seen as prioritising measurability over the flexibility to allow for student knowledge development. Whatever the case, what is more certain is that both constructive alignment and output-based education emphasise the importance of clearly defined/designed learning outcomes and aligning instruction and assessment with those outcomes.

In summary, output-based education focuses on the processes of learning, particularly the activities, tasks, and efforts that students engage in during their learning journey. It emphasises the 'outputs' or the products of the learning process, such as assignments, projects, presentations, and portfolios. Therefore, in the output-based paradigm, the emphasis is on completing tasks and demonstrating knowledge and skills through various assignments and assessments (Biggs & Tang, 2011). Here, drawing on the relevant literature (e.g. Entwistle, 2009; Entwistle & Ramsden, 2015; Kember et al., 2008; Gijbels et al., 2008; Baeten et al., 2013), for the benefit of contrasting comparisons, we summarise the key distinctions between the input-based and output-based educational paradigms in Table 1.

|  | Input-based education | Output-based education |
| --- | --- | --- |
| Focus | On the content and materials provided to students, following predetermined curriculum, emphasising the delivery of information and knowledge | On the activities and tasks completed by students during the learning process through the practical application of knowledge and skills |
| Assessment | Often centres around testing students' knowledge and comprehension of the content, typically through exams, tests and quizzes | Based on the completion of tasks, assignments, and activities that are geared towards evaluating students' ability to apply their knowledge and skills in authentic, real-world scenarios, such as projects, presentations, and performance/simulation-based assessments |
| Emphasis | On the acquisition of information and the coverage of content and success is often measured by the extent to which students absorb the provided material | On the process of learning and the effort put into completing tasks through the practical application and demonstration of knowledge and skills |

*Table 1: A summary of input-based education and output-based education.*

Returning to our ESLO model and its relationship to the above-discussed conceptual paradigms, the ESLO model draws on both constructive alignment and output-based learning experience. Firstly, as Figure 1 (below) shows, within the ESLO model, the first phase — the 'designing' learning outcomes phase — is completed; guided by constructive alignment (Biggs, 1996). To design and define learning outcomes, this first phase entails aligning TLAs and ATs to ensure students achieve the ILOs. Then, the second phase — the 'doing' phase — involves bringing about output-based learning experience and processes in facilitating TLAs within the output-based paradigm. Finally, in the third phase, the ESLO model takes an output-based perspective of learning outcomes.

This is because the model focuses on the specific learning outcomes that students should achieve after completing tasks through the practical application and demonstration of knowledge and skills. This phase emphasises the development of well-defined skills, competencies and attributes by the end of a particular learning experience. Such development should be evaluated based on evidence of those skills, competencies and attributes, and demonstrated by projects, presentations, or performance/simulation-based assessments. Thus, the third phase of the ESLO model — the 'diagnosing' phase — is centred on determining whether students have met the pre-defined/pre-designed learning outcomes.

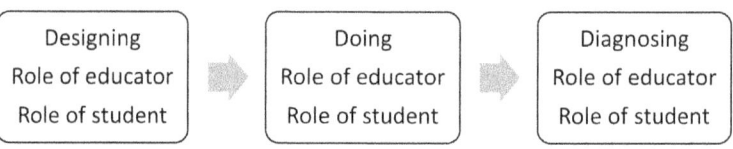

*Figure 1: The ESLO model and its three phases: designing, doing, diagnosing.*

As we stated previously, based on our experiences with curriculum development (Nygaard & Andersen, 2005; Nygaard et al, 2008; Enomoto & Warner, 2018; Warner & Enomoto, 2015), we have developed the ESLO model, which can help educators consciously and purposefully 1) design learning outcomes, 2) facilitate learning activities, and 3) diagnose students learning outcomes. In Table 2 below, we describe the role of educators and students in each of these three phases.

|  | Role of educator | Role of student |
|---|---|---|
| 1) Designing | - Begin by clearly designing/defining the ILOs, encompassing the knowledge, skills, and competencies students should attain by the end of a learning experience<br>- Ensure coherence between the ILOs and TLAs and assessment methods to promote deep learning strategies<br>- Align the curriculum, instruction, and assessment with the ILOs, adhering to constructive alignment and output-based principles | Students generally do not participate directly in the design phase, but their needs, learning preferences, and objectives should be considered while designing the ILOs, designing TLAs, and developing assessment methods<br>- By considering students' prior knowledge, skills, and diverse backgrounds, educators can develop a more inclusive, equitable, and relevant curriculum that caters to the learning needs of all students |
| 2) Doing | - Facilitate TLAs that align with the ILOs and engage students in meaningful learning experiences<br>- Foster a learner-centred approach, focusing on the desired learning outputs and promoting students' intrinsic motivation<br>- Adopt output-based principles to support achieving the desired learning outcomes, focusing on student engagement and satisfaction | - In this phase, students actively engage with the TLAs and participate in discussions, group activities, projects, and other learning experiences that align with the ILOs<br>- Students are encouraged to adopt a deep learning approach, reflecting on their own learning processes and becoming increasingly self-directed in acquiring knowledge and skills<br>- They collaborate with their peers, build interpersonal relationships, and contribute to a supportive learning community that fosters knowledge exchange and collective growth |

|  | Role of educator | Role of student |
|---|---|---|
| 3) Diagnosing | - Use ATs that closely align with the ILOs, ensuring a clear connection between learning outcomes and assessment criteria<br>- Encourage students to engage in deep learning strategies by carefully designing ATs that require them to apply their knowledge and skills in new and complex situations<br>- Employ various ATs, including formative and summative assessments, that offer diverse opportunities for students to demonstrate competence and understanding<br>- Regularly review and refine ATs to maintain alignment with the ILOs, address potential concerns related to narrow curricula, and overemphasise easily measurable outcomes or assessment practices hindering meaningful learning experiences | - Students are responsible for demonstrating competence and understanding through various ATs, showcasing their ability to apply knowledge and skills in different contexts and situations, by the end of a learning experience |

*Table 2: The role of educators and students in the three stages of the ESLO model.*

In this way, the ESLO model highlights the interconnected roles of designing, doing, and diagnosing learning outcomes, focusing on constructive alignment and output-based principles. By strategically connecting these elements, educators can create an effective learning environment that enhances student learning outcomes, promotes deep understanding, and fosters student motivation and engagement. At this juncture, we outline the three phases — designing, doing, diagnosing — in more detail.

## 1) Designing

First and foremost, it is important that educators design with a clear focus on ILOs, and that ILOs are aligned with TLAs and ATs to effectively measure and evaluate student performance. As we discussed above, this learning outcomes focus and alignment is crucial to ensuring that students achieve the desired learning successfully (Biggs, 1999). Designing learning outcomes requires a systematic and iterative process that involves several steps. In the first instance, we must identify the desired learning outcomes based on our students' course objectives and needs. Secondly, we need to formulate the learning outcomes in a measurable, observable, and relevant way to the course content and context. Finally, we must review and revise the ILOs based on student feedback, colleagues, and other stakeholders to continuously review, adjust and improve our teaching practices.

Research has shown that when learning outcomes, TLAs, and ATs are appropriately aligned, students will likely better engage with the material and demonstrate their understanding effectively (Fry et al., 2009). In addition, well-aligned courses not only improve learning outcomes but also student satisfaction (Gibbs, 1999). Moreover, alignment ensures that assessments accurately measure students' mastery of the ILOs, leading to a reliable and valid evaluation of student performance (Huba & Freed, 2000).

Significantly, Bloom's taxonomy has been utilised in designing learning outcomes since its inception in the 1950s (Bloom et al., 1956). The utilisation of Bloom's taxonomy provides educators with a hierarchical structure for organising learning outcomes and creating assessments that progressively challenge students' cognitive abilities (Wiggins & McTighe, 2005). The revised version, by Anderson and Krathwohl (2001), further adapts the taxonomy to better reflect the complexity and dynamics of learning, emphasising higher-order thinking skills. Other frameworks, such as Fink's (2003) taxonomy of significant learning and Wiggins and McTighe's (2005) understanding by design, can also serve as valuable resources for designing learning outcomes that foster meaningful learning experiences and promote critical thinking, problem-solving, and application skills. We mention those frameworks here because they may serve as inspirations when designing learning outcomes.

## 2) Doing

The link between TLAs and ILOs has been shown to have a significant impact on student learning. By aligning TLAs with specific learning outcomes, educators can create a more effective and efficient learning experience for students. One example of a TLA that can improve student learning is the use of case studies. By presenting students with real-world scenarios, instructors can help students apply theoretical concepts to practical situations. Past research has shown that the use of case studies can improve critical thinking skills and problem-solving abilities (e.g. Branch et al., 2014). Another TLA example that can enhance student learning is the use of collaborative learning (Forbes, 2020). By working together in groups, students can not only share discipline-specific knowledge, but also develop transferable skills such as teamwork, communication and leadership skills (Enomoto & Warner, 2014; Enomoto & Warner, 2018; Enomoto & Warner, 2022). Furthermore, peer learning (Donald & Ford, 2023) and vicarious learning (Bandura, 1994) through collaborative learning can also foster a sense of community (Lave & Wenger, 1991; 1998) in the classroom — be it physical or virtual (Enomoto & Warner, 2014). Studies have shown that collaborative learning can evoke affirmative interdependence (Scager et al., 2016) and lead both to improved academic performance (Forbes, 2020) and higher levels of student engagement (Johnson et al., 2014).

Moreover, the use of information communications technology has opened up 'new worlds' in the sphere of collaborative learning (and beyond) with the potential for motivating student learning and what Duță & Martínez-Rivera (2015:1466) term *"collaborative nuances"*. The potential of social media in TLAs is also being widely realised (Al-Rahmi & Othman 2013; Wandera et al., 2016; Alkhathlan & Al-Daraiseh, 2017; Sabah, 2023). As we outline in Section 3, all of the chapters in this book demonstrate how different TLAs, including some collaborative TLAs and case studies, have led to enhanced ILOs.

In summary, the link between TLAs and ILOs is crucial in improving student learning. By using a variety of TLAs, educators can create a more engaging and effective learning experience for students. This leads us to the third phase of the ESLO model, namely, diagnosing learning outcomes.

## 3) Diagnosing

Choosing and designing appropriate assessment tasks are critical in the evaluation of students' learning outcomes in the higher education sphere. As seen in Table 1 (above), the input-based educational value of quizzes and tests seemingly lies in their usefulness for a point-in-time assessment of students' knowledge and their understanding of specific concepts and topics. In contrast, widely used output-based assessment tasks include projects, presentations, portfolios and performance/simulation-based assessments, such as drama presentations (Enomoto & Warner, 2018). Appropriate output-based assessment tasks should be designed carefully based upon discipline-specific feedback needs and the ILOs. Moreover, output-based assessment tasks, such as projects (see Nygaard, 2023 in this book), should be set up so as to allow students scope to demonstrate their critical thinking, research, and writing skills — transferable skills.

Furthermore, other output-based assessment tasks such as presentations and portfolios can provide evidence of students' ability both to communicate effectively and to showcase their work over time. For example, portfolios, including e-portfolios, (Ciesielkiewicz, 2019) can function as a form of a 'living CV'; their development may be valuable as a transferable demonstrated skills bridge to a future workplace. As will be seen, at various junctures in this book, a key issue is, in terms of student learning outcomes, the conjoining of transferable skills and discipline-specific skills in contemporary higher education.

Effective use of any of these assessment tasks requires teachers to align the tasks with specific learning outcomes and to clearly communicate their expectations to the students. For students to achieve the learning outcomes specifically defined for the course, apposite assessment tasks should be developed to allow for the timely provision of feedback, which is both constructive (Warner & Miller, 2015) and dialogic (Beaumont et al., 2008). In this regard, as an effective mechanism of providing personalised and actionable feedback, apposite marking rubrics should be designed to function as a useful tool, not only for grading, but importantly for allowing students to identify their strengths and areas for improvement.

When working with the ILOs, it is also crucial to employ various assessment tasks, including formative and summative assessments, that offer diverse opportunities for students to demonstrate competence and understanding. Formative assessment is an ongoing process that helps educators and students identify strengths and weaknesses in learning (Black & Wiliam, 2006). Formative assessment can be conducted in the form of low-stakes quizzes/tests (Saccucci, 2023 in this book) to measure the extent of students' content knowledge and comprehension, which tend to follow the input-based educational paradigm. During learning activities, formative assessment serves to help reduce the gap between what the student understands and does not yet understand (Paterson et al., 2020).

On the other hand, summative assessment often involves the evaluation of students' learning outcomes through output-based assessment tasks at the end of a course or a significant period, such as a term or semester. Other output-based summative methods, such as authentic assessment, play important roles in the higher education assessment space. Of particular importance to learning outcomes is authentic assessment (Moss & Brookhart, 2019), which shifts the focus of assessment towards the evaluation of students' performance in real-life situations. This assessment method, which is clearly focused on transferable skills development (Bowd & Enomoto, 2023 in this book), is useful in determining students' ability to apply such skills to real-life situations.

It is crucial in the learning outcomes space to note that there is debate between the value of different types of assessment, with formative assessment as the 'good' assessment and summative assessment as the 'bad' assessment (Lau, 2016). As Lau (2016) points out, the Orwellian slogan 'Four legs good, two legs bad' can symbolically exemplify this debate. Yet, as she argues, well thought out and articulated summative assessments can impact positively on student learning outcomes. Indeed, past research has shown that the task appropriate and well-articulated use of different assessment methods leads to improved learning outcomes. For instance, Hattie and Timperley (2007) conducted a systematic meta-analysis of over 250 studies, finding that formative assessment significantly positively affected students' learning outcomes. The authors established that using formative assessment led to an improvement of up to 23% in students' learning outcomes. Similarly, Black and Wiliam (2006) showed that using formative assessment significantly improved students' learning outcomes. However, other research has shown that summative assessment can also improve learning outcomes. For instance, Bangert-Drowns et al. (1991) found that using summative assessment led to an improvement of up to 15% in students' learning outcomes whilst also resulting in an improvement in students' motivation to learn. Moreover, a review of relevant research indicates that tests and exams, used typically for summative assessment purposes, *"directly potentiates learning"* (Rohrer & Pashler, 2010:406).

In summary, assessment methods, be they formative, summative or authentic, can play a crucial role in enhancing student learning outcomes, as they help measure students' progress and identify areas that need improvement. The effective use of these assessment methods has been shown to improve student learning outcomes significantly. In this book, the chapter authors explore a variety of research-informed assessment methods that advocate for their positive use in enhancing student learning outcomes and it is to an overview of these chapters that we now turn.

## Section 3: The chapters in this book

Thus far, we have presented our own ESLO model as a tool which educators can use to work with enhancing students learning outcomes. We have also explored some of the literature pertaining to learning outcomes and the assessments thereof; what follows now is a brief synopsis of each of the fourteen other chapters of this book. All of these chapters are grounded within the ESLO model in the learning outcomes space. A variety of assessment methods are utilised, affording diversity in both approaches and strategies to help the reader improve and refine their educational practices to maximise the learning outcomes of their students.

Chapter 2, written by John D Branch, is titled: *Physician, Heal Thyself: Enhancing Student Learning Outcomes through Reflective Practice*. The author discusses how he integrates his personal educational values into his teaching strategy to enhance student learning outcomes. He identified 10 key educational values, such as learner-centred engagement and experiential learning, by undertaking an autoethnography for his Doctor of Professional Studies degree. The author demonstrates how these values inform his unique approach to teaching, viewing each course as a problem requiring a bespoke solution, connecting academic theories with real-world applications. Moreover, he emphasises the importance of continuous assessment throughout the learning journey, recognising that students learn at varying paces. This chapter provides a practical and inspiring approach to improving learning outcomes using reflective practice.

Chapter 3, written by Kayoko Enomoto and Richard Warner, is titled: *Enablers of Student Learning Outcomes Based on Eight Cases of Second Language Learning and Teaching in Higher Education*. The authors delve into eight instances of second language teaching and learning, highlighting eleven key factors that enhance both second language-specific and transferable skills. The authors emphasise the importance of regularly reviewing and adjusting learning outcomes to strike a balance between language-specific and transferable skills. As university language educators, they stress their role in conveying these outcomes through well-structured, scaffolded curricula. They analyse their theory-informed learning and teaching practices that promote and develop both types of skills. Using a collaborative auto-ethnographic approach, they self-reflect on their teaching methods, identifying enablers for concurrent development of second language and transferable skills. This chapter offers valuable insights into second language education, offering a holistic approach beneficial to university language educators and students alike.

Chapter 4, written by Janet De Wilde and Elena Forasacco, is titled: *Developing STEM Doctoral Students' Collaboration Skills as Learning Outcomes*. The authors underscore the significance of collaboration skills in STEM doctoral students. The authors explore the nuances of nurturing these skills, particularly when dealing with intricate challenges. They outline a three-stage scaffolded approach to cultivate collaboration skills, emphasising their importance in diverse intercultural and interdisciplinary contexts. The chapter also describes the implementation of these activities in an in-country program involving STEM students from multiple institutions. Feedback from students reveals insights into their perceptions of task management, problem-solving, and communication when collaborating across cultures and disciplines. Developing these skills enhances students' competitiveness and employability, making this chapter a valuable resource for understanding and fostering collaboration skills in STEM doctoral students within our interconnected world.

Chapter 5, written by Claus Nygaard, is titled: *Enhancing Student Learning Outcomes through Contextualised Learning Activities*. The author delves into the shift from input-based to output-based curriculum in university education. He illustrates the profound impact of this transition using two case studies. He emphasises the importance of tailored learning activities that enhance students' analytical skills and readiness for their future careers. The chapter describes undergraduate and postgraduate programs designed to blend theory with practical experience, preparing students to tackle real-world challenges. The author's evaluation reveals positive student feedback and strong job placement rates, validating the effectiveness of the curriculum transformation. This chapter provides a valuable blueprint for institutions aiming to improve student outcomes in response to evolving professional demands, making it highly pertinent to the book's overarching theme.

Chapter 6, written by Henriette van Rensburg, is titled: *Interactive Practices in a Library Makerspace Using Technology to Deliver Positive Student Outcomes*. The author explores how an academic library makerspace can foster innovation in a university. She focuses on crafting detailed learning outcomes for this creative environment, aiming to empower adult learners with practical skills. The makerspace serves as a hub for hands-on learning and innovation, allowing students to apply their skills and pursue independent projects. The chapter evaluates the shift towards an output-focused curriculum and questions the relevance of traditional grading systems in the era of artificial intelligence. It highlights the success of the university's innovative approach and its significance in promoting impactful student outcomes within academic settings.

Chapter 7, written by András Margitay-Becht and Udayan Das, is titled: *Enhancing Student Learning through Hidden Motivational Learning Outcomes*. The authors explore the art of crafting learning outcomes that inspire students, especially in challenging subjects. The authors focus on a pre-introductory programming course designed to change negative perceptions about programming. This course creates a supportive environment, integrating both explicit and implicit learning goals. The practical phase involves hands-on activities, reigniting student interest and motivation whilst equipping them with essential skills. Through formative assessments, surveys, and project analysis, the authors assess not only academic growth but also increased student confidence and enthusiasm for the subject. This chapter offers a unique approach to learning outcomes, emphasising student motivation and perspective transformation in higher education.

Chapter 8, written by Janet De Wilde and Elena Forasacco, is titled: *Enhancing Learning Outcomes for STEM Doctoral Students through Perspective Taking in Safe Spaces*. The authors emphasise the importance of safe learning environments and perspective-taking for enhancing STEM doctoral students' learning outcomes. This approach not only equips students with the necessary knowledge and skills for their doctorates, but also enhances their professional qualifications and employability. Practical implementation is conducted in writing and impact retreats where they facilitate active and collaborative learning through perspective taking. This chapter offers a unique perspective on enhancing learning outcomes through safe spaces and perspective-taking, especially relevant for STEM doctoral students.

Chapter 9, written by Shelly Jose, is titled: *Enhancing Learning Outcomes through a Student-Centred Learning-Teaching Process in a Master of Human Resource Management Program*. The author outlines his innovative approach to improving learning outcomes by adopting a student-centred learning and teaching paradigm in a Master of Human Resource Management program. The designing phase prioritises fostering creativity, innovation, and analytical skills, focusing on creating a psychologically safe learning environment. The doing phase draws from social learning theories, combining individual responsibility and collaboration to enhance student engagement. In the diagnosing phase, the author assesses the intervention's success, marked by increased student engagement. This chapter provides a blueprint for implementing a student-centred approach, particularly valuable for postgraduate programs, ensuring students are central to the learning-teaching process.

Chapter 10, written by John D Branch and David Wernick, is titled: *The Use of Debate Cases for Enhancing Students' Reasoning Skills as Learning Outcomes*. The authors explore the transformative potential of using debate cases to enhance students' reasoning abilities. The authors focus on hands-on classroom applications and resulting learning outcomes. In the designing phase, they detail the methodology of using debate cases to strengthen reasoning. Each case presents a managerial dilemma with two solutions, fostering spirited debates to ignite students' reasoning skills. The doing phase describes how the authors integrated debate cases into their teaching, benefiting students' reasoning, research, and project management skills. These cases also enhance student engagement and their overall learning experience. The diagnosing phase assesses the method's effectiveness from the students' perspective, emphasising their active participation as crucial. This chapter introduces a novel pedagogical tool, the debate case, highlighting its impact on critical reasoning skills in higher education.

Chapter 11, written by Kathryn Bowd and Kayoko Enomoto, is titled: *Bringing Employability to Life: Developing Employability Skill Sets and Understandings as Student Learning Outcomes*. The authors discuss enhancing student learning outcomes in a first-year undergraduate course, with a focus on demystifying employability. In the designing phase, the authors outline the curriculum, tailored to develop students' employability skills while also recognising their existing strengths and interests. In the doing phase, the 12-week curriculum unfolds, offering a diverse learning experience, including content delivery, interactive activities, and discussions that encourage student participation. The assessments align with learning outcomes and cater to individual needs. In the diagnosing phase, the authors assess the effectiveness of their Experiential Learning Curriculum Model. Feedback highlights increased student confidence, employability awareness, and a sense of community. This chapter adds significant value to the book by exploring understandings of employability in higher education.

Chapter 12, written by Bernie St. Aubyn and Amanda Andrews, is titled: *A Pedagogical Approach to Enhance Nursing Students' Written Communication Skills as Learning Outcomes*. The authors introduce an innovative pedagogical strategy aimed at enhancing the written communication skills of undergraduate nursing students, guiding them from novices to advanced beginners. In the designing phase, the authors identify the prerequisites for proficient written communication skills in UK nursing education, considering input from various stakeholders. They present 'The Training Trilogy' a pedagogical blueprint tailored to impart essential written communication skills to nursing students, particularly

Generation Z learners. In the doing phase, three distinct activities from the trilogy are detailed, showcasing hands-on and experiential learning techniques. The diagnosing phase involves feedback from students and educators to assess the strategy's success, identifying areas of excellence and potential refinements. This chapter is a valuable addition to the book, offering a tailored approach to enhancing written communication skills in nursing education, crucial for effective healthcare communication.

Chapter 13, written by Franco (Frank) Saccucci, is titled: *How Increased Volume of Low-Stakes Testing Improved Student Engagement and Performance without Additional Grading Burden*. The author explores the transformative impact of frequent low-stakes testing in the classroom, leading to improved student engagement and academic performance while alleviating educators' grading burdens and budget constraints. He details the rationale and methodology behind this approach, emphasising the integration of regular low-stakes quizzes to enhance memory retention and practical application of concepts. A peer-marking system is introduced to ease grading responsibilities and involve students in the assessment process. The author describes how short quizzes are seamlessly integrated into classroom sessions, creating a 'gamified' environment that boosts student enthusiasm and participation. This strategy has been successfully replicated across different institutions, maintaining quality and efficacy. Student surveys and observations confirm its positive impact on preparedness, engagement, and academic outcomes. This chapter is a valuable addition to the book, highlighting an innovative assessment approach benefiting both students and educators.

Chapter 14, written by Amanda Andrews and Bernie St. Aubyn, is titled: *Partnering with Clinical Provider Organisations to Enhance Learning Outcomes for Healthcare Practitioners*. The authors explore the symbiotic relationship between higher education institutions and clinical provider organizations to enhance learning outcomes for healthcare professionals. They emphasise the need for a harmonised approach that combines theoretical knowledge with practical clinical experience. Academic Advisors play a crucial role in guiding clinical providers toward applying knowledge effectively, aligning with Bloom's Taxonomy. Evaluation involves feedback from clinical providers, students, and Advisors, highlighting strengths, areas for improvement, and a shift towards self-directed learning. This chapter provides a fresh perspective on academia and clinical practice collaboration, emphasising its significance in improving educational outcomes for healthcare professionals.

Chapter 15, written by Sarah Swann, is titled: *Student-Centric Pedagogy: What Happens When Learning Outcomes Are Customised to Students' Own Interests*. Swann explores the transformative potential of tailoring learning outcomes to align with students' interests, ensuring a comprehensive and engaging learning experience. The author emphasises the integration of theoretical and practical elements from Childhood Studies and Education Studies, aligning academic prerequisites with students' practical actions for a holistic learning trajectory. This chapter details how the curriculum was implemented in her context, highlighting her pivotal role of the teacher in transitioning students from disenfranchised learners to empowered individuals. The final evaluation based on the written assessment feedback demonstrates the curriculum's success, pointing to its effectiveness and areas for further improvement. This chapter is valuable to the book, presenting a fresh perspective on student-centric pedagogy and the significance of tailoring learning outcomes to individual student interests.

---oOo---

This book showcases inspirational accounts of learning theory-informed methods of enhancing student learning outcomes in a variety of higher education contexts worldwide. We hope that reading these chapters will inspire you to continue developing your own learning and teaching methods — for enhancing student learning outcomes.

## About the Authors

Kayoko Enomoto is an Associate Professor, Head of the Department of Asian Studies and Associate Dean, Student Experience in the Faculty of Arts, Business, Law and Economics at the University of Adelaide, Australia. She can be contacted at this email: kayoko.enomoto@adelaide.edu.au

Richard Warner is an Adjunct Lecturer in the School of Education in the Faculty of Arts, Business, Law and Economics at the University of Adelaide, Australia. He can be contacted at this email: richard.warner@adelaide.edu.au

Claus Nygaard is a professor, PhD, and executive director at the Institute for Learning in Higher Education. He can be contacted at this email: info@lihe.info

## Bibliography

Alkhathlan, A. A., & Al-Daraiseh, A. A. (2017). An analytical study of the use of social networks for collaborative learning in higher education. *International Journal of Modern Education and Computer Science*, 9(2), 1.

Al-Rahmi, W. M., & Othman, M. S. (2013). Evaluating student's satisfaction of using social media through collaborative learning in higher education. *International Journal of Advances in Engineering & Technology*, 6(4), 1541.

Ambrose, S. A., Bridges, M. W., DiPietro, M., Lovett, M. C., & Norman, M. K. (2010). *How learning works: Seven research-based principles for smart teaching*. Jossey-Bass.

Anderson, L. W., & Krathwohl, D. R. (Eds.). (2001). *A taxonomy for learning, teaching, and assessing: A revision of Bloom's taxonomy of educational objectives.* Longman.

Baeten, M., Dochy, F., & Struyven, K. (2013). The effects of different learning environments on students' motivation for learning and their achievement. *British Journal of Educational Psychology*, 83(3), 484-501.

Bandura, A. (1994). Self-efficacy. In V. S. Ramachaudran (Ed.), *Encyclopaedia of human behaviour*. (Vol. 4). Academic Press.

Bangert-Drowns, R. L., Kulik, J. A., Kulik, C. C., & Morgan, M. T. (1991). The instructional effect of feedback in test-like events. *Review of Educational Research*, 61(2), 213-238.

Beaumont, C., O'Doherty, M., & Shannon, L. (2008). Staff and student perceptions of feedback quality in the context of widening participation. *Higher Education*, 1(August), 1-71

Biggs, J. B. (1996). Enhancing teaching through constructive alignment. *Higher Education*, 32(3), 347–364.

Biggs, J. B. (1999). What the student does: Teaching for enhanced learning. *Higher Education Research & Development*, 18(1), 57-75.

Biggs, J. B. (2003). Aligning teaching and assessing to course objectives. *Teaching and Learning in Higher Education: New Trends and Innovations.* University of Aveiro, 13-17 April 2003.

Biggs, J. B., & Tang, C. (2011). *Teaching for quality learning at university: What the student does.* (4th ed.). The Society for Research into Higher Education & Open University Press.

Black, P., & Wiliam, D. (2006). Assessment and classroom learning. Assessment in education: *Principles, Policy & Practice*, 5(1), 7-74.

Bloom, B. S., Engelhart, M. D., Furst, E. J., Hill, W. H., & Krathwohl, D. R. (1956). *Taxonomy of educational objectives: The classification of educational goals. Handbook 1 Cognitive Domain.* David McKay Company, Inc.

Boud, D., & Falchikov, N. (2006). Aligning assessment with long-term learning. *Assessment & Evaluation in Higher Education*, 31(4), 399–413.

Bowd, K., & Enomoto, K. (2023). Bringing employability to life: Developing employability skill sets and understandings as student learning outcomes. In K. Enomoto, R. Warner & C. Nygaard. (Eds.), *Enhancing student learning outcomes in higher education.* Libri Publishing Ltd.

Branch, J., Bartholomew, P., & Nygaard, C. (Eds.) (2014). *Case-based learning in higher education.* Libri Publishing Ltd.

Caspersen, J., & Frølich, N. (2017). Higher education learning outcomes–transforming higher education?. *European Journal of Education*, 52(1), 3-7.

Ciesielkiewicz, M. (2019). The use of e-portfolios in higher education: From the students' perspective. *Issues in Educational Research*, 29(3), 649-667.

Donald, W. E., & Ford, N. (2023). Fostering social mobility and employability: the case for peer learning. *Teaching in Higher Education*, 28(3), 672-678.

Duţă, N., & Martínez-Rivera, O. (2015). Between theory and practice: the importance of ICT in Higher Education as a tool for collaborative learning. *Procedia-Social and Behavioral Sciences, 180*, 1466-1473.

Eisner, E. W. (1979). *The educational imagination: On the design and evaluation of school programs.* Macmillan.

Enomoto, K., & Warner, R. (2014). Promoting student reflection through considerate design of a virtual learning space. In L. Scott-Webber, J. Branch, P. Bartholomew & C. Nygaard (Eds.), *Learning space design in higher education.* Libri Publishing Ltd.

Enomoto, K., & Warner, R. (2018). Developing undergraduate students' transferable generic skills through an innovative group drama project. In K. Enomoto, R. Warner & C. Nygaard (Eds.), *Innovative teaching and learning practices in higher education.* Libri Publishing Ltd.

Enomoto, K., & Warner, R. (2022). Partnering with student leaders: Active learning through integration of peer assisted study sessions into an undergraduate language course. In K. Enomoto, R. Warner & C. Nygaard (Eds.), *Active learning in higher education: Student engagement and deeper learning outcomes*. Libri Publishing Ltd.

Enomoto, K., & Warner, R. (2023). Enablers of student learning outcomes based on eight cases of second language learning and teaching in higher education. In K. Enomoto, R. Warner & C. Nygaard (Eds.), *Enhancing student learning outcomes in higher education*. Libri Publishing Ltd.

Entwistle, N. (2009). *Teaching for understanding at university: Deep approaches and distinctive ways of thinking*. Palgrave McMillan.

Entwistle, N., & Ramsden, P. (2015). *Understanding student learning (Routledge revivals)*. Routledge.

Ewell, P. T. (2001). *Accreditation and student learning outcomes: A proposed point of departure*. CHEA Occasional Paper. Council for Higher Education Accreditation.

Fink, L. D. (2003). *Creating significant learning experiences: An integrated approach to designing college courses*. Jossey-Bass.

Forbes, M. (2020). The value of collaborative learning for music practice in higher education. *British Journal of Music Education, 37*(3), 207-220.

Fry, H., Ketteridge, S., & Marshall, S. (2009). *A handbook for teaching and learning in higher education: Enhancing academic practice*. Routledge.

Fullan, M. (2007). *The new meaning of educational change*. Routledge.

Gibbs, G. (1999). Using assessment strategically to change the way students learn. In S. Brown & A. Glasner (Eds.), *Assessment matters in higher education*. Open University Press.

Gijbels, D., Segers, M., & Struyf, E. (2008). Constructivist learning environments and the (im)possibility to change students' perceptions of assessment demands and approaches to learning. *Instructional Science, 36*(5-6), 431-443.

Hadjianastasis, M. (2017). Learning outcomes in higher education: assumptions, positions and the views of early-career staff in the UK system, *Studies in Higher Education, 42*(12), 2250-2266.

Hattie, J., & Donoghue, G. M. (2016). Learning strategies: A synthesis and conceptual model. *NPJ Science of Learning, 1*, 1-13.

Hattie, J., & Timperley, H. (2007). The power of feedback. *Review of Educational Research, 77*(1), 81-112.

Havnes, A., & Prøitz, T. S. (2016). Why use learning outcomes in higher education? Exploring the grounds for academic resistance and reclaiming the value of unexpected learning. *Educational Assessment, Evaluation and Accountability, 28*, 205-223.

Huba, M. E., & Freed, J. E. (2000). *Learner-centered assessment on college campuses: Shifting the focus from teaching to learning.* Allyn & Bacon.

Hussey, S., & Smith, P. (2003). The uses of learning outcomes. *Teaching in Higher Education, 8*(3), 357–368.

Hussey, S., & Smith, P. (2008). Learning outcomes. A conceptual analysis. *Teaching in Higher Education, 13*(1), 107–115.

Jenkins, A. (2004). *A guide to the research evidence on teaching-research relations.* The Higher Education Academy.

Johnson, D. W., Johnson, R. T., & Smith, K. A. (2014). Cooperative learning: Improving university instruction by basing practice on validated theory. *Journal on Excellence in College Teaching, 25*(3&4), 85-118.

Kember, D., Ho, A., & Hong, C. (2008). The importance of establishing relevance in motivating student learning. *Active Learning in Higher Education, 9*(3), 249-263.

Krathwohl, D. R., Bloom, B. S., & Masia, B. B. (1964). *Taxonomy of educational objectives, the classification of educational goals. Handbook II: Affective domain.* David McKay Company, Inc.

Kuh, G. D., Kinzie, J., Schuh, J. H., & Whitt, E. J. (2006). *What matters to student success: A review of the literature.* National Postsecondary Education Cooperative.

Langan, A. M., Wheater, C. P., Shaw, E. M., Haines, B. J., Cullen, W. R., Boyle, J. C., Penney, D., Oldekop, J. A., Ashcroft, C., Lockey, L., & Preziosi, R. F. (2015). Peer assessment of oral presentations: Effects of student gender, university affiliation, and participation in the development of assessment criteria. *Assessment and Evaluation in Higher Education, 40*(6), 800–818.

Lau, A. M. S. (2016). 'Formative good, summative bad?'–A review of the dichotomy in assessment literature. *Journal of Further and Higher Education, 40*(4), 509-525.

Lave, J., & Wenger, E. (1991). *Situated learning: Legitimate peripheral participation.* Cambridge University Press.

Lave, J., & Wenger, E. (1998). *Communities of practice: Learning, meaning and identity.* Cambridge University Press.

Lizzio, A., Wilson, K., & Simons, R. (2002). University students' perceptions of the learning environment and academic outcomes: Implications for theory and practice. *Studies in Higher Education, 27*(1), 27-52.

Moss, C. M., & Brookhart, S. M. (2019). *Advancing formative assessment in every classroom: A guide for instructional leaders.* ASCD.

Nicol D. J., & McFarlane-Dick, D. (2006). Formative assessment and self-regulated learning: A model and seven principles of good feedback practice. *Studies in Higher Education, 31*(2), 199-218.

Nusche, D. (2008). Assessment of learning outcomes in higher education: Comparative review of selected practices. *OECD Education Working Papers, 15*, OECD publishing, © OECD.

Nygaard, C. (2023). Enhancing student learning outcomes through contextualised learning activities. In K. Enomoto, R. Warner & C. Nygaard (Eds.), *Enhancing student learning outcomes in higher education*. Libri Publishing Ltd.

Nygaard, C., & Andersen, I. (2005). Contextual learning in higher education: curriculum development with a focus on student learning. In R.G. Milter, V.S. Perotti & M.S.R. Segers (Eds.), *Educational Innovation in Economics and Business IX: Breaking Boundaries for Global Learning*. Springer Netherlands.

Nygaard, C., Courtney, N., & Bartholomew, P. (Eds.). (2013). *Quality enhancement of university teaching and learning*. Libri Publishing.

Nygaard, C., Højlt, T., & M. Hermansen (2008). Learning-based curriculum development. *Higher Education, 55*(1), 33–50.

Nygaard, C., Holtham, C., & Courtney, N. (Eds.). (2009). *Improving students' learning outcomes*. Copenhagen Business School Press.

Paterson, C., Paterson, N., Jackson, W., & Work, F. (2020). What are students' needs and preferences for academic feedback in higher education? A systematic review. *Nurse Education Today, 85*, 104236.

Pintrich, P. R. (2004). A conceptual framework for assessing motivation and self-regulated learning in college students. *Educational Psychology Review, 16*(4), 385-407.

Rohrer, D., & Pashler, H. (2010). Recent research on human learning challenges conventional instructional strategies. *Educational Researcher, 39*(5), 406-412.

Sabah, N. M. (2023). The impact of social media-based collaborative learning environments on students' use outcomes in higher education. *International Journal of Human–Computer Interaction, 39*(3), 667-689.

Saccucci, F. (2023). How increased volume of low-stakes testing improved student engagement and performance without additional grading burden. In K. Enomoto, R. Warner & C. Nygaard (Eds.), *Enhancing student learning outcomes in higher education*. Libri Publishing Ltd.

Scager, K., Boonstra, J., Peeters, T., Vulperhorst, J., & Wiegant, F. (2016). Collaborative learning in higher education: Evoking positive interdependence. *CBE—Life Sciences Education, 15*(4), ar69.

Simpson, E. J. (1972). *The classification of educational objectives in the psychomotor domain*. Gryphon House.

Suskie, L. A. (2018). *Assessing student learning: A common sense guide* (3rd ed.). Jossey-Bass.

Wandera, S., James-Waldon, N., Bromley, D., & Henry, Z. (2016). The influence of social media on collaborative learning in a cohort environment. *Interdisciplinary Journal of e-skills and Lifelong Learning, 12*, 123-143.

Warner, R., & Enomoto, K. (2015). Embedding research skills in the curriculum design of a pathway programme for international students. In C. Guerin, P. Bartholomew & C Nygaard (Eds.), *Learning to research – Researching to learn*. Libri Publishing Ltd.

Warner, R., & Miller, J. (2015). Cultural dimensions of feedback at an Australian university: A study of international students with English as an additional language. *Higher Education Research & Development, 34*(2), 420-435.

Wiggins, G. P., & McTighe, J. (2005). *Understanding by design*. (2nd ed.). Association for Supervision and Curriculum Development (ASCD).

Zeidner, M., & Saklofske, D. (1996). Adaptive and Maladaptive coping. In M. Ziedner & N. Endler (Eds.), *Handbook of coping: Theory, research, applications*. John Wiley & Sons.

Zimmerman, B. J. (2002). Becoming a self-regulated learner: An overview. *Theory Into Practice, 41*(2), 64-70.

Zull, J. E. (2004). *The art of changing the brain: Enriching teaching by exploring the biology of learning*. Stylus Publishing.

Chapter 2
# Physician, Heal Thyself: Enhancing Student Learning Outcomes through Reflective Practice

John D Branch

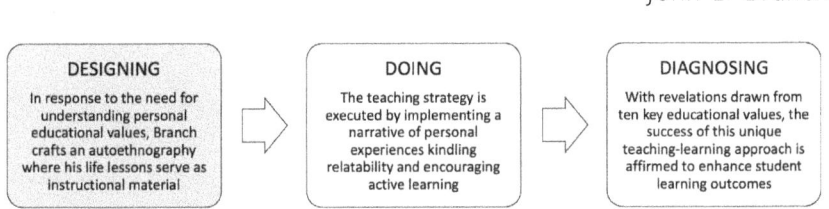

## Preamble

With his chapter, John D Branch contributes to this book, *Enhancing Student Learning Outcomes in Higher Education,* by showing how he incorporates his educational values as a marketing educator to enhance student learning outcomes. He achieves this by utilising a teaching strategy based on reflective practice. He relates to the three phases of the central ESLO model of the book in this way:

In the DESIGNING phase, he explains the steps he took to carefully plan and develop an autoethnography for his Doctor of Professional Studies degree. This insightful project helped him to discover 10 educational values as a marketing educator, which include learner-centred engagement, experiential learning, scaffolding, storytelling, and innovation. He explains how he designs his teaching strategy using reflective practice, by incorporating his educational values into his methodologies.

In the DOING phase, he shows how he adopts an engineering approach to his teaching design. This involves carefully planning and executing his teaching strategy, and considering each course or module as an engineering problem which requires a solution. This process helps him build a curriculum which relates academic concepts to real-world experiences, enabling the practical application of knowledge.

In the DIAGNOSING phase, he assesses his educational values, specifically examining how they have influenced his professional practice as a marketing educator, and how they enhance student learning outcomes. From a student's perspective, he views assessment as inseparable from the learning process, noting that the pace of acquisition and understanding of knowledge varies among students. Consequently, teachers ought to ensure that assessments are distributed throughout the learning process, rather than solely at the end. He shows how he had achieved this by utilising reflective practice.

## Introduction

As intimated by the title, the chapter is premised on the ancient wisdom of self-awareness. That is to say, I describe how autoethnography (an ethnography of the self) was part of my Doctor of Professional Studies research, in which I explored my professional practice as a marketing educator. This led me to discover 10 educational values upon which I base my teaching strategy using reflective practice to enhance student learning outcomes. I define learning outcome as the measurable knowledge, skill, or attitude that a student acquires as a consequence of a discrete unit of instruction. In contrast, a learning objective is normative, specifying what a student ought to know, do, or think following a discrete unit of instruction (a session, a module, or even an entire course of study).

The saying 'physician, heal thyself', or *medice, cura te ipsum* in Latin, is often attributed to Hippocrates, who is considered to be the father of medicine. But it was also engraved in stone at Delphi, and it appears in the Talmud as 'physician heal thine own lameness' (Massey, 2018). Jesus utters the words in Luke 4:23: *"And he said unto them, Ye will surely say unto me this proverb, Physician, heal thyself: whatsoever we have heard done in Capernaum, do also here in thy country"*. In all instantiations, however, the core sentiment is the same: attend to yourself (before attending to others).

More *apropos*, the chapter proposes that, in concert with the saying 'physician, heal thyself', enhancing student learning outcomes begins by enhancing teaching outcomes. Indeed, the chapter follows the emerging perspective in education that reflective practice is central to effective teaching. As suggested by Mamede et al. (2011:10), *"reflection on experience is the basic mechanism for learning and improvement of professional practice"*. And consequently, teachers at all levels ought to have the *"capacity and commitment to engage in autonomous self-development through systematic self-study, reflection and research"* (Zwozdiak-Meyers, 2012:3).

In 2019, therefore, I registered for the Doctor of Professional Studies degree at Middlesex University, which requires you to *"undertake a critical reflection on your personal and professional practice followed by a piece of doctoral level practice-focused research in your own context, organisation or community of practice"* (Middlesex University, 2023). At the time, I had been teaching for more than 25 years. But the degree afforded me the opportunity to explore — deliberately and critically — my professional practice as a marketing educator.

For my Doctor of Professional Studies research, I adopted Living Educational Theory, which provides teachers with both a philosophy and a method for theorising professional practice. As it is beyond the scope of this chapter, I shall not fully detail the Living Educational Theory I constructed in Section 1. However, central to Living Educational Theory is the notion that professional practice embodies a teacher's educational values. I conducted an autoethnography to discover my educational values, drawing on autobiography and hermeneutics. The result of my doctoral research was a 'living educational theory', which theorises my professional practice as an analogy that teaching is like engineering… with my educational values as the elementary unit.

## Chapter overview and key takeaways

The chapter has four main sections. In Section 1, I explain my rationale for pursuing the Doctor of Professional Studies degree and introduce Living Educational Theory. In Section 2, I overview the specific autobiographical procedures I employed to discover my educational values. I summarise my 10 educational values which I discovered, before I illustrate how my educational values are embodied in my professional practice by describing one specific pedagogy. In Section 3, I discuss my educational values with respect to enhancing student learning outcomes. Finally, in Section 4, I outline my plans to continue researching reflective practice.

Reading the chapter, you will understand:
1. The philosophy and method of Living Educational Theory;
2. The autoethnography which I conducted;
3. My 10 educational values;
4. The embodiment of my educational values in my professional practice; and
5. The link between enhancing student learning outcomes and reflective practice.

## Section 1: Background to my work with learning outcomes

In May 2001, following the submission of my PhD dissertation, I took up the position of Senior Lecturer at the Olin Business School of Washington University, a private institution of higher education in Saint Louis, United States. My teaching load consisted of six full-term modules of international marketing per year. I developed an active research agenda. And I established my 'social capital' in the business school by serving on several committees. To the outsider, therefore, it must have appeared that I had made it:

- PhD degree ☑
- Senior Lecturer position ☑

Soon, however, a disillusionment with marketing began creeping in…not with marketing *per se*, but rather the academic discipline of marketing. First came the realisation that the scientific research, on which I spent excessive time, had a marginal impact on the quotidian marketing practice. In other words, the academic discipline of marketing appeared to have very little overlap with real marketing. Second, I observed that, for many of my colleagues in the marketing department, the subject of marketing appeared to be almost entirely divorced from the students whose marketing mastery they professed to be nurturing. Student needs were seemingly of low importance, and their employability factored little in curriculum design. Third, and most jarring, was the revelation that to most of my colleagues in the marketing department, teaching was considered secondary. Indeed, they viewed teaching as trivial and insignificant in contrast to scientific research, the gravity of which, for them, was undeniable. I remember the Dean stating offhandedly at a faculty meeting that three out of five on teaching evaluations was adequate… although the average teaching evaluation score in the school was more than four out of five.

However, in 2008, I reconnected with my former University of Cambridge carrel-mate Claus Nygaard, who had taken up a position at Copenhagen Business School in Denmark after completing his doctoral degree in the academic discipline of strategic management. In a similarly short time, he had likewise become frustrated with the emphasis on subjects over students at Copenhagen Business School. Consequently, Claus launched a new association, *The Institute for Learning in Higher Education* (LiHE), which, as intimated by its appellation, focused on learning at the post-secondary level. This focus reflected the shift in higher education which was underway at the time: from a professor-centred, transmission-based philosophy to a student-centred, learning-based philosophy (I use the term professor throughout this context statement in the generic sense, not in terms of institutional rank.). Its scope was limited to vocational colleges, universities, and other higher education institutions. Claus contacted me in 2008 specifically to solicit a chapter proposal for an upcoming symposium whose theme, coincidentally, was 'Improving Student Learning Outcomes'. I submitted a chapter proposal on the use of analogies in teaching. The idea for the chapter arose one day in a conversation with a colleague who remarked that his go-to instructional tool was the 2×2 matrix (I have witnessed his teaching many times, and I certify that he can boil every management challenge down to two orthogonal dimensions.). With a smile, I added that my go-to instructional tool was the analogy.

Thankfully, my chapter proposal was accepted. The subsequent full chapter was also accepted. And I headed off to the Greek island of Aegina, to a small 1-star family-run resort, to the site of my first LiHE symposium…the first of many, as it turned out. Claus and I were the only business-school professors; the other participants came from various faculties and departments, including history, chemistry, and music. Like me, each professor had her/his subject-specific expertise. But we coalesced around the common goal of improving teaching and learning in higher education. At that moment, I realised that this rag-tag, non-denominational group of professors was my community of practice. Indeed, I had met my tribe; I had found my intellectual home. I also pinpointed my professional identity — that 'thing' which had eluded me since completing my PhD. Indeed, I could finally identify — at least in name, if not substance — who I was as a professional. I was not a marketer. Nope, I was not out there in the real-world practising marketing. Nor was I a marketing scholar conducting scientific research on marketing phenomena. Rather, I was a marketing educator!

Immediately, my scholarly activities, my memberships in professional associations, and even my daily conversations with colleagues shifted away from marketing towards teaching and learning. For example, I cancelled my subscription to the *Journal of Marketing* and joined the *Higher Education Special Interest Group* of the *American Marketing Association*. A psychological calm replaced the anxiety which had (unconsciously) accompanied my lack of professional identity, and I embarked on a decade of research and writing in and around the scholarship of teaching and learning, all to further my professional practice as a marketing educator.

## *Learning theory and methodology related to learning outcomes*

Pinpointing a professional identity, however, is not the same as knowing it. Indeed, although I had identified myself as a marketing educator, its meaning remained nebulous. Who was I, exactly, as a marketing educator? What did I see when I looked in the mirror? How did I present myself to others?

To be fair, a decade of research and writing in and around the scholarship of teaching and learning had doubtless improved my teaching abilities. And it is obvious to me now that the many chapters I wrote for LiHE anthologies (including that first chapter on the use of analogies in teaching) also went some way to unveil some facets of my professional identity. Consider one chapter in which I documented an instructional and assessment activity I developed, which used the board game RISK to introduce marketing strategy (Branch et al., 2011). It showed that I subscribe to the foundational tenet of experiential learning — that knowledge is constructed through experience transformation (Dewey, 1938). Nonetheless, a professional ambiguity lingered despite this chapter and other research and writing in and around the scholarship of teaching and learning. In the words of Bono, 'I still hadn't found what I was looking for'.

In 2019, therefore, I registered for the Doctor of Professional Studies degree at Middlesex University, which remedied this professional ambiguity, by enabling me to conduct a kind of archaeology of the self. Whereas the Doctor of Philosophy degree is fundamentally theoretical in nature, situated within the scientific literature of an academic discipline, and designed to improve human understanding of a phenomenon, the Doctor of Professional Studies degree is practice-oriented, situated within a professional environment, and designed to allow candidates to examine "*knowledge developed over time in a theoretical academic framework*" (QAA, 2015:8).

I adopted Living Educational Theory as the theoretical academic framework for my research, which offers a systematic approach to describing and explaining professional practice. It is attributed to Jack Whitehead, who spent most of his career as a professor of education at the University of Bath. Living Educational Theory was born in the early 1980s from Whitehead's critique of traditional scientific research in the academic discipline of education. Its clarification, formalisation, and propagation as a paradigm solidified throughout his more than four-decade career.

In short, Living Educational Theory is a paradigm for scientific research in the academic discipline of education in which a teacher theorises her/his professional practice. Using action research, she/he reflects on her/his educational values and the practice solutions developed from there. The outcome is a living educational theory which describes and explains her/his professional practice, with educational values as its elementary unit. The teacher substantiates this living educational theory by demonstrating how the educational values are embodied in her/his professional practice. In this regard, Living Educational Theory is distinct from traditional scientific research in the academic discipline of education, in the first instance when concerning theoretical claims. A living educational theory is not defined by a set of interconnected propositions (Whitehead, 1998b) which sit idly in the stacks of university libraries (Whitehead,

1989a). On the contrary, a living educational theory is organic, *"living in the public conversations of those constituting professional practice…growing in the living relationship between teachers, pupils and professional researchers and embedded with their forms of life"* (Whitehead, 1989b:4).

In addition, Living Educational Theory is also patently practice oriented. Just as necessity is the mother of invention, practical problems in the classroom trigger action research. In the words of Whitehead (1989a:34), *"I believe that you, like me, are experiencing a tension at work because you are not fully living your educational values in your practice"*. As such, Living Educational Theory ostensibly reverses the 'order of operations' in the academic discipline of education, with the theory *"now seen more and more as an extension of the practice rather than as vice versa or as two separate disciplines of the one activity"* (Whitehead, 1983:174). Thus, the output of the Living Educational Theory is distinct for its rhetorical form. Whereas a theory generated from traditional scientific research in the academic discipline of education is typically presented as abstract linguistic concepts and as relationships between these concepts, a living educational theory is presented as a dialogical and dialectical explanation.

Indeed, a teacher who adopts Living Educational Theory uses a more informal, conversational rhetorical form and weaves together values, context, and understandings to explicate her/his professional practice (Whitehead, 1998c). Dialectical in Living Educational Theory refers to the inner discourse which occurs when a teacher realises that she/he is not living her/his values. Often a teacher exists as a 'living contradiction', in the words of Whitehead (1998c), the reconciliation of which is the core of dialectics in general and the impetus for action. Stated plainly, a living educational theory divulges that a teacher's professional practice is often misaligned with her/his educational values. For example, a teacher might value student edification but often finds herself/himself 'teaching to the test'. Values, therefore, are not to be bracketed, as is common practice in more traditional scientific research in the academic discipline of education. On the contrary, a teacher who adopts Living Educational Theory recognises that action research *"is inherently value-laden because researcher values inevitably influence the choice of phenomenon, choice of method, choice of data, and choice of findings"* (Hirschman, 1986:238).

However, in Living Educational Theory, values play an even more central role because a teacher's professional practice cannot be divorced from her/his educational values. A teacher's educational values are embodied in her/his professional practice. Following Van Manen's argument (1990), a teacher who adopts Living Educational Theory uses her/his educational values as the explanatory principles in a living educational theory that explicates her/his professional practice. Indeed, as suggested by Whitehead (1998c:8), "[e]ach action-researcher has represented their explanation for their own professional learning within their social context as a unique constellation of values, understandings and actions. They have communicated the meanings of their values and understandings as they emerge through time and action." In effect, values become the elementary unit of a living educational theory. For a discussion of institutional values in higher education (see Margitay-Becht & Das, 2023 in this book).

## Section 2: My practice towards enhancing student learning outcomes

I conducted an autoethnography to identify my educational values. As Ellis et al. (2011) suggested, autoethnography uses both autobiography and ethnography. Of course, an autoethnographer *"does not live through experiences solely to make them part of a published document, rather, these experiences are assembled using hindsight"* (Ellis et al., 2011:2). Yet, stories of these experiences, which are written after the fact, become the autoethnographer's data, with the autoethnographer herself/himself serving as the data source.

I began the autoethnography by writing my autobiography of sorts. I qualify with 'of sorts' because I did not chronicle my entire life from my first memories to the present. Instead, I described specific events in my life which have been instrumental in my development — epiphanies in the language of Ellis et al. (2011). I also consider that an autobiography shows *"people in the process of figuring out what to do, how to live, and the meaning of their struggles"* (Bochner and Ellis, 2006:111). Consequently, by writing my autobiography — describing and reflecting on my lead up to, my entry into, and my time within, the higher education profession — I discovered the educational values embodied in my professional practice as a marketing educator.

I wrote the autobiography over two months in the summer of 2019. I drew on some earlier autobiographical work which I completed as part of my Master of Arts in Education degree, which I completed in 2004. My autobiography included descriptions of the specific events in my life that have been instrumental in my development and my reflections on these events. The rhetoric was informal and conversational in tone, consistent with both Living Educational Theory and autoethnography. I isolated my reflections from the main text with **_emboldened italics_**.

In the reflections, I attempted to re-frame the specific events in my life in a new context, which enabled me to view them from a different perspective — a methodological sleight of hand which Schön (1983) called a 'frame experiment'. The reflections were necessary because, as suggested by MacLure (1996:273), an interpretive researcher must move "*backwards to the past and forward again in order to try to make sense of the present*". In other words, the reflections precipitated movement from my autobiography being simply a description of the specific events, which were instrumental in my development, to my autobiography also explaining why these specific events were instrumental in my development. Indeed, the reflections helped me transform the specific events of my life into specific, meaningful events.

Now, to discover my educational values, I followed a hermeneutic procedure in which I treated the autobiography (specific events and reflections) as a text (see Ricoeur, 1981 for the idea of a text). I began with an interpretive reading of my autobiography to yield an initial understanding of its educational values. I then started breaking down my autobiography into meaningful elements using a paper-based coding and indexing system. More specifically, I developed codes for different meanings and indexed all instances of these meanings by tagging the textual units in my autobiography, which demonstrated the codes. I then reconstructed these codes in a new way, yielding a new understanding of my autobiography. This process of coding, indexing, and theorising continued until I believed that I had resolved the contradictions among and between the elements of the autobiography and the autobiography as a whole.

## *How my practice affects students' way of studying*

The final result of the hermeneutic procedure was a 'fresh description' of my autobiography— specifically, my 10 educational values embodied in my professional practice as a marketing educator (see Table 1 for a summary). To begin, I believe that students participate in higher education purposefully but that the purpose of higher education is equivocal. That is to say, higher education is not a happenstance for students. On the contrary, they elect to enter higher education institutions of their own free will, but they do so for different reasons. In parallel, higher education institutions operate under different philosophical assumptions, hold different strategic postures, and seek different organisational and societal outcomes. As a professor, therefore, I engage in higher education critically.

I believe that higher education ought to be student-centred. This belief is premised on the philosophical notion that knowledge is constructed – that people are born into a meaningless world and that this world only becomes meaningful when they ascribe meaning to it. Consequently, higher education is about learning, not teaching. Students are not passive receivers of information but active constructors of knowledge. As a professor, therefore, I do not transmit information; I facilitate learning.

I believe that knowledge is conceptually mediated. Human understanding of the world consists of a Peircian triad of an object (a tangible or intangible thing), the sign (or *representamen*) which is used to symbolise the object, and the conceptualisation (or *interpretant*) of the object (see Peirce Edition Project, 1998). Conceptual meaning consists of a linguistic structure linking concepts in a cognitive schema. In simple(r) terms, concepts are mental abstractions of reality. And they are the building blocks of knowledge. As a professor, therefore, I establish conceptual foundations.

| Educational Value | Meaning | Intentionality |
| --- | --- | --- |
| 1. Critical | The form and function of higher education is equivocal | I engage in higher education critically |
| 2. Learner-Centred | Higher education is about learning, not teaching | I facilitate learning |
| 3. Conceptual | Knowledge is conceptually-mediated | I establish conceptual foundations |
| 4. Contextual | Knowledge and learning are contextual | I account for contextual differences |

| Educational Value | Meaning | Intentionality |
|---|---|---|
| 5. Experiential | Learning occurs through experience | I curate experiences |
| 6. Scaffolding | Students need guidance to learn effectively | I scaffold learning |
| 7. Assessment | Students learn in different ways and at different rates | I assess learning |
| 8. Storytelling | People 'storify' their worlds | I tell stories |
| 9. Innovation | Higher education can be improved | I innovate |
| 10. Technology | Educational technologies continue to evolve | I experiment with educational technologies |

*Table 1: A summary of my educational values.*

I believe that all human knowledge is contextual. Indeed, the meanings people ascribe to the world are not immune to their extant knowledge, cultural backgrounds, or personal circumstances. Likewise, learning is contextual, people do not exist in a vacuum. On the contrary, learning occurs within specific learning environments, the characteristics of which impact learning mechanisms. As a professor, therefore, I account for contextual differences.

I also believe that learning occurs through experience – that the natural learning process is enhanced if learning is grounded in life experiences. I follow Kolb (1984), who models learning as a cycle of concrete experience, reflective observation, abstract conceptualisation, and active experimentation, and who, accordingly, defines experiential learning as the mental process by which knowledge is constructed through the transformation of experience. As a professor, therefore, I curate experiences.

I believe that all people have the capacity to learn but often need to be guided and supported in their learning. This guidance and support mirror the idea of scaffolding which was introduced by Wood et al. (1976), and which analogises the activities which are provided by a teacher to students as they move through the 'zone of proximal development' (see Vygotsky, 1978). As a professor, therefore, I scaffold learning.

I believe that students learn in different ways and at different rates. Learning is not linear, and the pace at which students learn varies. Consequently, the assessment of learning is a central activity of higher education, which ought to be implemented throughout (and not only after) a student's learning journey, and which ought to draw on different assessment methods. As a professor, therefore, I assess learning.

I believe that people are 'natural' storytellers. Indeed, I buy into the fundamental proposition in Jonathan Gottschall's book (2012) that one of the abilities which distinguishes *homo sapiens* from other primates is storytelling. The corollary of this proposition — one I have witnessed throughout my career— is that people 'storify' their worlds: they think in stories, share their lives in stories, and learn from stories. As a professor, therefore, I tell stories.

I believe that higher education can be improved. Indeed, higher education is always tentative — in a permanent state of flux — and has no end point, thereby recalling the proverbial journey rather than the destination. This tentativeness is caused by endogenous innovation: teachers, students, and other people 'in the business of' higher education who work continually to make it better — a process which Schumpeter (1975) called 'creative destruction'. As a professor, therefore, I innovate.

Finally, I believe that educational technologies continue to evolve as innovators adapt extant technologies or create new technologies to improve higher education. Educational technologies need not be 'high tech', and not all new educational technologies improve teaching and learning. As a professor, therefore, I experiment with educational technologies.

Now, the result of my doctoral research was a living educational theory that theorises my professional practice as an analogy that teaching is like engineering...with my educational values as the elementary unit. In essence, although I discovered my community of practice (professors whose goal is to improve teaching and learning in higher education) and pinpointed my professional identity (marketing educator), I am an engineer at my core. I constructed plastic models as a child. I rebuilt sports cars during my high school years. I studied engineering for my undergraduate degree. You can take me out of engineering...

Chapter 2

Accordingly, my teaching approach is the teaching approach of an engineer. When tasked with a new module, for example, I plan and execute it like an engineer. I treat a ninety-minute classroom session as if it were an engineering problem. And each case study or exercise I intend to use is engineered with precision, down to the board plan and pedagogical 'pastures' (classroom discussion themes). And my 10 educational values serve as Aristotelian' first principles' – the elementary ideas from which a concept, theory, or system is derived (see Swann, 2023 in this book), in which she describes how epistemology informs her module design.

A specific example (which I documented in a LiHE chapter) is my use of the ECTS for course design. The ECTS, short for European Credit Transfer and Accumulation System, was intended to facilitate student mobility by creating course transparency for institutions. It functions as a kind of common currency of higher education within the European Union (the educational equivalent of the EURO) by specifying the number of learning hours per credit, irrespective of the instructor's chosen pedagogy. One instructor, for example, might teach a 2-credit course in marketing by having its 60 learning hours spread over only two learning activities: 59 hours of face-to-face classroom lectures and a 1-hour examination. Another instructor, however, might assign 20 hours of readings, 10 hours of cases, 20 hours of team consulting project, and 10 hours of online discussions. From the perspective of the ECTS, the two courses are equivalent. The ECTS, with its arithmetic simplicity, appeals to the engineer in me. A 3-credit course equates to 144 learning hours. The course is spread over a 14-week semester. There is a 1-week Winter break and a shorter week in honour of Dr Martin Luther King, Junior. Do the math.

Similarly, and more importantly, the ECTS provides me with a tool to engineer a semester of learning activities. Indeed, I view the creation of a syllabus when designing a course as an engineering problem. And the ECTS enables me to engineer the pieces and parts logically and systematically. Curriculum, instructional, and assessment design are individual elements of a course, but they must be engineered to work together as a whole. My use of the ECTS for course design goes a long way to enhancing student learning outcomes. Numerous students have commented, for example, that the concision of learning activities and their corresponding number of learning hours contributes to their grasp of an overarching course 'narrative'. The granularity which ECTS demands makes it easier for students to track their learning; they can simply check off each learning activity as it is completed. Indeed, many students, especially part-time graduate students whose schedules are hectic with work and family commitments, have told me that they appreciate the focus of ECTS on learning hours which facilitates planning, allowing them to allocate the appropriate amount of time for each learning activity, and thereby enhancing their learning outcomes.

## How I prepare and organise my pedagogy to enhance student learning outcomes

In Living Educational Theory, a teacher's educational values are not isolated but instead are considered to be embodied in her/his professional practice. I shall illustrate how my educational values are embodied in my professional practice by describing one specific pedagogy: *Homerton Changemakers*, which is a three-year, integrated, co-curricular programme which I developed for Homerton College undergraduate students at the University of Cambridge. In brief, *Homerton Changemakers* aims to help Homerton College undergraduate students become changemakers. It is part of the College's *"long-term commitment to intelligent education combined with vision and practical hard graft: the tools for creating a more just, sustainable, inclusive world"* (Homerton Changemakers, 2023). The programme also supports Homerton College undergraduate students' mental and physical health during their three years of studies, emphasising self-clarification and self-fortification. It prepares them to thrive in a world which is increasingly ambiguous, complex, interconnected, and dynamic (ACID). And it increases the employability of Homerton College undergraduate students by encouraging both a mindset and a skill set which bolster their academic degrees.

*Homerton Changemakers* is particularly intriguing if viewed in the context of the purpose of higher education. The colleges of the University of Cambridge have traditionally (and perhaps not surprisingly) held a singular focus on academic achievement, with edification as the primary purpose of higher education. Other universities in the United Kingdom and elsewhere, however, have been pushing education of the 'whole student'. They have been emphasising student experience at university, and they have begun to redesign courses of study with a view to student employability.

*Homerton Changemakers* provides Homerton College undergraduate students numerous opportunities to iterate through the Kolb's experiential learning cycle (1984). The programme begins, for example, with a real-life, community-embedded challenge. But throughout the three years of the programme, students have opportunities for many other experiences, including inspirational TED-style talks from real changemakers, movie nights, workshops, international field trips, and internships. Built into the programme are the requisite time, opportunities, and support for the reflection, abstraction, and experimentation stages of the Kolb-ian learning cycle (1984). Moreover, my assessment of educational value is also evidenced in *Homerton Changemakers*. Indeed, assessment forms the backbone of the programme, with multiple and different types of assessments scattered throughout the three-year student journey. In Year 3, for example, students participate in a leadership workshop after completing an assessment identifying leadership style and traits.

Finally, storytelling is a cornerstone of *Homerton Changemakers*. In Year 1 of the programme, for example, Homerton College students participate in a storytelling workshop to explore stories' role in leadership and develop their skills as storytellers. Throughout the 3-year programme, students participate in a variety of experiences which rely on storytelling. And students are encouraged to document their three-year personal and professional journeys using an e-portfolio.

## Section 3: The outcome

In this section, I discuss my educational values with respect to enhancing student learning outcomes, first from the student perspective, and then from my teacher perspective.

### Student perspective

Living Educational Theory is premised on the notion that students benefit from reflective teachers, who continually strive to *"recognise problem areas, to imagine solutions, to try out solutions through a process of trial and error, to evaluate the outcomes and to modify the problems in light of the evaluation"*

(Whitehead, 1983:175). Therefore, reflective teachers engage in action research in their daily professional lives, which, *"seeks to bring together action and reflection, theory and practice, in participation with others, in the pursuit of practical solutions to issues of pressing concerns to people, and more generally, the flourishing of individual persons and their communities"* (Reason & Bradbury, 2001:1).

Action research is steeped in reflection — the *"process of becoming aware of one's context, of the influence of societal and ideological constraints on previously taken-for-granted practices, and gaining control over the direction of these influences"* (Carr and Kemmis, 1986:37). It leverages the personal knowledge (Polyani, 1974) of the action researcher. And it recasts research as an activity of practitioners rather than scientists proper because reflection and theory development occur *in situ* (Schön, 1983). Indeed, *"[w]hen someone reflects-in-action, he becomes a researcher in the practice context. He is not dependent on the categories of established theory and technique, but constructs a new theory of the unique case"* (Schön, 1983:24).

If teaching is *"viewed as consisting of practical problems requiring deliberation and action for their solution"* (Calderhead, 1989:44) for enhancing student learning outcomes then action research is seemingly an ideal research approach for reflective teachers. Indeed, action research is how a teacher addresses everyday practical questions of the kind, 'How do I improve this process of education here?' (Whitehead, 1998c). And in Living Educational Theory, action research is the 'natural' research tradition by which a teacher constructs her/his living educational theory…not as a one-off scholarly exercise, but as part of her/his quotidian routine.

As an example, I have been using computer-based simulations since 2002, when I adopted MarkStrat for a capstone marketing strategy course. With each use of a simulation, I assess student learning outcomes through a combination of competitive performance in the simulation and a written submission which takes the form of an annual report. I generally allocate 10-20% of a student's grade to the competitive performance and the remainder to the annual report, which allows a student to overcome poor performance with the annual report.

It was more than 15 years into my use of computer-based simulations, however, when I acknowledged that I was not exploiting the full power of simulations. I was well pleased with myself for having adopted simulations when many of my colleagues continued to rely on lectures.

The simulations were doubtless a hit with my students, whose engagement was higher than with other pedagogical methods. And anecdotal evidence suggested that student learning outcomes were superior relative to other pedagogical methods which I had previously used. However, I had failed to recognise that the notion of reflective practice, which I was adopting, could also be applied to students. Indeed, students can achieve deeper learning by engaging in active reflection. And I knew this. Several colleagues at LiHE symposia had written chapters on such topics as reflective practice, student journaling, and e-journals. I was simply not implementing it in my course, specifically not in the computer-based simulations.

Immediately following this recognition, I added a reflection component to the annual report. It was slightly awkward because CEO reflections on their learning do not generally appear in an annual report. Nevertheless, student learning outcomes were enhanced by 'forcing' students to share their thoughts about the simulation, their teams, the links between the simulation and the course concepts and theories, their mis-plays, and so on.

## Teacher perspective — my reflections

In Living Educational Theory, a teacher reflects on her/his practice using action research, through which her/his *"philosophy of education is engaged as a first person participant"* (Whitehead, 1992:1). This living educational theory captures in detail her/his educational values and the solutions which were developed therefrom. By documenting these reflections, she/he claims to know her/his professional practice…but subjects it to public scrutiny.

Unsurprisingly, one external examiner recalled during the *viva voce*, my use of the concept of love to introduce one of my ten educational values. He proceeded by noting that my living educational theory itself is relatively devoid of love. Consequently, since the *viva voce* (and channelling my inner Tina Turner), I have been pondering the question, 'What's love got to do with it?'. Is love the motivating force behind my professional practice? What does it mean when I proclaim that I love being a professor (a marketing educator)? And how, if at all, does love play into the way in which I serve my students?

Admittedly, my living educational theory is relatively devoid of love. I certainly hope that it does not read as a dispassionate treatise on my teaching – that my professional practice, which I have theorised as an analogy that teaching is like engineering, does not paint me as some robotic, heartless, and mechanistic marketing educator…because the exact opposite is true. I am passionate about my profession. The stay-at-home measures implemented due to the Covid-19 pandemic, and which kept me out of the classroom, left me feeling empty. And although it sounds somewhat sentimental, I consider students to be my *raison d'être*.

Love, it seems, has got a lot to do with it. The notion of love as the wellspring of my professional practice conjures up the Japanese concept of 'ikigai'. Translated as 'a reason for being', ikigai sits at the confluence of four dimensions: 1) what you love, 2) what the world needs, 3) what you can be paid for, and 4) what you are good at. According to Garcia (2017), ikigai defines the meaningfulness in your life. It is akin to Maslow's (1971) idea of self-actualisation. It is what makes you "*jump out of bed each morning*" (Oppong, 2018). I use ikigai frequently, usually when counselling students (both young and old) about their post-business school careers. And I almost always refer to myself as a 'poster child' for ikigai, boasting that I have found that sweet spot at the confluence of the four dimensions. I wonder, therefore, if a valuable complement/supplement to Living Educational Theory might be (as I have begun to sketch out here) an exploration of the motivating force at the root of professional practice. Indeed, it might be worth including love, passion, compulsion, conviction, or other conative force which drives professional practice as a key component of a living educational theory.

I also wonder if there is any kind of relationship between love and student learning outcomes. Indeed, can a loving professor have some kind of heliotropic effect on students? Cameron (2010) has documented this as part of a broader research agenda on positive organisations. A focus on the positive is life-giving for employees in organisations, just as light enhances thriving in living organisms. By extension, it seems logical that love would enhance learning in students. The concept of love in the context of professions also brings to mind the philosophy of servant leadership, which has recently gained popularity in management and popular literature. Servant leadership inverts the traditional hierarchical view of organisations in which a leader 'commands' employees from on high, emphasising instead that servant leaders situate employees above them and aim to empower and uplift them (Tarallo, 2018). Therefore, an interesting twist on servant leadership might revolve around the concept of love in the context of professions and, more specifically, around the obligation to serve students, which many teachers appear to have.

The philosophy of servant leadership also alludes to the topic of responsibility, which was also raised during the *viva voce*. Although I doubtless feel obligated to serve my students, as a marketing educator, I might also be responsible for serving other stakeholders within my community of practice. Truthfully, I had not given this much thought prior to the *viva voce*. To be fair, I have conducted teaching workshops for doctoral students as part of the doctoral consortium, which the *Society for Marketing Advances* runs each year at its annual conference. But beyond that, my engagement with a wider array of stakeholders has been limited. Perhaps publications like this chapter are a small step in that direction.

## Section 4: Moving forward

In Living Educational Theory, a living educational theory is considered to be organic, in a permanent state of flux — the 'living' in Living Educational Theory. Indeed, it morphs as the teacher reflects on her/his educational values and the practice-solutions developed therefrom. And, of course, new educational values might emerge to complement or supplant existing educational values. As an example, reflections on love, servant leadership, and responsibility have prompted me to consider the role of relationships in education. I am adamant that social interaction is not a necessary evil of being a professor. I phrased it thus, because I am convinced some colleagues genuinely dislike students (see Jose, 2023 in this book, who has identified different faculty member orientations).

I also recognise, however, that I can (and do) develop different types of relationships with different students. For example, in a recent cross-cultural business module, some students visited my office weekly, asking me for advice, chatting about my international travels, or discussing the module materials in greater depth. There were other students, however, with whom the interaction was limited to class time only, and even then, it remained at a very hierarchical student-professor level.

This reminds me of different stages in the evolution of marketing, each characterised by a different philosophical/operational approach to the interaction between a company and its customers. In the early years of marketing, for example, the relationship between a company and its customers was primarily transactional in nature, focused on the exchange between them. In the latter part of the twentieth century, customer relationship management emerged as the dominant marketing logic. It specified that a company ought to develop more intimate relationships with its customers. And more recently, there has been much talk about key account management, which advocates very intense relationships, but with a limited and select group of customers. I often describe these three different stages in the evolution of marketing according to three different types of relationships: acquaintances, friendships, and marriages. In a future research project, I plan to examine different types of student relationships, drawing on the different stages in the evolution of marketing. More germane to this anthology, I hope to explore how these different types of student relationships can enhance student learning outcomes.

## Conclusion

My Doctor of Professional Studies degree has been both personally and professionally rewarding. Indeed, constructing my living educational theory allowed me to crystallise my community of practice and my professional identity, which, although seemingly trivial, was revelatory. Perhaps more importantly, it afforded me the (once in a lifetime?) opportunity to engage in my profession at a depth and breadth which would be inconceivable under normal circumstances. Subsequently, I became a more conscious teacher, aware of how my educational values shape my professional practice and how, in turn, my professional practice re-shapes my educational values. In the spirit of the saying 'physician, health thyself', it allowed me to attend to myself as a marketing educator…thereby enhancing student learning outcomes.

Consequently, I encourage other teachers to explore their professional practices in this kind of *autocritique*, subjecting their own living educational theories to public scrutiny. In doing so, I am confident that they will also become more conscious practitioners, aware of how their educational values shape their professional practices, and, in turn, how their professional practices re-shape their educational values. More importantly, they will know themselves better as teachers, and thereby enhance their teaching outcomes, and ultimately enhance student learning outcomes. Physician, heal thyself, indeed.

## About the Author

John D Branch is Clinical Associate Professor of Business Administration at the Stephen M. Ross School of Business at the University of Michigan, USA. He can be contacted at this email: jdbranch@umich.edu

## Bibliography

Bochner, A., & Ellis, C. (2006). Communication as autoethnography. In G. Shepherd, J. John & T. Striphas (Eds.), *Communication as…Perspectives on theory*. Sage.

Branch, J., Hershey, L., & Vannette, D. (2011). The use of RISK® for introducing marketing strategy. In C. Nygaard, C. Holtham & N. Courtney (Eds.), *Beyond transmission: Innovations in university teaching*. Libri Publishing Ltd.

Calderhead, J (1989). Reflective teaching and teacher education. *Teaching and Teacher Education*, 5(1), 43-51.

Cameron, K. (2010). Five keys to flourishing in trying times. *Leader to Leader*, Winter, 45-51.

Carr, W., & Kemmis, S. (1986). *Becoming critical: Education, knowledge and action research*. Farmer Press.

Dewey, J. (1938). *Experience & education*. Kappa Delta Pi.

Ellis, C., Adams, T., & Bochner, P. (2011). Autoethnography: An overview. *Forum: Qualitative Social Research*. 12(1).

Garcia, H. (2017). *Ikigai: the Japanese secret to a long and happy life*. Penguin.

Gottshcall, J. (2012). *The storytelling animal: how stories make us human*. Houghton Mifflin.

Hirschman, E. (1986). Humanistic inquiry in marketing research: philosophy, method, and criteria. *Journal of Marketing Research*, 23, 237-249.

Homerton Changemakers. (2023). Retrieved July 3, 2023, from https://www.homerton.cam.ac.uk/homerton-changemakers

Jose, S. (2023). Enhancing learning outcomes through a student-centred learning-teaching process in a Master of Human Resource Management Program. In K. Enomoto, R. Warner & C. Nygaard (Eds.), *Enhancing student learning outcomes in higher education*. Libri Publishing Ltd.

Kolb, D. (1984). *Experiential learning: experience as the source of learning and development*. Prentice-Hall.

MacLure, M. (1996). Telling transitions: Boundary work in narratives of becoming an action researcher. *British Educational Research Journal, 22*(3), 273-286.

Mamede, S., Rikers, R., & Schmidt, H. (2012). The role of reflection in medical practice: continuing professional development in medicine. In A. McKee & M. Eraut (Eds), *Learning trajectories, innovation and identity for professional development*. Springer.

Margitay-Becht, A., & Das, U. (2023). Enhancing student learning through hidden motivational learning outcomes. In K. Enomoto, R. Warner & C. Nygaard (Eds.), *Enhancing student learning outcomes in higher education*. Libri Publishing Ltd.

Maslow, A. H. (1971). *Self-actualization*. Big Sur Recordings.

Massey, J. (2018). *Physical, heal thyself*. Naturopathic Doctor News & Review. Retrieved July 3, 2023, from https://ndnr.com/mindbody/physician-heal-thyself-2/

Middlesex University (2023). Doctor of Professional Studies (Transdisciplinary). Retrieved July 3, 2023, from https://www.mdx.ac.uk/courses/postgraduate/professional-studies-transdisciplinary

Oppong, T. (2018). Ikigai: the Japanese secret to a long and happy life might just help you live a more fulfilling life. *Thrive Global*. Retrieved July 20, 2023, from https://thomasoppong.com/ikigai-the-japanese-secret-to-a-long-and-happy-life-might-just-help-you-live-a-more-fulfilling-life/

Polyani, M. (1974). *Personal knowledge*. University of Chicago Press.

QAA. *Characteristics statement: Doctoral degree*. Retrieved July 3, 2023, from https://www.qaa.ac.uk/docs/qaa/quality-code/doctoral-degree-characteristics-statement-2020.pdf?sfvrsn=a3c5ca81_14

Peirce Edition Project. (1998). The essential Peirce: Selected philosophical writings. Volume 2: 1893-1913. In the *Peirce Edition Project*. Indiana University Press. (EP 2)

Reason, P., & Bradbury, H. (2001). *Handbook of Action Research: Participative Inquiry and Practice*. Sage.

Ricoeur, P. (1981). *Hermeneutics and the social sciences*. Cambridge University Press.

Schön, D. (1983). *The reflective practitioner: How professionals think in action*. Basic Books.

Schumpeter, J. (1975). *Capitalism, socialism and democracy*. Harper.

Swann, S. (2023). Student-centric pedagogy: What happens when learning outcomes are customised to students' own interests. In K. Enomoto, R.

Warner & C. Nygaard (Eds.), *Enhancing student learning outcomes in higher education*. Libri Publishing Ltd.

Tarallo, M. (2018). *The art of servant leadership*. SHRM. Retrieved May 28, 2020, from https://www.shrm.org/resourcesandtools/hr-topics/organizational-and-employee-development/pages/the-art-of-servant-leadership.aspx

van Manen, M. (1990). *Researching lived experience: Human science for an action sensitive pedagogy*. State University of New York Press.

Vygotsky, L. (1978). *Interaction between learning and development*. Harvard University Press.

Whitehead, J. (1983). The use of personal educational theories in in-service education. *Journal of In-Service Education, 9*(3), 174-177.

Whitehead, J. (1989a). Creating a living educational theory from questions of the kind, 'How can I improve my practice?' *Cambridge Journal of Education, 19*(1), 41-52.

Whitehead, J. (1989b). How do we improve research-based professionalism in education? A question which includes action research, educational theory and the politics of educational knowledge. *British Educational Research Journal, 15*(1), 3-17.

Whitehead, J. (1992). How can my philosophy of action research transform and improve my professional practice and produce a good social order? A response to Ortrun Zuber-Skerritt. In C. Bruce & A. Russell (Eds.), *Proceedings of the Second World Congress on Action Learning, Action Research and Process Management*. ALARPM.

Whitehead, J. (1998a). *Developing research-based professionalism through living educational theories*. Paper presented at: *Educational Studies Association of Ireland Annual Conference*. Dublin, Ireland: ESAI.

Whitehead, J. (1998b). *Creating educational theories through paradigmatic and post-paradigmatic possibilities*. American Educational Research Association Conference. San Diego, CA, United States.

Whitehead, J. (1998c). *Educational action researchers creating their own educational theories*. American Educational Research Association Conference. San Diego, CA, United States.

Wood, D., Bruner, J., & Ross, G. (1976). The role of tutoring in problem solving. *Journal of Child Psychology and Psychiatry, 17*, 89-100.

Zwozdiak-Meyers, P. (2012). *The teacher's reflective practice handbook: Becoming an extended professional through capturing evidence-informed practice*. Taylor & Francis.

Chapter 3
# Enablers of Student Learning Outcomes Based on Eight Cases of Second Language Learning and Teaching in Higher Education

Kayoko Enomoto and Richard Warner

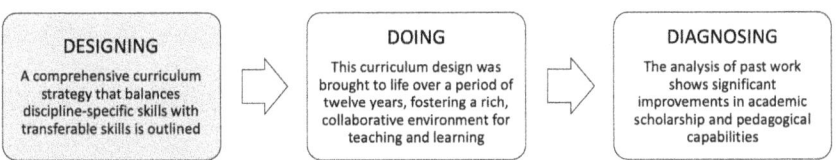

## Preamble

With their chapter, Kayoko Enomoto and Richard Warner contribute to this book, *Enhancing Student Learning Outcomes in Higher Education*, by analysing eight cases of second language learning and teaching. In so doing, they identified eleven enablers of learning outcomes that help develop language students' transferable skills in addition to their second language-specific knowledge and skills. The authors relate to the three phases of the central ESLO model of the book in this way:

In the DESIGNING phase, they emphasise the need to regularly review and reassess learning outcomes, 'balancing' second language-specific and transferable skills. They also outline their responsibility as university language educators in assisting students to understand learning outcomes. They achieve this through designing scaffolded second language curricula.

In the DOING phase, they present their experiences with curriculum design, brought to life over twelve years. This fosters a rich, collaborative environment for learning and teaching, developing both language-specific and transferable skills as learning outcomes. They illustrate the practical implementation of their curriculum design through collaborative academic dialogue and publication.

In the DIAGNOSING phase, they employ a collaborative auto-ethnographic method and analysis to reflect upon their pedagogical approaches, as documented in their published works. In so doing, they identify the enablers of student learning outcomes where both language-specific and transferable skills are developed 'in tandem'.

## Introduction

In this chapter, we analyse our practice of enhancing student learning outcomes through our past twelve years of teaching. We do so by retrospectively interrogating how we have worked with learning outcomes in eight cases of second language learning at the University of Adelaide, Australia, since 2011. We have published in-depth accounts and reflections on these eight cases in *The Learning in Higher Education Series* (Libri Publishing Ltd.). Therefore, in writing this chapter, we had the opportunity to adopt a collaborative auto-ethnographic (CAE) approach (Chang et al., 2016; Godber & Atkins, 2021) to reflect on how we have evolved our teaching practices to enhance student learning outcomes. CAE can be defined as *"a qualitative research method that is simultaneously collaborative, autobiographical, and ethnographic"* (Chang et al., 2016:17). We followed the CAE approach adopted by Godber and Atkins (2021) to undertake critical reflection on our teaching practices published since 2011 (for comparison, see Branch, 2023 in this book who uses an auto-ethnographic approach). This approach enabled us to engage in the process of collaborative reflection. In so doing, we questioned how we had enabled student learning outcomes in our courses/programs, followed by analysing and interpreting our underlying values and drivers for enabling student learning outcomes. Through this CAE interrogation of the eight cases documented in the published chapters, we posit eleven effective enablers of successful student learning outcomes that help students develop transferable skills 'in addition to' second language-specific knowledge/skills for the benefit of their studies and future careers.

Making learning outcomes explicit to students is important. As university educators, we have often witnessed a lack of student understanding of learning outcomes in a given course/program: what learning outcomes are; how and why they are embedded; and how they are assessed. We have observed that such a lack of understanding is commonly seen among students with less well-developed academic skills and discernment, who tend to adopt surface learning methods and strategies (Enomoto, 2012a:105). Therefore, it is essential that we, as educators, make a conscious effort to raise students' understanding of learning outcomes. Doing so necessarily involves unpacking why the stipulated learning outcomes are relevant to their short-term and long-term goals — one key to motivating students to achieve those learning outcomes.

We use this definition of learning outcomes: *"statements of what a learner is expected to know, understand and/or be able to demonstrate at the end of a period of learning"* (Adam, 2006: B23-1:1). In addition, as Adam (2006) also notes, learning outcomes can take various multidimensional forms, often combining: 1) skill sets, 2) knowledge, 3) understandings, 4) attitudes, and 5) abilities that a student acquires via successful experiential interaction through a set of higher education (HE) experiences. Our second language learning and teaching contexts at the University, have required us to contemplate how we can effectively combine this multidimensional form of learning outcomes as understandable learning outcomes in our course/program curricula, learning activities and assessments. In our specific contexts, learning outcomes have encompassed second language-specific knowledge/skills (such as grammar, vocabulary, reading, writing, listening and speaking) and transferable skills (such as self-regulated learning skills, research skills, reflective learning skills, communication skills, intercultural competence). Furthermore, learning outcomes are also an exemplification of a specific methodological approach, through which the curriculum is both expressed and described (Adam, 2006) which, in all our cases, balances both discipline specific and transferable skills.

## Chapter overview and key takeaways

This chapter has four main sections. In Section 1, we provide a background to our work with student learning outcomes by presenting our CAE narrative, describing our journey to and within the community of the Institute for Learning in Higher Education (LiHE). In Section 2, by conducting a CAE methodological and reflective inventory of our eight cases of enhancing second language students' learning outcomes in HE, we outline how we balanced the development of second language-specific knowledge/skills with transferable skills as learning outcomes. In Section 3, we interrogate the effectiveness of our theory-underpinned learning models and pedagogical approaches that we utilised through our LiHE journey. In Section 4, we discuss possible ways to meet emerging challenges in the learning outcomes space in HE, before we conclude our chapter.

Reading this chapter, you will gain the following three insights:
1. How we have designed curricula that enable students to develop transferable skills in addition to second language-specific knowledge/skills for the benefit of their studies and future work;

2. How we have informed our teaching practice with learning theories and pedagogical approaches to enable us to locate the positive enablers of desired student learning outcomes;

3. That the eleven enablers of our desired learning outcomes encouraged students to shift their focus away from marks/grades towards their learning processes.

## Section 1: Background to our work with learning outcomes

The chapter is set in the context of our being university educators, working in second language teaching, with Kayoko teaching Japanese as a second language and Richard teaching English as an Additional Language (EAL). We have remained working in these fields, following various iterations of degree/non-degree programs and courses (credit and non-credit bearing). Kayoko is situated in the School of Social Sciences, Richard in the School of Education, both within the Faculty of Arts, Business, Law and Economics at the University of Adelaide. We both share an Applied Linguistics background, from the University of Edinburgh, Scotland, and have been highly involved in second language teaching since the beginning of our time at the University of Adelaide, over 30 years ago. We have seen how market-driven fluctuations have impacted such teaching and learning scenarios in university policies. This situation is coupled with the fact that the rapid and continuing changes in digitally-enhanced new technologies have precipitated a revolution in how and in what learning spaces we learn, be it physical or virtual (Bartholomew & Bartholomew, 2014); including MOOCs (Laurillard, 2016). All these changes, at least in an Australian HE context, have also been set midst a scenario of considerable transformation, diversifying and broadening student cohorts, with substantial growth seen in the numbers of non-traditional students from lower socio-economic backgrounds (Bradley et al., 2008). This widening participation in Australian HE, with subsequent changes to the educational landscape, is largely the result of federal government strategy, particularly since 2009. Alongside the influx of the non-traditional student cohort, there has been a substantial increase in international students, as universities nationwide seek to offset government funding cuts.

The student cohort transformation was, for both of us as university educators, pivotal in our reflections upon determining pathways to achievable learning outcomes for all types of students, including:

- traditional local students;

- non-traditional students-often first in family and/or low socio-economic status; and

- international students (often from non-English speaking countries).

Informing such reflections were our observations, from meeting past students, that not all students who had achieved high grades necessarily became high achievers in their chosen careers. Indeed, based on our former students' (formal and informal) career updates and information, it is not uncommon to discover that those students who had achieved low to medium grades actually had successful career progression. This provided us with useful insights for our reflection; what stood out was that these low to medium grade students possessed well-developed leadership, teamwork, digital literacy and communication skills. However, it was often the case that these skill sets were not part of course assessments. As university educators, this led us to make the conscious decision that transferable skills development, incorporated within our courses and programs, was critical for our students' working futures. Our decision was in line with the Threshold Concepts Framework of Meyer and Land (2003), whereby transferable skills are integrated into learning outcomes and aligned with threshold concepts.

In our particular contexts, such transferable skills development needed to be 'balanced' against language-specific knowledge/skills and that student learning outcomes reflect such a balance. Therefore, we viewed it as our goal that learning outcomes in our language courses and programs were characterised not only by second language-specific knowledge/skills, but also by the development of transferable skills (Oliver, 2011), which could be utilised by students in their other courses and beyond into the workplace. With this goal in mind of improving student learning outcomes for all students, this generic skills transferability (Enomoto & Warner, 2018) was paramount.

This realisation drew our attention to the question of considering the enablers of learning outcomes in balancing second language-specific knowledge/skills and transferable skills development. The goal of achieving such a balance led us to innovate our teaching practices underpinned by appropriate learning theories. Yet, to attain such a balance, we faced an all-too-common attitude, succinctly espoused in the following comment from a student in 2010. The student asked (verbally) in an orientation lecture: *"I need to pass this course to get my degree. 50% is a pass. A pass is a degree. So, how much work do you think I need to do to pass this course?"* (Enomoto & Warner, 2013:185). Such questions were by no means uncommon, and were indicative of some students viewing accumulation of the number of 'credit units' prescribed for their degree as their only university learning goals.

Moreover, this evidenced to us that such students demonstrated an understanding deficit in terms of the value of 'learning processes'. They seemed unaware that what they absorb from such learning processes may eventually reduce their academic load and positively impact both their marks and futures, both short and longer term. This required *"a pedagogically viable strategy to shift students' focus away from marks and reduction in workload and towards their learning processes"* (Enomoto & Warner, 2013:183). Thus, raising students' awareness of the value of learning processes became a crucial element in our curricular design, to develop their second language-specific knowledge/skills and transferable skills as learning outcomes.

To achieve such learning outcomes, we needed to facilitate students to shift their focus away from marks/grades towards their learning processes. To do so, required us to create learning tasks whereby higher-order thinking skills, including critical thinking and problem-solving skills (Brush & Saye, 2002), could be developed. These higher-order thinking skills are requisite for success in developing both second language-specific knowledge/skills and transferable skills in our academic contexts. They happen when a student acquires new knowledge, stores it in their memory and organises, correlates or evaluates it, incorporating the sub-skills of analysis and synthesis, the highest skill levels in Bloom's Taxonomy (Bloom et al., 1956), updated by Krathwohl (2002), to realise a learning outcome (Abosalem, 2016).

As previously stated, these student learning outcome considerations were fed into the second language-specific knowledge/skills and transferable skills foci for developing our courses and programs in both Japanese and academic English for EAL students. We felt we were ploughing a lonely furrow, as both our institution and second language students alike tended to focus more on developing second language-specific knowledge/skills than balancing second language-specific and transferable skills. We were a silo, rather than representative of a majority of academics. Moreover, within this evolving academic teaching and learning environment, characterised by significant student cohort changes, there was little opportunity for local collegiate reflection on the impacts of the rapidly changing student landscape. Academics within our discipline areas, time-poor, when faced with different, increasingly diverse student cohorts, with commensurate increased class sizes and workloads, had little time to give us meaningful collaboration and feedback on our learning-outcome-focussed endeavours.

## International collegiality

Set against this landscape, we needed to look internationally for collegial support for such endeavours and find a teaching and learning-related publishing space, where we could share and receive feedback on our written work on the importance of balancing second language-specific knowledge/skills and transferable skills. At this juncture, we had the great fortune of discovering LiHE, which has provided us with such a collegial working space over the years. There has been the collegiality we sought, but LiHE has also provided a safe space, working with like-minded HE academics from around the world. This has helped us both to improve our own writing (and get published) and to offer our insights into the writing of others in this safe space, in a mutually supportive environment. Our journey with LiHE actually began with our participating separately in two different LiHE Symposia and publishing separate chapters in two different edited books in the same year, 2011.

The LiHE symposia adopt a collegial, collaborative academic writing publication model; this collaborative model was initiated and innovated by a group of academics who founded LiHE in 2007. Since then, the model has continuously evolved, incorporating and reflecting participants' collegial, constructive feedback and suggestions each year. The teaching and learning theme-based symposium, the cornerstone of the organisation's activity, echoes the Ancient Greek format, whereby co-creation is fundamental (Scott-Webber et al., 2014). The symposium, be it face-to-face or online (during the COVID-19 pandemic), brings together chapter writers, all of whom have had their chapter proposals — relevant to each theme of the LiHE edited book series — triple-blind peer-reviewed prior to acceptance. At the LiHE symposium, all the chapter writers work not only on their own chapter, but also collegially, in revising the chapters of their peers, and cooperate to construct a synthesised compilation. The chapter writers then submit their completed chapter after a few weeks, following which the carefully edited manuscript is forwarded to the publisher — Libri Publishing Ltd., UK.

Having both attended LiHE symposia in 2011, we quickly realised that our shared interests and values, as student-centred educators, made it a logical step for us to collaborate together. Our collaboration was not only to sound off ideas between each other but also to use those ideas to enlighten our teaching practices, including what informs and drives those practices, and to reach a broader audience for these practices through publication. Our reflections on the value and positive impact of our collaborations motivated us to take a CAE-guided contemplation of our LiHE journey as HE academics. Not counting this chapter, we have published eight chapters in this LiHE book series during our journey.

## Section 2: Inventory of our practice towards enhancing student learning outcomes

To write this chapter in itself, indeed, is part of our LiHE journey; at this point, we retrospectively reflect on what we have done to enable learning outcomes that balance second language-specific knowledge/skills and transferable skills in our curricular design since 2011. In order to do so, we deemed it crucial to bring about students' awareness and recognition that developing transferable skills (such as communication, digital literacy, critical thinking, problem-solving, and teamwork) are as equally relevant to their futures as developing second language-specific knowledge/skills. Coincidentally, in 2011, the Graduate Attributes for the Australian Qualifications Framework was published, requiring all universities, including our university, to also espouse core attributes that graduates should attain. In 2011, the University of Adelaide expressed these graduate attributes as follows:

- *"The ability to locate, analyse, evaluate and synthesise information from a wide variety of sources in a planned and timely manner;*
- *An ability to apply effective, creative and innovative solutions, both independently and cooperatively, to current and future problems;*
- *A proficiency in the appropriate use of contemporary technologies;*
- *A commitment to continuous learning and the capacity to maintain intellectual curiosity throughout life;*
- *An awareness of ethical, social and cultural issues within a global context and their importance in the exercise of professional skills and responsibilities."* (University of Adelaide, 2011 in Enomoto, 2012b:349).

However, at that time, the notion of graduate attributes appeared as a new institutional directive, rather than a grass-roots learning and teaching initiative. It was, as yet, unfamiliar to a majority of academics. Consequently, it appeared to be left to individual academics to embed the articulated attributes into curricula, as there were few institutional guidelines on how to realise those attributes as student learning outcomes.

Since then, Australian universities have endeavoured to integrate similar graduate attributes into curricula and teaching practices, and many universities have also developed their own institution-specific graduate attributes, particularly extending to the sphere of graduate employability. Yet, the literature defines the concept of employability in various ways (Römgens et al., 2020; Healy, 2023). Moreover, we have observed that employability seems to be used in HE institutions as a 'fuzzy' umbrella term to describe discipline-specific expertise and those capabilities and personal qualities which are transferable to meet the demands of today's workplace and beyond. This fuzziness perhaps is plausible, given the fact that contemporary student cohorts are more diverse than ever before, in terms of the changing goal posts in career goals, resulting in more diversity in their potential future pathways. Such pathways may likely involve several career shifts, in response to rapidly evolving workplace demands. Ongoing discussions surrounding the importance of employability, indeed, have occurred at our university resulting in the Graduate Employability Framework (University of Adelaide, 2021; also discussed in Bowd & Enomoto, 2023 in this book).

To continue our reflective journey, we adopted a CAE approach (Chang et al., 2016; Godber & Atkins, 2021) to allow ourselves to interrogate each other to ascertain our motivations for bringing about student learning outcomes in our own teaching practices chronologically. Since 2011, we have drawn upon theoretical frameworks such as Vygotsky's Zone of Proximal Development (ZPD) and Scaffolding (Vygotsky, 1978; see De Wilde and Forasacco, 2023 in this book, who detail the concept of ZPD), Bloom's Taxonomy (Bloom et al., 1956; see Andrews & St. Aubyn, 2023 in this book) updated by Krathwohl (2002), and the SOLO (Structure of the Observed Learning Outcome) Taxonomy (Biggs & Collis, 1982) to inform and develop the enablers of student learning outcomes as our models/approaches. Furthermore, working within the theoretical framework of constructive alignment (Biggs, 1996), our starting point has been the intended student learning outcomes, from which we align student learning activities and assessment tasks. If learning outcomes change, the aligned learning activities and assessment tasks must also be realigned for relevant effective learning to occur. Therefore, we do not underestimate the significance of continually reviewing and reassessing learning outcomes, and being agile enough to amend them appropriately in response to a rapidly-changing learning and teaching landscape.

As part of this CAE approach, we undertook the process of mind mapping as a useful research tool to determine enablers of student learning outcomes through our teaching and learning endeavours. Davies (2011:3) defines mind maps as *"a [visual] network of connected and related concepts"* and indeed, as he points out: *"Free-form, spontaneous thinking is required when creating a mind map…the aim of mind mapping is to find creative associations between ideas"*. As researchers, it was this spontaneous process that helped us firstly to brainstorm and then to organise our thinking threads, by way of creating a non-linear diagram to link each of our ideas, conceptual themes, and relevant information and relationships around our central topic – enablers of learning outcomes. This mind mapping process informed the analyses, interpretation and categorisation of our values and drivers for enabling student learning outcomes. Then, we interrogated each of our eight chapters in order to see how those values and drivers have been historically represented in our teaching practices since 2011.

Consequently, what clearly stood out was that our sustained embedding of the transferable skills development through our learning and teaching practices was showcased in each of our eight LiHE publications. At the same time, we also realised that we had, indeed, started to embed transferable skills as learning outcomes consequent to thinking about our students' longer-term benefits beyond university. In Section 3 below, we will demonstrate what enablers of student learning outcomes emerged through the eight chapters that reflect our teaching and learning endeavours since 2011.

## Section 3: The outcome of our LiHE publishing journey – our reflections

Our mind mapping process informed how we structured our CAE inventory in Table 1. We analysed and interpreted each of our eight book chapters in terms of categories:

1. Publication number;
2. Year of publication;
3. Chapter title;

Chapter 3

4. Underpinning learning theories/pedagogical approaches as enablers of learning outcomes;

5. Resulting transferable-skills-related learning outcomes.

Table 1 shows that since 2011, we have used a range of learning theories and theory-underpinned pedagogical approaches to achieve transferable-skills-related learning outcomes appropriately balanced with second language — Japanese and EAL – specific knowledge/skills development. In so doing, we encouraged students to understand and value their learning processes as crucial manifestations of 'learning' directly pertinent to their longer-term future benefits; not solely their short-term gains in terms of marks or grades.

| Pub # | Year | Chapter title | Underpinning learning theories/pedagogical approaches as enablers of learning outcomes | Resulting transferable-skills-related learning outcomes |
|---|---|---|---|---|
| 1 | 2011 Richard | Enabling postgraduate students to become autonomous ethnographers of their disciplines | • Control-Wedge-Based Scaffolded Curriculum Model (Cadman & Grey, 2000), ZPD and Scaffolding Theory (Vygotsky, 1978)<br>• Tripartite Relationship Model (Cargill & Cadman, 2005)<br>• Students as Researchers Approach (Paltridge, 2007)<br>• Community of Practice (Wenger, 1998) | • Intercultural competence<br>• Research skills<br>• Reflective learning skills<br>• Independent learning skills<br>• Critical thinking skills |

Enablers of Student Learning Outcomes Based on Eight Cases of Second Language Learning

| Pub # | Year | Chapter title | Underpinning learning theories/pedagogical approaches as enablers of learning outcomes | Resulting transferable-skills-related learning outcomes |
|---|---|---|---|---|
| 2 | 2011 Kayoko | Fostering high quality learning through a scaffolded curriculum | • Control-Wedge-Based Scaffolded Curriculum Model (Cadman & Grey, 2000)<br>• ZPD and Scaffolding Theory (Vygotsky, 1978) | • Research skills<br>• Critical thinking skills<br>• IT skills/digital literacy (including in Japanese)<br>• Independent learning skills<br>• Oral presentation skills |
| 3 | 2013 Kayoko & Richard | Building student capacity for reflective learning | • Experiential Learning Model (Kolb, 1984)<br>• Community of Practice (Wenger, 1998)<br>• ZPD and Scaffolding Theory (Vygotsky, 1978) | • Reflective learning skills<br>• Self-regulated learning skills (including time management and organisational skills)<br>• Increased self-efficacy |
| 4 | 2014 Kayoko & Richard | Promoting student reflection through considerate design of a virtual learning space | • Situated Learning Theory (Lave & Wenger 1991; Wenger, 1998)<br>• Social Learning Theory (Bandura, 1977; 1994), ZPD and Scaffolding Theory (Vygotsky, 1978) | • Reflective learning skills<br>• IT skills/digital literacy (including in Japanese)<br>• Independent learning skills<br>• Communication skills<br>• Research skills<br>• Self-regulated learning (including time management skills)<br>• Increased self-efficacy |
| 5 | 2015 Richard & Kayoko | Embedding research skills in the curriculum design of a pathway programme for international students | • Experiential Learning Model (Kolb, 1984)<br>• Control-Wedge Model (Cadman & Grey, 2000)<br>• ZPD and Scaffolding Theory (Vygotsky, 1978) | • Research skills<br>• Independent learning skills,<br>• Teamwork skills<br>• Intercultural competence |

Chapter 3

| Pub # | Year | Chapter title | Underpinning learning theories/pedagogical approaches as enablers of learning outcomes | Resulting transferable-skills-related learning outcomes |
|---|---|---|---|---|
| 6 | 2018<br><br>Kayoko & Richard | Developing undergraduate students' transferable generic skills through an innovative group drama project | • Process Model of Intercultural Competence (Adapted from Deardorff, 2011)<br>• ZPD and Scaffolding Theory (Vygotsky, 1978) | • Teamwork skills<br>• Communication skills<br>• Intercultural competence<br>• IT skills/digital literacy (including in Japanese)<br>• Research skills<br>• Critical thinking skills |
| 7 | 2021<br><br>Richard & Kayoko | An innovative assessment method to evaluate independent learning and academic writing skills | • Teaching-Learning Cycle Model (Adapted from Caon-Parsons & Dimmell, 2016; Kolb & Kolb, 2005)<br>• ZPD and Scaffolding Theory (Vygotsky, 1978) | • Independent learning skills<br>• Intercultural competence<br>• Communication skills<br>• Teamwork skills<br>• Reflective learning skills |
| 8 | 2022<br><br>Kayoko & Richard | Partnering with student leaders: active learning through integration of Peer Assisted Study Sessions into an undergraduate language course | • Students as Partners Model (Healey et al., 2014; 2016)<br>• 360° Feed-forward Active Learning Model (Enomoto & Warner, 2022), ZPD and Scaffolding Theory (Vygotsky, 1978) | • Communication skills<br>• Digital literacy (including in Japanese)<br>• Self-regulated learning skills, including time management<br>• Reflective learning skills<br>• Leadership skills |

*Table 1: An inventory of eight book chapters conducted through a CAE approach.*

In Figure 1 (below), we visualise the above column 'Underpinning learning theories/pedagogical approaches as enablers of learning outcomes' that we utilised through these eight chapters that have manifested our teaching and learning practices since 2011.

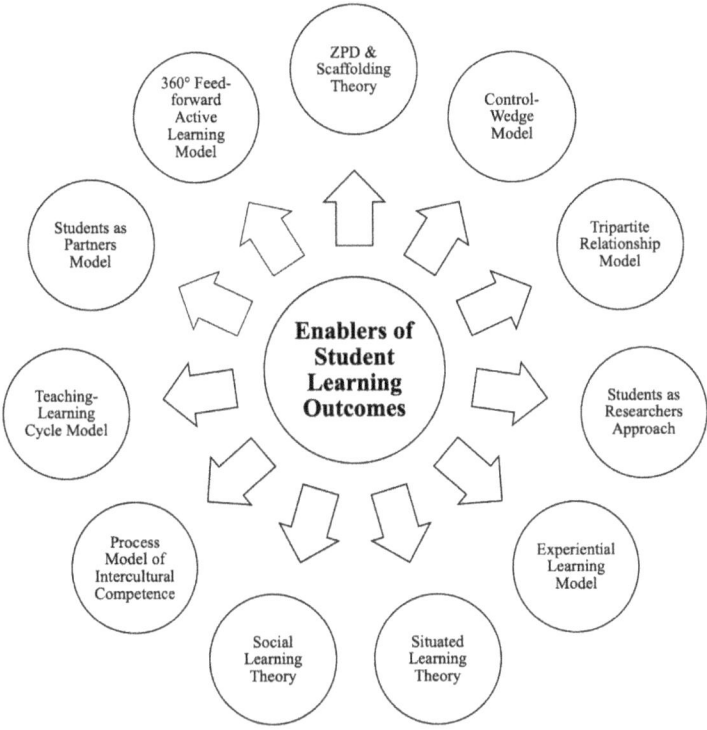

*Figure 1: Enablers of student learning outcomes.*

## Publication 1 (2011): Enabling postgraduate students to become autonomous ethnographers of their disciplines

As Table 1 shows, chronologically, we began our LiHE publishing journey in 2011, at that time a separate journey. Richard published in the context of two international postgraduate semester-length academic development programs at the University of Adelaide: the Integrated Bridging Program (IBP) for research students and the Introductory Academic Program (IAP) for coursework students. The pedagogy that both programs followed was informed by the conviction that postgraduate education should integrate the postgraduate into the broader academic community environment (Picard, Warner & Velautham, 2011), as well as into their specific discipline-based *"community of practice"* (Lave & Wenger, 1991:69).

Already, at this very early stage of the LiHE journey, the issue of transferability was paramount, such as in postgraduates needing to demonstrate marketable skills that were transferable on a global stage. As can be seen in Table 1, one of the theory-driven enablers of learning outcomes was the Control-Wedge Scaffolded Curriculum Model (Cadman & Grey, 2000). This model is characterised by a student-centred gradual shift in control from educator to student as a course or program development, with a corresponding increase in student autonomy. In summary, this publication outlines the enablers of learning outcomes, which included the following transferable skills:

- Intercultural competence;
- Research skills;
- Reflective learning skills;
- Independent learning skills;
- Critical-thinking skills.

## *Publication 2 (2011): Fostering high quality learning through a scaffolded curriculum*

The Control-Wedge Scaffolded Curriculum Model (Cadman & Grey, 2000) also functioned as a learning outcome enabler in Kayoko's LiHE chapter in the same year. This chapter related to a different student cohort, namely a third-year undergraduate course titled Advanced Japanese (for non-native speakers of Japanese) from various disciplines. Yet, the issue of transferability was also foregrounded in this highly scaffolded course, which was framed so that, in this second language learning context, skills developed from scaffolded tasks could be utilised in other learning scenarios in the students' own disciplines (Enomoto, 2011).

Furthermore, several learning outcomes, relevant to transferability skills, forthcoming from this Advanced Japanese course, namely, research skills, critical thinking skills and independent learning skills, were synonymous with those in the postgraduate programs outlined in the previous paragraph. Such synergies, in our respective second-language fields of operation, were an important consideration in our decision to publish together within LiHE. In summary, this publication outlines the enablers of learning outcomes, including the following transferable skills:

- Research skills;
- Critical-thinking skills;
- IT skills/digital literacy (including in Japanese);
- Independent learning skills;
- Oral presentation skills.

## Publication 3 (2013): Building student capacity for reflective learning

Our first joint LiHE chapter publication took place in 2013, when we collaborated on a book chapter which focused on a first-year beginners Japanese 1A course, with an approximate mix of 50% international students and 50% local students from both traditional and non-traditional backgrounds (Enomoto & Warner, 2013). As in our individual chapters outlined above, our pedagogical requisite guided us to balance second language-specific knowledge/skills, the community of practice (Lave & Wenger, 1991) element, with more transferable skills. In addition, we were mindful of the importance of having a strategy that was sufficiently pedagogically viable to work towards shifting students' focus away from grades and workload and more towards their learning processes. The principal learning outcome enabler was the Experiential Learning Model (Kolb, 1984), whereby the scaffolded reflective learning (inherent to the course) as learning processes are expedited through students' contemplations that translate their own experiences into learning (Enomoto & Warner, 2013).

Moreover, a learning-outcomes-related theme, tying together this third study with the previous two (individual) studies, lies in the independent/self-regulated learning skills elements, which might not be unexpected given the shared focus on skills transferability. In summary, this publication outlines the enablers of learning outcomes, including the following transferable skills:

- Reflective learning skills;
- Self-regulated learning skills (including time management and organisational skills);
- Increased self-efficacy.

## Publication 4 (2014): Promoting student reflection through considerate design of a virtual learning space

In 2014, our collaborative chapter further developed the notion of community of practice (Lave & Wenger, 1991) in terms of utilising a blog as a scaffolded reflective learning space related learning outcome enabler. We drew on Lave and Wenger's (1991) situated learning theory to help inform such an enabler, as they determine that learning is situated, thus necessitating participatory engagement on the part of the learners, which lies within the aforesaid student community of practice (Enomoto & Warner, 2014). We argued that our community of practice enabled our students to develop their reflective skills in writing their blogs and give input, in the form of comments and feedback, to their peers. Moreover, such activities could well lead to what Bandura (1994) terms vicarious learning, on the part of the students, where behaviour can be altered because a person observes and models the behaviour of others — in our case through the medium of a blog as a reflective learning space.

The importance of the development of reflection as a transferable-skills-related learning outcome is also noted in two of the previous chapters summarised in Table 1, namely Publications 1 and 3. In addition, the development of research skills and independent skills, again in the context of transferable-skills-related learning outcomes, are foregrounded in this 2014 publication, as they are in Publications 1 and 3 for independent learning skills, and Publications 1 and 2 for research skills. There was also a shared focus on digital literacy, with Publication 2 as a transferable-skills-related learning outcome. In summary, this publication outlines the enablers of learning outcomes, including the following transferable skills:

- Reflective learning skills;
- IT skills/digital literacy (including in Japanese);

- Independent learning skills;
- Communication skills;
- Research skills;
- Self-regulated learning, including time management skills;
- Increased self-efficacy.

## Publication 5 (2015): Embedding research skills in the curriculum design of a pathway programme for international students

The following year, 2015, saw us turn our attention to a different student cohort. We presented a chapter on embedding student research skills into the curriculum design for a direct-entry pathway program, the Pre-enrolment English Program (PEP), for international EAL students at the University. As a crucial part of the program, students were required to complete the 'Independent Learning Skills' component, whereby learning is accomplished via engaging in scaffolded tasks and activities, one of which was the 'Independent Research Paper' (Warner & Enomoto, 2015). Akin to key learning-outcome-related enablers underpinning the PEP were Kolb's (1984) Experiential Learning Model (summarised above relevant to our 2013 publication) and the Control-Wedge-Based Scaffolded Curriculum Model (summarised above relevant to both 2011 publications).

The transferability element in PEP was, in a sense, partially reversed from those outlined in our other studies though, in that the 'Independent Learning Skills' component related to both the second language-specific (the student determined 'Independent Research Paper' related to individual student's discipline area) and more generic transferable skills and attributes. On the other hand, the major focus of this publication, namely research skills, clearly aligns with these transferable-skills-related outcomes in Publications 1, 2 & 4. In addition, the students were gaining transferable skills in intercultural competence, operating in an academic environment different from their domestic academic experiences, a specific transferable skill related outcome they share with Publications 1 and 6. Moreover, the 'Independent Learning Skills' component of our 2015 publication also coordinates with findings pertinent to transferable-skills-related outcomes in Publications 1, 3 and 4. Interestingly enough, we also found another unexpected transferable learning outcome correlating with another learning outcome from the previous publication: increased self-efficacy. In summary, this publication outlines the enablers of learning outcomes, including the following transferable skills:

- Research skills;
- Independent learning skills;
- Teamwork skills;
- Intercultural competence;
- Increased self-efficacy.

## Publication 6 (2018): Developing undergraduate students' transferable generic skills through an innovative group drama project

Our next chapter, published in 2018, was again pertinent to a Japanese as a second language learning context; this time in terms of a final (3$^{rd}$) year undergraduate capstone course at the University. This chapter focused on a group drama project, based on a student-determined Japanese socio-cultural issue, as a pedagogy for developing various transferable skills as major learning outcomes (Enomoto & Warner, 2018), which were carefully embedded in a scaffolded curriculum. As principal enabler of one such learning outcome, namely intercultural competence, in this chapter, we adapted the Process Model of Intercultural Competence of Deardoff (2011). This model offers four cyclical process dimensions: (PD1) Individual's Attitudes, leading to (PD2) Individual's Cultural Knowledge, Comprehension and Skills, leading to (PD3) Individual's Desired Internal Outcome, leading to (PD4) Desired External Interactional outcome, leading back to PD1. Thus, intercultural competency can be constantly extended. Intercultural competence was also a transferable learning outcome highlighted in Publication 1.

There were three other transferable learning outcomes in the 2018 chapter, which could also be found in some of our previous chapter publications, such as digital literacy in Publications 2 & 4, independent learning skills in Publications 1,3,4 & 5, and research skills in Publications 1, 2, 4 & 5. In summary, this publication outlines the enablers of learning outcomes, including the following transferable skills:

- Teamwork skills;
- Communication skills;
- Intercultural competence;
- IT skills/digital literacy (including in Japanese);
- Research skills;
- Critical thinking skills.

## Publication 7 (2021): An innovative assessment method to evaluate independent learning and academic writing skills

In 2021, our subsequent chapter was the first of two chapters published following online LiHE symposia, which occurred owing to the COVID-19 pandemic. This chapter, which again focused on EAL students studying the Pre-enrolment English Program at the University, this time showcased an innovative four-stage assessment method, utilising both the English for Academic Purposes teaching team and faculty-based academics. The method was created to evaluate the 'Independent Learning Skills' component (see 2015-chapter detail above) and the academic writing skills of the PEP students (Warner & Enomoto, 2021). The learning outcome enablers were driven by the Teaching-Learning Cycle Model adapted by Caon-Parsons & Dimmell (2016), based on the work of Kolb & Kolb (2005). A four-stage cycle characterises this theory-informed model:

Stage 1: Concrete experience of taking action;

Stage 2: Reflective observation of that experience;

Stage 3: Conceptualisation based on evaluation and analysis;

Stage 4: Active experimentation of further action.

The experiential learning cycle provided a scaffolded and structured iteration for students to engage interactively in critical reflection, including intercultural communication, and for teachers and students to monitor and analyse student progress (Warner & Enomoto, 2021). Moreover, the cycle allows students to develop gradual control of their learning, thus enabling them to grow their independent learning skills and research skills as learning outcomes. The independent learning skills learning outcomes are also common to our previous LiHE Publications 1, 3, 4 & 5, whereas the research skills learning outcomes are found in Publications 1, 2, 4, 5 & 6. The increasing focus on teamwork skills in our work, as a learning outcome in our 2021 chapter, is also manifested by its inclusion in Publications 5 & 7. In summary, this publication outlines the enablers of learning outcomes, including the following transferable skills:

- Independent learning skills;
- Intercultural competence;
- Communication skills;
- Teamwork skills;
- Reflective learning skills.

## Publication 8 (2022): Partnering with student leaders: active learning through integration of Peer Assisted Study Sessions into an undergraduate language course

Our most recent jointly written book chapter publication took place in 2022, which was published following the second LiHE online symposium. This chapter focused on active learning, in the context of Japanese 2A, a second-year undergraduate course at our university, which incorporated students' (voluntary) participation in Peer Assisted Study Sessions (PASS), which itself is a program with international accreditation (Enomoto & Warner, 2022). The learning outcome enablers underpinning our transferable-skills-related learning outcomes were the Student as Partners framework (Healey et al., 2014; 2016) and our self-determined 360° Feed-forward Active Learning Model (Enomoto & Warner, 2022). In the Student as Partners framework, students act as active (and often collaborative) participants in developing their own learning instead of passive recipients of course-related content. Such active participation requires students to engage in learning processes and reflections, encouraged via authentic and germane learning activities (Prince, 2004), initiated by the PASS leader in this case. The second learning outcome enabler, the 360° Feed-forward Active Learning Model, is a scaffolded learning cycle that allows student voices (concerning areas of difficulty and coverage) to be heard and acted upon in each of its three dimensions:

> Dimension 1: Lecture by course coordinator (feed forward into tutorial);
>
> Dimension 2: Tutorial by tutors (feed forward into PASS);
>
> Dimension 3: Peer-assisted study sessions by PASS student leader (feed forward into lecture).

Transferable-skills-related learning outcomes that resulted from students' participation in PASS, mirroring those from our previous LiHE publications, can be seen in digital literacy (also seen in Publications 2, 4 & 6) communication skills (also in Publications 4, 6 & 7) and reflection skills (Publications 1, 3, 4 & 7). In summary, this publication outlines the enablers of learning outcomes, including the following transferable skills:

- Communication skills;
- Digital literacy (including in Japanese);
- Self-regulated learning skills, including time management;
- Reflective learning skills;
- Leadership skills.

To summarise, the CAE approach we adopted to document our LiHE journey has enabled us to realise that all our theory-underpinned pedagogical approaches are centred around 'balancing' between second language-specific knowledge/skills and transferable skills, as learning outcomes showcased in each chapter. Furthermore, it is important to note here that this balancing approach — which we have continued to adopt to this day — has stood the test of time and remains clearly and directly relevant to students' futures and their lifelong learning. To exemplify this, we can cite the most recent student comment (below) from the formal (online) University Student Evaluation of Learning and Teaching, conducted in 2023:

> "The learning of Japanese, especially in this course, requires much more critical thinking than I thought learning originally a language would. Learning and memorising vocabulary and grammar is only a small part of the language learning process. It then requires a deep analysis of the building blocks which make language work, which helps to build critical thinking skills. This course has helped me to greatly improve my critical thinking, and the skills have rolled over into other subjects, which is why I feel it is such a valuable course, and I will continue on my language journey throughout uni".

The comment above clearly evidences the 'sustained' benefit and value of our balancing approach between second language-specific knowledge/skills and transferable skills to enhance student learning outcomes as a whole. However, such balancing also means that, in each publication, rather than aiming to develop all kinds of transferable skills, we targeted the development of different sets of transferable skills as language students' learning outcomes. To demonstrate this, we summarise in Table 2, which transferable skills were developed in each of the eight publications. In addition, Table 2 also signals the five most commonly repeated transferable skills learning outcomes as follows:

- o Independent/Self-regulated learning skills;
- o Research skills;
- o Reflective learning skills;
- o Communication skills;
- o IT skills/digital literacy (including second language).

| Transferable-skills-related learning outcomes | Pub #1 | Pub #2 | Pub #3 | Pub #4 | Pub #5 | Pub #6 | Pub #7 | Pub #8 |
|---|---|---|---|---|---|---|---|---|
| Research skills | ✓ | ✓ | | ✓ | ✓ | ✓ | | |
| Communication skills | | | | ✓ | | ✓ | ✓ | ✓ |
| Intercultural competence | ✓ | | | ✓ | ✓ | ✓ | | |
| Increased self-efficacy | | | ✓ | ✓ | ✓ | | | |
| Independent/Self-regulated learning skills (including time management and organisation) | ✓ | ✓ | ✓ | ✓ | ✓ | | ✓ | ✓ |
| Critical thinking skills | ✓ | ✓ | | | | ✓ | | |
| Reflective learning skills | ✓ | | ✓ | ✓ | | | ✓ | ✓ |
| IT skills/digital literacy | | ✓ | | ✓ | | ✓ | | ✓ |
| Oral presentation skills | | ✓ | | | | | | |
| Teamwork skills | | | | | | ✓ | ✓ | ✓ |
| Leadership skills | | | | | | | | ✓ |

*Table 2: A summary of transferable skills as learning outcomes across the eight book chapters.*

Yet, it needs to be borne in mind that the presented documentation is retrospective. Given the fast-changing AI-enhanced technologies that are becoming increasingly available to educators and students, the enablers of learning outcomes are likely to require significant readjustments. In Section 4 (below), we will discuss how these rapid technological developments might impact our values and teaching practices in HE.

## Section 4: Moving forward

We have seen, through our CAE-informed retrospective journey over the past 12 years, that there has been strong continuity in terms of balancing our course/program learning outcomes by embedding both second language-specific knowledge/skills and transferable skills. As a result of this CAE retrospective, what has become increasingly clear to us is the fundamental importance of 'scaffolding' framed around the ZPD theory (Vygotsky, 1978). Across all the enablers of student learning outcomes, it is critical to carefully embed staged scaffolds in a timely manner to work effectively (Enomoto, 2011; Enomoto & Warner, 2014; Wilson & Devereux, 2014). Such scaffolding should comprise soft and hard scaffolds (Brush & Saye, 2002), which must support learning second language-specific knowledge/skills and transferable skills to achieve the intended learning outcomes.

As we point out in Section 3, the key transferable skills targeted and enabled as the learning outcomes across the years, have been:

o   Independent/Self-regulated learning skills;

o   Research skills;

o   Reflective learning skills;

o   Communication skills;

o   IT skills/digital literacy (including second language).

However, out of these five commonly embedded skills since 2011, we have observed and experienced the increasing necessity to develop students' IT skills/digital literacy skills. Our students' digital capabilities are now, more than ever, directly pertinent to their success both at university and in their chosen career pathways. Furthermore, we believe it is vital to clearly acknowledge that students' IT skills/digital literacy at university will not remain static and sufficient in the workplace of the future. Thus, we propose that what is needed, in this digital capabilities space, is to develop student capacity to acquire and develop new IT/digital capabilities and be flexible enough to continually adapt to emerging technologies.

Such adaptability is faced not only by students, but also by educators working with them in HE institutions. Thus, as university educators, if we are to prepare students sufficiently to meet the demands of future workplaces, one of the imminent challenges lies in exploring how we can build student capacity to continue developing their own digital capabilities to adapt to future technologies that might emerge. Indeed, this also requires us to develop our own digital capabilities by continually updating our digital knowledge and skill sets.

One of the imminent challenges we already face today is the emergence and availability of AI-enhanced technologies in education. The AI landscape is rapidly changing, presenting ongoing challenges, which need to be addressed by establishing our collective understanding of its evolving capabilities and worth in HE. Currently, there appear to be many AI-related discussions and concerns from HE institutions and external stakeholders, particularly concerning the academic integrity of course/program assessments and potential negative impacts on graduates' qualities and capabilities.

To establish collective understanding of AI capabilities and deficits, we advocate for clear guidelines for educators on how to use AI-enhanced technologies in our teaching practices and assessment tasks. This in turn requires us to reassess and amend the existing learning outcomes in our courses/programs, considering any additional workload repercussions. Furthermore, at a course/program level, for course/program coordinators to effectively implement such guidelines, HE institutions must have institutionally-determined clear governance policies on the use of AI-enhanced technologies in assessments, for example. This is so that course/program coordinators can provide clear advice to students about their expectations and boundaries regarding AI use in specific assessment tasks. However, such policies and guidelines will need to be constantly updated to respond to the capabilities of AI technology and its rapidly expanding nature.

When framing current concerns around the use of AI enhanced technologies in an HE context, we must recognise that we are indeed in a fluid state of transition. Both our understanding of AI-enhanced technologies and the responsible use thereof are still advancing. Yet, we should not underestimate the potential positive impacts of AI-enhanced technologies on learning and teaching in HE. For example, we can encourage students to embrace and use AI tools as part of their independent learning skills, with the proviso that they must exercise their human dimension, including the ability to make sound judgements and interrogate through critical thinking and ethics when engaging with AI technologies. Thus, HE institutions need to explore effective ways to develop students' 'information literacy' that enables them:

1) to confidently discriminate whether the information AI-powered tools generated for them are true, neutral or biased in opinion/argument;

2) to appropriately identify when it is better not to use AI-powered tools, but to utilise their own creativity and originality as humans.

We propose that the human dimension is multifaceted and includes a sense of responsibility, fairness, ethics, creativity, resilience, and self-regulation. Yet, it is this human dimension that AI in its current form cannot always effectively teach our students. In today's HE context, all transferable skills and personal attributes remain both relevant and necessary as student learning outcomes pertinent to their future careers. Therefore, whilst we advocate for actively incorporating the available AI-technologies into the learning processes, we recognise the impending requirement for embedding and enabling the human dimension in their learning outcomes. Currently, as it stands, there are many ways in which AI can be incorporated into a learning tool specifically targeting learning outcomes (see Nygaard, 2023 in this book for further discussion).

## Conclusion

In this chapter, through our CAE-guided LiHE retrospective, we have presented insights into how we utilised our theory-underpinned models and pedagogies to balance second language-specific knowledge/skills and transferable skills in our course/program designs since 2011. We also demonstrated how we used such models and pedagogies as enablers of balanced student learning outcomes. Furthermore, as part of the balance, we showed how our models and pedagogical approaches encouraged a student focus shift away from marks/grades towards their learning processes. The enablers of student learning outcomes (Figure 1) we demonstrate in this chapter still have relevance in our learning and teaching practices today.

We have analysed how we designed a curriculum to develop our students' transferable skills in each of the eight LiHE chapter publications and reflected upon our own learning process as university educators. We also demonstrated how we balanced the development of second language-specific knowledge/skills with transferable skills as learning outcomes. Based on our own learning process, we suggest that the readers might take on board the following five steps in their own teaching practice. The readers can utilise these steps in order to reach an optimum balance between discipline-specific and transferable skills in a program/course:

1. Categorise your current espoused Program/Course Learning Outcomes into two categories: discipline-specific and transferable skills;
2. Identify the current balance between discipline-specific and transferable skills development in your Program/Course Learning Outcomes;
3. Reassess whether the current balance is conducive to and fit for purpose in terms of your students' employability and future careers in the 21$^{st}$ century;
4. Amend your Program/Course Learning Outcomes with a new balance between discipline-specific and transferable skills development;
5. Realign learning activities and assessment tasks with discipline-specific and transferable skills in the new Program/Course Learning Outcomes.

In this way, we emphasise the continual need to review and reassess learning outcomes to move with the changing times, especially in the digital capabilities space for students and us as university educators. This is to allow healthy, responsible and purposeful engagement with AI-enhanced technologies in HE to occur. For enhancing student learning outcomes, it is, more than ever, vital to explore how we can effectively develop the human-dimension associated attributes, including a sense of responsibility, fairness, ethics, creativity, resilience, and self-regulation, as a significant part of transferable skills development.

## About the Authors

Kayoko Enomoto is an Associate Professor, Head of the Department of Asian Studies and Associate Dean, Student Experience in the Faculty of Arts, Business, Law and Economics at the University of Adelaide, Australia. She can be contacted at this email: kayoko.enomoto@adelaide.edu.au

Richard Warner is an Adjunct Lecturer in the School of Education in the Faculty of Arts, Business, Law and Economics at the University of Adelaide, Australia. He can be contacted at this email: richard.warner@adelaide.edu.au

## Bibliography

Abosalem, Y. (2016). Assessment techniques and students' higher-order thinking skills. *International Journal of Secondary Education, 4*(1), 1-11.

Adam, S. (2006). An introduction to learning outcomes. In E. Froment, J. Kohler, L. Purser & L. Wilson. (Eds), *EUA Bologna handbook*. Raabe.

Andrews, A., & St. Aubyn, B. (2023). Partnering with clinical provider organisations to enhance learning outcomes for healthcare practitioners. In K. Enomoto, R. Warner & C. Nygaard (Eds.), *Enhancing student learning outcomes in higher education*. Libri Publishing Ltd.

Bandura, A. (1977). *Social learning theory*. Prentice Hall.

Bandura, A. (1994). Self-efficacy. In V. S. Ramachaudran (Ed.), *Encyclopedia of human behavior*, Vol. 4. Academic Press.

Bartholomew, N., & Bartholomew, P. (2014). Social and cognitive affordances of physical and virtual learning spaces. In L. Scott-Webber, J. Branch, P. Bartholomew & C. Nygaard (Eds.), *Learning space design in higher education*. Libri Publishing Ltd.

Biggs, J. (1996). Enhancing teaching through constructive alignment. *Higher Education, 32*(3), 347-364.

Biggs, J., & Collis, K. (1982). *Evaluating the quality of learning: The SOLO taxonomy (structure of the observed learning outcome)*. Academic Press.

Bloom, B. S., Engelhart, M. D., Furst, E. J., Hill, W. H., & Krathwohl, D. R. (1956). *Taxonomy of educational objectives: The classification of educational goals. Handbook I: Cognitive domain*. David McKay Company.

Bowd, K., & Enomoto, K. (2023). Bringing employability to life: Developing employability skill sets and understandings as student learning outcomes. In K. Enomoto, R. Warner & C. Nygaard. (Eds.), *Enhancing student learning outcomes in higher education*. Libri Publishing Ltd.

Branch, J. D. (2023). Physician, heal thyself: Enhancing student learning outcomes through reflective practice. In K. Enomoto, R. Warner & C. Nygaard (Eds.), *Enhancing student learning outcomes in higher education*. Libri Publishing Ltd.

Bradley, D., Noonan, P., Nugent, H., & Scales, B. (2008). *Bradley review of Australian higher education: Final report*. Canberra, ACT: Department of

Education, Employment and Workplace Relations, Commonwealth of Australia.

Brush, T., & Saye, J. (2002). A summary of research exploring hard and soft scaffolding for teachers and students using a multimedia supported learning environment. *The Journal of Interactive Online Learning, 1*(2), 1-12.

Cadman, K., & Grey, M. (2000). The 'action teaching' model of curriculum design: EAP students managing their own learning in an academic conference course. *EA Journal, 18*(2), 21-36.

Caon-Parsons, S., & Dimmell, P. (2016). *Pre-enrolment English Program (PEP) review- Stage 2 December 2016*. English Language Centre, University of Adelaide.

Cargill, M., & Cadman, K. (2005). Revisiting quality for international research education: Towards an engagement model. In *2005 Australian Universities Quality Forum*, 45-49.

Chang, H., Ngunjiri, F., & Hernandez, K. A. C. (2016). *Collaborative autoethnography* (Vol. 8). Routledge.

Davies, M. (2011). Concept mapping, mind mapping and argument mapping: What are the differences and do they matter? *Higher Education, 62*(3), 279-301.

Deardorff, D. K. (2011). Assessing intercultural competence. In J.D. Penn (Ed.), *New directions for institutional research, 149*. John Wiley & Sons.

De Wilde, J., & Forasacco, E. (2023). Developing STEM doctoral students' collaboration skills as learning outcomes. In K. Enomoto, R. Warner & C. Nygaard (Eds.), *Enhancing student learning outcomes in higher education*. Libri Publishing Ltd.

Enomoto, K. (2011). Fostering high quality learning through a scaffolded curriculum. In C. Nygaard, N. Courtney & C. Holtham (Eds.), *Beyond transmission: Innovations in university teaching*. Libri Publishing Ltd.

Enomoto, K. (2012a). A study skills action plan: integrating self-regulated learning in a diverse higher education context. In X. Song & K. Cadman (Eds.), *Bridging transcultural divides: Asian languages and cultures in global higher education*. University of Adelaide Press.

Enomoto, K. (2012b). Promoting deeper learning through a scaffolded language curriculum: Double tasking language-specific and research-skills development. In J. Hajek, C. Nettelbeck & A. Woods (Eds.), *The next step*. The University of Melbourne.

Enomoto, K., & Warner, R. (2013). Building student capacity for reflective learning. In C. Nygaard, J. Branch & C. Holtham (Eds.), *Learning in higher education – Contemporary standpoints*. Libri Publishing Ltd.

Enomoto, K., & Warner, R. (2014). Promoting student reflection through considerate design of a virtual learning space. In L. Scott-Webber, J. Branch, P. Bartholomew & C. Nygaard (Eds.), *Learning space design in higher education*. Libri Publishing Ltd.

Enomoto, K., & Warner, R. (2018). Developing undergraduate students' transferable generic skills through an innovative group drama project. In K. Enomoto, R. Warner & C. Nygaard (Eds.), *Innovative teaching and learning practices in higher education*. Libri Publishing Ltd.

Enomoto, K., & Warner, R. (2022). Partnering with student leaders: active learning through integration of peer assisted study sessions into an undergraduate language course. In K. Enomoto, R. Warner & C. Nygaard (Eds.), *Active learning in higher education – student engagement and deeper learning outcomes*. Libri Publishing Ltd.

Godber, K. A., & Atkins, D. R. (2021). COVID-19 Impacts on teaching and learning: A collaborative autoethnography by two higher education lecturers. *Frontiers in Education*, 6, 1-14.

Healey, M., Flint, A., & Harrington, K. (2014). *Engagement through partnership: students as partners in learning and teaching in higher education*. The Higher Education Academy.

Healey, M., Flint, A., & Harrington, K. (2016). Students as partners: Reflections on a conceptual model. *Teaching and Learning Inquiry*, 4(2), 8-20.

Healy, M. (2023). Careers and employability learning: pedagogical principles for higher education. *Studies in Higher Education*, 65(1), 106–125.

Kolb, D. A. (1984). *Experiential learning: Experience as the source of learning and development*. Prentice-Hall.

Kolb, A.Y., & Kolb, D.A. (2005). Learning styles and learning spaces: enhancing experiential learning in higher education. *Academy of Learning Management and Education*, 4(2), 193-212.

Krathwohl, D. R. (2002). A revision of Bloom's taxonomy: An overview. *Theory into Practice*, 41(4), 212-218.

Lave, J., & Wenger, E. (1991). *Situated learning: Legitimate peripheral participation*. Cambridge University Press.

Laurillard, D. (2016). The educational problem that MOOCs could solve: Professional development for teachers of disadvantaged students. *Research in Learning Technology*, 24, 1-17.

Meyer, J. H. F., & Land, R. (2003). Threshold concepts and troublesome knowledge: Linkages to ways of thinking and practising within the disciplines. *ETL Project Occasional Report 4*, 1-12.

Nygaard, C. (2023). Enhancing student learning outcomes through contextualised learning activities. In K. Enomoto, R. Warner & C. Nygaard

(Eds.), *Enhancing student learning outcomes in higher education*. Libri Publishing Ltd.

Oliver, B. (2011). *Assuring graduate outcomes*. Sydney: Australian Learning and Teaching Council.

Paltridge, B. (2004). *Approaches to teaching second language writing*. [Paper presentation]. 17th English Australia Conference, Adelaide, Australia.

Picard, M., Warner, R., & Velautham, L. (2011). Enabling postgraduate students to become autonomous ethnographers of their disciplines. In C. Nygaard, N. Courtney & L. Frick (Eds.), *Postgraduate education – Form and function*. Libri Publishing Ltd.

Prince, M. (2004). Does active learning work? A review of the research. *Journal of Engineering Education, 93*(3), 223-231.

Römgens, I., Scoupe, R., & Beausaert, S. (2020). Unraveling the concept of employability, bringing together research on employability in higher education and the workplace. *Studies in Higher Education, 45*(12), 2588-2603.

Scott-Webber, L., Branch, J., Bartholomew, P., & Nygaard, C. (2014). Practising learning space design. In L. Scott-Webber, J. Branch, P. Bartholomew & C. Nygaard (Eds.), *Learning space design in higher education*. Libri Publishing Ltd.

University of Adelaide. (2021). *Graduate employability framework*. Retrieved August 9, 2023, from https://www.adelaide.edu.au/learning/strategic-projects/student-employability

Vygotsky, L. S. (1978). *Mind in society: The development of higher psychological processes*. Harvard University Press.

Warner, R., & Enomoto, K. (2015). Embedding research skills in the curriculum design of a pathway programme for international students. In C. Nygaard, P. Bartholomew & C. Guerin (Eds.), *Learning to research – Researching to learn*. Libri Publishing Ltd.

Warner, R., & Enomoto, K. (2021). An innovative assessment method to evaluate independent learning and academic writing skills. In K. Enomoto, R. Warner & C. Nygaard (Eds.), *Teaching and learning innovations in higher education*. Libri Publishing Ltd.

Wenger, E. (1998). *Communities of practice: Learning, meaning and identity*. Cambridge University Press.

Wilson, K., & Devereux, L. (2014). Scaffolding theory: High challenge, high support in Academic Language and Learning (ALL) contexts. *Journal of Academic Language and Learning, 8*(3), A91-A100.

Chapter 4
# Developing STEM Doctoral Students' Collaboration Skills as Learning Outcomes

Janet De Wilde and Elena Forasacco

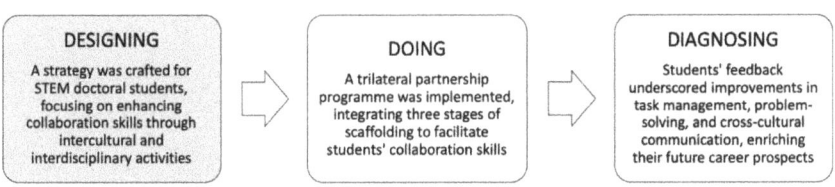

## Preamble

With their chapter, Janet De Wilde and Elena Forasacco contribute to this book, *Enhancing Student Learning Outcomes in Higher Education*, by explaining how they develop STEM doctoral students' collaboration skills when solving complex challenges. To achieve this, they have designed learning activities with three stages of scaffolding to develop collaboration skills. The authors relate to the three phases of the central ESLO model of the book in this way:

In the DESIGNING phase, they outline the need to enhance STEM doctoral students' collaboration skills. They describe how the desired learning outcomes — which form a sub-set of abilities for developing collaboration skills — are achieved through learning activities in intercultural and interdisciplinary contexts.

In the DOING phase, the authors explain how they implement such learning activities, designed with three stages of scaffolding, within an in-country programme for STEM doctoral students. They offer the programme in a trilateral partnership with two of their international partner universities overseas. Students in different years of their doctoral candidature, from a range of STEM disciplines in the three different universities, take part in the programme.

The DIAGNOSING phase incorporates feedback and reflection, where the authors evaluate the effectiveness of their in-country programme based on the students' responses through an anonymous feedback form. Their evaluation includes doctoral students' perceptions of their ability to effectively manage tasks, problem-solve and communicate, whilst working with others from different cultural and disciplinary backgrounds. Developing their collaboration skills complements the students' existing competitive capacity and attributes fostered within their research-intensive university culture, thus resulting in enhanced employability for their future careers.

## Introduction

In our research-intensive institutions in the UK, perhaps due to their already existing competitive culture, doctoral students appear to have limited opportunities to develop their collaboration skills during their candidature. Our doctoral students are often equipped with highly developed capacity and readiness for 'competition'; after all, their university entry selection process was highly competitive and rigorous. Moreover, during their time as doctoral students, their well-developed capacity and readiness to compete with others, appears to be further encouraged by the research-intensive institutional culture. Significantly, however, encouraging such a competitive culture can sometimes result in our students' seemingly having underdeveloped collaboration skills, those skills which are crucial for the increasingly globalised workplace and research environments. Indeed, collaboration-related skill sets are one key facet of the notion of employability (see Bowd & Enomoto, 2023 in this book), and students' collaboration skills can be developed through carefully scaffolded learning activities, even when it appears to be more challenging to do so in some disciplines/programs more than in others (Enomoto & Warner, 2018).

This chapter describes how we designed, embedded and scaffolded learning activities carefully, in three stages, to effectively facilitate STEM (Science, Technology, Engineering, Mathematics) doctoral students to develop collaboration skills as their learning outcomes. We implemented such scaffolded learning activities in our in-country programme in a trilateral partnership with two of our international partner universities: one in Europe and the other in Asia. Participating student cohorts typically consisted of those in different doctoral candidature years, from a range of STEM disciplines in the three different universities; such a mixed cohort worked together for five days at one of the three universities. The country where the in-country programme is to be held, is rotated between the three universities every year. This programme, therefore, provides participating students with unique environments — both intercultural and interdisciplinary — to develop their collaboration skills, which will be further detailed in the subsequent sections.

## Chapter overview and key takeaways

Section 1 explains how we identified the need to focus on developing STEM doctoral students' collaboration skills to complement their competitive capacity and attributes that already exist within the research-intensive university culture. Section 2 provides details of the learning activities we designed, with three stages of scaffolding, to develop collaboration skills. Section 3 describes the outcomes of the learning activities, which occurred in intercultural and interdisciplinary contexts provided by the trilateral institutional partnership, and evaluates a range of student quotes highlighting their experiences. Section 4 outlines our reasons for continuing to develop more contextualised collaboration learning activities to enhance our STEM doctoral students' collaboration-related skill sets.

Reading this chapter, you will gain the following three insights:

1. How we can utilise the experiential learning cycle to achieve the Programme Learning Outcomes that form a sub-set of abilities for developing collaboration skills;

2. How we can embed three-stages of scaffolding into learning activities to develop STEM doctoral students' collaboration skills;

3. How we can effectively develop doctoral students' collaboration skills in intercultural and interdisciplinary contexts.

Chapter 4

## Section 1: Background to our work with learning outcomes

As university educators, we work in the area of the professional development of doctoral students. We have worked together for several years, in the same UK research-intensive institution, in roles with a remit to address postgraduate professional development. We share the same working ethics, approach and ethos, and in our time together, we have endeavoured to address the challenge — enhancing STEM doctoral students' collaboration skills as their learning outcomes. Fostering students' capacity and readiness for competition in our research-intensive institution, and developing their collaboration skills, are not mutually exclusive; the former does not have to occur at the expense of the latter. Indeed, as will be seen, developing collaboration skills can complement these students' competitive capacity and attributes fostered within their research-intensive university, and further enhance their future employability in either academia or industry.

With this background, we present a case study — an in-country programme — we designed and implemented in a trilateral partnership with two of our international partner universities that are STEM research-intensive: one in Europe and the other in Asia. Each year, one of the three universities takes turns to host the programme in their own country. Participating doctoral students are diverse in terms of their cultural, linguistic and discipline backgrounds. A total of around 40 students from the three universities, participate in each programme, working in intercultural and interdisciplinary groups. Participating students actively engage in learning activities that are carefully scaffolded in three stages and designed to develop collaboration skills. The in-country programmes typically run over five days, preceded by a two-hour online welcome event. Each group has a teacher who supervises the student discussions, whilst maintaining a supportive, constructive, and non-judgmental space. Creating such a safe learning space is essential for students to feel comfortable in sharing ideas and giving and receiving feedback (see De Wilde & Forasacco, 2023 in this book).

From our institution's perspective, in-country programmes, including our programme, are supported as part of the institutional strategic plan to develop and strengthen connections with international partner institutions and research groups. Doctoral students, through their participation in these in-country programmes also have the opportunity to complete a research visit in one of these partner institutions. Indeed, such a research visit will likely be beneficial to our doctoral students, as they can explore their doctoral research projects through new lenses, whilst additionally creating new opportunities for joint research projects. Doctoral students' participation in our in-country programme is voluntary, rather than being a compulsory component of their doctoral studies. Yet, the demand has been high, largely because both students and supervisors understand the potential benefits of the programme for both the students' and research groups' futures. We, therefore, select participants based upon their willingness to enhance their collaboration skills as learning outcomes.

Before we were given the opportunity to design and develop our in-country programme for STEM doctoral students, we initially participated as teachers in other professional development programmes for doctoral students to learn from and build upon them. In these other programmes, as teachers, we were witness to doctoral students excelling when undertaking competitive learning activities. However, at the same time, we also recognised that these competitive learning activities were just playing to their existing skills sets and reinforcing them. We felt something crucial was missing, as we saw the doctoral students were not challenged sufficiently to develop less well-developed skill sets. This experience led us to identify a missing piece — collaboration skills — and the importance and benefits of immersing students in an intercultural and interdisciplinary context to bring about intercultural and interdisciplinary collaborations (Lo-Philip et al., 2015; Behrnd & Porzelt, 2012) in our new design of an in-country programme- specifically for STEM doctoral students' professional development.

We were given the opportunity to 'redefine' the learning outcomes of STEM doctoral students' professional development during their candidature when, in 2017, our research-intensive university strategised the strengthening of new international partnerships with equally research-intensive partner universities overseas. This is when we came to focus on collaboration skills, in the design of a new in-country programme that takes place in the trilateral institutional partnership with one university in Europe and the other in Asia. It is important to note that our partner institutions shared our ethos, agreed with the need to complement and balance the competitive culture with collaboration, and thus strongly supported the rationale for the new collaboration skills focused programme. They trusted us, allowing us the freedom to develop a new in-country programme design that can capitalise on the interplay between the notions of collaboration and competition.

Table 1 shows the Programme Learning Outcomes that form a sub-set of abilities for developing collaboration skills — through the learning activities designed specifically for the in-country programme for STEM doctoral students.

| Programme Learning Outcomes | Students will develop their ability: |
| --- | --- |
| 1 | to exercise perspective taking and cultural awareness appropriately |
| 2 | to network and communicate effectively |
| 3 | to influence intercultural and interdisciplinary groups |
| 4 | to be creative and manage tasks to develop collaborative ideas and solve challenges |

*Table 1: Programme Learning Outcomes of the in-country programme.*

These Programme Learning Outcomes 1-4 are a sub-set of abilities that are essential to developing collaboration skills. To enable these Programme Learning Outcomes in our new programme design, we encourage students to clearly recognise that being one of the other — competitive or collaborative — is insufficient in group learning activities. The dominance of the former could lead to an interpersonal fallout, resulting in a dysfunctional group with the likelihood of sub-optimal results. Similarly, the dominance of the latter could lead to a 'static' project, owing to too much compromise and insufficient drive for creativity. In the structure of our programme design, competition and collaboration are determined as interrelated behaviours on the same spectrum, with the notion of competition and the notion of collaboration at either end. Thus, the degree of the two notions can move along the spectrum to create the right energy for the task at hand. Moreover, competition may intersect collaboration and vice versa, when students combine their discipline-specific knowledge and skills to develop an interdisciplinary group project (Oliver, 2004).

For our doctoral students, to work within the context of increasingly globalised workplaces and research environments as future professionals — be it in academia or in industry — engaging in intercultural and interdisciplinary collaborations through developing the requisite sub-set of abilities (Table 1), is fundamental to solving their complex future challenges. This realisation pointed us to the framework of the United Nations Sustainable Development Goals (UNSDG) (United Nations, 2015). In the programme, to solve complex UNSDG global challenges, our doctoral students must develop and be able to apply the sub-set of abilities for developing their collaboration skills as learning outcomes (Table 1).

## How we redefined the four learning outcomes for STEM doctoral students' professional development

Effective collaborations take place when members are open, flexible, adaptable, and receptive to diversity. The concept of openness is one key personal attribute that can facilitate the acceptance of cultural diversity (Caligiuri et al., 2000). Individuals with high openness are expected to work and collaborate well in an intercultural and interdisciplinary context. Likewise, according to Caligiuri et al. (2000), one's high openness to cultural diversity equally indicates their cultural agility comprising three elements: cultural adaptation, minimisation and integration (Table 2).

| Behaviour | Definition |
| --- | --- |
| Cultural adaptation | Collaborators adapt to cultural differences in their context and adjust the work norm to the different cultures |
| Cultural minimisation | Collaborators smooth cultural differences to create consistency and limit variations. Finding compromises is the most effective strategy |
| Cultural integration | All collaborators work together across cultures to create norms and approaches accepted by all cultures |

*Table 2: Elements of cultural agility (adapted from Caligiuri, 2013).*

Indeed, when redefining the four learning outcomes (Table 1), these three elements of cultural agility were considered as attributes of collaboration. We identified that the students would develop their self-awareness and perspective taking by participating in our in-country programme. Accordingly, the programme must necessarily develop students' intercultural competence. This is because developing intercultural competence is fundamental to increasing cultural awareness and agility, promotes self-reflection, and, importantly, gives the agency of development to students so that they are actively responsible for their own and the group's development (Cotton et al., 2019).

We incorporated those attributes of collaboration in our in-country programme by designing a three-stage-scaffolding approach. To support the enhancement of the first three learning outcomes 1-3 (Table 1), we have designed learning activities which are effective experiential opportunities. These learning activities encourage engagement, learning from others' perspectives, reflection, critical and creative thinking, openness, and adaptability. Concurrently, these activities also facilitate intercultural competence to be developed. As Enomoto and Warner (2018) state, developing intercultural competence is a demanding task when students work in a culturally and linguistically different environment from their own. Thus, our in-country programme is inherently contextualised and experiential so as to effectively encourage doctoral students to develop their intercultural competence.

We based the enhancement of the learning outcomes 3 and 4 (Table 1) on group projects that seek solutions for UNSDG global challenges. Through these projects, we aim to enhance students' group working competencies to strike a balance along the collaboration and competition spectrum. The interface between competition and collaboration can be worked on within a group; for example, group members could collaborate and share knowledge and learn from each other to create a more competitive group. As another example, groups might positively use competition to create collaboration by identifying the motivations of individual group members to use as motivators for the whole group.

## Learning theory and methodology related to learning outcomes

Our design is based on active learning approaches rooted in social constructivism (Vygotsky, 1967), where students learn and make meaning together. We adopted Kolb's (1984) experiential learning approach as it incorporates reflection, which is essential for developing self-awareness, and considers learning a continuous process involving transforming experiences into knowledge, skills, attitudes, and behaviours. This theory supports the notion that students learn best when they actively engage in contextualised experiences, reflect on those experiences, conceptualise abstract ideas based on their reflections, and then apply those concepts in new situations. The four key elements of this theory, known as the experiential learning cycle (Kolb, 1984; also see Bowd & Enomoto, 2023 in this book; Branch & Wernick, 2023 in this book), are:

1. Concrete experience: students actively engage in a real-world experience or situation, from a hands-on experiment to a practical activity.

2. Reflective observation: after the experience, students reflect on what they have observed, paying attention to their thoughts, feelings, and reactions during the experience. This reflection helps individuals gain a deeper understanding of the experience.

3. Abstract conceptualisation: based on their reflections, students try to make sense of the experience by conceptualising abstract ideas or creating theories. This step involves connecting the experience with existing knowledge and theories.

4. Active experimentation: students apply the concepts and theories they have conceptualised to new situations, actively experimenting and testing their ideas and theories. This step encourages students to engage in problem-solving and critical thinking actively.

In our design, we also incorporated Bruner's scaffolding concept (Bruner, 1971) as a supportive framework to help students effectively acquire new knowledge and skills. The three-stages of scaffolding are:

- Stage 1: Breaking down complex tasks into smaller and more manageable parts facilitated by the teacher or more knowledgeable students. This process helps students understand the components of the task, thus preventing them from feeling overwhelmed.

- Stage 2: Providing support to work on tasks: the teacher supports students by demonstrating strategies, offering guidance, and supplying necessary resources. This support can take various forms, such as modelling the process, asking leading questions, offering hints or cues, or providing templates or frameworks.

- Stage 3: Fading the support: as students become more competent and confident, the teacher's support is gradually reduced or removed. This process allows students to gradually take responsibility for their learning, encouraging independent thinking and problem-solving.

Using Bruner's three-stages of scaffolding, our approach is based on social constructivism and Vygotskys' Zone of Proximal Development (ZPD) (Vygotsky, 1967). The ZPD incorporates the range of tasks a student can accomplish with guidance and assistance from a more knowledgeable individual. This zone represents the gap between a student's current ability level and their potential for growth and development. Learning occurs most effectively within the ZPD, where students engage in tasks just beyond their current capabilities. This approach supports and emphasizes the importance of social interaction and collaboration in learning to expand the individual's ZPD. Figure 1 visualises how our learning activities can follow the three-stages of scaffolding to create students' social learning experience in order to enhance collaboration skills through social interactions.

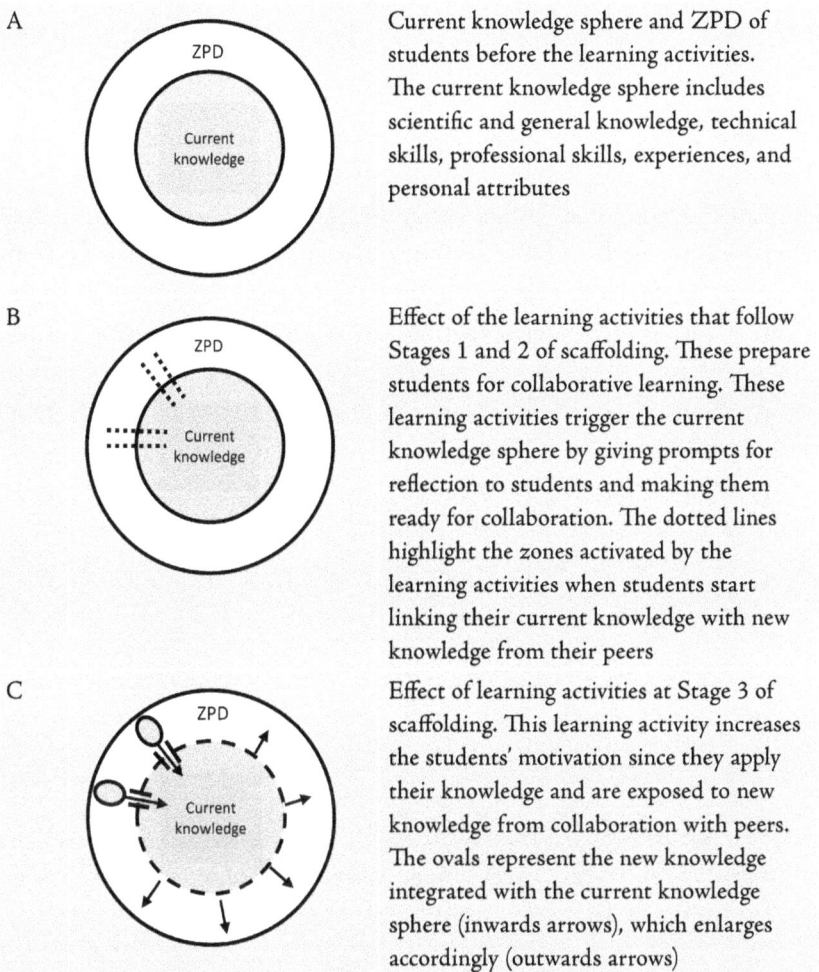

Figure 1: Visual explanation of the effect of scaffolding activities on students' learning. A) students' ZPD before the three-stages activities; B) effects of Stage 1 and Stage 2 on the students' ZPD; C) effect of Stage 3 on the student's current knowledge and ZPD (adapted from Forasacco, 2018).

## Section 2: Our practice towards enhancing students' learning outcomes

Our five-day in-country programme aims to enhance students' collaboration skills through developing the sub-set of abilities we outlined in Table 1 as the Programme Learning Outcomes. The programme is implemented in partnership with international partner institutions overseas. In this case study, we focus on the programme design that we developed and run in partnership with two international partner universities: one in Europe and the other in Asia. In this case study, participating doctoral students were from a range of STEM backgrounds from both our university and partner universities.

In such international partnerships, we undertake the role of leading the programme design and development. In addition, we also collaborate and work closely with our partner universities. We do so in order to 'adapt' the programme design around the afore-mentioned UNSDG global challenges, as group projects that participating students work on. During the in-country programme, the learning outcomes are developed through a three-stage scaffold based on active learning approaches (see also Figure 1):

- Stage 1: learning activity designed to support the development of an inclusive environment through perspective taking. Students analyse and reflect on language differences to increase their understanding of each other's communication skills.

- Stage 2: learning activities to practice the components of collaboration skills, from communication to planning.

- Stage 3: applying these enhanced collaboration skills to develop a collaborative group project.

It is important to note that we introduce and run a debrief session at the end of each learning stage, essential for students to reflect on their work and performance, and prepare well for the next learning stage.

## How our practice affects students' way of studying

In our STEM context, doctoral students usually work in research groups where they 'individually' develop a part of a large project. Results from those individual projects are then combined to obtain comprehensive findings. With this system, students work in groups, but rarely collaborate in developing their projects. Sometimes the peer-pressure drives them more towards competition rather than towards collaboration. Yet, given that collaboration is the fulcrum of every research project in the contemporary research world, the need for enhancing collaboration skills is clear when considering the future careers of doctoral students.

The learning activities we designed support the development of collaboration skills by expanding the students' ZPD (see Figure 1). In Stage 1 and Stage 2, each learning activity is tailored for and focuses on a specific component of collaboration, such as communication, time, and resource management. Then, in Stage 3, students combine and apply those components to finalise their learning (also see Nygaard 2023 in this book), in the form of a project showcasing their collaboration skills development.

- Stage 1: 'Words' exchange – Normalise the silence': this activity enhances inclusivity by adding a new level of understanding of our multi-lingual environment. Students translate a short phrase from English to their native language (jargon or dialect). They then explain the differences in the structure (including words and alphabets) between English and their native language. Visualising those differences helps all students understand the process applied by non-native English speakers to communicate in English, and 'silence' represents a reflection tool for those students as well as a cultural behaviour. Namely, 'silence' is a component of turn-taking in intercultural conversations (e.g. question-answer, discussions) and also depends on unwritten cultural behaviours, such as avoiding overlapping speaking and respecting speakers (for example Stivers et al., 2009).

- Stage 2: with Activities 1-5 (below), students practice verbal and visual communication, creativity, time management, planning and resources management. Each activity lasts 30 minutes and is in a specific room, with groups moving around the rooms.

- Activity 1: 'Interdisciplinary intersection' supports the development of creative verbal communication and management skills. Each student is blindfolded and has a set of plastic shapes; there are five sets of shapes in five different colours, two of which are in the teacher's hands and not visible to students. Each student needs to describe their shapes to identify the two shapes in the hands of the teacher. Since students are blindfolded, they need to apply their creative verbal communication skills to describe the shapes and use inclusive language for words and analogies.

- Activity 2: 'Professor Puzzle' (Table 4) is about planning, task sharing and management. This activity is composed of eight connected tasks. After students understand the task, they split the group into sub-groups based on their individual knowledge and skills so that each sub-group completes a task that all together completes the activity.

- Activity 3: 'Lab attack' promotes the enhancement of planning skills. Each student in the group should cross a grid with hidden obstacles in it. Only one student at a time enters the room with the grid; when they hit a hidden obstacle, they leave the room and verbally describe the followed pathway to their group to prepare a new student to cross the grid avoiding the obstacles.

- Activity 4: 'Janél protein' is about creative verbal communication and organisation. The group selects a leader who is the only group member able to see the structure of pseudo-protein. The leader describes the structure to the other group members, who need to build a copy of the structure, as close as possible to the original. This task complements 'Interdisciplinary intersection' as an additional opportunity for students to use inclusive language.

- Activity 5: 'Drawable drawings' enhances creative, non-verbal communication skills. In each group, students work in pairs to draw items belonging to different categories (e.g. inventions, sports) starting with a specific letter. The rest of the group needs to guess those items. We designed this task to prompt the use of drawings as inclusive communication tools useful to facilitate explanations in intercultural and interdisciplinary audiences.

- Stage 3: students in their groups apply their enhanced collaboration skills to develop a collaborative project aiming to solve a UNSDG global challenge. Working on their project, students combine their group's knowledge, skills and experiences and network with other groups to find potential collaborators to complement the group's skill set (e.g. business skills).

Table 3 summarises the connections between learning activities and the Programme Learning Outcomes.

| Learning outcomes | Students will develop their ability: | Stages and activities where learning outcomes are enhanced |
|---|---|---|
| 1 | to exercise perspective taking and cultural awareness appropriately | Stage 1: 'Words' exchange – Normalise the silence' |
| 2 | to network and communicate effectively | Stage 2: verbal and non-verbal communication (Interdisciplinary intersection, Janél protein, Drawable drawings) |
|   |   | Stage 3: networking among groups |
| 3 | to influence intercultural and interdisciplinary groups | Stage 3: group discussion during the preparation of the project |
| 4 | to be creative and manage tasks to develop collaborative ideas and solve challenges | Stage 2 activities |
|   |   | Stage 3 group project |

*Table 3: Mapping learning activities to the Programme Learning Outcomes.*

## How we prepare and organise our pedagogy to enhance students' learning outcomes

The preparation and organisation of our in-country programme are firmly guided by the learning outcomes that we redefined. As outlined previously, we first redefined the learning outcomes that can be brought to life for our doctoral students in the context of increasingly globalised workplaces and research environments as future professionals. Then, we

Chapter 4

designed learning activities aligned to these learning outcomes to create a contextualised learning opportunity for students, as explained in Nygaard (2023, in this book). As Table 3 shows, each learning activity is aligned with one or two stipulated learning outcomes. When designing these learning activities, we collaborated and applied the set of abilities that all feed into developing the students' collaboration skills. For developing creativity and task management (learning outcome 4), for example, we developed the 'Professor Puzzle' activity (Table 4), that prompts students to share tasks and manage resources, including different skill sets, knowledge and experiences that each group member brings to the table when working in groups. We designed eight interconnected tasks (Table 4). Each task has its clues, and all tasks are linked through a narrative: each group of students is part of a research group, and they need to complete the eight tasks to meet the Principal Investigator's requirements and have the research contract signed.

| | Tasks | Results and connections |
|---|---|---|
| | On the table, students find: | |
| 1 | A globe: students identify four cities based on four given clues | Once students identify the four cities, they start a 'tour around the world' from London to City 1, then City 2, City 3 and City 4. The order they move from city to city corresponds to directions (north, south, east and west). Those directions are the key to opening a first padlock |
| 2 | A map of Paris: students identify four landmarks based on four given clues | Similar to task 1, once students identify the four landmarks, they start a 'tour around Paris'. The four directions of the tour open a second padlock |
| | | |

The two padlocks lock a backpack; when opened, students have access to the other five activities. As a result of those activities, students will obtain a 4-digit code to open another padlock.

| 3 | Puzzle with clues to identify a number and a letter and clues to use it combined with the Sudoku | Once students have completed the puzzle, they will be able to identify the number and letter required. This number and letter combination identifies a number on the Sudoku |
| 4 | Sudoku to complete | Once completed, students use the letter and number identified with the puzzle to find a number. This number is the first part of a combination to open another padlock |

Developing STEM Doctoral Students' Collaboration Skills as Learning Outcomes

|   | Tasks | Results and connections |
|---|---|---|
| 5 | Catalogue of equipment for laboratories with clues to identify two products | When students identify the two products with other clues, they identify a number, which is the second part of the combination |
| 6 | Periodic table with clues to highlight a set of elements | The highlighted elements draw a number on the periodic table, which is the third part of the combination |
| 7 | Cards with dinosaurs with clues to select two dinosaurs | Once students select two dinosaurs, other clues prompt them to define the fourth number of the combination |
| The four numbers obtained open a bag that contain the final task: | | |
| 8 | A set of coloured cars with clues | Using the clues, students need to order the eight cars, following the spectrum of light wavelengths (purple, blue, green, yellow, orange, red) |
| When a group aligns the cars in the right order, they have successfully completed the task. | | |

Table 4: A synthesis of tasks in the 'Professor Puzzle'.

We correlate these activities with clear and specific information for groups by:
1. clarifying that completing the task is not essential, but they should work towards the completion by blending and using their knowledge and skills;
2. listing the main skills they need to apply to work on the task;
3. providing step-by-step instructions.

Importantly, partner university's staff members manage the Stage 2 Activities 1-5 (above), creating a fair and unbiased environment; each staff member then identifies the group that best performed in their activity and gives feedback and a prize to the group. After receiving the feedback, each group has a debrief session with their teachers to discuss how they worked and collaborated and what they might improve to enhance their collaboration skills further. During debrief sessions, after each stage of activities, teachers prompt groups to reflect on and discuss their performances with questions, supporting the individual's and group's reflection. Based on the teacher's observations during the activities, those questions prompt students to evaluate their performances critically and safely without creating conflicts.

## Section 3: The outcome

We present here the student perspective on our programme using students' quotes collected in the anonymous feedback form we ask students to complete at the end of each programme. In this chapter, we have incorporated feedback collected since our first programme in 2017, from about 200 students.

### Student Perspective

The programme is a full-time experience, given that students are always engaged in activities to enhance their collaboration skills through developing the sub-set of abilities outlined in the Programme Learning Outcomes (Table 1). For example, the achievement of the learning outcome 1, 'ability to exercise perspective taking and cultural awareness appropriately' is synthesised in Figure 2. As described in Section 2, in the activity 'Words' exchange — Normalise the silence', each student translates a simple sentence in their own language and explains to the group the translation, highlighting similarities and differences. Figure 2 shows the whiteboard with some translations developed during the 2023 programme in Singapore. On purpose, students decided to focus on culturally and linguistically non-cognate languages spoken in Africa and Asia. This whiteboard allowed students to enhance their intercultural and interdisciplinary awareness through perspective taking since, for the first time, they could visualise what non-native English speakers face when communicating in English.

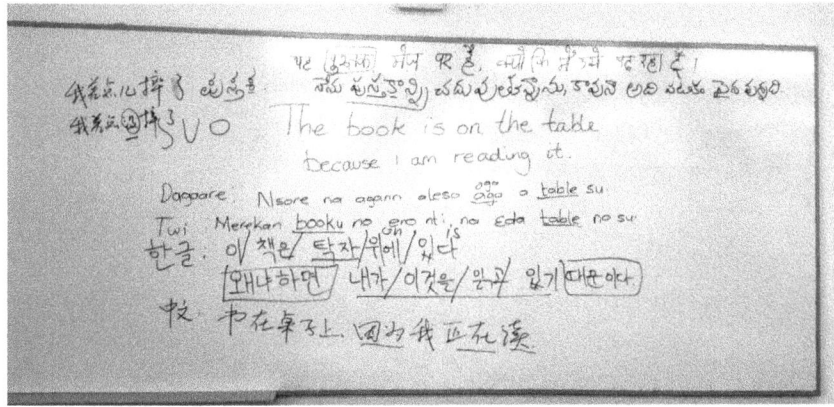

*Figure 2: Results of the activity 'Words' exchange – Normalise the silence'. In the centre is the English phrase translated by students in some languages and dialects from Asia and Africa.*

The achievement of the other learning outcomes is synthesised with quotes from students:

- Ability to network and communicate effectively:
  o *"The expectations of connecting and networking was fulfilled"*
  o *"I have been able to collaborate and learn from all others in my team"*
- Ability to influence intercultural and interdisciplinary groups:
  o *"The teamwork and collaborations especially with people from multiple country backgrounds make it very interesting and inspiring to hear the ideas that one would never thought of"*
  o *"My expectation was to meet new people from other cultures and disciplines and to learn from them and this was fully satisfied"*
- Creativity and task management to develop collaborative ideas and solve challenges:
  o *"It was nice to see how an international team of strangers can work together and develop an idea in just five short days! It requires the*

use of many skills and was definitely demanding, but very rewarding in the end"

o "I did not expect team building challenges like we had on day 2 but it was so much fun! It definitely improved the dynamic and efficiency of our group!"

*Teachers' perspective – our reflections*

After each programme, we reflect and debrief about the students' experiences and our own experiences. Each programme represents a learning experience for us; our collaborations have improved since the first programme in 2017, with the programme improving accordingly. Our first reflection is connected to the environment that we have created: there is no competition among teachers from all partner institutions; we work collaboratively to create a meaningful student experience. The effectiveness of our collaboration appears clear and visible to participating students. We seemingly are role models for them, unconsciously representing the success of the programme. Along with effective collaborations, the design and development of successful programmes like this one also depend on our shared ethos: *"Focus on the process, not on the product. The product-programme will be successful if the design process is well thought"*.

The programme's effectiveness also lies in the flexibility and adaptability of our approach. Since 2017, we have collected suggestions from students and implemented them into the programme and activities. For example, we have introduced technology — in response to the students' request to facilitate pre-programme interactions. Each programme has a Teams Class that is a platform to initiate students' discussions, as well as a repository of preparatory material about collaboration skills in intercultural and interdisciplinary contexts. We have also introduced an online event, before the in-person programme, when teachers and students meet to define the programme's expectations and start group work by introducing ourselves and creating group rules for an effective collaboration.

Prior to 2017, the programme was decontextualised and for both us and the students it was difficult to see (and believe in) the rationale of the learning activities. Our reflections, creativity, flexibility, and adaptability help support the changes in the learning activities to make these contextualised experiences clearly connected to the learning outcomes and also help to lead to a meaningful debriefing related to collaboration skills. The current learning activities allow students to practice collaborative skills and allow us to discuss with students, specific aspects of collaboration, such as verbal communication.

Our latest introduction (June 2023) is the 'Words' exchange – Normalise the silence' activity. We had been trying to add the linguistic component to the programme since 2017, but we had never found a way to do it without disrespecting some cultures. Only when we started to think through the lens of perspective taking (Gehlback, 2004), did we introduce languages in the programme through the learning activity whereby students described how their languages work compared to English. This activity increases the understanding of differences and similarities in languages, as well as cultural differences in turn-taking among the group in an unbiased, non-judgmental, and critical way. After this activity, we observed a sudden increase in engagement with communications in all students, which in previous programmes we observed only at the end of Day 2.

We also reflect on how we bring our own bias to our programme. We have personal experiences and cultural influences which impact upon how we think about the design and development of learning activities. Our experiences can both positively and negatively affect this development process. However, what makes a positive difference is how we discuss openly and share all these factors as teachers. We carefully adjust and shape the learning design through debate and discussion, there is trust between us. Trust between teachers is crucial, as is allowing time and space to develop this trust. Where there is not this trust, as reflected in some of our earlier experiences, there is no debate and shaping, and hence learning activities are often not fully formed and effective. The aim of any programme should be to develop the student, not glorify the teacher. To be able to be fully open and to be able to say, "*This doesn't make sense to me*" or "*I don't understand this*" is crucial in any design process. When this ability to be fully open is missing, the design is not optimised; hence the learning outcomes are not enhanced. Thus, open and trusting collaboration between teachers is crucial to enhance learning outcomes, especially when the learning outcome is focused on collaboration.

## Section 4: Moving forward

Finding the balance between collaboration and competition within professional development is often neither recognised nor discussed. We discussed and debated this balance when creating learning outcomes and learning activities for developing collaboration. Moreover, we identified that the intercultural and interdisciplinary contexts our students experienced was crucial to consider when developing effective collaboration.

Moving forward, we will raise awareness of the need for competition-collaboration balance and the need to expose students to intercultural and interdisciplinary contexts to enhance their practice. Too many challenges in education and the workplace arise because we develop specialist skills with determination and focus (analytical ability) but with no awareness of which skills are not developing (e.g. collaboration skills) with the associated consequences. So many leaders are impressive at speaking but have not developed their listening ability. The consequences of this can mean that many voices may go unheard, thus not creating a sense of belonging. Scientists are experts at experimentation and problem-solving but often at the expense of communication skills, as discussed by De Wilde and Forasacco (2023 in this book). Our work here on enhancing learning outcomes that utilise intercultural and interdisciplinary contexts to enhance collaboration skills is just the start. The conversation needs to be broader and deeper. Our future global workforce needs to develop intercultural skills to enable this collaborative-competitive balance in their transactions. Taking this work forward, we will develop more contextualised collaboration learning activities that are engaging and meaningful for students and explore learning outcomes that enhance a balanced and agile approach to personal and professional development.

## Conclusion

In this chapter we have explained how our past experiences have influenced our current practice. Our observations of the professional development led us to identify the need to focus on the enhancement of collaboration skills. If we had focussed only on developing the students' competitive abilities, students would not have taken the time to develop their collaboration skills. From the experience of undertaking the learning activities we designed, our students are better able to work with diverse colleagues in intercultural and interdisciplinary contexts as they progress through their careers.

We have also indicated that enhancing learning outcomes is better achieved through using a balanced approach to learning activity design. Our observations have shown that it is all too easy to design learning activities that play to student strengths i.e., competitive abilities. Students find competitive activities familiar and, as such, easy to participate in, rather than more challenging learning activities that address their more underdeveloped skills. When designing a learning activity, teachers should be aware of not only what they are developing but also of what they are not. In this way, reconsidering the design may lead to more balanced learning outcomes. Finally, we have learnt to value our collaboration and to bring our ethos to designing and creating learning activities that successfully and meaningfully develop the students' collaboration skills.

From our perspective, as university educators, our approach to enhance collaboration skills could be considered as a transferable approach applicable in other contexts. Therefore, we suggest to the reader the following points that could be taken into account to enhance students' collaboration skills as learning outcomes:

- Developing a shared understanding and perspective is core to effective collaboration among students, as well as among teachers when working together.

- For programmes to be meaningful for students, we must contextualise learning activities to be visibly applicable in real-life.

- Learning activities enhancing collaboration need to be designed in a challenging way so that students cannot complete the learning activities individually, but only by working collaboratively.

- For each learning activity we must explain the rationale and the connection with the learning outcomes.

- Valuing collaborations with other teachers support the design of learning activities and strengthen the value of your work; your work will represent your collaboration skills, students will see it, they will understand the benefits of collaboration and they will be keen on enhancing their collaboration skills.

Irrespective of the level of students (undergraduates or doctoral students), these points can be considered and applied where curricula include group activities and assessments, to prepare students for collaboration.

## About the Authors

Janet De Wilde is a Professor of Engineering and Education and Director of Queen Mary Academy at Queen Mary University of London, UK. She was at Imperial College London when the case study presented was designed and developed. She can be contacted at this email: janet.dewilde@qmul.ac.uk

Elena Forasacco is a Senior Teaching Fellow in the Graduate School at Imperial College London, UK. She can be contacted at this email: e.forasacco@imperial.ac.uk

## Bibliography

Behrnd, V., & Porzelt, S. (2012). Intercultural competence and training outcomes of students with experiences abroad. *International Journal of Intercultural Relations*, 36, 213-223.

Bowd, K., & Enomoto, K. (2023). Bringing employability to life: Developing employability skill sets and understandings as student learning outcomes. In K. Enomoto, R. Warner & C. Nygaard. (Eds.), *Enhancing student learning outcomes in higher education*. Libri Publishing Ltd.

Branch, J. D., & Wernick, D. (2023). The use of debate cases for enhancing students' reasoning skills as learning outcomes. In K. Enomoto, R. Warner & C. Nygaard (Eds.), *Enhancing student learning outcomes in higher education*. Libri Publishing Ltd.

Bruner, J. S. (1971). "The Process of Education" Revisited. *The Phi Delta Kappan*, 53(1), 18-21.

Caligiuri, P. M. (2013). Developing culturally agile global business leaders. *Organizational Dynamics*, 42, 175-182.

Caligiuri, P. M., Jacobs, R. R., & Farr, J. L. (2000). The attitudinal and behavioural openness scale: Scale development and construct validation. *International Journal of Intercultural Relations*, 24, 27-46.

Cotton, D. R. E., Morrison, D., Magne, P., Payne, S., & Heffernan, T. (2019). Global citizenship and cross-cultural competency: Student and expert understandings of internationalization terminology. *Journal of Studies in International Education*, 23(3), 346-364.

De Wilde, J., & Forasacco, E. (2023). Enhancing learning outcomes for STEM doctoral students through perspective taking in safe spaces. In K. Enomoto, R. Warner & C. Nygaard (Eds.), *Enhancing student learning outcomes in higher education*. Libri Publishing Ltd.

Enomoto, K., & Warner, R. (2018). Developing undergraduate students' transferable generic skills through an innovative group drama project. In K. Enomoto, R. Warner, & C. Nygaard (Eds.), *Innovative Teaching and Learning Practices in Higher Education*. Libri Publishing Ltd.

Forasacco, E. (2018). *Active learning in doctoral students' professional skills development: A case study of students' experiences of Graduate School provision*. Master in Education dissertation, Imperial College London.

Gehlback, H. (2004). A new perspective on perspective taking: A multidimensional approach to conceptualizing an aptitude. *Educational Psychology Review*, 16(3), 207-234.

Kolb, D. A. (1984). *Experiential learning: Experience as the source of learning and development*. Prentice Hall.

Lo-Philip, S. W. Y., Carroll, C., Li Tan, T., Ann, O. Y., Heng Tan, Y., & Hwee Seow, S. (2015). Transforming educational practices: Cultural learning for short-term sojourners. *International Journal of Intercultural Relations*, 49, 223-234.

Nygaard, C. (2023). Enhancing student learning outcomes through contextualised learning activities. In K. Enomoto, R. Warner & C. Nygaard (Eds.), *Enhancing student learning outcomes in higher education*. Libri Publishing Ltd.

Oliver, A. L. (2004). On the duality of competition and collaboration: Network-based knowledge relations in the biotechnology industry. *Scandinavian Journal of Management*, 20, 151-171.

Stivers, T., Enfield, N. J., Brown, P., Englert, C., Hayashi, M., Heinemann, T., Hoymann, G., Rossano, F., de Ruiter, J. P., Yoon, K-E., & Levinson, S. C. (2009). Universals and cultural variation in turn-taking in conversation. *Proceedings of the National Academy of Sciences*, 106(26), 10587-10592.

United Nations (2015). *Transforming our world: the 2030 agenda for sustainable development*. Resolution Adopted by the General Assembly on September 25, 2015, 42809, 1-13.

Vygotsky, L. S. (1967). Play and its role in the mental development of the child. *Soviet Psychology*, 5(3), 6-18.

Chapter 5
# Enhancing Student Learning Outcomes through Contextualised Learning Activities

Claus Nygaard

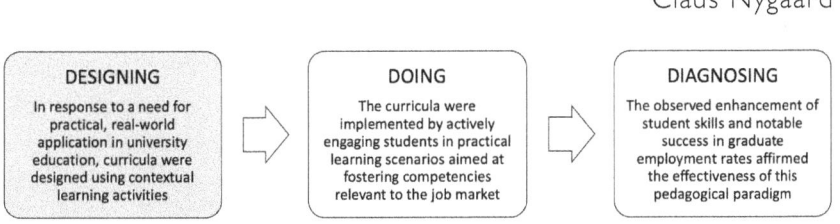

## Preamble

With his chapter, Claus Nygaard contributes to this book, *Enhancing Student Learning Outcomes in Higher Education,* by showing two cases of curriculum transformation from input-based to output-based curricula. He relates to the three phases of the central ESLO model of the book in this way:

In the DESIGNING phase, he engages with the shift from input-based to output-based curricula in university teaching and learning. He describes how implementing contextualised learning activities aims to enhance students' analytical thinking and practical skills relevant to their future careers.

In the DOING phase, he shows how teaching and learning activities relate to real-world contextual environments for practical learning experiences. Explicit references are made to the execution of an undergraduate course and a postgraduate programme. Both were designed to integrate theory with practice and provide tools and techniques necessary for problem-solving in real-world situations. These actively precipitated students to take responsibility for their learning through internships, case studies, and project-based learning activities.

In the DIAGNOSING phase, he shows the evaluation of student learning outcomes in the two curricula. The analysis of student feedback and success rates in securing employment indicated positive results, underlining the effectiveness of the implemented curriculum design.

## Introduction

In this chapter, I show how I – together with inspiring colleagues — have been engaged in a significant transformation of university teaching and learning by shifting focus from input-based to output-based curricula (Jarvis et al., 1998; Rassow, 1998; Nygaard et al., 2009). This transformation to output-based curricula has led us to base our courses and programmes on contextualised learning activities. As such, we have moved away from strictly discipline-oriented didactic teaching based on decontextual learning theory and engaged in subject-oriented teaching based on contextual learning theory.

Our transformation as teachers has paralleled the broader transformation in higher education (HE), which has occurred through various approaches and strategies. One example is implementing problem-based learning (PBL), which encourages students to work in interdisciplinary teams to solve complex, real-world problems (Savery, 2006). PBL encourages critical thinking, collaborative problem-solving, and the integration of knowledge from different disciplines (Woods, 2007). Another example is the creation of interdisciplinary programmes and degrees that bring together knowledge from various fields. For instance, the emergence of environmental studies programmes, which draw on natural sciences, social sciences, and humanities, demonstrates the growing recognition of the need for interdisciplinary approaches to complex environmental issues (Vincent & Focht, 2009). Furthermore, many universities have implemented capstone projects that require students to apply their knowledge and skills in an interdisciplinary context. These projects typically and often involve collaboration with external organisations and stakeholders, giving students hands-on experience in addressing real-world problems (Gardner & Jones, 2011).

Overall, the shift to contextualised learning activities that incorporate interdisciplinary paradigms and methodologies has been supported by an expanding body of research emphasising the importance of such approaches in preparing students for the complexities of today's job market and global challenges (Newell, 2013; Frodeman et al., 2010). In Section 3, I will return to some of these challenges when I further anchor the chapter in theory and methodology related to learning-centred HE.

The transformation of our teaching aims to better align students' learning with the knowledge, skills, and competencies needed in their future careers. As a result, we have strived to meet the expectations of a tripartite of key stakeholders: students (first and foremost), prospective employers, and universities. It has been our guiding principle that contemporary HE is not merely about imparting the 'right knowledge' to students, but instead providing them with opportunities to develop those skills and competencies (Nygaard et al., 2009), which are both transformative and relevant to the job market (Harvey et al., 1992; Harvey & Knight, 1996; Falconer & Pettigrew, 2003).

We have worked from the belief that teachers must address at least three central challenges that stem from this transition to output-based curricula:

1. Actively connecting academic disciplines with current professional practices in private, public, and non-profit sectors;

2. Defining, assessing, and linking students' knowledge, skills, and competencies to national and international qualification frameworks, as exemplified by the Bologna process and the Dublin Descriptors in Europe, and most importantly, about student learning;

3. Employing teaching and study methods that embrace the new paradigms of contextual learning to account for all aspects of students' learning outcomes fully.

This chapter explores the intricacies of student learning outcomes in HE and discusses those factors contributing to their successful development. By examining and discussing existing research, I will shed light on the approaches of HE institutions to ensure students have the skills and competencies to thrive in their future careers (Jarvis et al., 1998; Rassow, 1998; Nygaard et al., 2009). Furthermore, I will also investigate the challenges and opportunities that arise as HE institutions navigate this transition and strive to meet the expectations of their diverse stakeholders.

Chapter 5

*Chapter overview and key takeaways*

The chapter has five main sections. Section 1 presents my background in working with student learning outcomes. It takes the form of a personal narrative to give the reader an understanding of how I approach teaching and learning. Furthermore, this section serves to stress that the teacher and their teaching methods are interrelated on a deeper personal level. In Section 2, I argue why a shift in curricula from input-based and discipline-oriented to output-based and subject-oriented is greatly needed in HE. Some may say I do so to legitimise my practice. Still, I will say I do so because it is for the students' benefit if HE transforms. In Section 3, I present the contextual learning theory, because it underpins output-based and subject-oriented curricula. In Section 4, I give concrete examples of how some of the output-based and subject-oriented curricula I have been involved in have helped enhance student learning outcomes, supporting my argument with student data. In the final Section 5, I look forward to what may be the subsequent transformation of the learning paradigm in HE.

Reading the chapter, you may gain the following insights:

1. Arguments for why a shift in curricula from input-based to output-based is highly needed in HE;

2. An insight into the theory of contextual learning underpinning output-based education; and

3. Concrete examples of how output-based and subject-oriented curricula have helped enhance student learning outcomes.

## Section 1: My background in working with student learning outcomes

I began my professional career as a software programmer in 1988, programming and selling self-developed learning software to Danish primary schools. Therefore, given my software-related interest, I am pleased to have my chapter included in this book alongside the chapter by Margitay-Becht & Das (2023), who show how a software programming course has been designed, this time in an HE context, with a particular focus on enhancing IT students' learning outcomes. In my case, I established a company with a schoolteacher, and we sold learning software designed to help pupils learn Danish grammar, History, Geography, and Political Science. It was a suite of learning software that could facilitate a move from one-size-fits-all classroom lecturing to individual training and learning. Using the learning software, the pupil could engage in various tasks, exercises, and quizzes. They could play text adventure games set in the stone age or answer questions about the political climate in Denmark, which would respond with figurative exit polls. We had a great deal of enjoyment in both the creation and programming of these engaging learning activities. In our minds, we would beat and be bigger than Microsoft (Apple did not have a foothold in Denmark then). Soon, though, we learned an important lesson.

Most schoolteachers in Danish primary schools were not geared towards changing how they taught. They preferred keeping the pupils in the classroom so they could lecture, write on the blackboard, and ask the same question to all pupils, although only one pupil could reply. The teacher would read from a book while all pupils listened. It would be the same book for all pupils simultaneously. However, they were at different academic levels, learning styles, ambitions, and so on. Most teachers had decided (maybe without conscious awareness) that they owned the learning process – not the pupils.

Hence, after only two years, we closed our company. It was depressing because it should have been a 'no-brainer' to start using learning software, by which each pupil could own their learning process, scaffold their learning, and document their progress by printing out detailed certificates that showed their strengths and weaknesses within a discipline. If, for example, they were conjugating Danish verbs, the teacher could see from their certificate which person, number, and tense the individual pupil had already mastered to perfection or did not. That could help the teacher cluster pupils into groups and differentiate the teaching. However, it was not to be. I was 20, and maybe my ideas did not sit well with the older generation of schoolteachers. I do not think it was age-related, though, given that my business partner, Jens-Erik Kjeldsen, the schoolteacher, was 52 at the time. He is now 87 years old and still actively engaged with computers, using virtual reality while exercising on his treadmill. No, it was not age – it was culture. The primary schools, as institutions, kept reproducing the same old culture – where the teacher owned their classroom and the learning process, and pupils were good pupils if they were compliant and remained silent while the teacher lectured.

I started as a PhD student at Copenhagen Business School seven years later. I was shocked to find that the institution reproduced the same cultural norms that I had experienced at the primary schools. Most teachers practised syllabus-driven didactic teaching. All students on a programme were moving through the same sequential row of courses planned and plotted into the overall programme, following a political resource game institutionalised through academics spending time on the study boards. After one year into my PhD, I was offered a course coordinator role. I was soon elected as my department's academic representative on the study board, which governed the bachelor programme on economics and business administration. I was surprised that we rarely talked about student learning. Our hour-long meetings were used to discuss things like the overall finances of the bachelor programme, the money and time allocated to each course, and the dropout rate of students. We were looking at spreadsheets and making decisions based on forever historical data. And most important, we could not 'rock the boat'. The sixteen courses offered as part of the bachelor programme were nested in four departments: Organisation (where I came from), Finance, Marketing, and Accounting. If somebody suggested a change that, in any way, threatened the power balance between the departments, meaning that a department would lose teaching hours on the programme, 'all hell would break loose'. Someone would start preaching about the last reform in the 1970s, how difficult it was to reach where we now were, and why anyone would dare to destroy the good collaboration between the four departments. So instead, we would look at the syllabus for a particular course and said something like: *"The textbook is from 1992. Isn't there a new edition out from 1995?"* Those were the kind of changes we made.

In 2000, I was offered a position at CBS Learning Lab, a support unit of the Vice-Chancellor's office at Copenhagen Business School. The unit was founded in 1996 with two aims: 1) to reduce the dropout rate at Copenhagen Business School, which was over 20% for some programmes, and 2) to help master students complete their dissertations on time. The director at CBS Learning Lab was the now late Ib Andersen, a visionary academic, extremely knowledgeable, generous, and empathic in his approach. He was a living example of a director who practised self-determination theory (Deci & Ryan, 2008) without being aware of the theory. He used its three basic psychological needs in his everyday leadership: 1) autonomy: the need for individuals to feel control and agency over their actions and decisions; 2) competence: the need to feel effective and capable in one's activities, and to experience a sense of mastery and growth in one's skills and abilities; and 3) relatedness: the need to feel connected to and valued by others, as well as to experience a sense of belonging and social support. This involves forming meaningful relationships and feeling attached to a community or group.

Moreover, Ib Andersen taught us, by example, that these principles should be an integral part of any learning process we would engage in. And since CBS Learning Lab was a staff unit engaged in quality enhancement of all study programmes at Copenhagen Business School, we could participate in and affect several turnaround processes where individual courses of entire study programmes moved away from syllabus-driven didactic teaching to a new learning-based paradigm. Section 3 will present some learning-based activities I have enjoyed outside the CBS Learning Lab.

## Section 2: the need for contextualised learning activities

While I navigated my way through the tenure track from PhD student to professor, the landscape of the modern workforce gradually changed. The commodification of the Internet — through browser technology — was perhaps the most dominant factor that greatly impacted entire value chains across all industries and sectors. It became apparent to (some of) us that the increasing demands of the knowledge economy required a significant shift in how HE institutions develop curricula. We needed to examine the learning process, because what we had been teaching was no longer adequate. Navigating this complexity presented a challenge for HE institutions, particularly in contemporary societies, where organisational structures within and between companies experienced significant transformations due to the decline of the old economy (Best, 1990; Lash & Urry, 1994). With the emergence of new technologies and shifting professional roles and identities, there was a growing demand for novel skills and competencies. Firms increasingly required adaptability as a competitive edge, achieved mainly by hiring versatile employees with a wide range of transferable knowledge, abilities, and expertise (Assiter, 1995; Harvey & Knight, 1996). Traditional input-based and discipline-oriented curricula were no longer sufficient to meet the needs of either learners or employers. As a result, we started focusing on developing flexible, interdisciplinary, and transferable competencies that equip students to thrive in the dynamic and complex world of work.

One key argument for this shift was the evolving nature of the job market, which demanded employees with diverse skills and knowledge. The traditional discipline-oriented curricula, focusing on narrow areas of expertise, did not provide students with the interdisciplinary and transferable competencies vital in today's job market. Another significant factor driving the need for change in HE curricula was the growing importance of flexibility in the workplace. Employees were increasingly expected to learn, adapt, and develop their competencies while working in loosely coupled networks and multitasking between integrated or disintegrated projects. With their heavy dependence on syllabus-driven didactic teaching and rigid course structures, traditional input-based curricula did not nurture the adaptable and self-directed learners that the modern job market requires (Maskell & Törnqvist, 2001).

Since we observed these changes, we began transforming from input-based to output-based curricula, focusing on students' learning process, fostering their ability to learn how to learn, and encouraging them to take greater ownership of their educational journey. By developing transferable skills and competencies, rather than acquiring discipline-specific knowledge, our approach better-equipped students to navigate the fluid and ever-changing landscape of the contemporary job market.

Moreover, it became increasingly clear that the traditional one-size-fits-all approach to education was no longer tenable. As our understanding of how individuals learn and process information grew, it became increasingly apparent that diverse teaching and learning methods were necessary to cater to the needs of all students. An output-based and learning-centred approach to curriculum development provided the flexibility and adaptability needed to accommodate these diverse learning styles and preferences, ensuring that all students had the opportunity to succeed and reach their full potential.

In summary, the rapidly changing demands of the modern job market, and the growing importance of interdisciplinary, transferable skills (Enomoto & Warner, 2023 in this book) and competencies, required a significant shift in how we thought about and developed curricula. Transforming to an output-based and learning-centred approach, focusing on the learning process, adaptability, and development of transferable skills, was far better suited to prepare students for the challenges and opportunities of the current and future workforce. Based on my experiences, I believe that by embracing this new approach and moving away from traditional input-based and discipline-oriented curricula, HE institutions can better fulfil their role in scaffolding students' development of the skills and competencies needed to thrive in the knowledge economy. However, it requires a specific understanding of learning, namely contextual learning, which I will present in Section 3.

## Section 3: From decontextual learning to contextual learning

Arguing for the benefits of contextual learning is, in a way, meaningless if I do not briefly describe its counterpart, decontextual learning. Therefore, I shall do so below in brief.

### Decontextual learning

Decontextual learning is an approach to education that views learning as an individual psychological process. It emphasises the acquisition of knowledge through the study of academic literature, often disregarding the importance of context and social aspects of learning. I argue that decontextual learning is the traditional approach in HE, in which knowledge is seen as absolute and bound to the books. Advocates of decontextual learning believe that finding the right book for a course and teaching its content will produce competent students. In decontextual learning, knowledge is perceived as an object that can be transformed into learning across independent entities and contexts. This implies that learning occurs when the teacher lectures, and all students are considered equal learners (they learn by transfer). Their learning outcomes depend mainly on their efforts and abilities to acquire the knowledge presented in books and by teachers. In Table 1, I sum up key aspects of decontextual learning.

| Definition of learning | Definition of knowledge | Ways of acquiring knowledge | The relation between knowledge and competencies |
|---|---|---|---|
| To learn is to acquire knowledge | Knowledge is an object. Knowledge is propositional and found in books and papers. Knowledge is decontextual and can be transformed into learning across independent entities and contexts | By reading books and papers from teaching in classrooms | To be competent is to possess knowledge about relevant rules and principles. Competencies are universally transferable |

*Table 1: Key aspects of decontextual learning (Nygaard & Andersen, 2005).*

As a university teacher and learning consultant, I have seen many teaching and learning activities based on decontextual learning. These five dominant activities are easily recognisable:

1. Lectures: in a traditional lecture setting, the instructor delivers information to a large group of students who passively absorb the knowledge. Students are expected to learn and understand the material independently, without much interaction with their peers or the instructor. This method often focuses on the content of academic literature and may not incorporate real-world examples or contexts.

2. Independent reading and study: decontextual learning often involves students engaging in extensive independent reading and study of academic literature. Students are expected to gain knowledge and understanding from the text, without necessarily relating the material to real-world situations or their own experiences.

3. Rote memorisation: a teaching method that emphasises rote memorisation of facts and figures without considering the context or application of the information is an example of decontextual learning. Students are expected to memorise the material without necessarily understanding its relevance or connections to broader concepts.

4. Standardised testing: decontextual learning can also be seen in standardised testing, where students are assessed on their ability to recall facts and information from academic literature without applying the knowledge to real-world scenarios. These tests often focus on individual performance and do not encourage collaboration or contextual understanding of the material.

5. Traditional problem sets and exercises: in some courses, students are given problem sets and exercises that focus solely on applying theories and formulas without incorporating real-world examples or situations. These assignments often emphasise the technical aspects of the subject matter, and do not encourage students to consider the broader context or application of their knowledge to diverse scenarios. This approach can limit students' critical thinking and problem-solving skills, as they are only exposed to abstract, decontextualised problems.

Whilst this approach has been prevalent for many years, the critique has been that it often overlooks the importance of context and social aspects of learning. By disregarding the role of context, decontextual learning may fail to provide students with opportunities to 'apply' their knowledge in real-world situations, limiting their ability to develop critical thinking, problem-solving, and communication skills. The critique has led to a shift towards contextual learning approaches that offer students a more holistic and effective learning experience. By incorporating context and social interactions, teachers can create more meaningful and compelling learning experiences for students, better preparing them for success in their future academic and professional endeavours. Let me look further at contextual learning.

## Contextual learning

Contextual learning is an educational approach that emphasises the relationship between academic knowledge and real-world applications. This approach acknowledges that learning is a social and embedded process, affected by the learner's identity and social position within ongoing systems of social relations. Contextual learning, then, is a theory that posits that learning is *"...a contextual process tied to particular situations...a process affected by the identity of the learner... a process affected by the social position of the learner...and by the learners' embeddedness in social collectivities"* (Nygaard & Holtham, 2008:13-14). It argues that learning occurs best when it is connected to real-world situations and experiences, making what has to be learned more relevant and meaningful for the learner. It also acknowledges that the learner is contextually embedded. Granovetter (1992:53-58) describes embeddedness in this way: *"...the argument that the behaviour and institutions to be analysed are so constrained by ongoing social relations that to construe them as independent is a grievous misunderstanding... Actors do not behave or decide as atoms outside a social context, nor do they adhere slavishly to a script written for them by the particular intersection of social categories that they happen to occupy. Their attempts at purposive action are instead embedded in concrete, ongoing systems of social relations"*.

Such ongoing systems of social relations exist between, for example, the learner, their peers, teachers, mentors, role models, institutions and organisations. Thus, learners are embedded in learning contexts. As McDermott (1999:15) writes: *"...context is not so much something into which someone is put, but an order of behaviour of which one is a part"*. This definition focuses on the learning process (the order of behaviour) rather than the structure of the learning context (classroom, lecture theatre). The argument that systems are 'ongoing' and the context is a 'behavioural order' implies that relationships between individual students, their peers, teachers, administration, and other key actors in HE are never stable but continuously evolving. As a result, the auditorium, classroom, or student working group cannot be considered a stable structure over time. Each meeting of students, teachers, and other vital individuals creates a unique system of social interactions, which means the learning context constantly changes and is never identical.

This approach moves beyond the traditional view of learning as an isolated psychological process. This is because it emphasises the importance of the learning context, the learner's identity, and the social position of the learner in shaping the student's learning experience and, hence their learning outcomes. Learning is seen as an intersubjective process between embedded learners, where the learning context is in a dualistic relationship with learners. Earlier, I wrote about contextual learning (Nygaard & Andersen, 2005; Nygaard & Holtham, 2008; Nygaard & Bramming, 2008; Nygaard, 2015) and formulated five statements that sum up its characteristics:

1. "learning is never a simple repetition of previous learning. People learn based on their experiences and expectations.

2. *learning is both an individual and social process.*

3. *learning is a contextual process tied to particular situations.*

4. *learning is a process affected by the identity of the learner.*

5. *learning is a process affected by the social position of the learner… and by the learners' embeddedness in social collectivities."* (Nygaard & Holtham, 2008:13-14).

Table 2 below sums up the key aspects of contextual learning.

| Definition of Learning | Definition of knowledge | Ways of acquiring knowledge | The relation between knowledge and competencies |
|---|---|---|---|
| Learning is an ongoing process that involves more than acquiring knowledge | Knowledge is an artificial object. Knowledge is not propositional. Knowledge cannot be expressed in books and papers. Knowledge is situated and acquired during social activity | Solving assignments or discussing information with others | To be competent is "to be able to". Competencies are tied to the situations at hand. Competencies are not universally transferable |

*Table 2: Key aspects of contextual learning (Nygaard & Andersen, 2005).*

As a university teacher and learning consultant, I have also seen many teaching and learning activities based on contextual learning. These five dominant activities are also easily recognisable:

1. Project-based learning: students work on real-world projects, applying their knowledge and skills to solve complex problems or create tangible products. This approach encourages students to actively engage with the subject matter, collaborate with peers, and understand the relevance of their learning in real-life situations (Meier & Nygaard, 2008).

2. Case studies: Using case studies in teaching involves presenting students with real-world scenarios or examples that illustrate the concepts being taught. Students are encouraged to analyse the case, apply theories and principles, and discuss potential solutions. This approach helps students see the practical applications of their learning and fosters critical thinking and problem-solving skills (Branch et al., 2015).

3. Internships and work placements: Contextual learning can occur through internships and work placements, where students gain practical experience. By working in real-world settings, students can apply their academic knowledge to professional situations, develop valuable skills, and gain a deeper understanding of the context in which their learning occurs (Piihl et al., 2015).

4. Role-playing and simulations: Role-playing and simulations allow students to step into the shoes of professionals or other individuals in specific situations. By participating in these activities, students can better understand the context in which decisions are made and the implications of their actions. This approach encourages students to apply their learning practically and engagingly, fostering empathy and critical thinking skills (Nygaard et al., 2012).

5. Collaborative learning and group work: Contextual learning often involves students working together in groups to explore concepts, solve problems, or complete projects. These collaborative activities enable students to learn from their perspectives, experiences, and insights, fostering a deeper understanding of the subject matter and its practical applications. Moreover, group work helps students

develop essential skills, such as communication, teamwork, and leadership, which are valuable in their future academic and professional endeavours (Meier & Nygaard, 2008).

## Four requirements stemming from contextual learning

In HE, contextual learning is crucial in enhancing student learning outcomes. It allows students to apply their knowledge and skills in real-life situations, fostering a deeper understanding of the subject matter. In the wake of the five statements that characterise contextual learning mentioned above (Nygaard & Holtham, 2008:13-14), if curricula are based on contextual learning, there are at least four requirements:

**Requirement 1: Connection to real-world situations**
Contextual learning emphasises the importance of connecting academic knowledge to real-world contexts, allowing students to see the relevance and applicability of their learning. This can be achieved through case studies, internships, project-based learning, or collaborations with industry partners.

**Requirement 2: Social and collaborative learning**
Contextual learning recognises that learning is both an individual and social process. Students are encouraged to work in groups, discuss, and share their knowledge with peers. This collaborative approach fosters a sense of community and allows students to learn from one another's perspectives and experiences.

**Requirement 3: Learner's identity and social position**
Contextual learning acknowledges that each student brings their unique identity and social position to the learning context. By considering these factors, educators can create inclusive learning environments that cater to diverse student needs and backgrounds.

**Requirement 4: Adaptive and dynamic learning contexts**
As learning contexts change over time, contextual learning encourages educators to adapt their teaching strategies and materials to meet the evolving needs of their students better. This flexibility allows for a more

personalised learning experience and ensures students remain engaged and motivated.

### Impact on student learning outcomes

Contextual learning has positively affected student learning outcomes in HE. Students can better understand and retain the material by connecting academic knowledge to real-world situations, improving performance in assessments and examinations. Additionally, the social and collaborative nature of contextual learning helps develop critical thinking, problem-solving, and communication skills, which are essential for success in the workforce. Furthermore, focusing on the learner's identity and social position in contextual learning allows for more inclusive and equitable learning environments, helping close achievement gaps and promoting greater academic success for all students. Finally, the adaptive and dynamic contextual learning approach ensures that students remain engaged and motivated throughout their educational journey, contributing to higher satisfaction and retention levels.

For me, contextual learning is vital in enhancing student learning outcomes. By connecting academic knowledge to real-world situations, fostering social and collaborative learning, considering the learner's identity and social position, and embracing adaptive and dynamic learning contexts, teachers can create more meaningful and effective learning experiences for their students. As a result, students are better equipped with the skills and competencies needed to succeed in their future endeavours, both within academia and the professional world.

## Section 4: Two examples of programmes based on contextualised learning activities

In this section, I present two curricula I have contributed to, based entirely on contextualised learning activities. The two examples are the *BETA* course we designed in 2010 and the Camp Future programme, which we designed in 2012. Both ran for more than a decade.

## The BETA course

The first example is the *BETA* course, which was part of the Bachelor's programme in Business Administration and Organisational Communication at Copenhagen Business School. It was designed to integrate theories, methods, and practice while enhancing students' professional development. The course design began about 18 months before its scheduled start. It was grounded in ongoing research from the involved teachers and researchers. It incorporated current business practices and encouraged students to take responsibility for organising their curriculum.

To achieve this, we established five guiding principles:
1. students must take responsibility for and organise a part of their own curriculum,
2. the *BETA* course curriculum will include current business practices,
3. the *BETA* course is based on a practice-oriented pedagogy,
4. students must be able to apply theories, work methodically, reflect critically, develop personal and interpersonal competencies, and
5. the *BETA* course will be grounded in ongoing research from teachers/researchers involved in developing and teaching courses.

These principles were based on contextual learning theories, which led to the development of five modules for the course, each covering a half-year semester. The total workload of *BETA* was 31 ECTS (European Credit Transfer and Accumulation System, which equals 930 student work hours), making it a significant course in terms of time and workload. A blended learning approach was employed, combining face-to-face interaction in the classroom with asynchronous communication through a learning management system called SiteScape Forum. This system facilitated daily communication, file sharing, and academic debate among administrators, teachers, and students. In the month leading up to the course, a conference call and a detailed 36-page manual were uploaded to the SiteScape Forum. The manual outlined the course plan, student expectations, learning goals, and pedagogy. A reading list was

Chapter 5

also provided, and students were responsible for acquiring the necessary learning materials.

Here, I shall only focus on the first part of the course, the mini-conference. It served as the foundation for integrating theories, methods and practices. Students prepared for the mini-conference by reading relevant literature, researching the participating companies, and submitting questions for a Q&A session with the managing directors of two companies. The mini-conference began with presentations from these two managing directors, who discussed their companies' economic challenges. Students were required to prepare questions for the Q&A session beforehand, encouraging them to engage with the course material and do empirical research on the companies. After the Q&A, the managing directors gave the students an assignment to analyse the two case companies' economic challenges using the theories from the course, write a report and prepare a presentation on the key findings.

Students worked in groups to analyse the companies' challenges over the next four days. On day three, teachers invited retired managing directors from private companies to join in for a workshop with student groups. During the workshop, students discussed their analysis of the two case companies economic challenges with the seasoned managers, thereby receiving valuable feedback on their work in progress. The workshop and group discussions encouraged social and collaborative learning, fostering a sense of community and allowing students to learn from one another's perspectives and experiences. Students then submitted their final reports, which were evaluated by teachers based on the curriculum's learning requirements. The best reports were nominated, and two winning groups were selected to present their findings to the managing directors and the entire class. Both teachers and managing directors provided feedback, offering valuable insights to students as they learned to master the new academic field.

The competitive element of presenting to the managing directors added motivation, and the course's various pedagogical tools contributed to its success. BETA students performed better than those in traditional courses and taught themselves theories and methods typically aimed at graduate students. The course structure was designed to be adaptive and dynamic, incorporating various pedagogical tools to suit the evolving needs of its students. For example, the mini-conference, workshops, and online communication allowed for ongoing adaptation and responsiveness to students' learning needs, ensuring that they remained engaged and motivated throughout the course.

In summary, the *BETA* course was a unique and innovative approach to teaching business economics, which focused on integrating theories, methods, and practices, while emphasising real-world applications, social and collaborative learning, and adaptability. By combining traditional classroom instruction with online communication and engagement with industry professionals, the course successfully prepared students to apply their knowledge and skills in real-world situations and fostered their professional development. In Table 3 below, I reflect on the BETA course and how its learning activities were designed to meet the four requirements stemming from contextual learning.

| The four requirements of contextual learning | Contextual learning activities of the BETA course |
| --- | --- |
| 1. Connection to real-world situations | In the case of *BETA*, the connection to real-world situations is evident through the involvement of managing directors from the two case companies in the curriculum. These directors presented their companies' economic challenges and engaged in a Q&A session with the students. Students then worked in groups to analyse these challenges and develop solutions using the theories and methods they had learned in the course. Furthermore, the students participated in the workshop with the retired business managers, who served as mentors. This direct engagement with real-world business challenges and managers allowed students to see the relevance and applicability of their learning. |
| 2. Social and collaborative learning | BETA emphasised social and collaborative learning through group work, workshops, and online communication. Students worked in groups to analyse the challenges of companies and present their findings. They also participated in workshops where they discussed their analysis with their peers and teachers, who acted as supervisors and coaches. They fostered a sense of community and encouraged students to learn from each other's perspectives and experiences. |

Chapter 5

| The four requirements of contextual learning | Contextual learning activities of the BETA course |
|---|---|
| 3. Learner's identity and social position | *BETA* addressed its students' unique identities and social positions by allowing them to take responsibility for organising their curriculum and working in diverse groups. They could bring their individual perspectives and experiences to the learning process. This collaborative approach created an inclusive learning environment catering to diverse student needs and backgrounds. |
| 4. Adaptive and dynamic learning contexts | *BETA* demonstrated adaptability and dynamism in its learning context through various pedagogical tools and the blended learning approach. By combining face-to-face interaction in the classroom with asynchronous communication through a learning management system, *BETA* offered flexibility and personalisation to suit the evolving needs of its students. Additionally, the course structure, including mini-conferences, workshops, and online communication, allowed for ongoing adaptation and responsiveness to the student's learning needs, ensuring that they remained engaged and motivated throughout the course. |

*Table 3: How the BETA course met the four requirements of contextual learning.*

**Student's learning outcomes in the *BETA* course**

Following the BETA course, it was formally evaluated like all courses at Copenhagen Business School are evaluated. It received positive feedback from students, who found it inspiring, engaging, and educational. Here are some quotes (my translation from Danish to English) from four female and four male students who shared their experiences:

- "Honestly, the BETA course was so inspiring! The way we like got to work with real companies and their challenges made me feel like I was making a difference." (Female student 1).

- "I've learned so much in this course! The mix of theory and practice made the concepts stick. I feel much more confident that I can use this knowledge in my future career." (Female student 2).

- "The group work and collaboration in BETA were fantastic. It was really engaging to bounce ideas off each other and learn from my peers." (Female student 3).

- "I loved how the BETA course pushed us to think critically and apply what we learned. I've never felt this confident about my skills before." (Female student 4).

- "BETA was a game-changer for me. Getting hands-on experience with real-world situations made the learning so much more engaging and relatable." (Male student 1).

- "I've got to say, the BETA course was amazing. Working with actual companies and tackling their challenges was super inspiring and motivating. I feel like I've grown so much during this course." (Male student 2).

- "The blend of classroom learning and online interaction in BETA was perfect. It kept me engaged throughout the course, and I feel like I learned a lot." (Male student 3).

- "I really appreciated the collaborative atmosphere in the BETA course. It made learning enjoyable, you know, and I think I've gained valuable insights from working with my classmates." (Male student 4).

These quotes from students clearly highlight the success of the BETA course in providing an inspiring, engaging, and educational experience, preparing them for their future careers with a solid foundation in business economics.

## The Camp Future programme

Camp Future was an innovative 10-week postgraduate training programme designed to help unemployed university graduates develop an entrepreneurial mindset and secure employment. Developed in 2012 and running until 2022, the programme successfully assisted over 900 graduates in finding jobs. An average of 64% of participants secured employment during or shortly after completing the programme. The programme was structured into two main parts: six weeks of learning-centred teaching and case-based fieldwork, followed by a four-week internship with the case company. Throughout the programme, students were matched with a case company and tasked with solving a real business challenge relevant to that company. These challenges varied widely and covered areas such as marketing, product development, and corporate strategy.

Camp Future's curriculum was based on a learning-centred action plan (Bolhuis, 2003; Nygaard & Bramming, 2008), placing students' learning at the programme's centre. Students were expected to take individual action from day one and engage in trial and error, while working as reflective practitioners to solve their assigned business challenges. This approach aimed to develop a culture of deep learning, with students actively engaged in their learning process and focused on making a qualitative and positive impact on the companies they work with (Marton & Säljö, 1976; Ramsden, 1988).

Throughout the six-week teaching period, students spent 10 days with their teachers and 20 days working independently on their case-company projects. During the ten days of face-to-face teaching, students were introduced to various tools and techniques to analyse and address their business challenges. Some of these tools included wicked problem analysis, Porter's Five Forces analysis, and customer value analysis, all tools related to business economics and marketing. In addition to learning how to utilise these tools best, students also participated in academic workshops, collaborating with peers on the tools for their respective business cases. Furthermore, students received individual supervision and teacher feedback to help refine and improve their solutions. At the end of the six-week teaching period, students presented their solutions to the case company's management team and an implementation plan for their proposed solution. Following this presentation, students embarked on a four-week internship with their case company, implementing their implementation plans and gaining valuable real-world experience. Camp Future utilised various technological platforms to support student learning and engagement throughout the course. These e-learning technologies aimed to enhance the programme's effectiveness, ensuring that students were actively involved in their learning process even when not in the classroom.

In summary, Camp Future was a unique and impactful postgraduate training programme that combined learning-centred teaching, case-based fieldwork, and internships to help unemployed university graduates develop an entrepreneurial mindset and secure employment. By focusing on solving real business challenges and providing students with the tools and support, the programme has successfully assisted hundreds of graduates in their transition from unemployment to meaningful employment. The combination of classroom learning, hands-on experience, and technological support made Camp Future a valuable and effective programme for graduates seeking to kick-start their careers.

In Table 4 below, I reflect on the Camp Future course and how its learning activities were designed to meet the four requirements stemming from contextual learning.

| The four requirements of contextual learning | Contextual learning activities of Camp Future |
| --- | --- |
| 1. Connection to real-world situations | In Camp Future, students were directly connected to real-world situations by working with case companies to solve real business challenges. For example, students could be asked to "create a social media strategy for our company" or "design a curriculum for our new corporate talent management programme". By working on these real-world problems, students saw the relevance and applicability of the tools and techniques they learned in the programme, making their learning experience more meaningful and practical. |
| 2. Social and collaborative learning | Camp Future emphasised social and collaborative learning through academic workshops, group discussions, and peer feedback sessions. For instance, students worked together during workshops to apply the tools they have learned to their respective business cases, fostering a sense of community and allowing them to learn from each other's perspectives and experiences. This collaborative approach helped students develop their problem-solving, communication, and teamwork skills, which are essential for success in the job market. |

| The four requirements of contextual learning | Contextual learning activities of Camp Future |
|---|---|
| 3. Learner's identity and social position | The programme considered each student's unique identity and social position by offering diverse business challenges and creating an inclusive learning environment. Students came from various educational backgrounds, such as finance, marketing, engineering, and art. They were given business challenges that aligned with their expertise and interests. This approach ensured that students felt valued and included in the learning process, allowing them to draw from their backgrounds and experiences to contribute to the collaborative learning environment. |
| 4. Adaptive and dynamic learning contexts | Camp Future's curriculum was designed to be adaptive and dynamic, accommodating students' diverse needs and learning styles. Throughout the programme, students worked independently on their case company projects. They engaged in face-to-face teaching sessions, academic workshops, and supervision. Teachers provided individual feedback and support to help refine and improve students' solutions, ensuring that the learning process was tailored to each student's needs. Additionally, the programme continuously evolved and adapted its teaching strategies and materials to keep up with industry developments and trends, ensuring students remained engaged and motivated throughout their learning journey. |

*Table 4: How the Camp Future Programme met the four requirements of contextual learning.*


**Students' Learning Outcomes in the Camp Future programme**
The success of Camp Future can be measured by the learning outcomes its participants achieve. The programme was designed to help unemployed university graduates develop an entrepreneurial mindset and secure employment. The following section presents qualitative and quantitative evaluation results for students participating in the Camp Future programme.

Feedback from participating students was overwhelmingly positive.

Many students reported that the programme exceeded their expectations and helped them develop valuable skills in the job market. Common themes that emerged from the qualitative evaluation include:

1. Enhanced problem-solving skills: Students reported that the programme helped them develop their problem-solving skills by providing them with real-world challenges to solve. The collaborative learning environment and guidance from teachers and case company mentors also helped them develop critical thinking skills.

2. Improved communication skills: Many students reported that the programme helped them develop their communication skills. Working with case company mentors and presenting their solutions to management teams helped students develop their ability to communicate effectively with various stakeholders.

3. Entrepreneurial mindset: Students reported that the programme helped them develop an entrepreneurial mindset, which they found valuable in the job market. The programme encouraged students to take ownership of their learning and develop solutions to real-world challenges, which helped them develop an entrepreneurial approach to problem-solving.

4. Real-world experience: Students reported that the programme provided valuable real-world experience, which potential employers highly valued. The four-week internship with the case company allowed students to apply the skills and knowledge they had learned in the programme to real-world situations.

The quantitative evaluation of the Camp Future programme was based on the number of graduates who secured employment during or shortly after completing the programme. The programme successfully assisted over 900 graduates in finding jobs, with an average of 64% of participants securing employment during or shortly after completing the programme. Asked if they would recommend the course to others, a class of students would often respond with 100% yes; no class ever going below 91% answering with a yes.

The Camp Future programme successfully assisted unemployed university graduates in developing an entrepreneurial mindset and securing employment. The programme achieved this through learning-centred teaching, case-based fieldwork, and internships with case companies. The programme's success can be measured by the high number of graduates who secured employment after completing the programme and the positive feedback from students who participated.

## Section 5: Moving forward in higher education

Three and a half decades after I launched my software company and programmed learning software for Danish primary schools, technology again 'knocks on the front door' of educational institutions. This time it is 'knocking very loudly' in the form of artificial intelligence (AI), as 'personified' by ChatGPT, Bart and Bing Chat Enterprise. Undoubtedly, HE institutions must evolve to keep pace with these rapid changes. Faced with AI's growing influence, universities must adapt their approach to teaching and learning, ensuring that students are equipped with the skills and knowledge needed to thrive in an AI-driven world. It is, therefore, alarming to see how (at present) the majority of the educational sector in Denmark has spent months trying to either ignore ChatGPT, Bart and Bing Chat Enterprise or ban them. The Danish minister of education even suggested that the educational system might have to revert to pen and paper to avoid students cheating. One of the key challenges I see facing HE is preparing students for a job market that will be increasingly influenced by AI technologies. Undoubtedly, AI is revolutionising how we work, live, and interact. As such, HE institutions must adapt their curricula to prepare students for a future where AI plays a central role rather than reverting to pen and paper.

Firstly, AI technologies can automate many tasks once performed by humans, particularly those that involve routine and repetitive work. This means the job market is shifting toward roles that require higher levels of cognitive, creative, and emotional intelligence – skills that are less susceptible to automation. An output-based and subject-oriented curriculum can help students develop these critical competencies, providing them with the tools they need to remain relevant and competitive in an AI-driven job market.

Secondly, the rise of AI creates new, specialised roles that demand a deep understanding of the technology and its applications across various domains. HE institutions must incorporate AI-related subjects and skills into their curricula to ensure students can fill these emerging roles. This includes offering courses in AI, machine learning, data science, and other related fields and integrating AI concepts and applications into existing subject areas.

Additionally, the rapid pace of AI development necessitates that students become lifelong learners who can adapt to new technologies and continuously update their skills throughout their careers. An output-based and subject-oriented curriculum that emphasises learning how to learn, critical thinking, and problem-solving will better prepare students for this reality, fostering a mindset of continuous growth and adaptability.

AI also has the potential to transform the way education is delivered and experienced. Personalised learning powered by AI algorithms can tailor educational content and experiences to individual needs, preferences, and learning styles, enabling more effective and engaging learning experiences. HE institutions must consider leveraging AI technologies to enhance their teaching and learning methods, emphasising the need to shift away from traditional, input-based curricula.

Moreover, as AI raises ethical, social, and legal concerns, HE institutions must address these issues in their curricula. Students must be educated on the responsible use and development of AI technologies and their potential consequences and societal challenges. This requires an interdisciplinary approach to education, focusing on the intersection of technology, ethics, and social implications.

To conclude, the rise of AI and its profound impact on the job market, the nature of work, and how we learn highlights the urgent need for HE institutions to change their curricula. By adopting an output-based and subject-oriented approach, HE can better prepare students for the challenges and opportunities of an AI-driven future. This involves developing essential cognitive, creative, and emotional intelligence skills, fostering a mindset of lifelong learning, integrating AI-related subjects and applications into a wide range of disciplines, leveraging AI technologies to enhance teaching and learning, and addressing AI's ethical and social implications. Only by embracing this transformative shift in HE can we ensure that students have the knowledge, skills, and competencies to navigate and succeed in the rapidly evolving world shaped by artificial intelligence.

## Conclusion

In this chapter, I have highlighted the shift from input-based to output-based curricula in HE and the importance of contextualised learning activities in enhancing students' learning outcomes. The transformation of teaching and learning to better align with the demands of the job market and the expectations of various stakeholders has led to adopting of interdisciplinary paradigms and methodologies, such as shown in the BETA course and the Camp Future programme. Moreover, the chapter has discussed the challenges and opportunities that arise as HE institutions navigate this transition and strive to meet the diverse expectations of their stakeholders. Ultimately, this chapter has provided valuable insights into the theory and practice of output-based and subject-oriented curricula, offering concrete examples of how these approaches have helped enhance students' learning outcomes.

By aligning academic disciplines with current professional practices, defining and assessing students' knowledge, skills, and competencies, and employing teaching and study methods that embrace contextual learning, HE institutions can equip students with the skills and competencies necessary to thrive in their future careers. The chapter has argued that this shift in curricula is greatly needed in HE and that preparing students for the complexities of the job market and the global challenges of the 21st century is essential. Ultimately, the chapter serves as a call to action for HE institutions to continue to evolve and adapt their teaching and learning practices to meet the changing demands of the world around us, aptly demonstrated through the growth of AI technologies.

## About the Author

Claus Nygaard is a professor, PhD, and executive director at the Institute for Learning in Higher Education. He can be contacted at this email: info@lihe.info

## Bibliography

Assiter, A. (Ed.) (1995). *Transferable skills in higher education*. Kogan Page.

Best, M. H. (1990). *The new competition. Institutions of industrial restructuring.* Polity Press.

Bolhuis, S. (2003). Towards process-oriented teaching for self-directed lifelong learning: a multidimensional perspective. *Learning and Instruction, 13*(3), 327–47.

Branch, J., Bartholomew, P., & Nygaard, C. (Eds.) (2015). *Case-based learning in higher education.* Libri Publishing Ltd.

Deci, E. L., & Ryan, R. M. (2008). Self-determination theory: A macro theory of human motivation, development, and health. *Canadian Psychology/Psychologie canadienne, 49*(3), 182–185.

Enomoto, K., & Warner, R. (2023). Enablers of student learning outcomes based on eight cases of second language learning and teaching in higher education. In K. Enomoto, R. Warner & C. Nygaard (Eds.), *Enhancing student learning outcomes in higher education.* Libri Publishing Ltd.

Falconer, I., & Pettigrew, M. (2003). Developing practical competencies: A case study. *Management Learning, 34*(1), 11-30.

Frodeman, R., Thompson Klein, J., & Mitcham, C. (Eds.) (2010). *The Oxford handbook of interdisciplinarity.* Oxford University Press.

Gardner, P., & Jones, G. (2011). Integrating work experiences into higher education: a practical guide to work-based learning. Higher Education Academy.

Granovetter, M. (1992). *The sociology of economic life.* Westview Press.

Harvey, L., & Knight, P. T. (1996). *Transforming higher education.* Society for Research into Higher Education/Open University Press.

Harvey, L., Burrows, A., & Green, D. (1992). *Democratising quality.* American Association for Higher Education, 7th Conference on Assessment in Higher Education, Miami Beach, June 1992.

Jarvis, P., Holford, J., & Griffin, C. (1998). *The theory & practice of learning.* Kogan Page.

Lash, S., & Urry, J. (1994). *The end of organised capitalism.* Polity Press.

Margitay-Becht, A., & Das, U. (2023). Enhancing student learning through hidden motivational learning outcomes. In K. Enomoto, R. Warner & C. Nygaard (Eds.), *Enhancing student learning outcomes in higher education.* Libri Publishing Ltd.

Marton, F., & R. Säljö (1976). On qualitative differences in learning – outcome and process. *British Journal of Educational Psychology, 46*(1), 4–11.

Maskell, P., & Törnqvist, G. (2001). Universiteternes rolle i den lærende region. In P. Maskell & H. Siggard Jensen (Eds.), *Universiteter for fremtiden. Universiteterne of videnssamfundet.* Rektorkollegiet.

McDermott, R. P. (1999). On becoming labelled – the story of Adam. In P. Murphy (Ed.), *Learners, Learning & Assessment* Paul Chapman Publishing, Ltd.

Meier, F., & Nygaard, C. (2008). Problem-oriented project work – organisational challenges. In C. Nygaard & C. Holtham (Eds.), *Understanding learning-centred higher education*. Copenhagen Business School Press.

Newell, W. H. (2013). The state of the field: Interdisciplinary theory. *Issues in Interdisciplinary Studies, 31*, 22–43.

Nygaard, C. (2015). Rudiments of a strategy for technology-enhanced university learning. In C. Nygaard, J. Branch & P. Bartholomew (Eds.), *Technology Enhanced Learning in Higher Education*. Libri Publishing Ltd.

Nygaard, C., & Holtman, C. (2008). The need for learning-centred higher education. In C. Nygaard & C. Holtham (Eds.), *Understanding learning-centred higher education*. Copenhagen Business School Press.

Nygaard, C., & Andersen, I. (2005). Contextual Learning in Higher Education. In R. G. Milter, V. S. Perotti, M. S. R. Segers (Eds.), *Educational innovations in economics and business IX. Breaking boundaries for global learning.* Klüwer/Springer Verlag.

Nygaard, C., & P. Bramming (2008). Learning-centred public management education. *International Journal of Public Sector Management, 21*(4), 400–416.

Nygaard, C., Courtney, N., & Leigh, E. (Eds.) (2012). *Simulations, games and role play in university education*. Libri Publishing Ltd.

Nygaard, C., Holtham, C., & Courtney, N. (2009). *Improving students' learning outcomes*. Copenhagen Business School Press.

Piihl, J., Rasmussen, J. S., & Rowley, J. (2015). Internships as case-based learning for professional practice. In J. Branch, P. Bartholomew & C. Nygaard (Eds.), *Case-based learning in Higher Education*. Libri Publishing Ltd.

Ramsden, P. (1998). *Learning to lead in Higher Education*. Routledge.

Rassow, L. C. (1998). Outcome-based higher education: assessing the undergraduate international business major. *Journal of Studies in International Education, 2*, 59-80.

Savery, J. R. (2006). Overview of problem-based learning: definitions and distinctions. *Interdisciplinary Journal of Problem-based Learning, 1*(1), 9–20.

Vincent, S., & Focht, W. (2009). *Interdisciplinary environmental education on the nation's campuses: Elements of field identity and curriculum design*. National Council for Science and the Environment.

Woods, D. R. (2007). *Problem-based learning: how to gain the most from PBL*. Donald R. Woods.

Chapter 6

# Interactive Practices in a Library Makerspace Using Technology to Deliver Positive Student Outcomes

Henriette van Rensburg

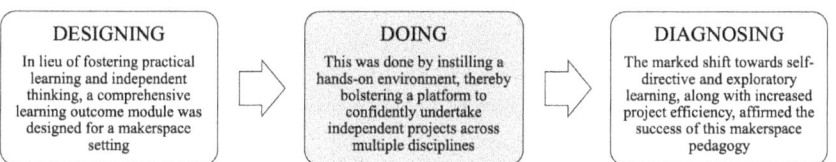

| DESIGNING | DOING | DIAGNOSING |
|---|---|---|
| In lieu of fostering practical learning and independent thinking, a comprehensive learning outcome module was designed for a makerspace setting | This was done by instilling a hands-on environment, thereby bolstering a platform to confidently undertake independent projects across multiple disciplines | The marked shift towards self-directive and exploratory learning, along with increased project efficiency, affirmed the success of this makerspace pedagogy |

## Preamble

With her chapter, Henriette van Rensburg contributes to the book, *Enhancing Student Learning Outcomes in Higher Education,* by describing how an academic library makerspace contributes to a university's innovation culture. She relates to the three phases of the central ESLO model of the book in this way:

The DESIGNING phase revolves around the conceptual blueprint of detailed learning outcomes. A creative ecosystem, an academic library makerspace, is designed to foster an atmosphere of innovation and practical learning within the university. The planned outcomes primarily aim to inculcate essential skills that adult learners can utilise effectively within this makerspace setting, ensuring a comprehensive learning approach.

In the DOING phase, the strategy developed in the earlier phase is executed within a practical learning environment. The application of these learning outcomes into the makerspace creates a propensity for learners to apply their skills and confidently undertake independent projects. The implementation also reveals potential implications and benefits for the varying stakeholders involved, providing a tangible perspective on the learnt skills.

Within the DIAGNOSING phase, a careful evaluation of the successful transition to output-based curricula and the effectiveness of the implemented learning outcomes takes place. There is a critical assessment of the traditional grading system's relevance in the face of rapidly advancing artificial intelligence technologies. Also, a noticeable shift of learners' preference towards a self-directed and exploratory approach to learning is reflected. These highlight the overall effectiveness of the innovative approach implemented within the university.

## Introduction

A makerspace is an environment where lecturers, researchers and students can get together *"to share resources and knowledge, work on projects, network, and build"* (Educause, 2013). I define learning outcomes as 'the need to know', including the skills adult learners learn within the makerspace setting, allowing them to use equipment and undertake projects more independently and confidently than before. In addition, this chapter has the potential implications and benefits of the research findings for educators, administrators, and policymakers. All such stakeholders are interested in enhancing student learning outcomes in higher education using makerspaces *and* other innovative learning environments that provide suitable facilities and support for learning; an ecosystem that includes the activity and the learning outcomes.

In the current global knowledge-intensive population, the need for higher education has become more prevalent, both for individuals and societies (Altbach et al., 2019; Information Resources Management Association, 2022). Higher education educators *"want students to achieve the educational, societal, and life effects that result from students being educated"* (The Glossary of Educational Reform, 2014:1). How can we improve students' learning outcomes in higher education? Ludwig et al. (2017:33) identified in their study that STEM (Science, Technology, Engineering, Mathematics) students learning outcomes improved *"when engaging in makerspace activities by creating tangible solutions to health-related problems"*. They discovered these students could identify and learn capabilities that will be critical in their future work.

Student outcomes usually refer to the expected goals of a learning experience, course, or program; they can also refer to the actual grades they achieve or fail to achieve during their education or later in life (The Glossary of Educational Reform, 2014). Lock et al. (2020:5) echo this by stating that *"risk-taking and learning from failure are critical components of making"* and learning. The Covid-19 pandemic challenged many educators and universities to respond to the challenges by changing and adapting in many ways to serve this changing world (Altbach et al., 2019). Halverson and Sheridan (2014) emphasised the emerging role of *making* in education. Learning occurs when learners make concrete artefacts through real-life learning and authentic opportunities and it is a creative and collaborative way to transform teaching and learning (van Rensburg & Piper, 2019). UNSW Art & Design Australia (2015) emphasises that their makerspace is an environment where students are no longer just consumers but can direct the learning outcomes themselves.

This study provides a snapshot of how a makerspace can play a key role in enhancing students' learning outcomes in a multi-campus regional university in Queensland, Australia. This type of project-based learning is often called 'constructivist learning', an idea developed by the educational psychologist, Papert (Blikstein, 2013). He believed that learning is best done from experiences, through building a physical object or something shareable with others; this is especially effective when the project is chosen by the student and self-directed (Yusoff & Aziz, 2020).

At the library makerspace, we often receive a wide range of specific requests from students and staff regarding personal projects, research or within different curricula. They learn hands-on skills with our latest digital fabrication technologies, at their own pace and to their own interest. Makerspace staff members want students and staff to feel confident with digital fabrication technologies for independent use. Benefits include capable and high-achieving graduates who, with admirable portfolios, prove to be more innovative and thus more employable.

## Chapter overview and key takeaways

In Section 1, I describe the background to our work on enhancing students' learning outcomes in the university library makerspace and education areas, and examine the underpinning learning theory — Knowles' theory of andragogy. Following this, in Section 2, I demonstrate our project-based practice towards enhancing student learning outcomes focussing on how our practice affects students' way of studying, and outlining the qualitative methodology used, namely the visual elicitation method, to ascertain our findings. Section 3 is where I present the findings of the study in the outcome section, from the perspectives of students, staff and the author; using Knowles' six concepts of andragogy to categorise the findings. Section 4 looks forward to possible future expansion of the university library makerspace, with a greater amount of physical space for use in curricular spanning a broader variety of subject areas. I conclude the chapter by re-iterating the value of makerspace in successfully engaging students in many different areas of tertiary study.

Reading this chapter, three insights will be gained:

1. The value of incorporating Malcolm Knowles' six principles of Andragogy (Knowles, 1984) into a library makerspace;

2. The importance of learner-centred, as well as problem-centred, project-based challenges for enhancing student learning outcomes; and

3. How a library makerspace can play a key role in building students' confidence, experience, orientation to learning, motivation and independence.

## Section 1: Background to our work with learning outcomes

As an experienced university educator in Technology Education, I am interested in andragogy and the importance of the students' learning journeys. In this research project, I worked closely with the Community Engagement Coordinator, running the library makerspace at the university. The Coordinator contributes significantly to developing a research and evidence-based library culture and work collaboratively to support decision-making and service improvement. This includes practice-based research in the university library makerspace. The Coordinator and I also collaborate with other educators, curriculum designers and researchers to ensure that the makerspace activities align with students' learning outcomes and support their academic development.

There is a connection between university activities and improving students' skills development. Data from the 3D printer usage in the makerspace during the past three months indicated 1,000 printing activities. Each 'print' also often contains multiple parts, activities or jobs, and this number shows the incredibly high demand for the makerspace 3D printers. There is often a waiting list for machine time during the semester. The university library makerspace is a place for hands-on learning with equipment including 3D printers, 3D scanners, laser cutters, electronics and more. "*Going beyond the physical location itself, they centre around building and creating in a collaborative environment*" (Bell et al. 2023:1). All students and staff members from any study area and faculty can use the space daily during weekdays between 10 am to 2 pm and undertake projects within research, course curriculum or extra-curricular areas. To begin their experience in this area, participants receive free 3D prints of up to 500 grams, where they can choose to print something from thingiverse.com or myminifactory.com. They learn how to set up a 3D print in the slicing software, change the printing material and set up the 3D printer. Generally, students choose something extra-curricular to print, which is low-pressure and encourages elements of play.

After completing a combination of online and hands-on inductions, students can obtain swipe card access to the makerspace between library opening hours (weekdays from 8 am to 6 pm and weekends from midday to 5 pm). This allows students to work independently on their projects within the makerspace. The goal is to build capacity in the students, allowing them to work unaccompanied and confidently. Rather than operating a printing space for students to send jobs to without interacting with the equipment, the focus is on skill building, not on the project output.

The makerspace allows students to gain hands-on skills that may not be present in their studies and receive one-on-one instruction for hands-on skills that they would otherwise not receive in a standard class. This allows students to undertake projects in their own interest areas and create portfolio projects that make them more employable upon completing their studies. The makerspace also acts as a 'third place' outside work or home where students can meet others and learn together, often sparking serendipitous collaborations across study areas, students, staff members and the public. Bogue and Ouillon (2023) describe makerspace third spaces as increasing social connectedness and building community, providing support in times of crisis. Through their research, Bogue and Ouillon (2023) experienced the evolevement of the Fab Lab into a more general community facility, offering advice and support on various issues and a space for people to talk, socialise, and share skills and knowledge. University makerspaces *"represent an opportunity for interdisciplinary access to technology and resources for digital fabrication and varied creative projects…however, a gap in the research literature on makerspaces on university campuses, including within libraries"* (Bell et al., 2023:1). Indeed, many researchers note the need for empirical research on the role of makerspaces in the Australian higher education context (Baker, 2021; Bell et al., 2023; van Rensburg & Piper, 2019; Wong & Partridge, 2016).

The university library makerspace staff members also experience challenges and face obstacles in the daily conducting of the makerspace. Sometimes it is difficult to find technical personnel to run the space. Competent staff and assistants are equally as important as the equipment; a successful and sustainable makerspace cannot function with just one and not the other. Although students and staff are offered safety inductions and guidance on the correct equipment usage, the university staff members are always aware of the level of risk when operating in the space. A part of developing hands-on skills in a makerspace is accepting that this is always a low-risk environment for participants. Makerspace users must accept some level of risk to reap the benefits of learning hands-on skills. It needs to be a safe learning space where students are allowed to fail. Sometimes a student can initiate a 3D print job incorrectly, which can damage the equipment or cause a print failure. Accepting that this can happen, and preparedness for mitigating these problems, is key in allowing students to fail and keep going with the learning experience.

## *Learning theory and methodology related to learning outcomes*

In more traditional pedagogy, education is viewed as a passive *"transmittal of knowledge and skills that had stood the test of time"* (Knowles, 1970:40). Yet, Knowles' theory of andragogy, which is based on self-directed independent learning, is philosophically opposed to such a behaviorist approach, and developed into a kind of movement within academia. Savićević (1991) noted that the research body revolving around andragogy has also expanded, and related research since has continued to develop (for example Knowles et al., 2015; Tezcan, 2022). As an educator, I follow the adult learning principles associated with andragogy (Knowles, 1990; Knowles et al., 2015) to underpin the development of the university library makerspace and when conducting the workshops. This theory-informed pedagogical approach improved students' outcomes and can be achieved by better application of skills, improved job performance, increased self-value, active and increased engagement in learning. The need for a different learning approach to pedagogy became obvious in reaction to the global societal changes that required adults to learn to their own advantage and with an instantaneous ability to apply what was learned (Savićević, 1991). The adult learning theory is based on Kolb's (1984) experiential learning, whereby learning is engrained by doing (Cherry, 2022). Adult learners are *"encouraged to explore the subject matter firsthand and learn from their mistakes. As a result, they are less likely to make those mistakes in the workplace and continually develop their experiential knowledge"* (Pappas, 2013). Successful adult learning is rooted in the basic principles that steer adult learners, namely, *"an acknowledgement of the knowledge and experience gained by adult learners and the idea that the learner — and not the instructor — is central to the process"* (Conaway & Zorn-Arnold, 2016:38). Such self-directed, independent learning is reflected in Knowles' (1984) six concept approach to adult learning, namely andragogy, and is the theoretical framework that underpins this study.

### 1. Experience

Conaway and Zorn-Arnold (2016) described two elements of experience, namely, time and dimension, experience being the mental re-creation and outcome of time past; it can also interpret the present and predict the future. Learners can draw meaning from both physical and/or psychological past experiences. Conaway and Zorn-Arnold (2016) further stated that educators can provide hands-on experience, for example, makerspace projects and science experiments. Adult learners rely on their own experiences as a framework for growth, they learn by integrating past experiences with new concepts and interpreting them in new, meaningful ways. Moreover, as Pappas (2013) notes, *"as a person matures, he/she accumulates a growing reservoir of experience that becomes an increasing resource for learning"*. Stewart (2021) extends this in her belief that adults' existing knowledge bases and life experiences make them more likely to be sceptical of new information- they learn best by challenging and testing new ideas.

## 2. Self-directedness
Self-directedness refers to the ability of an individual to make autonomous choices and decisions and to take full responsibility for their outcomes, it is a skill that develops with experience and age (Conaway & Zorn-Arnold, 2016:39). Self-directed learning *"empowers adults to adapt accordingly to fluid and complex social contextual changes...and advantages of fostering self-directed learning competence avoidance of knowledge and skill obsolescence"* (Morris, 2019:57).

## 3. The learners need to know
Adult learners become aware that they need to know more skills and information to reach their goals. They want to know why information is important (Conaway & Zorn-Arnold, 2016). Adult learners already know the benefits of learning. At the same time, Bloomquist and Georges (2022:59) described it as *"an intricate combination of identities, practices, and outcomes used to prepare people to address complex problems"*. Margitay-Becht and Das (2023 in this book) also note that their students needed to be interested in the course to be motivated and successful: *"the students read the syllabus, including the course descriptions and learning outcomes, and select a class that they find appealing"*.

## 4. Readiness to learn
Often there is a high failure rate among beginner students when they do not realise the importance of working hard. They are successful when they realise that an incident has motivated them to take control of their lives and has led them to enrol in university (Mikheeva et al., 2021; Conaway & Zorn-Arnold, 2016; Omar et al., 2020).

## 5. Orientation to learning
Adult students see the future as now; their alignment with learning is learner-centred (versus teacher-centred) and problem-centred, where they can apply what they are learning (Conaway & Zorn-Arnold, 2016).

**6. Intrinsic motivation**

Pedagogy focuses mostly on children and is situated in an extrinsically motivated environment, where the learner's behaviour is driven by a reward (Ozuah, 2005). In most countries, children are obliged to attend school, whereas adults study because they want to, due to personal growth and development. According to Morris (2019), adults are motivated by their needs, personally meaningful values, and interests when pursuing their goals. Students incorporate the critical principles of andragogy of goal orientation, self-direction, and intrinsic motivation and embrace a more active learning role (Caldwell et al., 2020).

## Section 2: Our practice towards enhancing student learning outcomes

University makerspaces are characterised by a user base that includes students and staff from any discipline. The university library makerspace is a vibrant hub of activity, hosting workshops, and a place where staff and students use makerspace equipment for projects, curriculum classes and industry placement projects. It fosters spaces where students can work on open-ended projects within their curriculum and as extra-curricular projects have many benefits. With the rise of AI text generation and ChatGPT-style technology, the way educators assess and grade learning outcomes are debatable. Assigning grades can have detrimental effects on the priority of the learning outcome versus the number received. and research indicates three reliable effects when students are graded- they tend to think less deeply, avoid taking risks and lose interest in the learning itself (Kohn, 2006). Challenge and project-based learning is more engaging for students and focuses on the process rather than the outcome (Kohn, 2006).

There is a growing movement for 'ungrading' in tertiary education. Stommel (2021) made the case that grades only are not a good incentive, feedback or marker of learning. They also encourage competitiveness over collaboration and do not reflect the idiosyncratic, subjective, emotional character of learning and are not inherently fair. Conaway and Zorn-Arnold (2016) stated that for adult learners, the future should be learner-centred, not teacher-centred. Learning is no longer an act of depositing, whereby students are the depositories and the teacher a depositor. This results in a lack of creativity and transformation; knowledge only emerges through invention and re-invention, arguing for a project and challenge-based approach. Makerspaces will very likely become more common with a shift in focus to project-based learning as educators evolve away from graded learning that is too easily replicated with AI technology tools.

*How our practice affects students' way of studying*

Project-based activities undertaken in the university library makerspace include the industry placement subject program, where students can pair with a local business and the makerspace to create a 3D printed or electronic solution to a problem. For example, students may create a custom learning aid for the science department, in their area of interest, or collaborate with a local hand therapy business on developing an aid for a client with a disability. These problem and solution-based projects are chosen with the student's desired career pathway in mind, tailored to their interests and inspirations. The final project is duplicated for the client and the student to keep, allowing the student to build up a portfolio of projects that aids in future employment.

A current student is working with the local hand therapy business to create a dexterity trainer for clients to increase proprioception and re-train muscles. In consulting with the hand therapist and the makerspace manager, she has created a list of minimum deliverables for the project. Using iterative design principles, the student learns how to utilise Autodesk Fusion 360 software, creating a 3D model from a sketch concept. After multiple rounds of client feedback, 3D printing and design improvements, the final product is delivered to the hand therapist and made available as an open-source download on the makerspace website. These types of projects benefit the university and local community and equip students to work independently with digital fabrication technologies, gaining a powerful problem-solving skillset.

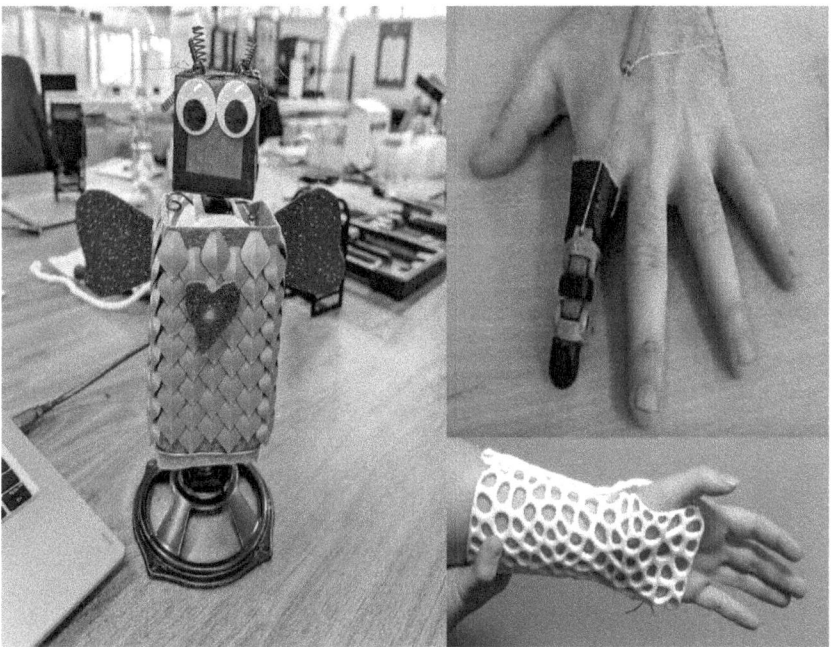

*Figure 1: Snapshots from the makerspace.*

The university library makerspace also offers a variety of workshops, including 3D Printing Basics, Arduino and Electronics, Autodesk Fusion 360 Basics, how to build a website and more. The Built a Bot two-day workshop is a project-based session where participants can design and build their own robot character. Using two servo motors and an LED light, they can make a creature of their own design come to life. This session combines the 3D printing and Arduino workshops to form a workshop intensive where students can take ownership of their project and learning and also take home their own creations. This workshop often receives glowing reviews, and sessions are held for university students, staff, and local teachers as professional development sessions.

A new makerspace workshop, the Future Makers Entrepreneurship Workshop, has recently been introduced at the university. This runs one day a week for three weeks to introduce students to basic business skills and side hustles. Many students are interested in solving problems or starting their businesses but do not have the skills to get started. This workshop uses the Lean Startup Methodology to test business ideas with the least monetary investment possible, focusing more on customer validation and time investment. This workshop has also received excellent reviews from participants.

Evidence of learning outcomes in the university library makerspace is collected from multiple sources. The qualitative evidence presented in this chapter has been developed from a research case study, in addition to user feedback and observations from the library staff within the makerspace. This case study research undertaken in the library makerspace sought an interpretive understanding of users' experiences of participation. This was a qualitative study that responded to two research questions:

- How do university makerspace adult users actively engage with the space and its activities to enhance their learning outcomes?

- What can adult users own experience of participation tell us about the value of using the makerspace for research, course curriculum, and extra-curricular as a framework for growth underpinned by andragogy?

The study employed a visual research method during the data collection phase to explore users' insights. Visual methods in qualitative research rely on visual mediums, such as photographs, to create data and meaning. The method chosen was a visual elicitation method (Orr et al., 2020), similar to photo elicitation and photo voice methods, including a visual element in our methodology aligned with the nature of the makerspace itself, as the makerspace is a tactile and hands-on environment that involves visual outputs. A purposive and convenience sample was used in this case study, with participants selected based on their sustained use of the makerspace for course curriculum, extra-curricular, or research purposes.

Four semi-structured interviews were conducted, with three student participants and one academic staff member. Two student participants had been introduced to the makerspace through their coursework and proceeded to do professional placements within the makerspace. A third student used the makerspace for extra-curricular projects, which included personal projects and community-based volunteering work. The thirty minutes interviews were conducted online via Zoom. These participants were invited to share visual media to describe their makerspace use at any stage. This could include photos, objects, designs, or any other visual media. It provided a unique way for participants to participate in the interview and share work that was meaningful to them and how they engaged with the space. Throughout the interviews, the visual research method helped to guide conversations about projects and the context in which they existed. The shared objects and visual media also provided the opportunity for reflection during the interviews. This helped the participants to connect the outputs of individual projects to the skills, knowledge, and support that had contributed to them.

## Section 3: The outcome – perspectives of student, staff and the author

University ethical clearance was given before the original research started. Four semi-structured interviews were conducted via Zoom, with three student participants and one academic staff member. In this case study, the author was given permission to analyse the pre-existing data set. All the excerpts below are from the student participants taken from the pre-existing data set, unless otherwise indicated, for example (Staff participant).

### Experience

Stewart (2021) claimed that adults' existing knowledge bases and life experiences make them more likely to be doubtful of new information, they learn best by testing new ideas. Burke (2015) stated that problem-based learning problems and activities are excellent ways for students to build and strengthen their knowledge. Yet, often students and staff in our study experienced initial hesitancy or apprehension in using the university library makerspace. This was coupled with curiosity and a feeling of wanting to be involved and experience what was on offer:

- *and not being able to go in there without…thinking that I'm intruding… to be honest, I thought it was…like part of the Creative Arts…and I didn't really have anything to do with it for a long time".*

In addition, an academic staff participant felt more confident in the development of his own skills:

- "We just started off really simple, and then, probably about six months later, I bought my own 3D printer" (Staff participant).

- "And I've always been a problem solver, I think that's in my nature. And I'm crafty as well. So it has really, it's just, it's given me so much more to do with that, which has been really great" (Staff participant).

Thus, the participants' initial hesitation changed to being confident makerspace users.

## Self-directedness

A mature learner's self-concept moves from:

> "one of being a dependent personality toward one of being a self-directed human being…Since adults are self-directed, instruction should allow learners to discover things and knowledge for themselves without depending on people. However, learners should be offered guidance and help when mistakes are made" (Pappas, 2013).

The willingness of makerspace users to share expertise created a positive and participatory environment. Adult learners are inclined to descend more toward learning experiences that offer some sort of social development benefit (Pappas, 2013). There was an understanding that:

- "everyone that goes in there is willing to help everyone and listen to what you're doing and give you their ideas".

Makerspace provided an opportunity to develop social and reciprocal connections based on a shared interest and experience. This allowed for connection outside of one's own academic program, encouraging input in projects from students with different academic backgrounds and new sources of expertise and knowledge. Thus, the makerspace may be conceived as an informal social learning space where students can meet new people. Some students responded that the makerspace is:

- "a place to meet up with other likeminded students wanting to make things"

- "I mean, you go in with the idea of what you want to do but being able to bounce the ideas off (the coordinator) or if she's not there, another *person that's in there. Yeah, collaborative, you know, getting everyone's opinion".*

Irrespective of whether discussion and problem-solving were collaboration, this sharing of knowledge and community was described by all student participants. The makerspace was experienced as a site of community connection. Being able to *"bounce ideas off", "get input",* or receive *"ongoing advice from peers or the coordinator".* Furthermore, one student participant described how, as a science student, *"talking to someone that's an engineering student that I really wouldn't cross paths with otherwise at the university. That's really nice".*

## The learners need to know

Bouchrica (2023:1) clearly stated that *"adult learners have the need to know the value of what they are learning and know the why's behind the need to learn them".* Sometimes a barrier to participation included understanding the purpose of the makerspace. Students using the makerspace recognised its value in contributing to their skills development. One student who had undertaken their course placement in the makerspace expressed the value of what was learnt: *"It really has been invaluable — it's given me a whole new set of skills".* Importantly, comments from other students identified the need to know the value of their learning:

- *"Initially, I went into this thinking I would do pre-med and go into med…or even research, but this has taught me a lot about how technology and science really work together to create things that really help people".*
- *"I didn't expect this to now be such a big part of my life, where you know, nearly every day I'm thinking about what I can print, what I can design, what, how I can make something better for, for my son, for my husband, for my parents for gardening, and like I can make a tool for that. Yeah, it's made a huge difference, and I didn't think it would".*
- *"So it really has changed and had a big impact on so many different parts of my life".*
- *"So it's not something that you can see a lot in the space right now in that space that I work in. So having that element of technology in*

*science and seeing how everything works out is, like, really cool".*

Thus, the participants became aware that they needed to gain more skills and acknowledged the benefits of hands-on learning.

## Readiness to learn

Adult learners usually fund their own learning or are sponsored by their employers; they still study by choice and are ready to learn. This makes them more attracted to study (Pappas, 2013). Students responded as follows:

- *"I use the space as a way of taking a new perspective on things".*
- *"So it's given me a lot of hope in my life decisions in a way to help me see that what I've done in my placement it is something that I could do in the future".*
- *"…going from an idea, translating it onto the computer, and then getting something physical at the end".*
- *"I learned how to take, take basically an idea from your head, or maybe like a little sketch that you've drawn, turn it into a model on the computer, and then turn it into something physical that, you know, now I've got, and I can work with".*
- *"Now I come home, and I have a whole new take on problem-solving… around the house".*
- *"It's led me to where I have now, with my honours".*

In this way, the above participants acknowledged the importance of working hard to be successful. They realised that taking part in makerspace activities of their own choice motivated them while they took control of their learning and lives.

## Orientation to learning

For adult learners, the orientation to learning is for immediate use rather than future application. The learning orientation of adults tends to incline towards focusing on the problem or the cause of why a problem emerged (Bouchrica, 2023). Students and a staff member responded as follows:

- "My accommodation doesn't have much in space other than some hanging space. So I made a piece that can go onto a hanging line that interlocks...it's designed so it can easily hold any pots and pans or such".
- "I didn't want to damage anything in the place I'm renting. And I want something that would both fit but also be both easily reusable, easily modified".
- "For work, a lot of it is just about improving productivity...Like they're not exciting things, but they make our work projects just go a little bit better". (Academic participant)
- "...to be honest, I was just like, I just need to get this placement out of the way so I can graduate".
- "I'm very study driven...so it was driven by placement and studies. So...not really driven by creativity, unfortunately".

These comments clearly indicate that the participants saw the future as now, and that their alignment with learning was learner-centred and problem-centred, where they could apply what they were learning.

## Intrinsic motivation

Adults are more motivated by internal personal factors rather than external pressures. Intrinsic motivation gives adult learners choices instead of making an activity a requirement. The following excerpts from the student participants expressed their intrinsic motivation:

- "And then [the Coordinator, Community Engagement] had mentioned that you could do a couple of free prints as a student. So there were a few of us that were, like, some awesome stuff. Let's go back and find something...then that was how it started".
- "I tend to use the space as a way of taking a new perspective on things. That's actually why I came up with the design... for the hanging hook...".
- "I wanted to go back because I was excited for it. But you know, seeing the 3d printers and all the stuff she has there. It's a little bit like...I'm not gonna know how to do this".

These comments demonstrate that the participants engaged in the library makerspace activities because they wanted to, due to personal growth and development. The 'Build a Bot' workshop is a two-day, project-based workshop where participants can design and build their own robot character. Some of the student participant feedback for this session included the following:

- "This course was really challenging, I am so glad I came along. I am a little bit amazed that I learnt how to do (what I consider) to be pretty hard stuff. Thank you for supporting the development of my self-efficacy. I really achieved some great success. Even more importantly, I actually have developed the crazy belief that I can do it, I have enough base knowledge to get started to develop further I can actually do robotics!".

- "The design thinking activities were truly transformative for my practices. Your task was extremely engaging, open-ended and supported me to use my creativity and reflective thinking. I don't think I would have gained the knowledge I have now if I had not been able to explore and experience like you supported us to do".

- "This workshop I was so nervous about because it was like nothing I had ever done before. But thanks to you I did get it, I understood, and I feel much more confident teaching these curriculum objectives and cross-curriculum priorities now. I feel as though I could now Including more learning using the same framework in different curriculum areas".

Thus, although the participants found the workshop challenging and engaging, they learnt from the hands-on experience and became confident in their own skills and abilities.

The Future Makers Entrepreneurship Workshop is a business-skills focussed session where students learn lean start-up methodology to create their own business or side hustle. Feedback from this session included the following:

- "My favourite part of the workshop was the lean methodology to figure out MVP and 'see how it sticks' attitudes. Allows me to try lots of things but know how long to try before moving on".

- "Thank you very much for doing this. It has opened my mind up to different opportunities and ways of thinking. I have more confidence to try different things with the lean methodology".

These findings are parallel to those of van Rensburg and La Thanh (2021:149), who also found that *"students tend to have a positive attitude toward using technology"*. The skill-sets gained by the students in our study sit within the categories of Knowles' theory of andragogy (Knowles, 1984), and they are:

- Experience
- Self-directedness
- The learners need to know
- Readiness to learn
- Orientation to learning
- Intrinsic motivation

Thus, the study has shown the value of incorporating Knowles' six principles of Andragogy into a library makerspace to develop students' skills and attributes as learning outcomes.

## Section 4: Moving forward

Makerspaces are agents of change influencing how educational stakeholders conceptualise learning, how they engage in designing and facilitating learning, as well as how technology is used in teaching and learning (Peterson & Scharber, 2018). Along with the venture into the infrastructure to support and enhance student learning and outcomes, the university library makerspace strives for the best possible design and to facilitate authentic learning experiences. Through illustrative examples, makerspace staff seeks to acknowledge strategies and challenges encountered in supporting robust learning through making. Lock et al. (2019:9) echo this by stating: *"Design and creativity are making their way to the forefront of educational considerations, and Makerspaces can address the needs of the future"*. van Rensburg and Piper (2019:14) also note the benefit of including and combining makerspace activities in adult education: *"Makerspace can be used by all educators and students…and it is a creative and collaborative way to transform teaching and learning…with many beneficial and positive effects for all the stakeholders"*. These exemplifications tie in with Knowles' (1984) six-concept approach to adult learning, namely experience, self-directedness, the learners need to know, their readiness to learn, their orientation to learning, and intrinsic motivation as student learning outcomes.

Ludwig et al. (2017:33) identified that STEM students in their study achieved their *"course objectives when engaging in makerspace activities by creating tangible solutions to health-related problems"*. Their students could recognise and learn capabilities — as their learning outcomes — that will be significant in their future work. This links to the future expansion of the university library makerspace, where there will be more physical space for curriculum engagement across a wider variety of subjects with different equipment available as the space expands. For example, food science students may use food 3D printers, or future materials research students may be able to use the makerspace to try out new plastic recycling techniques. A larger makerspace will benefit all the stakeholders across the university community, allowing for organic cross-collaboration and serendipity in networking and learning. More leadership positions will soon be available for students, allowing them to teach other makerspace users skills and gain more advanced skills. Having students as partners with makerspace skill delivery will make it more accessible for new first-time users and should give the space a closer connection to respond to users' needs.

In future, there may be more interplay between vocational studies and tertiary studies, bringing together hands-on skills with the technical and theoretical aspects as the world becomes more integrated with online connectivity, IoT (internet of mymini) and automation.

## Conclusion

We have shown in this chapter that makerspace can successfully engage students in many different areas of study within higher education. Makerspace hands-on activities improve students' skill development and eventually allow them to work unaccompanied and confidently. It can assist in empowering motivated, self-directed, and experienced adult learners and educators to achieve positive outcomes in self-chosen activities whenever they are ready for this hands-on learning. Makerspace gives students the opportunity to gain skills and experience that may not be part of their curriculum, yet make them more employable upon completion of their studies. Makerspace can be used as a 'third place' outside classes, work or home where participants can meet others and learn together. New collaboration across study areas, students, academics and the public can be formed to increase social connectedness and build community. Interactive practices in makerspace require interaction between educators and students using technology to deliver exciting and positive outcomes for all participants. Following Malcolm Knowles' six-concept approach to adult learning, andragogy is the underpinning framework of this chapter: 1) experience, 2) self-directedness, 3) the learners need to know, 4) readiness to learning, 5) orientation to learning, and 6) intrinsic motivation contributed to practices that derived positive learning outcomes for all. The findings of this study could successfully be applied to many different disciplines in higher education. Experiential learning, the process of learning by doing, is used to connect theories and knowledge to real-world situations. We conclude by stating that learning and *"life is a journey, not a destination"* (Branch & Wernick, 2023 in this book).

## Acknowledgement

I acknowledge the contributions of Stephany Piper for sharing her knowledge and expertise, which has helped me to write this chapter. She is the Community Engagement Coordinator, running the Library Makerspace at the University of Southern Queensland.

## About the author

Henriette van Rensburg, is an Associate Professor of Digital Literacies and Inclusion in the faculty of Business, Arts, Education and Law at the University of Southern Queensland, Australia. She can be contacted at this email: vanrensb@usq.edu.au

## Bibliography

Altbach, P, G., Reisberg, L., & Rumbley, L.E. (2019). *Trends in global higher education: Tracking an academic revolution.* (Vol. 22). Brill.

Baker, A. H. (2021). *Exploring student perspectives on informal and formal learning in university makerspaces* [Doctoral thesis, Clemson University]. TigerPrints.

Bell, E., Piper, S., & O'Sullivan, C. (2023). Users' experiences in a regional academic makerspace: a case study. *Journal of the Australian Library and Information Association, 72*(2)135-149.

Blikstein, P. (2013). Digital fabrication and' making' in education: the democratization of invention. In J. Walter-Herrmann & C. Büching (Eds.), *FabLabs: Of machines, makers and inventors*. Transcript Publishers.

Bloomquist, C. D., & Georges, L. (2022). Interdisciplinary leadership: A leadership development model for scholar-practitioners. *Journal of Leadership Education, 21*(4), 58-75.

Bogue, K., & Ouillon, S. (2023). Third place social infrastructure, after and in crisis: Insights from a local case study. *Global Social Challenges Journal, 1* (aop), 1-18.

Bouchrika, I. (2023). *The andragogy approach: Knowles' adult learning theory principles*. Retrieved July 3, 2023, from https://research.com/research/what-is-empirical-research

Branch, J. D., & Wernick, D. (2023). The use of debate cases for enhancing students' reasoning skills as learning outcomes. In K. Enomoto, R. Warner & C. Nygaard (Eds.), *Enhancing student learning outcomes in higher education*. Libri Publishing Ltd.

Burke, J. (2015). *Making sense: Can makerspaces work in academic libraries?* Paper presented at ACRL 2015, March 15-18, 2015. Advancing Learning Transforming scholarship Association of College & Research Libraries.

Caldwell, K. L., Vicidomini, D., Wells, R., & Wolever, R. Q. (2020). Engaging patients in their health care: Lessons from a qualitative study on the processes health coaches use to support an active learning paradigm. *Global Advances in Health and Medicine, 9*, 1-9.

Cherry, K. (2022). *Learning by doing. This is the basis for the experiential learning theory*. Retrieved July 3, 2023, from https://www.verywellmind.com/experiential-learning-2795154

Conaway, C., & Zorn-Arnold, Barbara. (2016). The keys to online learning for adults: The six principles of andragogy. *Distance Learning, 12*(4), 37-42.

Educause. (2013). *7 things you should know about Makerspaces*. Retrieved July 3, 2023, from https://library.educause.edu/resources/2013/4/7-things-you-should-know-aboutmakerspaces

Glossary of Educational Reform (2014). *Student outcomes*. Retrieved July 3, 2023, from https://www.edglossary.org/student-outcomes/

Halverson, E. R., & Sheridan, K. M. (2014). The maker movement in education. *Harvard Educational Review, 84*(4), 495-504.

Information Resources Management Association (2022). *Research Anthology on Remote Teaching and Learning and the Future of Online Education* (4 Volumes). Retrieved July 3, 2023, from https://www.irma-international.org/open-access/

Knowles, M. (1984). *Andragogy in action: Applying modern principles of adult learning.* Jossey-Bass.

Knowles, M. (1970). *The modern practice of adult education: From pedagogy to andragogy.* The Adult Education Company.

Knowles, M. (1990). *The adult learners: A neglected species.* Gulf Publishing Co.

Knowles, M. S., Holton, E. F., & Swanson, R. A. (2015). *The adult learner: The definitive classic in adult education and human resource development* (8th ed.). Routledge.

Kohn, A. (2006). The trouble with rubrics. *English Journal, 95*(4), 12-15.

Kolb, D.A. (1984) *Experiential learning: Experience as the source of learning and development.* Prentice-Hall, Inc.

Lock, J., Gill, D., Kennedy, T., Piper, S., & Powell, A. (2020). Fostering learning through making: Perspectives from the international maker education network. *International Journal of E-learning & Distance Education, 35*(1), 1-26.

Ludwig, P. M., Nagel, J. K., & Lewis, E. J (2017). Student learning outcomes from a pilot medical innovations course with nursing, engineering, and biology undergraduate students. *International Journal of STEM Education, 4*(1), 33-14.

Margitay-Becht, A., & Das, U. (2023). Enhancing student learning through hidden motivational learning outcomes. In K. Enomoto, R. Warner & C. Nygaard (Eds.), *Enhancing student learning outcomes in higher education.* Libri Publishing Ltd.

Mikheeva, M., Schneider, S., Beege, M., & Rey, G. D. (2021). The influence of affective decorative pictures on learning statistics online. *Human Behavior and Emerging Technologies, 3*(3), 401-412.

Morris, T. H. (2019). Adaptivity trough self-directed learning to meet the challenges of our ever-changing world. *Adult Learning, 30*(2), 56-66.

Omar, H., Khan, S., Haneline, M., & Chooi Gait Toh, C.G. (2020). Attitudes of dental and chiropractic students towards a shared learning programme – an interprofessional learning model. *European Journal of Dental Education, 25*(3), 592-599.

Orr, E. R., Ballantyne, M., Gonzalez, A., & Jack, S. M. (2020). Visual elicitation: methods for enhancing the quality and depth of interview data in applied qualitative health research. *Advances in Nursing Science, 43*(3), 202-213.

Ozuah, P. (2005). First there was pedagogy and then came andragogy. *Einstein Journal of Biology and Medicine, 21*(2), 83-87.

Pappas, C. (2013). *The adult learning theory – andragogy – of Malcolm Knowles.* eLearning Industry. Retrieved April 29, 2023, from https://elearningindustry.com/the-adult-learning-theory-andragogy-of-malcolm-knowles

Peterson, L., & Scharber, C. (2018). Learning about makerspaces: Professional development with K-12 inservice educators. *Journal of Digital Learning in Teacher Education, 34*(1), 43-52.

Savićević, D. M. (1991). Modern conceptions of andragogy: A European framework. *Studies in the Education of Adults, 23*(2), 179-201.

Stewart, H. (2021). The secret to making adult learning stick? Make it all about you. *Training & Development, 48*(4), 28-30.

Stommel, J. (2021). *Ungrading: An introduction.* Retrieved July 3, 2023, from https://www.jessestommel.com/ungrading-an-introduction/

Tezcan, F. (2022). Andragogy or pedagogy: Views of young adults on the learning environment. *International Education Studies, 15*(1), 136-147.

UNSW Australia, Art & Design. (2015). *The campus makerspace.* UNSW Australia.

van Rensburg, H., & La Thanh, T. (2021). Impacts of using technology-enhanced language learning in second language academic writing at a Vietnamese university. In K. Enomoto, R. Warner & C. Nygaard (Eds.), *Teaching and learning innovations in higher education.* Libri Publishing Ltd.

van Rensburg, H., & Piper, S. (2019). *Enabling students to learn hands-on technical skills using makerspace in a higher education academic library.* Conference Proceedings 2019- Singapore Learning Design and Technology Conference 1-8.

Wong, A., & Partridge, H. (2016). Making as learning: makerspaces in universities. *Australian Academic & Research Libraries, 47*(3), 143-159.

Yusoff, A. S. M., & Aziz, N. N. (2020). Conceptualisation of School Makerspace to Support Constructivism and Project-Based Learning in Public Schools in Malaysia. *Journal of Advanced Research in Social and Behavioural Sciences, 21*(1), 53-74.

Chapter 7
# Enhancing Student Learning through Hidden Motivational Learning Outcomes

András Margitay-Becht and Udayan Das

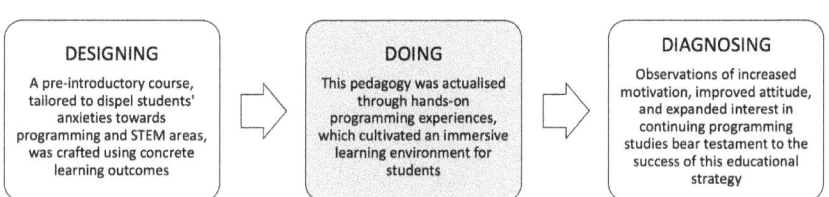

## Preamble

With their chapter, András Margitay-Becht and Udayan Das contribute to this book, *Enhancing Student Learning Outcomes in Higher Education*, by explaining how it is possible to construct learning outcomes in a way that enables, encourages and supports students to explore topics and areas of intellectual growth. More specifically, they focus on those topics and areas students previously found difficult, uninteresting or 'outright terrifying'. They relate to the three phases of the central ESLO model of the book in this way:

In the DESIGNING phase, they show how they designed a pre-introductory programming course. Here, the focus is on planning a course that considers learners' attitudes and perspectives and aims to change negative associations with areas like programming. The course aims to offer a safe exploration environment where students' fear of programming is alleviated, while incorporating explicit and implicit learning outcomes.

In the DOING phase, they describe the actual implementation of the designed course. In practice, the course's structure includes various activities such as software designing and construction of programs. In this phase, students are exposed to new programming concepts, given hands-on experience, and introduced to computational thinking. This implementation phase fosters learners' interest and motivation while preparing them for real-world challenges.

In the DIAGNOSING phase, the authors evaluate the success of the course through formative assessment, gathering feedback from a survey conducted before and after the course, and assessing the students' final projects. The primary goal here is not necessarily to measure the academic progression but rather the growth in learners' confidence, shifting perspective towards programming, and overall interest and motivation in the subject.

## Introduction

In this chapter, we define student learning outcomes as the collection of all changes that happen to a student due to participating in a learning experience. Such changes involve explicit skills (such as learning the basics of programming and the use of the computational thinking framework), implicit changes (such as an altered perception of a field or themselves), and their own abilities in the given field. This broad understanding of learning outcomes is critical as it encompasses most of the benefits the students gain from attending institutions of higher learning. Improving their learning outcomes improves the value proposition; the students receive increased results for the same cost (both in time and money). As such, learning outcomes need to be structured so as to be appropriate for the target audience, at both ends of the educational pipeline. Firstly, as university educators, we must ensure that, by graduation, the students possess all the skills they need to succeed in the labour market (see Nygaard, 2023 in this book for more on this issue). Secondly, we must ensure that the material starts at a level appropriate for first-year students of any given context and educational system. Learning outcomes for higher education institutions also need to facilitate the personal growth of their students; many 18- and 19-year-olds are still forming notions about themselves, the world, and their place in the world. Properly structured learning outcomes can provide additional help with such personal growth.

There are many different ways of categorising learning outcomes, but a common approach is breaking them down along the three major domains of learning established in Bloom's Taxonomy: cognitive, psychomotor and affective (Hoque, 2017). Cognitive learning, and thus cognitive learning outcomes, focus on the knowledge of the students and the application of that knowledge, such as recognising Mozart's music, being aware of the major events of the industrial revolution, or being able to apply the net present value formula to evaluate and compare investment opportunities. The psychomotor domain of learning, and thus the corresponding learning outcomes, focus on skills and movement of the students, for example, the ability to play one of Mozart's pieces, type with high speed and accuracy on a keyboard, or score a goal. The affective domain describes learning related to emotions or attitudes of a given area, like learning to like Mozart's music, understanding the value of history, or discovering the importance of accounting. To fully enable student learning, all of these learning outcomes must align to ensure that college graduates are ready to face the challenges inherent within the market environment.

Our approach, that we dubbed motivational learning outcomes, focus on a subset of the affective learning outcomes, specifically targeting the students' emotional reaction and valuation of a given topic, in our case, computer science. Indeed, certain fields of study tend to be viewed as inherently challenging for students, often creating feelings of apprehension or worry for them. This situation applies to our case — computer science. Therefore, in our learning and teaching context, the emotional journey does not start at neutral but rather in a negative position. As a result, our students require more emotional support than in most other fields of study.

In this chapter, we describe a pre-introductory computer science course we developed specifically targeting incoming first-year university students who do not plan to study computer science. The purpose of the course, the true enhanced learning goal we want to achieve, is to address students' fear of programming and showcase to them that coding can be a highly rewarding experience. These motivational learning outcomes not only fulfil these students' expectations and guide them towards better performance in areas they expect to grow (cognitive domain), but change their motivations, educational direction, and expand their educational trajectory (affective domain). This then, can lead to an enhanced learning path for the student throughout their academic career at the college or university, help better prepare them for the real world's challenges, and improve their starting position in their adult life.

Chapter 7

*Chapter overview and key takeaways*

The chapter has four main sections. In Section 1, we describe our motivation for focusing on student learning outcomes and showcase the literature pertaining to the area of concern: fear of and disinterest towards programming. In Section 2, we showcase the course we have constructed, with sufficient detail that it could serve as a blueprint for others. Section 3 contains the class outcomes, followed in Section 4, by thoughts on how the approach could expand to a university-wide phenomenon, before we conclude this chapter.

Reading this chapter, you will gain the following insights:

1. How motivational outcomes can drive interest in subject areas perceived by students as challenging;

2. How you can construct learning experiences facilitating these learning outcomes;

3. What opportunities and challenges are present in delivering these experiences.

# Section 1: Background to our work with learning outcomes

In this section, we describe both why we personally find it important to work on student learning outcomes, and also what the literature says specifically about learning outcomes related to trying to learn programming.

*Our reasons for working on students' learning outcomes*

Becoming a university educator is an expensive decision, especially in fields where the gap between corporate and educational salaries is significant, such as in computer science or economics. The key reason for us to decide to be educators, was always the motivation to improve students' learning outcomes: we pay the price in reduced personal wealth but hope to increase the world's welfare by improving the lives of thousands.

Dr. Das has extensive experience introducing newcomers to Computer Science and Programming. He served previously as Director of Technology Programs at Loyola University Chicago where he oversaw educating adult learners in the School of Continuing and Professional Studies. One of his key innovations and achievements was removing restrictive prerequisites from the Introductory Programming course. Additionally, there was measurable improvement in the gender and racial diversity of the programs. Before Loyola, he also oversaw a non-profit bootcamp training program that helped underserved students start careers in the IT field. Those students, who primarily came in with high school completion, were able to complete programming training and begin entry level positions in IT. Finally, he has worked as a volunteer computer skills, HTML, and programming instructor at a Community Technology Center offering free classes to community members. His philosophy is that, if early programming instruction is interesting and less abstract, this will widen the number of people pursuing programming and computer science. Apart from this, basic knowledge of computing and computational problem solving is a critical skill in the $21^{st}$ century in all major professions.

Dr. Margitay-Becht started his educational career focusing on teaching Economics and Business Strategy to Bachelors and Masters level students. He quickly encountered the issue that most students were struggling with mathematical concepts. Hence, as a form of support, he started to teach students basic computer literacy skills that they could utilize to understand quantitative concepts. Over the past two decades, he has worked to increase the computational understanding of all of his students, working with his department to change the Economics program to have a significantly more robust computational foundation. Moreover, as associate dean, he has supported the creation and launch of a Bachelor's level data science program to align student opportunities and market demand in the San Francisco Bay Area.

**Institutional reasons**
The authors found an excellent life-long partner for their learner-centred pursuits in Saint Mary's College of California. Founded by the Lasallian Christian Brothers, followers of Jean-Baptiste De La Salle, the institution

was placed on firm Lasallian footing. As explained in The Brothers of the Christian Schools (2009:20), "*The method of teaching developed by De La Salle [...] was based on both an abiding respect for the students and a realistic assessment of what they needed to become mature members of society*". During its founding in 1863, the key focus of Saint Mary's College was student outcomes. Figure 1 below is the mission statement from that time, which has been expanded and compared to the traditional Lasallian curriculum with the addition of Bookkeeping.

## ST. MARY'S COLLEGE,

### SAN FRANCISCO.

---

### THE OBJECT OF THIS INSTITUTION

is to impart a sound, practical Education, at the lowest possible cost, thereby placing its advantages within reach of all. The Course of Instruction, besides the usual English branches, comprises Mathematics, Bookkeeping, Ancient and Modern Languages, so that boys, whether destined for mechanical, commercial or professional pursuits, can select such studies as will best fit them for future avocations.

TERMS—$150 per year, half-yearly in advance. NO EXTRA CHARGES OF ANY KIND.

Students can enter at any time, commencing their accounts with the month in which they enter.

For further information application may be made to any of the Catholic Clergymen of the State, or to

REV. J. F. HARRINGTON,
President.

*Figure 1: SMC Mission Statement, 1863.*

These values could be reflected in the institutional learning outcomes of the College (Saint Mary's College, 2014). The forty-seven learning outcomes listed describe a student who fits into the globally integrated modern society, firmly rooted in timeless and modern values.

More recently, Saint Mary's College has been undergoing large-scale changes, more closely integrating into the American education system, adopting the industry-standard Carnegie system. The updated mission statement once again re-affirms these values: *"The mission of Saint Mary's College is…to create a student-centered educational community"* (Saint Mary's College Mission Statement, Saint Mary's College, 2023).

**Student-centric mentoring culture**
Saint Mary's College prides itself in its faculty-driven, student-centric mentoring structure. Each student starts their Saint Mary's experience in an immersive experience called First Year Advising Cohort, in which they are led by a professor and a more experienced student peer mentor through the adjustment from high school to college life. This experience is followed up by three years of intensive advising experience, where faculty members (advisors) are paired with students in their programs to provide continuous support to their students.

Both authors had the pleasure of serving as academic advisors in the above roles, and Dr. Margitay-Becht was in charge of administering the advising office – overseeing all the academic advising activities for the university. In these roles, we had the opportunity to meet and get to know our students, to learn their goals, motivations, backgrounds and challenges. This direct contact strongly supports our immense responsibility as faculty members: improving learning outcomes improves lives directly. The relationship is not abstract: enhanced learning outcomes lead to better, freer, happier, more fulfilled students, alumni and citizens.

**Educational management experience**
Dr. Das is the program director of Saint Mary's Computer Science program. Including pre-Saint Mary's experience, he has 5 years of program management in higher education and 6.5 years of program management overall. Dr. Margitay-Becht was the associate dean of the Business School during the pandemic years. These leadership roles provided excellent opportunities to discover improvement opportunities, as other faculty,

staff, students and even parents found it important to express challenges and desired changes. This enabled facilitating conversations, leading not only to learning outcome enhancements, but the creation of new programs for students and new cooperations among faculty members to be able to better serve – and even better integrate — our communities.

## Learning theory and methodology related to learning outcomes

The theoretical issues that lead to the development of our approach can be summarised by the quartet of:

1) fear of programming (and mathematics);

2) the challenges of introductory courses to increase student excitement;

3) the importance of computational thinking;

4) constructionist approach supported by an easy-to-use programming language.

**Math and programming phobia**

It is a well-known phenomenon that a significant portion of the population is afraid of Mathematics. According to the 2012 PISA results (OECD, 2012:NP), 30% of students have anxiety doing mathematics:

> "One way that a student's negative self-belief can manifest itself is in anxiety towards mathematics. Some 30% of students reported that they feel helpless when doing mathematics problems: 25% of boys, 35% of girls, 35% of disadvantaged students, and 24% of advantaged students reported feeling that way".

Reports worldwide show that 'math phobia' is present across cultures: for example, we can find it among the college students in the United States (Atuahene & Russell, 2016), Economics students in Germany (Büchele & Feudel, 2023), Maths students in Italy (Di Martino & Gregorio, 2019), and Engineering students in the Philippines (Wenceslao, 2022).

Nonetheless, because Mathematics is a prerequisite to most studies in Science, Technology and Engineering (STEM); feeling alienated from Mathematics can lead to a student believing they have no place in the STEM world. To address this, Seymour Papert, one of the designers of the Logo programming language aimed at teaching children programming, suggested in his seminal work Mindstorms: Children, Computers and Powerful Ideas (Papert, 1980:viii) to utilise the attractiveness of computers and programming to help children overcome their fear of mathematics: *"The computer is the Proteus of machines. Its essence is its universality, its power to simulate. Because it can take on a thousand forms and can serve a thousand functions, it can appeal to a thousand tastes".*

Papert failed to foresee that programming would become perceived as something hard and arcane and math-adjacent, translating some of the fear of mathematics onto programming itself. While for some, coding became the pathway to overcome math phobia, for others, math phobia led to programming phobia. Indeed, it is common enough that workshops, open to all, are being organised to help teachers overcome this fear (Frederick et al., 2017).

Connolly et al. (2009) found that, even among computer science students, a third of them have anxiety about taking a computer language course. A decade later, similar results were found by Alford et al. (2017), when investigating engineering students' attitudes towards programming before and after taking their first introduction to programming course. They found that a significant majority of them agreed or strongly agreed with the statement: *"I find computer programming intimidating"* (Alford et al., 2017:7). Interestingly after taking the course, women were slightly less intimidated by programming than before — yet the change was only a slight improvement. Our takeaway message from this research was that a key element in designing our enhanced learning outcome was to provide students with:

- an experience that dispels their fear of programming;
- changes their perceptions of coding and themselves; and
- builds their resolve to grow in the field.

### Interest and joy: focus on a pre-introductory experience?

Creating a pre-introductory experience for students is also important, as introductory classes are not necessarily designed to raise or maintain students' interest. When students encounter a subject in an introductory class, it might even deter them from continuing. We experienced this among the students we advise, as some students, who were preparing to be programmers for some time, decided against continuing after an introductory course — while praising the instructor and the course as a whole for their high quality. Similarly, Alford et al. (2017) reported that student interest in programming significantly decreased after taking an introductory course. When teaching non-IT students the basics of programming, Wyeld and Nakayama (2018) experimented with a more visual approach by utilising an HTML and JavaScript-based game creator platform. They found that this approach improved the students' realisation of the programming potential and somewhat reduced their fear of coding, but overall, the students were still heavily reliant on external help. Fifteen years earlier Solomon (2004) demonstrated the importance of appropriately choosing the first programming language to introduce students to programming. He warned that using a language that looks overly complicated and arcane would 'scare away' students, and instead recommended using easier to read languages as an introduction to programming. Yet, even twenty years later, many universities still use C or C++ as the introductory programming language, replicating the alienating effect Solomon discussed.

Höök and Eckerdal (2015:6) found that while the amount of time a student spent practicing was the most important factor in good performance in an introductory programming course, those who did well reported that they found programming fun. This seems to confirm that finding programming fun is not just an issue of retention but also of success. Our takeaway from this research was twofold. Firstly, we wanted to ensure to create an environment where the students can experience the joy of creation and the excitement of coding that is not always possible to facilitate in an introductory course. The name of the class, 'Coding is fun', was driven by this desire. Our secondary takeaway was to use a programming language that is as easy to use and as visual as possible, that is why we start the learning experience with Scratch (See Figure 2).

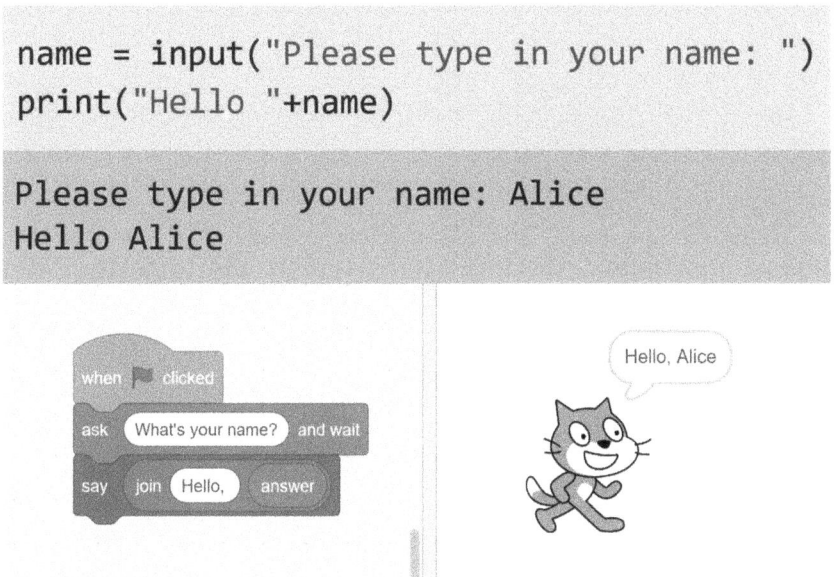

*Figure 2: Comparison of Python (top) and Scratch (bottom) codes.*

**Computational thinking**

The notion of computational thinking was introduced by Papert (1996), but popularised by Wing when she re-introduced the term in her influential article Computational Thinking (2006) and her many follow-up works both as a researcher and as the Corporate Vice President of Microsoft Research (Wing, 2008; Wing, 2011; TU Wien TV, 2016; Martin, 2016). Indeed, *"computational thinking involves solving problems, designing systems, and understanding human behavior, by drawing on the concepts fundamental to computer science"* (Wing, 2006:1), highlighting the fact that the tools and techniques represented by computational thinking have applications far beyond programming itself. Examples for non-programming use of computational thinking can be found, for example, in Moore et al (2021) that showcase how computational thinking can be used to create and analyse a 'Hero's journey', or de Paula et al. (2018) who showed how computational thinking, art and literature can be brought together through game making. Farah et al. (2020) showed that computational thinking can also be brought to Business and Economics students, and

Liao et al. (2022) indicated that improving non-STEM students understanding of computational thinking can improve their overall experience at the universities.

The incredible, potentially society-transforming impact of computational thinking was recognised by many nations and national governments, and many countries modified or are modifying their K-12 learning outcomes to include computational thinking (For some examples, see Falkner et al., 2014; Brown et al., 2014; Mannila et al., 2014; Kilhamn & Bråting, 2019). However, when implementing these curricula, computational thinking often narrows to just programming (Kilhamn & Bråting, 2019; Taslibeyaz et al., 2020; Pears et al., 2021), ignoring the other components.

**Scratch and constructivism**
Utilising the Scratch programming language also aligns well with constructivist learning approaches. Constructivism grew out of Piaget's ideas about learning, essentially focusing on allowing the student to construct knowledge in a learner focused environment (Harlow et al., 2007). Constructivist approaches had suggested using programming and computer science as one possible medium of constructivism, even before the term constructivism became mainstream, for example, Papert (1980) in Mindstorms, explicitly referencing Piaget. Scratch itself has been used as a language of choice for constructivist and constructionist educational approaches, both in small-scale pilot projects and large-scale, nationwide educational approaches (Noss et al., 2020). This approach is closely linked to the maker movement, specifically focusing constructionist approaches that see students create an actual real-world object. For a description of an interesting makerspace project see van Rensburg (2023) in this book.

While Scratch is primarily a language that targets middle school students, it is also an excellent language if one is trying to keep the complexity of computer science education to a minimum. For example, Davies (2008) deliberately reduced the access of complex programming concepts to his students, and instead introduced a simple set of pseudocode instructions, with which the students had to solve high level conceptual problems. We find that a similar approach can be implemented in a pre-introductory course using a simpler, more learning focused programming language. This enables the students to focus on the conceptual aspects of computational thinking and less on the minutiae of coding syntax.

Our takeaway from this research is to 'double down' on using Scratch as our introductory language and emphasise computational and design thinking principles, allowing the students to see how far reaching the utility of these concepts are, both inside and outside of computer science.

## Section 2: Pre-introductory courses for motivational learning outcomes

To address all of the above concerns, we created an elective course designed to provide students with an opportunity to experience the joys of programming without having to worry about the usual stressors associated with an introductory programming course.

### An introduction to our practice

Since we created an optional elective experience, it needed to be offered in a way that is both accessible to the students (in the sense that they can fit it into their course schedule) and sufficiently appealing for them to devote their time to it.

**American-style vs. European-style Bachelor's degrees**
Before discussing the details of our practice, it is critical to highlight some key differences between US and European-style institutions of higher education, especially with the focus on the structure and delivery of Bachelor's degrees.

The European-style universities traditionally have tended to create Bachelor's degrees that are highly focused on their discipline, creating a robust, deep learning experience suitable to those already committed to a given career path and the corresponding field of study. This enables these programs to give their students deep, theory-backed and practice-focused experience, usually delivered in 3 years.

As opposed to the above, the American-style universities have a set of shared experiences among all students, referred to as "the core" or "general education requirements". These classes are usually taken at the beginning of the students' college or university career to provide foundational knowledge and even opportunity for academic exploration before a student chooses a field of study to major in. Because of these broader exploratory opportunities, American-style universities usually deliver their Bachelor's degrees in 4 years (or 2+2 years for those who first pursue an associate's degree).

The authors understand that teaching in an US-style institution is more conducive to providing accessible experiences with motivational learning outcomes. On the one hand, since the students are expected to take more classes outside of their majors, they have more time exploring, such as taking a pre-introductory course. On the other hand, the students themselves are usually more interested, receptive, and expectant of courses leading to a broader educational experience than students in European institutions. At the same time, the authors believe that courses focusing on motivational learning outcomes can benefit students from all nations and cultures, if for no other reason than to re-affirm their major and career decisions.

**Creating learning outcomes to empower exploration**

We have created a stand-alone, prerequisite-free, first-year-targeting, open-for-everyone course called "Coding is fun". This course was delivered during the January term of Saint Mary's College, a month-long intensive-study term set aside for educational experiences aiming at exploration outside one's major field of study. The students read the syllabus, including the course descriptions and learning outcomes, and select a class they find appealing. In this context, our course carried the following description:

*Course description and outline*

*This course is aimed at students with no programming experience but would like to get a quick introduction to the field. Programming is a highly creative activity that can be rather fulfilling, but the stigma surrounding it can scare potential students away. This course focuses on a series of fun interactive activities that will see the students discover for themselves the basics of computational thinking. This course aims to show that programming can be fun, and that anyone can do it. No prior computer programming experience is required.*

*Learning outcomes*

*At the end of this course students will be able to:*
- *understand the basics of computational thinking;*
- *demonstrate the understanding of computational thinking through a small programming project.*

*Skills*

*Aside from the above programming-focused gains, the class will also focus on developing the life skills crucial for success in today's competitive job markets. Key skills that will be focused on (in alphabetical order):*
- *critical thinking skills: programming is critical thinking. Covering the basics of computational thinking will further develop and practice the students' critical thinking skills:*
- *computer literacy: students will learn basic computer literacy skills;*
- *quantitative reasoning: students will practice quantitative reasoning skills;*
- *basic project management: by undertaking a final project, the students will practice creating and following a simple project plan.*

The key idea was that the learning outcome we considered most important, the motivational learning outcome, did not appear in the explicit list of learning outcomes. We offer esoteric learning outcomes (computational thinking is not a buzzword that easily attracts students). Still, in the skills section promise transferable competencies we expect our target audience would want to pursue. In the San Francisco Bay Area, computer literacy and critical thinking skills are well known to students, high school career counsellors and parents as crucial skills in the job market of the 21st century. Coincidentally, these skills are extremely easy to teach in introductory level programming classes. By connecting the skills for which there is demand for, with a promise of accessible education, we managed to successfully target students who are receptive to the enhanced, hidden motivational learning goals of the course, which could be summarised as follows:

At the end of this course, the students will:
- understand that programming is an activity well within their skillset;

- be able to improve their own programming knowledge using freely available resources on the internet.

With the aspirational learning outcome, the students will find joy in programming at the end of the course.

**A pre-introductory programming experience**

We categorised this course as a pre-introductory programming class for three reasons. Firstly, it was a 1-unit course, requiring the equivalent of 1-hour-a-week effort from the students (condensed into 3 hours four times during January), as opposed to the usual 3- or 4-units for introductory classes. In the context of computer science education, our class would not replace an introductory course, instead provide the students with some background and emotional fortitude so that taking an introductory course (should they later decide to do so) would be easier.

Secondly, while we made it a point to deliver the key components of the basics of programming (algorithmic thinking, variables, loops, conditional statements), the focus was not on them. In a traditional introduction to programming class the material uses examples to illustrate programming concepts. Even if the examples are interesting and exciting, the key focus is on the coding. In our class, we reversed the experience: the students were focused on creating a programming product, and the programming concepts came up as a way of getting closer to the completion of the product or improving the final program.

Finally, the programming language of choice was a mixture of Scratch and Python. While the latter is a common university-level introductory language, the Scratch programming language (Scratch, 2023) is more often used in middle schools. Scratch aims to make programming more accessible for everyone (Resnick et al., 2009), while Python is an easy-to-use language for production environments in many computer science and data science contexts. Thus, despite Python being a language that is decidedly easier to understand and learn than C or C++, Scratch is even more user-friendly for students just familiarising themselves with programming. By starting our class in Scratch, we ensured that any university student could follow and engage with the material. Once the students understood and internalised the concepts, and practiced them by creating their own Scratch programs, we could then introduce the students to the exact same concepts in Python to show that the simplicity carries over.

The course had a lot of built-in flexibility. The authors knew they wanted to start the student experience using Scratch for ease of access. After the initial class, the students were allowed to vote on whether they wanted to continue fully in Scratch or switch over to Python. In the end, due to the large demand, both the Scratch and the Python tracks ended up running, and some students completed both on their own time, despite the fact that they received no extra credit or improvement on their grade for this at all. We considered it great feedback; our intent on inducing self-motivation in the students seems to have succeeded.

### The structure of the class

As an intensive, January-term 1-Carnegie-unit course, the course was designed to meet only four times during the month in an online format.

Prior to the first meeting, we invited our students to fill out a pre-questionnaire to learn a bit about their background, expertise in programming, and general attitude towards computer science. Before finalising the actual structure of the class, we consulted these results to fine-tune the student experience.

The first class was designed to ease the class into the mindset of programming smoothly and to progress quite quickly to empower them with the basics of algorithmic thinking. We started the class by a round of introductions, then fired up Scratch, and designed two programs. The first was the mandatory "Hello World" program that simply printed out a greeting — this case, from the mouth of a cartoon cat. Because of the approachable nature of Scratch programming, this code was easily expanded to animating the cat figure, and even adding a bouncing ball could be done with a handful of instructions. Within 15 minutes of coding, the students created their first program, which included multiple graphical animations. Immediately, this was the promise delivered: the students felt that coding was easy and doable, and they have nothing to fear.

Before we even started working on our second piece of code, we had already started to introduce the basics of the promised computational thinking by first *designing* the program (a simple ball-clicking game). Here the students gained hands-on experience in:

- how to think through the different parts of the program they need to create;

- how they can break down complex tasks into easier tasks;
- how they can turn a specific idea into a general solution method; and
- how they can think through if their proposed solution will achieve the desired goals.

In short, before they even saw the second piece of code in their lives, they had actively engaged in computational thinking and designing a piece of software. The rest of the first class was taken up by actually creating the code, and while doing so, incrementally introducing newer and newer programming concepts (how variables work, how events are handled, what a loop is, how simple Boolean statements work). By the end of their first class, the students designed and built a fully functional simple computer game and appeared to be excited to learn more.

We intended the second class to be either more Scratch or a switch over to Python. After the first class, we felt that the hidden learning goal was already achieved, the students were excited and unafraid of programming. We possibly had succeeded too much, as we were asked to provide both the Scratch and the Python experience, so we did just that. During the normal class time, we held our second Scratch class, where we first started by expanding the ball clicking game by making it more game-like (this enabled us to re-hash some of the topics covered last time, but instead of having a 'What did we learn last week?' conversation, the students used their knowledge to add new features to the game). We had also added comments to our code, learned more complex logical and nested if statements, and finally the concept of functions. The second half of the class was spent designing a different kind of game that gave the opportunity to discuss more advanced event management, cloning and backdrop changes, which could enable the creation of more complex projects for the students.

During the same week, an extra class session was added to introduce Python basics. While students were required to attend only one of the two class sessions over the second week, most of them were present for both. We considered it helpful to add the Python component, as this showed the students that the 'fun' and 'game-like' things they had created with Scratch have their counterparts in the 'serious' programming language of Python. So, if Scratch is doable and easy and fun, that translates to

Python being doable and easy and fun. The three hours allotted to this class was insufficient to cover everything. As a result, a *second* optional extra class session was created over the third week, which drew similarly high attendance.

The third official class was focused on discussing design thinking and computational thinking. We consider these methods critical not just for computer science in particular or engineering in general, but solution approaches which can be used in all walks of life. Design thinking is *"an analytic and creative process that engages a person in opportunities to experiment, create and prototype models, gather feedback, and redesign"* (Razzouk & Shute, 2012:1). It connects ideas from Economics, Marketing, Engineering and Innovation Management to help understand markets, market needs, market niches and a way to design a product or service that could succeed in these niches. It also emphasises the importance of maintenance and further development, processes that are just as valid when writing software as when writing novels or starting a non-profit organisation to save the whales. We also discussed the framework of computational thinking, focusing on decomposition, pattern identification, abstraction algorithm design, reasoning and evaluation; a series of equally universal steps. We celebrated, when some students realised that they followed the steps discussed in computational thinking during their design process in the first class. For the rest of the class period, we conversed on how students can use these approaches to select, design and implement their final projects.

The time between the third and final class was devoted to optional consultation opportunities for the students, in case they needed synchronous help with some tasks. We were gratified to find that most students felt empowered to use existing online resources to find solutions to their problems, or approach us for asynchronous help over E-mail or Slack (see more below), instead of resorting to these consultation periods when preparing their final projects.

The final class period was devoted to the students showcasing their projects, and they 'took our breath away'. They created far more intricate designs than could be expected from what amounted to two long class sections of introductory materials in Scratch or Python (for an example, see Figure 3). We had repeatedly emphasised that our expectations for the final project were low. As long as they can demonstrate that they

Chapter 7

understand the basic functionality of a programming language they have successfully passed the course. Not a single student followed this minimalist approach. It became obvious, relatively quickly, that they had spent significantly more time outside the classroom expanding their understanding of programming than how much time we had spent together (even with the stretched 6-meeting schedule instead of the preliminarily designed 4). They were motivated to learn more, build more, and show more.

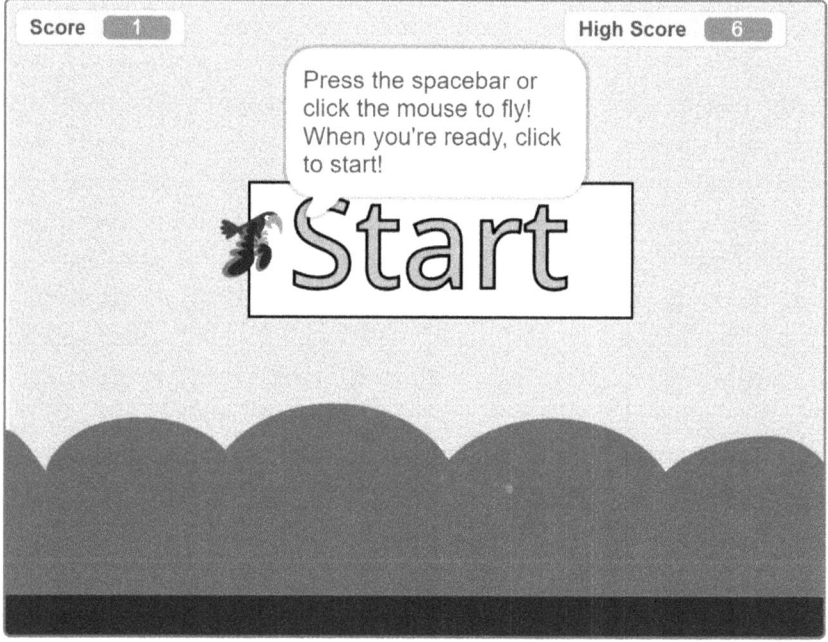

*Figure 3: Flappy Birds recreated as a final project.*

## How our practice affects students' way of studying

Our expectation towards our students was very simple and clear: keep up with the class material, create a project, and we will support you. This simplicity served two purposes:

1) to drive home the point that there is nothing to be afraid of in the class; and

2) to empower them to scale the learning according to their own desires.

We were very excited to find that the students welcomed this approach. The risk was there that the students will be disengaged, but instead we found unexpected excitement and self-motivation. Students attended class, those whose schedule allowed attended the extra classes, read the material and further expanded their knowledge on their own.

To ensure that the material remained non-threatening, assessment of student learning happened exclusively on a project basis. The students had complete freedom to choose any project they wished to create and were free to choose any programming language they wish (even outside Python or Scratch, though they all stuck to these two). In lieu of homework, we provided the students with ample time to prepare their projects and ensured that both the instructors and volunteer peer helpers (three computer science students from higher grades) provided consultation times outside the class to provide help with the project.

The course also had its own Slack channel. Slack is a platform that enables participants to easily share information and documents, have one-on-one conversations, or even have thematic communications channels set up for discussing certain topics. In our Slack, we had separate channels for discussing questions regarding the programming languages we used, the class project, and logistical conversations. For example, this latest channel was used when we were trying to gauge student interest in the material to be covered, so conversations and votes on this channel shaped the course structure.

We are not certain we would be brave enough to use this approach in a traditional class like an introduction to programming course, but that is exactly the point of this course. Our only true purpose was to change our students' mindset, and empower them to brave further exploration. We consider it an exciting extra success that we managed to change their learning patterns and empower their self-learning further.

## How we prepare and organise our pedagogy to enhance students' learning outcomes

The key preparation for the class was a three-pronged approach: a substantial amount of preparation, just-in-time delivery and thorough follow-up. We had started to create this one-month-long course over six months before it started. To offer the greatest possible flexibility for the students, we planned out different trajectories and allowed the students to select which one should be realised.

The material was delivered in a just-in-time format, however. None of the preparations were shared with the students prior to the class, instead, they were revealed through engagement with the students. The students were challenged to perform a task (at times individually, at times in groups), and were asked to report back the difficulty they encountered. This allowed them to apply their established coding knowledge but also explore its limits, and the students returned with well-formed needs of extra capability – which then was provided for them. We also made sure to point out that many resources are available on the internet to find help in any programming languages, and some assignments directly asked the students to search for solutions to programming problems on their own. This approach increased engagement as the material was delivered in a more organic manner, but could run the risk of insufficient depth and lack of support.

To alleviate that risk, thorough lecture notes were posted to the course website and the Slack channel after the class. These notes included annotated code samples, summarised the conversations regarding the programming challenges, re-iterated the argument why new coding skill was needed — or how existing programming knowledge could be re-purposed to solve a task, and what possible expansion opportunities were within reach that were not discussed in the course. In addition to the lecture notes, annotated code was available for all the coding projects discussed. Once the second programming language started, a separate set of notes were published showing parallels between the approaches of the two languages (as shown in Figure 4).

### 3: Calculating the area of a circle

```
r = float(input("What is the radius of the circle? "))
area = 3.14 * r * r
print(area)
```

```
What is the radius of the circle? 10
314.0
```

Unlike in Python, we don't need to worry about type conversion in Scratch. If the answer appears to be a number, the calculation will run:

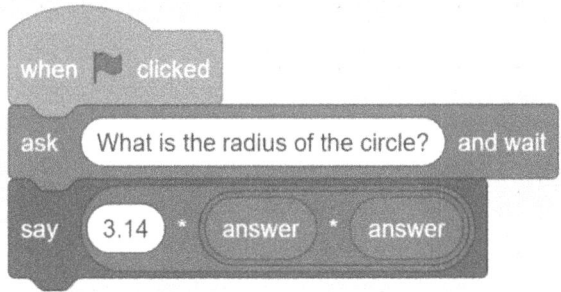

Try for yourself what will happen if the user enters a non-numeric answer!

*Figure 4: Excerpt from the class notes, showcasing the similarities and differences in implementing a simple greeting programme.*

## Section 3: Outcomes

Since the purpose of the course was to change students' minds about programming, when discussing learning outcomes, we consider the actual grades the students received immaterial. Instead, our principal focus lay on assessing their attitudes, that is the learning taking place in the affective domain (Bloom & Krathwohl, 1956).

Chapter 7

## Student perspective

When we envisioned this course, we were trying to target first-year non-computer science students who were potentially interested in programming but felt intimidated by it. As shown in the course outline, we specifically said no prior programming experience was needed, and (thankfully) we have attracted this targeted audience. A total of 27 students started the course, though three dropped out of the class without attending a single section. Out of the 24 students who began the course, we lost only 1 student; 23 of them completed the class. We were also delighted to have received a rather mixed subject demographic of students. Though the largest population were Psychology and Undeclared majors, we also had students from social sciences, natural sciences and business-related fields (see Figure 5).

To evaluate any change of student perceptions as a result of taking the class, we asked the students to take a survey both before the course started and also after the final presentations were completed. Most of the survey questions were simple multiple-choice options — to reduce confusion about interpreting their meaning — although we provided the opportunity to expand on the answer for each question. For the rare student who chose this option we evaluated their answer and categorised it appropriately.

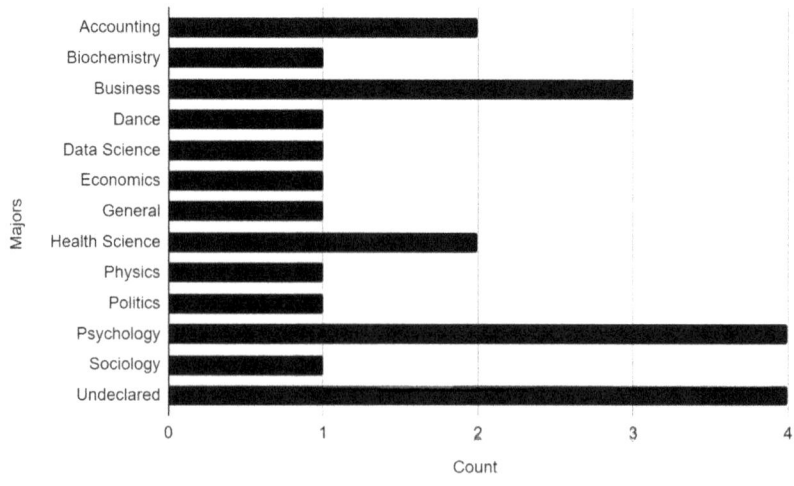

Figure 5: Breakdown of students by major of study.

In our initial survey we asked the students how challenging they thought the class was going to be. Since the course description explicitly promised that no prior programming experience was required, it is not surprising that no student said that programming will be too much for them. However, of the remaining 23, 19 said they think they can *probably* do it, and only four students were confident that the class would be no problem. Regarding the usefulness of programming in their life, except for the two health science majors, all students said it will probably be useful, with seven being certain of it.

|  | Somewhat harder than expected | About as hard as expected | Somewhat easier than expected | A lot easier than expected |
|---|---|---|---|---|
| Too hard for me | 0% | 0% | 0% | 0% |
| I can probably do it | 13% | 33% | 33% | 0% |
| I can for sure do it | 0% | 7% | 7% | 7% |

*Table 1: Student perception of programming difficulty: pre(rows) and post(column).*

About half of the students had a positive experience in the class, the majority of the rest a neutral experience, with two negative experiences.

An overwhelming majority of the students considered programming to be more important to them after the class than before.

The post survey was filled out by a smaller population of students, only 15 of them provided their thoughts. As seen in Table 1, most of the students found that programming was about as hard or easier as they expected. Although two students found that coding was a little harder than they anticipated, both said in the follow-up questions that they will continue to learn coding on their own. One of them said that they consider programming more important than before the class, and are less afraid of it now than before taking the course. In terms of perception of the utility of programming in their real life, most respondents said their appreciation of the usefulness of programming has increased due to the course (Table 2).

|  | I think programming will be somewhat less important for me than before the course | I think programming will be as useful for me as I thought before the course | I think programming will be somewhat more useful for me than I thought before the course | I think programming will be a lot more useful for me than I thought before the course |
| --- | --- | --- | --- | --- |
| I probably won't use it | 0% | 7% | 7% | 0% |
| I will probably have to use some of it down the road | 7% | 7% | 33% | 7% |
| It will be something I will definitely have to use at some point | 0% | 0% | 20% | 13% |

*Table 2: Student perception of the usefulness of programming before the class (rows) and after the class (columns).*

Finally, we also asked the students if they were interested in learning more programming. With the exception of two students, all respondents reported that they will increase their coding knowledge in one form or another. Nearly half plan on doing it using the study skills they have learned in the class, and study further on their own, but we had three students planning on taking a class, and another three intended to complete a minor or a certificate in the field.

Potentially even more interesting than the quantitative feedback was the qualitative feedback provided by 11 students. They expressed much more interest and a lot less fear before. One student said:

> "I went from I feel very nervous to being confident in my future ability to code much more complicated stuff".

Another added:

> "I feel like I have greater understanding of why coding is so significant in the economy today. The paint store I work at, in my opinion, could benefit so much from a little creativity and programming skills. Honestly the couple of lessons from this quarter credit have really sparked an interest in how I see coding being a problem solving tool".

Excitingly, a student who came into the course with a lot of negative preconceptions about programming left with a much more positive approach, that was captured by her final project as well:

> "...it's become a lot more positive and less disgusted [sic]because for a while it was a scary gross subject that I automatically assumed I'd suck at but really it's just one big puzzle and I love puzzles".

Overall, we feel that this course was an eye-opening experience for a significant majority, and whether they continue on their own or in an institutional setting, the positive experiences and feeling of empowerment will propel them to an enhanced learning experience.

## Student follow-up

As part of the post-course survey, we asked the students their intention to continue studying programming. After all, the purpose of the class was to encourage students to brave programming; having had a good experience is not enough. Encouragingly, over 85% of the students reported that they will continue studying programming. Moreover, 20% of them decided to continue by taking an official introductory course, and a further 20% planned to continue their studies to a minor or a certificate.

## Teacher perspective

Our greatest takeaway from the course was that it was a worthwhile endeavour that needs to be continued and expanded. This was clearly supported by the students, evidenced by the most common feedback item that we received which stated that the 1 Carnegie unit (equivalent to 1 hour a week worth of work in a standard long semester) — which in reality was closer to 1.5 Carnegie units delivered — was much too short. The students were asking for a full 3-Carnegie-unit experience, and so the class will be delivered in triple the time in the future. We were also mindful to ensure to provide different kinds of support structures for the students (written materials, code examples, consultation with the professors, Slack-channel, student mentors), and not all of these channels were fully utilised by the students. We maintain that during the initial time of offering these kinds of classes it is probably better to offer excessive support if it is affordable. Once the pattern of students' utilisation of these resources are established, then they can be rationalised down to something more sustainable. We are also planning on using some of the extra time to introduce smaller projects and tasks earlier, to drive up enthusiasm and engagement that we observed towards the end of the course earlier.

## Section 4: Moving forward

We have found this class experience to have been highly valuable for the students, but also feel that it is possible to increase the student experience further. The primary – and biggest – change we are going to make is to expand the course from a 1-Carnegie-unit to a 3-Carnegie-unit experience, and be able to provide the students with a slower, deeper experience spanning Scratch and Python programming languages. The extra time will be used to:

a) slow down and expand on the Scratch portion, including some mini-projects for the students for more constructivist learning;

b) introduce Python in greater detail, allowing the students to create more serious projects themselves, and further cementing their confidence in their own programming abilities;

c) create a more robust overlap between the pre-introductory experience and the introductory programming class (in Python), creating an easier start for those students who want to pursue a deeper understanding of programming.

In addition, we are striving to create a version of the course that will be available for the students during the traditional, long semesters, increasing the potential outreach of the course yet further.

We feel that this approach also has opportunities in the university-wide environment for Saint Mary's College. It could be possible to create pre-introductory learning experiences to other majors. This course, expanded as described above, could serve as the pre-introductory experience for Computer Science and Data Science, but a similar class could be designed for Business, Accounting, Economics, Science etc. majors, to allow students some hands-on, applied experience in these otherwise complicated, theoretical and quantitative fields, that could re-affirm their determination to pursue the field.

We also feel that pre-introductory learning experiences can be utilised to *enhance* student learning: it could offer a way for students pursuing a major to explore, try out different fields, and shore up their knowledge with a few classes or a minor on the other fields. For example, a Computer Science major could explore a minor in Accounting, to help them create customised software solutions for small businesses. An Economics major could explore a minor in Data Science to be able to create more stunning data visualisations. A Business major could pursue a minor in Biology to prepare them for a career in Biotech.

## Conclusion

To conclude, we found that a highly effective way of enhancing student learning outcomes is to provide them with a pre-introductory experience, specifically designed to address well-known issues of fear and lack of interest regarding computer science. Our course raised their level of interest so that close to 90% of respondents — who all are majoring in a different field of study — said that they will want to pursue learning about computer science in one way or another. In order to deliver our motivational learning outcomes, we created the course focusing at every step of the way on the expected emotional response from the students:

- We designed the class to be project-based, so the students saw application, utility and exciting opportunities from the very beginning of the class;

- We ensured that the course retained this project focus throughout, culminating in student-chosen final project frequently driven by student emotions (some re-creating old time favourites like flappy bird, others improving childhood experiences like space shooters, yet others combining their love for music with programming when creating a simple synthesizer with player-piano features, or a student that used her final project to re-connect with her little brother living in a different state and working on a game for him);

- We kept the level of the material accessible through the just-in-time delivery of new materials: they only learned of a new programming concept after they already felt the need for having it, thus connecting an internal understanding of need with a revealed solution for more meaningful understanding;

- We continuously focused on gathering and responding to student feedback, down to re-structuring the course mid semester to provide the students with the increased learning they asked for.

As mentioned previously, the biggest course delivery challenge we found, when delivering the course, was that of time. In future, we will need to allow approximately triple the amount of time for course delivery; complemented by an extension in student support structures, including materials extension and student mentors.

We were also pleased that we were able to provide our students with mental frameworks which have transferability of use in other life contexts, whether they continue to pursue programming or not. Such mental framework development lies in addition to the delivery of a promised introduction to programming and a (hoped for) motivational learning outcome, with a strong emphasis placed on Computational and Design thinking. These skills created further enhanced learning outcomes for the students that will affect them beyond the pre-introductory course, and even beyond their life in higher education.

## About the Authors

András Margitay-Becht is an Associate Professor of Economics at the School of Economics and Business Administration at Saint Mary's College of California, USA. He can be contacted at am17@stmars-ca.edu

Udayan Das is an Associate Professor of Computer Science at the School of Science at Saint Mary's College of California, USA. He can be contacted at udd1@stmars-ca.edu

## Bibliography

Alford, L., Dorf, M. L., & Bertacco, V. (2017). Student perceptions of their abilities and learning environment in large introductory computer programming courses. In *2017 ASEE Annual Conference & Exposition Proceedings*, 28867.

Atuahene, F., & Russell, T. A. (2016). Mathematics readiness of first-year university students. *Journal of Developmental Education*, 39(3), 12.

Bloom, B. S., & Krathwohl, D. R. (1956). *Taxonomy of educational objectives: The classification of educational goals. Book 1, cognitive domain.* Longman.

Brown, N. C. C., Sentance, S., Crick, T., & Humphreys, S. (2014). Restart: The resurgence of computer science in UK schools. *ACM Transactions on Computing Education*, 14(2), 9:1-9:22.

Büchele, S., & Feudel, F. (2023). Changes in students' mathematical competencies at the beginning of higher education within the last decade at a German university. *International Journal of Science and Mathematics Education*, 1-23.

Connolly, C., Murphy, E., & Moore, S. (2009). Programming anxiety amongst computing students — A key in the retention debate? *IEEE Transactions on Education*, 52(1), 52–56.

Davies, S. (2008). The effects of emphasising computational thinking in an introductory programming course. *2008 38th Annual Frontiers in Education Conference*, T2C-3-T2C-8.

de Paula, B. H., Burn, A., Noss, R., & Valente, J. A. (2018). Playing Beowulf: Bridging computational thinking, arts and literature through game-making. *International Journal of Child-Computer Interaction*, 16, 39–46.

Di Martino, P., & Gregorio, F. (2019). The mathematical crisis in secondary–tertiary transition. *International Journal of Science and Mathematics Education*, 17(4), 825–843.

Falkner, K., Vivian, R., & Falkner, N. (2014, January). The Australian digital technologies curriculum: challenge and opportunity. In *Proceedings of the Sixteenth Australasian Computing Education Conference-Volume 148*, pp. 3-12.

Farah, J. C., Moro, A., Bergram, K., Kumar, A., Gillet, D., & Holzer, A. (2020). Bringing computational thinking to non-STEM undergraduates through an integrated notebook application. In *Proceedings of 15th European Conference on Technology Enhanced Learning*.

Frederick, C., Pierce, M., Griggs, A., Sun, L., & Ding, L. (2017). Get rid of your student's fear and intimidation of learning a programming language. *Publications*. Retrieved July 30, 2023, from https://commons.erau.edu/publication/573

Harlow, S., Cummings, R., & Aberasturi, S. M. (2007). Karl Popper and Jean Piaget: A rationale for constructivism. *The Educational Forum*, 71(1), 41–48.

Höök, L. J., & Eckerdal, A. (2015). On the bimodality in an introductory programming course: An analysis of student performance factors. *2015 International Conference on Learning and Teaching in Computing and Engineering*. Retrieved July 30, 2023, from https://ieeexplore.ieee.org/document/7126236

Hoque, M. (2017). Three domains of learning: Cognitive, affective and psychomotor. *The Journal of EFL Education and Research (JEFLER)* 2, 45–51.

Kilhamn, C., & Bråting, K. (2019). Algebraic thinking in the shadow of programming. In *Proceedings of the Eleventh Congress of the European Society for Research in Mathematics Education*, 566-573.

Liao, C. H., Chiang, C.-T., Chen, I.-C., & Parker, K. R. (2022). Exploring the relationship between computational thinking and learning satisfaction for non-STEM college students. *International Journal of Educational Technology in Higher Education*, 19(1), 43.

Mannila, L., Dagiene, V., Demo, B., Grgurina, N., Mirolo, C., Rolandsson, L., & Settle, A. (2014). Computational thinking in K-9 education. *Proceedings of the Working Group Reports of the 2014 on Innovation & Technology in Computer Science Education Conference*, 1–29.

Martin, F. (Director). (2016, September 16). *What is computational thinking? With Jeannette Wing*. https://www.youtube.com/watch?v=fSoknljUI4Q

Moore, J., Sanchez, J., & Tudor, A. (2021). Weaving a storytelling tapestry using computational thinking. In *International Association of School Librarianship Annual Conference Proceedings*.

Noss, R., Hoyles, C., Saunders, P., Clark-Wilson, A., Benton, L., & Kalas, I. (2020). *Making constructionism work at scale: The story of Scratchmaths*. MIT Press.

Nygaard, C. (2023). Enhancing student learning outcomes through contextualised learning activities. In K. Enomoto, R. Warner & C. Nygaard (Eds.), *Enhancing student learning outcomes in higher education*. Libri Publishing Ltd.

OECD (2012). *Key findings—PISA 2012*. Retrieved July 30, 2023, from https://www.oecd.org/pisa/keyfindings/pisa-2012-results.htm

Papert, S. (1980). *Mindstorms: Children, computers, and powerful ideas*. Retrieved July 30, 2023, from https://mindstorms.media.mit.edu

Papert, S. (1996). An exploration in the space of mathematics educations. *International Journal of Computers for Mathematical Learning*, 1(1), 95–123.

Pears, A., Tedre, M., Valtonen, T., & Vartiainen, H. (2021). What makes computational thinking so troublesome? *2021 IEEE Frontiers in Education Conference (FIE)*, 1–7.

Razzouk, R., & Shute, V. (2012). What is design thinking and why is it important? *Review of Educational Research*, 82(3), 330–348.

Resnick, M., Maloney, J., Monroy-Hernández, A., Rusk, N., Eastmond, E., Brennan, K., Millner, A., Rosenbaum, E., Silver, J., Silverman, B., & Kafai, Y. (2009). Scratch: Programming for all. *Communications of the ACM*, 52(11), 60–67.

Saint Mary's College (2014). *Institutional learning outcomes, Bachelors degree*. WASC. Retrieved July 30, 2023, from https://wascsenior.app.box.com/s/g5hhepp8bgfc8hr7s75o8fv66l3a6i80

Saint Mary's College (2023). *Saint Mary's College mission statement*. Retrieved March 30, 2023, from https://www.stmarys-ca.edu/about/saint-marys-college-mission-statement

Scratch (2023). *Scratch—Imagine, program, share*. (2023). Retrieved January 30, 2023, from https://scratch.mit.edu/

Solomon, J. (2005). Programming as a second language. *Learning & Leading with Technology*, 32(4), 34-39.

Taslibeyaz, E., Kursun, E., & Karaman, S. (2020). How to develop computational thinking: A systematic review of empirical studies. *Informatics in Education*, 19(4), 701–719.

The Brothers of the Christian Schools. (2009). *Saint John Baptiste de La Salle—Founder. Educator, Saint*. District of San Francisco.

TU Wien TV (Director). (2016, July 4). *Jeannette Wing: Computational thinking*. https://www.youtube.com/watch?v=YVEUOHw3Qb8

van Rensburg, H. (2023). Interactive practices in a library makerspace using technology to deliver positive student outcomes. In K. Enomoto, R. Warner & C. Nygaard (Eds.), *Enhancing student learning outcomes in higher education*. Libri Publishing Ltd.

Wenceslao, P. (2022). Mathematical readiness of freshmen engineering students (K-12 2020 Graduates) in Eastern Visayas in the Philippines. *Asian Journal of University Education*, *18*(1), 191.

Wing, J. (2011, March 6). Research notebook: Computational thinking — What and why? *The Link Magazine*, *6*, 20-23

Wing, J. M. (2006). Computational thinking. *Communications of the ACM*, *49*(3), 33–35.

Wing, J. M. (2008). Computational thinking and thinking about computing. *Philosophical Transactions of the Royal Society A: Mathematical, Physical and Engineering Sciences*, *366*(1881), 3717–3725.

Wyeld, T., & Nakayama, M. (2018). Visualising the code-in-action helps students learn programming skills. *2018 22nd International Conference Information Visualisation (IV)*, 182–187.

Chapter 8
# Enhancing Learning Outcomes for STEM Doctoral Students through Perspective Taking in Safe Spaces

Janet De Wilde and Elena Forasacco

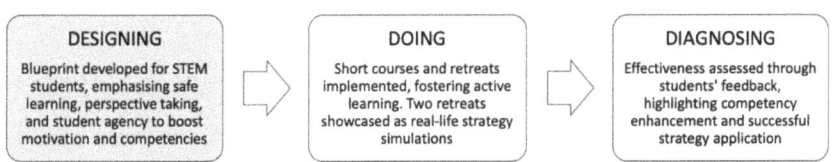

| DESIGNING | DOING | DIAGNOSING |
|---|---|---|
| Blueprint developed for STEM students, emphasising safe learning, perspective taking, and student agency to boost motivation and competencies | Short courses and retreats implemented, fostering active learning. Two retreats showcased as real-life strategy simulations | Effectiveness assessed through students' feedback, highlighting competency enhancement and successful strategy application |

## Preamble

With their chapter, Janet De Wilde and Elena Forasacco, contribute to this book, *Enhancing Student Learning Outcomes in Higher Education*, by explaining the importance of creating safe learning spaces and encouraging perspective taking for STEM doctoral students to enhance their learning outcomes. They show how this enhancement provides students with knowledge and competencies useful to complete their doctorate, whilst improving their professional portfolio. They relate to the three phases of the central ESLO model of the book in this way:

In the DESIGNING phase, a conceptual blueprint is elaborated to develop an educational framework aimed at increasing the students' motivation and competencies. Key learning outcomes specific to STEM doctoral studies are detailed, and guiding design principles are also described. The importance of creating safe and non-judgmental learning environments is emphasised, with strategies: facilitating perspective taking, adopting ungraded assessment approaches and fostering student agency.

During the DOING phase, these strategies are implemented through short courses and retreats, encouraging active and collaborative learning.

Two retreat case studies — a writing retreat and an impact retreat — serve as real-life simulations to demonstrate how these strategies are put into practice. These retreats present students with opportunities to explore new approaches in a conducive and supportive learning environment while enabling reflection, learning and adaptation of constructive strategies beneficial for their doctoral studies and future careers.

Finally, the DIAGNOSING phase involves the assessment of the effectiveness of these learning strategies. This involves analysing the qualitative feedback and perspectives of the students, as well as examining the change, growth, and enhancement of competencies in students through their practical application of teachings during these retreats.

## Introduction

This chapter describes our teaching approach that creates safe and non-judgmental spaces where STEM (Science, Technology, Engineering, Mathematics) doctoral students can become open minded, inspired, and motivated to work towards achieving their learning outcomes. To demonstrate how this approach works, we present two retreat case studies: a writing retreat and an impact retreat for doctoral students. Creating safe and non-judgemental spaces is vital for peer learning to effectively occur, because students need to feel safe and not judged so as to be able to fully explore ideas together and to have an open mind for new concepts (Holley & Steiner, 2005). Through our experiences as university educators, we often observe, if the learning space has a power imbalance and is perceived as judgemental, it is likely that barriers to discussion and learning will emerge and closed mindsets will set in. Hence, our priority as university educators has been to create safe and non-judgemental spaces to facilitate our doctoral students to become open minded, inspired, and motivated, whilst they learn.

To be open minded, inspired, and motivated, however, our doctoral students also require the type of feedback that helps increase their self-awareness of how they are learning. Therefore, we utilise ungraded assessments to provide such feedback in stages, in the forms of teacher- and peer-feedback, with the goal of raising students' self-awareness of how they are learning. In addition, embedding perspective taking activities within safe, non-judgemental learning spaces can further facilitate students to understand and appreciate the perspectives of others and the motivation and rationale behind others' perspectives (Gehlbach, 2004).

Thus, the two retreat case studies we present in this chapter — a writing retreat and an impact retreat — both aim to create such a safe, non-judgemental physical learning space that utilises ungraded assessment feedback and perspective taking activities to enhance doctoral students' learning outcomes. Each retreat has its own set of intended learning outcomes (to be detailed in Section 2). However, the two retreats share the key learning outcome — developing communication skills and strategies — that students need to achieve not only to complete their STEM doctoral studies, but also to enhance their employability-related portfolios for the job market. We defined learning outcomes focussed on communication skills and strategies because we work in STEM universities, and employers have often commented upon the lack of those skills in STEM graduates (McGunagle & Zizka, 2020). To design each of the two retreats, we developed together the six guiding principles (below):

1. Learning outcomes are enhanced and achieved when students are willing to learn and not forced;

2. The safe, non-judgmental learning space is crucial because when students feel safe and relaxed, they become open to ideas and are more willing to learn;

3. Learning activities are active and embody social collaboration to encourage peer learning;

4. Learning activities are designed to include students' perspective taking to provide the opportunity for students to understand the perspectives of different audiences and stakeholders;

5. Through staged ungraded assessments, students can focus more on learning processes than achieving a high grade; highly competitive student cohorts tend to forsake deeper learning for a higher grade;

6. The retreat design fosters student agency; students should feel they are responsible for their own learning.

In this chapter, we will demonstrate how these principles are put into practice in the writing retreat and the impact retreat to enhance STEM doctoral students' learning outcomes.

Chapter 8

*Chapter overview and key takeaways*

This chapter has four main sections. In Section 1, we explain how learning outcomes can be achieved through the creation of safe, non-judgemental learning spaces and the use of ungraded assessment feedback. This is followed by Section 2, where we describe the two retreat case studies to demonstrate the connection among safe, non-judgemental learning space, ungraded assessment feedback and perspective taking to enhance STEM doctoral students' learning outcomes. In Section 3, we show and highlight the benefits of this teaching approach. In Section 4, we outline our future aim when working with these students- to further develop our students' efficacy, agency, and responsibility. We then conclude our chapter.

Reading this chapter, you will gain the following three insights:

1. The importance of creating a safe, non-judgmental learning space to encourage STEM doctoral students to become open minded, inspired, and motivated;

2. The use of ungraded assessment feedback to facilitate peer learning to effectively take place;

3. The importance of embedding perspective taking in learning activities to develop STEM doctoral students' communication skills and strategies.

## Section 1: Background to our work with learning outcomes

We have extensive experience in different learning and teaching contexts, with a wide range of student cohorts, in higher education. As university educators, we have deep awareness that all students — regardless of their socio-economic, cultural, linguistic backgrounds — need, first and most of all, to feel 'safe' in order to learn effectively. We adopt the concept of safe space, both physical and emotional, that is supportive and conducive to enhancing learning outcomes in our teaching approaches. Core to our approaches is to give to our adult learners (doctoral students) the ownership (student agency) of their own learning through peer learning in the forms of ungraded assessment peer-feedback to increase their 'thirst' for learning.

In our roles within a UK research-intensive STEM institution, we started our work on enhancing learning outcomes in 2015, when a management change enabled us to reassess and renew our existing doctoral learning outcomes. Consequently, we were able to make renewed learning outcomes more meaningful and relevant to doctoral students' futures by way of linking their learning outcomes directly to the skills required in the 21$^{st}$ century job market. In so doing, we became particularly interested in embedding the practice of perspective taking in learning activities, so as to develop communication skills and strategies as key learning outcomes. Developing doctoral students' communication skills and strategies is, indeed, vital to help reduce communication barriers, such as language and cultural barriers, in the increasingly globalised job market, be it in academia or in the private sector. This interest led us to reach out to global employers to understand their skills needs and to research relevant literature on global employability (Villarroel et al., 2018; Isomöttönen et al., 2019; Lu et al., 2022; also see Bowd & Enomoto, 2023 in this book).

Our first goal was to design activities that enabled the students to practice and develop the graduate attributes desired by global employers, namely:

- An ability to work collaboratively with teams of people from a range of backgrounds and countries;
- Excellent communication skills and strategies: both speaking and listening;
- A high degree of drive and resilience;
- An ability to embrace multiple perspectives and challenge thinking;
- A capacity to develop new skills and behaviours according to role requirements;
- A high degree of self-awareness;
- An ability to negotiate and influence clients across the globe from different cultures;
- An ability to form professional, global networks;

- An openness to and respect for a range of perspectives from around the world;
- Multi-cultural learning agility (e.g. able to learn in any culture or space).

Although 'being a doctoral student' might be an individual process, we wanted to transform this individual task into a collaborative task following the notion of social competency development (De Wilde & Cavalli, 2021). In our teaching and learning environment, our retreats are attended by students from different departments/disciplines and they are at different years/stages of the doctoral candidature. Therefore, bringing about active peer-to-peer interactions in the classroom is essential so as to make students see our retreats as opportunities to learn, as well as to simply talk and share experiences. Therefore, for us, the concept of 'collaboration through ungraded assessment teacher- and peer-feedback' became a catalyst for the success of our retreats.

Our second goal was to design a learning space, both physical and emotional, to facilitate collaboration and maximise the students' learning. Learning spaces do not always facilitate the development of social competencies in students, and limited social exchanges mean limited learning (De Wilde & Cavalli, 2021). As teachers, we often observe that, if a physical learning space has fixed tables and chairs, it generates limited student movement, student participation and input, interactions and collaborations that many students desire to engage in the classroom. Such issues are exemplified by the student comments from a previous iteration of one of the courses:

- *"Plenaries were interesting but perhaps needed to be more interactive"*
- *"I think that although the teacher offered great advice, he could have allowed the group to come to their own decisions or conclusions with regards to the learning outcomes"*
- *"There was some repetition, and it could have been tailored for us"*

Following our analysis of these student feedback comments, our first step was to develop a flexible classroom design that challenges student perceptions of the teacher-student power differential. We designed our physical space in such a way that each classroom contains different sub-environments, each of them suitable for an activity, and that students can move around the sub-environments to complete learning activities. This simple physical change enabled students to remove physical and emotional constraints, and to feel safe and free when exploring new ideas and collaborating to enhance their learning outcomes (Forasacco, 2021).

Our initial implementation provided us with evidence that confirms the importance of learning space, especially for our residential retreats where students work together as a learning community over two or more days. We developed and implemented our flexible classroom design in the two retreat case studies, to effectively facilitate relaxation, exploration, and practice of ideas by our doctoral students. However, our initial implementation was not without any challenges. Some doctoral students did not expect a highly active environment, whilst others were not ready to 'surrender' their traditional perceptions of what constitutes the teacher-student power relationship. The latter group were likely to be thus influenced because of their cultural background.

An example of these influences was seemingly demonstrated when running group discussion sessions, wherein we created a micro-environment with chairs only, without tables, with the purpose of removing physical barriers. We arranged these chairs so that students and teachers could 'sit next to each other' in a circle. At the beginning of the discussion session, student engagement was quite slow, so the lead teacher had to prompt many questions to start the discussion. When analysing feedback comments from these discussion sessions, we found that many students, and even one of our colleagues, felt 'uncomfortable' with the learning space that discourages student perceptions of a traditional teacher-student power relationship. So, to overcome this, we designed and embedded scaffolded activities (to be detailed in Section 2) in both short courses and retreats to sufficiently prepare students for this type of active, interactive environment that discourages the student perception of teacher-student power relationship.

## Learning theory and methodology related to learning outcomes

We base the design of our retreats on social constructivism (Vygotsky, 1978) facilitated through active learning approaches and contextualised learning activities (Nygaard, 2023 in this book). We want our students

Chapter 8

to experience cooperative learning- the learning obtained through social interdependence (Gleason et al., 2011:3). Our approach emphasises the influence of peers in our students' cognitive development (O'Donnell & King, 2014). We are ambitious for our doctoral students to increase their confidence and learning through peer interactions in problem-solving activities. These gains are not achievable through mere knowledge transmission (Thorne & Lantolf, 2007; Aubrey & Riley, 2020). As facilitators, we prompt the students' current knowledge through discussing new ideas; then students adapt and internalise the new knowledge. We use group activities to consolidate this new knowledge as described by social constructivism theory (Aubrey & Riley, 2020). For our context, social constructivism is especially important, since our students are adult learners that bring their existing knowledge and life experiences. Both the knowledge and these experiences are valuable assets which can be shared and built upon during a course for the enhancement of learning outcomes for all students.

Similarly, we also support the notion that skills development happens in stages. We introduce suitable scaffolding activities to facilitate social learning to support students during their learning, and we gradually remove it when we observe engaged students (Bruner, 1977; Van de Pol & Elbers, 2013; Malik, 2017). Our design of a suitable scaffolding is crucial in these retreats and is applied to every step of our retreats. Scaffolding is used in the introduction, where we connect the learning outcomes to the stages of the retreat; in the instructions for activities; and in the guidelines to support meaningful and constructive peer-feedback and peer-discussion. With this staging, we ensure that students:

1) share skills during learning activities;

2) critically evaluate the new skills, whether and how it may be beneficial according to their needs; and

3) internalise the useful parts of these new skills (Bonk & Kim, 1998; Thorne & Lantolf, 2007).

In addition, we have observed that working together as a group on tasks can help develop students' (non-discipline specific) transferable skills through raising their awareness of others. Through such awareness of others, students can become team-mates working together to achieve a shared goal — by respecting different ideas and expertise, finding compromises and *"interthinking"* (Mercer & Howe, 2012:15). At the same time, the students likely increase both self- and peer-awareness, as their behaviours and attitudes towards collaborating and developing transferable skills change (Ozuah, 2005). According to Adams (2006), the more the learning environment becomes safe, non-judgmental and constructive, the more students feel free to express their ideas, resulting in improved collaboration and positive attitudes towards peer-to-peer feedback. Indeed, past studies (e.g. Gleason et al., 2011; Bonk & Cunningham, 2012) show that feedback from other students is an essential component of social constructivism — as a pedagogical tool — to improve the performance and enhance the learning outcomes.

It is important to us that we design our activities and social learning around real-life experiences. Thus, our doctoral students should be able to apply and practice their professional skills in simulations, enabling reflection on solutions to real-life cases (Ambrose et al., 2010; Kermis & Kermis, 2010). We utilise ungraded authentic assessments to enable these real-life simulations and to increase the students' motivation and engagement. As adult learners, we encourage our students to feel at the centre of learning (Kogan & Laursen, 2014) and to develop a 'mindful commitment' (Silcock, 2003:49). Therefore, students define how they want to work on the simulation whilst peers and experts provide them with meaningful, constructive formative feedback. Our approach, applied also in different contexts (such as Newton et al., 2020; von Renesse & Wegner, 2022), removes the effect of the 'teacher judging' the students. As a result, students are less stressed and can focus more on the process of learning, such as what skills they need to apply to work on the simulation. Furthermore, the real-life simulations designed for our retreats allow for authentic feedback from experts to strengthen the students' learning and their awareness of their own skills and capabilities to enhance their employability (Villarroel et al., 2018).

## Section 2: Our practice towards enhancing doctoral students' learning outcomes

Our practice aims to enhance the professional development of doctoral students and is two-fold: short blended courses (3 hours) and retreats (2-day and 5-day retreats). The practice focuses on the development of professional competencies and skills needed, not only during their doctoral studies, but also during their future careers in academia or in the private sector. Our doctoral students have the formal obligation to attend courses within the 4-year doctorate, they can attend any of our courses and retreats at any time during their doctorate. These courses and retreats are specifically designed to further improve institutional doctoral completion rates and employability performance indicators.

Our principles for learning design described earlier suit our context, as our doctoral students are adult learners who enhance their learning using their life and work experiences (Knowles, 1990). Adult learners co-learn best through social interactions; considering each other's experiences as sources of knowledge, building on the 'theory' they know from information sources (Bonk & Kim, 1998). This co-learning requires active and collaborative learning spaces. Our courses and retreats are attended by students from different departments, with different backgrounds and at different levels of their research projects. We have around 50 students attending a course or retreat at a time. This variety provides students with meaningful opportunities for peer-learning and peer-discussions through multi-stage learning activities with related ungraded assessments. We ensure these activities scaffold students' learning through practice and reflection on their practice, towards the enhancement of the learning outcomes. We set the ethos that the teacher is a facilitator who keeps peer-exchanges focussed on the learning outcomes. We also ensure that the teacher has the role of creating and maintaining a safe, supportive, constructive, and non-judgmental space. In such a space, students are more comfortable sharing their work and ideas, giving and receiving feedback, discussing doubts, and finding solutions.

## *How our practice affects students' way of studying*

We present two case studies to describe our innovative practice to enhance the learning outcomes: the writing retreat and the impact retreat.

### Case study 1: writing retreat

Here we explain the writing retreat as a case study: it is a residential retreat and represents an educational space that includes physical space and time for writing and sharing experiences. During the retreat we equip students with writing strategies (such as planning and resources management techniques), to support their thesis writing process and enhance the quality of their writing. We facilitate students to reflect on the quality of their writing and their writing process; adapt the writing strategies to their own needs; and build up their own writing strategies. This increases their writing efficacy and efficiency, useful for their writing in their future careers (De Wilde, 2019). By using this active approach, we are considering the nature of our students as adult learners; they prefer learning environments where they can self-direct their learning. First, we encourage that through self-reflection, students can increase their awareness of those competencies they need to enhance; then they adapt the suggested strategies to their own writing approach. Afterwards, we provide the writing sessions which represent large real-life simulations where students feel motivated to apply those strategies to improve the quality of their theses.

Our approach differs from the 'boot-camp' offered by many universities since they focus on the product (= thesis) based on the quantity produced (= word count). These bootcamps are frequently about sitting in silence and writing as much as possible. This bootcamp approach is pressurised and often uses minimal sharing opportunities, for example 'Shut-up and write' (Aitchison, 2020). Moreover, the organisers may announce how many words each student has written and praise the top number of words regardless of quality or critical thinking applied. Our approach, on the other hand, creates a non-stressful environment where the mind is free to explore the process of writing and the meaning of what they need to communicate (De Wilde, 2019).

The learning outcomes we defined for this retreat are:

- Plan and manage the thesis-writing process;
- Set clear and achievable goals for writing;
- Write clear, precise, and organised academic text;
- Structure and connect the narrative of your research writing;
- Maintain the momentum and your wellbeing.

We strive to ensure these learning outcomes are achieved due to active learning approaches, with students acquiring the suitable 'writing processes and strategies' in stages. Teachers are the initiators and facilitators of the process, students are the authors of their learning, they self-direct their learning.

In the first learning stage, before attending the retreat, students complete short activities that we designed- to prepare them for and enter in the mindset of the retreat. They watch short content videos with the writing strategies to make the thesis writing process more effective. We show the students how to create the thesis structure and critically select the content to write in each section and define the writing timeframe for each section to plan the writing. From our pre-course activities, which support an initial self-reflection, students can realise what they might need to change, and seeing the benefits of those changes; hopefully maximising their motivation to participate and engage at the retreat.

At the retreat, in the second learning stage, teachers exemplify the application of the strategies from the videos. This is followed by a Q&A session for students to clarify any doubts they might have; then students have writing time in order to apply those strategies.

In the third learning stage, learning is socially constructed through the ungraded peer-assessment process, designed to enhance the students' learning. This stage is based on perspective taking; since students are living the same experience (i.e., writing their theses), they well understand each other (emotions, feelings, doubts and issues). We prompt them to share the suggestions they would like to receive from their peers. Students work in groups, share their theses, then give and receive constructive and authentic peer-feedback. We provide reflective questions, to scaffold both this peer-discussion and the self-reflection on their own theses, while giving feedback to their peers. Students also receive authentic feedback from teachers in individual consultations where the discussion focuses on the student's thesis, they receive specific suggestions and support to improve their thesis and solve their doubts.

Our multi-stage learning approach creates a transformational retreat as, previously, writing was seen as a hurdle by most of the STEM students with whom we work. Our retreat provides students with strategies to approach writing with the same scientific mindset they apply to their projects. Students are enabled with new writing strategies; enhancing their communication and their learning constitutes an important part of their professional portfolios.

## Case study 2: impact retreat

We created an impact retreat to facilitate the understanding of impact amongst doctoral students, based on activities that simulate real-life experiences. Our impetus to create this retreat arose from a heightened requirement from UK funding agencies to communicate and share the impact of any research they fund (Sutton, 2020). This requirement arose because for many years research outcomes tended to stay within the academic sector and it was difficult for hospitals, industry, and other organisations to be aware of and benefit from these outcomes. Hence our doctoral students need to learn how to address impact in their research outputs.

We designed the impact retreat to have scaffolding over a few days, so that students could gradually understand, appreciate, and take the perspective of different stakeholders, similar to the approach taken by St. Aubyn & Andrews (2023 in this book). We encouraged student reflection on the meaning of impact for audiences and the students also reflected on their own research.

The learning outcomes we defined for the impact retreat are that the student will be better able to:

+ Recognise impact and pathways to impact in their research;

+ Identify and participate in impact activities for their research and for global challenges;

+ Assess audiences' requirements and use appropriate communication strategies;

+ Employ negotiation and influencing skills;

+ Evaluate and employ communication approaches for impact.

We set these learning outcomes into practice in the following ways. We arrange that students work together in five groups of 10 (50 students in total) to create an environment for social constructivism (Vygotsky, 1978) to operate. We ensure the students work together on activities designed to encourage them to combine their prior experience and knowledge to construct new knowledge and understanding.

The first activity is to reflect on what impact looks like from the view of five different audiences:

- the public;
- charity;
- industry;
- academic; and
- policy makers.

Each group takes an audience; considers its needs; reflects on its attitudes, bias and preconcepts towards scientific discoveries; identifies what impact looks like for the audience; and then creates a mind map diagram of the outcome on a sheet of paper (or on a Padlet or equivalent sharing software if working online). We then rotate the sheet of paper (or Padlet) they have been working on to another group, who add to the first group's knowledge and perspective. We do this rotation five times so that every group works on each audience, groups socially construct the learning. At the end, we give the original group back their first audience, they study the collated knowledge and give feedback to the room. We have applied this technique many times over several years and it is always remarkable to see how much knowledge and perspective taking is created. The next activity, after a break, makes the learning meaningful: we ask students to look at their research and work out what their impact would be for each audience. This activity enables adult learners to connect any learning to their own practice.

On the second day we have activities to learn how to communicate, explain, and negotiate with each audience based on the increased understanding and perspective taking achieved with the first activity. We ask students to create either poster presentations or slide presentations to practice how to explain their research with their peers, in preparation for the final day.

On the last day we arrange the final key activity which is a real-life simulation that allows students to practice and finalise the learning of the retreat. We invite in four actual professionals, one representing each sector — charity, academia, industry, policy— and also a member of the public with no/little knowledge in science, to have a meaningful, authentic formative assessment. The student groups must negotiate with each professional and the member of public for ten minutes to explain a project and to gain the professional's/member of the public's support for the project, asking for funding, and/or branding, and/or equipment loan. We request that students form pairs for the negotiation, so that each member of the group must have the experience of negotiation (for example, 2 students negotiate with the member of the public, another 2 negotiate with the industry professional, another 2 with the charity professional, another 2 with the academic, and finally another 2 students with the policy maker).

One special stipulation from us is that whilst each pair is negotiating, the others in the group, who are not negotiating, must remain silent but can supply post-it notes to prompt the negotiators. We apply this stipulation to ensure inclusivity and that all our students, even shy or quiet students, can engage in the experience. It also prevents any one student dominating the negotiation stage. During this activity, our students learn to consider the perspectives of the audiences; tailor and apply a suitable communication style; engage the professional/member of the public with their project; influence them regarding the quality and impact of the project, and negotiate fundings to develop the project. We have witnessed how students benefit from this activity, because it provides the opportunity to practice with professionals and a member of the public, and to receive a meaningful and authentic formative assessment from them. This authentic feedback is especially important for our adult learners, because they can connect it directly with their own practice and prepare them for their future careers.

We provide the professionals and the member of the public with criteria to act as assessors, evaluating the students according to professionalism, communicating well, and how well the student has understood their particular perspective. From our experience, this final day is immensely enjoyed by the students. The active learning feels real, and they learn how to switch between perspectives. Thus, overall, in the impact retreat, the learning outcomes are achieved through peer reflection, sharing, and learning to see beyond themselves.

## How we prepare and organise our pedagogy to enhance students' learning outcomes

The pedagogy of our retreats involves bringing people together to reflect on and build upon their competencies, share their experiences, and provide technical and non-technical peer-support. We have ensured that the role of the teachers is key in facilitating a safe and sharing community. We fully believe that *'authentic relationships between teachers and learners'* (Illeris, 2014:9) are needed for the developing of emotional trust at the retreat. We have designed our retreats so that this building of authentic relationships is possible as students have a longer time with teachers and peers. This extended contact facilitates the development of trusting and authentic teacher-student and student-student relationships and allows for the enhancement of the learning outcomes. Furthermore, extended time spent in a space different from their conventional learning space enhances the opportunities for these relationships to deepen and allow for perspective taking to occur. We identified that this change in the physical environment prompts students to change their mental and emotional perspectives and encourages social perspective taking. We, therefore, focussed the design of our retreats and pedagogy around the creation of suitable physical space and emotional space. The physical space includes the organisation of the rooms and the material, and the emotional space refers to the approaches we apply to relate to and work with students.

**Physical space**
We recognise that the physical space we use as a learning setting is fundamental for creating a safe environment to learn. University spaces are often designed to demonstrate power, for example with imposing columns at the entrance and high atriums. According to Foucault (1984:252), imposing spaces imply that the power is in the hands of the establishment rather than yours. We recognise this as an important point, as power implies influence and control, and if this is being exercised the mind is not so free. Accordingly, doctoral students often feel disempowered by supervisors and/or the university. We recognise that a retreat embodies the concept of creating a distance from the source of control and the removal of boundaries.

Retreats are conceptualised so as to allow our minds to explore freely. Thus, we explored physical spaces that we could use. We selected a 17th-century historical country house in which to hold our retreats. This country house is currently used as a non-profit educational centre that can be used by UK universities at low cost. We chose this setting as it is surrounded by a park containing spectacular scenery. Here we have observed that students feel safe, because they are far from their normal contexts, such as far from non-supportive colleagues and from issues with supervisors. In the environment we have selected, they work on activities, discover, and analyse new concepts, and develop solutions with a more objective mindset. This country house has different learning spaces that we allocate to the different activities.

For the writing retreat, since we need to create a safe space, as well as a motivational writing space, we hold the short talks and Q&A sessions in large teaching rooms with no spatial division between teachers and students to facilitate interactions and increase the sense of safety. For consultations and writing time, we are in rooms used as old libraries and reading rooms, with books and paintings, which create relaxing and motivational writing spaces. The peer-discussions are managed by students, peer-meetings happen either outside, with students in discussion whilst walking around the park, or in rooms with an informal set-up (e.g. sofas, piano). In both 'spaces' we observe students feeling relaxed, and they come back to their writing full of ideas and re-energised by the peer-meeting.

For the impact retreat, since it is based on group activities, we mainly use large teaching rooms where each group has its own table and space to work and move around, removing physical restrictions and facilitating exchanges among groups. For the final negotiation activity which allows students to summarise and practice the learning, we use five meeting rooms organised to represent the five scenarios of the negotiations. This representation supports students to enter in the mindset of the scenario; for example, the academic professor is in a room with the features of an office, while the member of the public is in a room looking like a living room.

**Emotional space**
With respect to the emotional space, our main pedagogical approach is the application of a coaching approach (open questioning; Starr, 2016) during group and individual discussions. Since our students are adult learners with meaningful previous experiences, the coaching approach facilitates the application of these experiences further to develop their projects as well as their competencies. Students reflect upon and share their past experiences, from learning to issues and solutions; in so doing they can develop new learning and solutions.

We dedicate part of the preparation of the emotional space to the definition of scaffolded guidelines for activities and discussions to enable students to apply the coaching approach while working with their peers. Our guidelines for activities include clear and detailed descriptions of the aims, connection to the learning outcomes and step-by-step instructions. We also ensure that each activity has tailored prompts to support group discussions, students' reflection on the activity and on their own work, as well as providing non-judgmental peer-feedback. For example, we share guidelines at the writing retreat which include questions to support the assessment of each chapter of their thesis. Example of our open questions are: 'Why is the problem you have solved with your project relevant and significant? Why is the method appropriate? What other methods could you have considered? In what ways does the structure support the answers to your research question?' During the peer-feedback sessions, students ask those questions and both students (the questioner and the recipient) reflect on their theses.

We use guidelines at the impact retreat that are designed to increase the students' awareness of research impact and its effect on their individual research projects. We design each activity as an opportunity for students to practice the learning connected to a learning outcome, and its instructions include:

- an introduction, where we explain the aim of the activity and its rationale;
- step-by-step instructions to facilitate the preparation and completion of the activity;
- reflective questions to support peer-feedback and to transform the learning from a real-life simulation to a real-life context.

We ask that following the activity, teachers facilitate the debrief, providing students with a set of questions as a guidance for reflection upon their learning, and its importance in relation to their doctorate and future career. For example, with the negotiation activity, students practice the appropriate communication styles to apply with the different audiences. Instructions includes the step-by-step preparation and presentation of their projects, as well as questions for the group debrief about their performances. We also scaffold the students understanding of feedback from the representatives of the audiences. Then, we create a second set of questions to support students applying the professional's feedback in a real context. Being aware that group activities might create competition between groups, our approach highlights the importance of the activity and its development (process), rather than focussing on the result of the activity (product). This approach is actioned thus, in order to minimise any competitiveness distracting from the learning process.

## Section 3: The outcome

In this section, we present the outcomes of the retreats in terms of student learning outcomes and our own outcomes as teachers.

### Student Perspective

Here we present the students' perspectives on the enhancement of the learning outcomes for the writing retreat and the impact retreat, as well as on the importance of the physical and emotional spaces towards this enhancement.

We obtained the students' perspectives with a two-stage qualitative research: in- depth interviews with 10 students and anonymous students' feedback over a period of 6 years, from 2016 onwards (about 200 students). We analysed data using embodied phenomenology (Merleau-Ponty, 2002; Davidson, 2000) as a theoretical approach since it considers space (or environment) and memories (or lived experiences) as crucial factors when understanding the current experience of participants. Students reported back their lived experiences during the retreats, giving us authentic feedback. Phenomenology also allowed us to consider and include in our analysis unique perspectives as well, giving limited importance to the frequency of answers (Dowling, 2007).

**Writing retreat**
We received the following quotes from students which synthesise the students' learning for each learning outcome.

- Plan and manage the thesis-writing process:
  - *"I gained clarity in my thinking about how to manage various aspects of my specific thesis and how to better manage the overwhelming task"*
  - *"This has really motivated me to get organised – with my space, my data and my thoughts!"*
- Set clear and achievable goals for writing:
  - *"I will set clear achievable goals and work according to the plan so I can manage my time well"*
- Write clear, precise, and organised academic text:
  - *"I found one to one meetings with members from the Centre of Academic English very useful, despite being a native English speaker"*
- Structure and connect the narrative of your research writing:
  - *"It was great to check my overall structure and flow as well as get some feedback on my writing style"*
  - *"Try not overload the thesis with info but present my project as a story"*
- Maintain the momentum and your wellbeing:
  - *"However, [although] it is only [a]writing retreat, [the]coaches were very informative about physical and mental health which is very important but easy to forget for PhD students while they are concerned about their thesis"*
  - *"Take more time to write and create a good environment for it. I realise that I need a regular change of scenery and somewhere I feel comfortable to keep motivated"*: the student reflected on their own learning- this quote synthesizes their resolution for keeping their writing momentum;
  - *"It provided a momentum push"*

## Impact retreat

We received the following students' quotes synthesize the students' learning at this retreat:

- Recognise impact and pathways to impact in your research:
    - *"My research has huge impact on not only academics and businesses, but also on the government and public"*
    - *"I found it very interesting and useful, I feel that I became more aware of my research in a larger picture, as well as learnt about various expectations in academia no one talked about before (i.e. finances and grants)"*
- Identify and participate in impact activities for your research and for global challenges:
    - *"I would be participating in more social engagement activities confidently"*
    - *"Do more active delivery of my research"*
- Assess audiences' requirements and use appropriate communication strategies:
    - *"I realise there is another language for different audience that we have use to have more impact on our research"*
- Employ negotiation and influencing skills:
    - *"The negotiation part was really interesting and helpful. It was a very realistic simulation, and the coaches were perfect in their roles. This helped a lot in understanding what to expect when you are going to negotiate with the 4 different audience proposed"*
- Evaluate and employ communication approaches for impact:
    - *"Draw-up a statement of impact to guide me through my research"*
    - *"I will reread my writing for conferences and general work through the lens of whether what I have written is as impactful as it can be"*

Based on these comments we realised that students benefit from the retreat due to the suitable physical and emotional space created at the retreat.

**Physical space**

Along with the enhancement of the learning outcomes, students highlighted the importance of the physical space since our retreats are constructed away from the campus in a new space, with social elements and support built in: *"I also loved the venue. It is important to be somewhere away from the city, where you can hear your thoughts"*. Students also mentioned mental associations of being *"thrown on an island"* or *"in the Himalayas"* which show that the students recognise that this space provides the chance to gain new perspectives (De Wilde, 2019).

Students perceived this physical learning space, away from the usual context, as a supportive emotional space, comfortable and safe: *"The lovely ambiance and easy way to focus on work!"*. Both teachers and students dedicate time to listen respectfully to each other and the learning is facilitated: *"It felt like a really safe and comfortable space to ask the questions – which was so helpful as I went away from the session with practical solutions and strategies for everything"*, *"The serenity of the atmosphere and the vision of the venue are properly aligned with the aim of the course. It's a good choice!"* and *"Venue stunning and very well-suited"*. In this physical space, students collaborated together to complete activities to enhance their learning, without competition: *"I love the activities where we got many chances to practice in the second day what we learned in the first day of the retreat"* and *"I liked the way interactive activities were designed to engage all the participants"*. Indeed, students' perspectives covered different angles of the retreats. The students' experiences, and associated feelings were varied but being around others who were also focussed on the same activity had a significant impact: *"That I'm not doing as badly as I thought I was! Also, the realisation of being peer-examined hit me – and boosted my confidence"*.

**Emotional safe space**

At our retreats, we learnt that the students' perceptions of teachers were positive. This student comment highlights the efficacy of the coaching approach for the creation of an open and safe space *"The coaches were very approachable and made the atmosphere conducive for all to learn and participate"*. They commented on the individual support: *"I'm very grateful for her [teacher] time and help, and the opportunity to have this one-to-one support tailored specifically to my needs"*. Furthermore, our efforts to create a community was recognised by students: *"I especially liked how the program provided some free time to take a walk around and spend time with other students to connect"* and *"The feeling that I am not alone and that I have help"*.

Importantly, students at the writing retreat felt in a learning community, as in Moore (2003). Our retreat promotes a shift from the solitary writer to a community-based, collaborative social act, as demonstrated by one of our students: *"I also enjoyed the shared experience with the other students…I enjoyed sitting…in the same room, and – well everyone typing away and everyone thinking not necessarily a lot of interaction, but this was…a fruitful space to focus ourself".* We recognise that the thesis writing experience can be very isolating, often students believe they need to be alone to write well. However, by bringing them together at the retreat, we are enabling a resource: graduate students' most underused resource is 'each other' (Simpson, 2012:105). Hence, this contact with others at the same stage is a significant aspect of the retreat experience: *"I think it was useful to be around a lot of people that were writing up, at least for me, in our department I am the only one at our stage, we are a very small group, so it was a really useful exercise for me".*

Through the communities we created at the retreats, enhancement of students' wellbeing was evidenced. One student shared that they had gained comfort from meeting fellow students: *"What is the main thing about the retreat is also meeting people who are writing and who are struggling as well and suddenly you feel less alone, you feel you are not alone to struggle"* and *"I was nervous about participating in some of the activities but the team made it easy for everyone to get involved".* We understand that a valuable part of journey to becoming a researcher is through 'sharing insecurities' (Wegener et al, 2016:1093). Through being at our retreats, students experienced and recognised that this struggle with insecurity and uncertainty is a natural stage to go through.

Our students also seemed to recognise the sense of a shared goal, like that found by Castle and Keane (2016:277) who highlighted the value in the 'sense of a shared project and the ability to discuss issues and challenges with others.' One student emphasised *"The good thing is, like, I was able to meet people who were almost submitting their thesis, very close to the submission, and others like were in the middle and others like me that were just starting with the background".* Another student enjoyed the diversity of the retreat group, and they were able to discover different perspectives:

*"It's nice to meet a lot of other people from different backgrounds different disciplines, different stages, and understand what stage they are at and what they're doing and their perception of things".*

## Teacher perspective – our reflections

Currently we have delivered about 20 writing retreats and 10 impact retreats. Following each retreat, we meet to reflect upon the experience and analyse the students' feedback to improve the design to further address the students' needs and enhance their professional practice.

During this reflective process, what we learnt first of all was the importance of using a safe and supportive physical and emotional space to enhance the students' learning. During the pilot of the writing retreat, we underestimated this aspect, and the retreat was an emotionally draining experience for all of us, teachers and students, with very limited learning (it was more like putting a patch on a problem, than prompting the students' learning). Also; based on students' comments, our second personal learning point concerned the importance of the physical space to remove the stress; *"London can have a lot of physical anxiety all around so that's, that was completely absent, that was good"*. We also saw that it was crucial to enable students to take responsibility for their learning; *"to take breaks in that way because you could take a sensible amount of time off just to walk round and get fresh air"*.

Our third personal learning point was to shift the focus to learning about the process of writing rather than concentrating on the product. Learning outcomes are enhanced when a set of conditions are met from both sides, teachers need to create a good process, students need to follow and apply that process to obtain a meaningful product. At the retreats, we provide students with strategies and scaffolded real-life simulations; students apply those strategies working on these real-life simulations.

Our fourth personal learning point was to apply a coaching approach (open questions) when interacting with students. This was done so as to prompt them focussing on solutions more than on issues; the coaching behaviour reassures students and helps them to relax and feel comfortable. In these conditions they work better because they realise that they can overcome issues and are not afraid of making mistakes. These realisations ensure that the students are primed to be more effective and productive, creating text for their thesis that is well planned, structured and of high quality. Owing to the coaching approach, we also work to break down any possible perceived barriers of superiority between teachers and students, helping students to feel safe and comfortable to discuss with us any doubts they might have.

Our fifth personal learning point was to acknowledge the effectiveness of meaningful, authentic, ungraded feedback from peers. Hence, we developed a scaffolded approach in the retreats to support students understanding of the perspectives of their peers, value their respective experiences and knowledge, and think outside the box. Accordingly, students can work towards reduction of their biases, approach their peers with fresh more objective eyes and hopefully provide valuable and meaningful feedback and suggestions.

Reflecting on our experience as teachers, we have realised how those retreats shifted our own thinking and professional practice. Retreats are also learning opportunities for us; we have enhanced our own confidence and self-efficacy with writing by applying strategies we discuss at the retreats, such as writing the purpose of the paragraph using a statement of intent for each paragraph to create the narrative. Now we have greater confidence in our own writing, and furthermore, we are now more aware of the value of our contribution. We have also learnt the balance between recognising emotions and supporting emotions, yet having a professional separation to guide students.

## Section 4: Moving forward

To consider moving forward, we need to reflect on where we started. Our students are high-achieving adults who have arrived at a competitive institution through a highly competitive process. They were being taught under the previous management in a style which reinforced the superiority of experience and knowledge combined with divisions between teachers and students. What we have asked of the students, in their time with us, is to step back from competing and to take their next learning step through a process of collaborative creative experiences. We have also asked them to see, through discovery and discussion, the perspectives of others. This may not seem a big step to a reader that resides in a collaborative context, but in our STEM context, it was a significant change of practice and a change of learning.

Taking this learning forward, we must consider applying this in other contexts and to explore it in greater depths. Our future aim for working with these students, is to increase further our students' efficacy, agency, and responsibility. Too many students at doctoral level develop anxiety, and/or imposter syndrome. Furthermore, often wellbeing is compromised during the doctoral experience. Through our approach of perspective taking and collaborative learning we can enable students to flourish in a community. We welcome all students, particularly doctoral students, to our academic community and we have a responsibility to ensure that the community they join is a flourishing one.

For universities, we would like to see applying collaborative peer learning in safe emotional spaces with enriching physical spaces more widely adopted. We are aware of institutional strategies that adopt authentic learning and hence this approach more suitable for them. We wish for institutions to think more creatively about their learning spaces for doctoral students. These spaces need to be created with peer collaboration at the centre, and wherever possible to remove the physical and psychological barriers between teachers, supervisors, and students.

We recognise that this chapter is focused on doctoral students who are smaller in number than undergraduate students and hence many of the concepts can be more easily applied to them. However, we raise the issue of learning spaces, safe emotional spaces, and physical spaces for doctoral students, because at this level of study their learning environment is often overlooked. From our experience, we can say that a safe space is mainly created by the teachers' ethos, mindset, and behaviours, and it can be created anywhere if care is taken. For example, we had online retreats during the Covid-19 pandemic and students seemed to experience the same sense of a safe space. Currently, some of our retreats are also held within the university premises, however we are careful to select rooms that are usually not used for teaching and are close to a public park. This is perceived by students as a change of scenery, since they are in rooms new for them, and they can still appreciate the tranquillity of the park. Moving forward, we will further advocate for doctoral students' enhancement of learning and learning outcomes via the safe space and perspective taking pathways we have followed.

## Conclusion

Based on our experience at the retreats, learning outcomes are enhanced when the teaching focusses on the process needed to achieve the learning. Our retreats provide students with strategies to use to learn and to enhance their current learning, and opportunities to apply those strategies with real-life simulations in a safe space. Importantly, each stage of the learning process is connected to ungraded assessments to maximise the students' learning. This approach is beneficial for students in their current positions, and in their future educational and professional careers.

Focussing on the process even further might be an interesting and necessary approach to take, especially for assessments, considering the increasing importance of Artificial Intelligence (AI) in the educational context. AI is able to assist in creating enhanced products, such as essays, computer code and images; students can obtain good marks if they use AI during their studies. However, the end results may lack individuality, and identifying the contribution of the student is complex. This controversy emphasises that many current assessment processes are poorly designed since they focus on grading the students' product(s), independently from their learning. These processes seemingly serve to encourage students not to study to learn but to get a high grade. Our retreats might represent examples for other teachers to overcome the limitations of the current assessment systems: focus on the learning process, assessing each stage and ensuring that assessment for learning is a core principle.

## About the Authors

Janet De Wilde is a Professor of Engineering and Education and Director of Queen Mary Academy at Queen Mary University of London, UK. She can be contacted at this email: janet.dewilde@qmul.ac.uk

Elena Forasacco is a Senior Teaching Fellow in the Graduate School at Imperial College London, UK. She can be contacted at this email: e.forasacco@imperial.ac.uk

# Bibliography

Adams, P. (2006). Exploring social constructivism: Theories and practicalities. *Education, 34*(3), 243-257.

Aitchison, C. (2020). Writing groups and retreats: Writing groups, writing retreats, boot camps and other social writing events for doctoral writers. In S. Carter, C. Guerin & C. Aitchison (Eds.), *Doctoral writing: Practices, processes and pleasures.* Springer.

Ambrose, S. A., Bridges, M. W., DiPietro, M., Lovett, M. C., & Norman, M. K. (2010). *How learning works: Seven research-based principles for smart teaching.* John Wiley and Sons.

Aubrey, K., & Riley, A. (2020). *Understanding and using challenging educational theories.* Sage Publications Ltd.

Bonk, C. J., & Cunningham, D. J. (2012). Searching for learner-centred, constructivist, and sociocultural components of collaborative educational learning tools. In *Electronic collaborators. Learner-centred technologies for literacy, apprenticeship, and discourse.* eBook. Routledge.

Bonk, C. J., & Kim, K. A. (1998). Extending sociocultural theory to adult learning. In M. C. Smith & T. Pourchot (Eds.), *Adult learning and development: Perspectives from educational psychology.* Taylor and Francis Group, Routledge.

Bowd, K., & Enomoto, K. (2023). Bringing employability to life: Developing employability skill sets and understandings as student learning outcomes. In K. Enomoto, R. Warner & C. Nygaard. (Eds.), *Enhancing student learning outcomes in higher education.* Libri Publishing Ltd.

Bruner, J. S. (1977). *The Process of Education.* 25th edition (1999), Harvard University Press.

Castle, J., & Keane, M. (2016) Retreating to write: Are publications the only important outcome? *Alternation, 23*(1), 265-284.

Davidson, J. (2000). A phenomenology of fear: Merleau-Ponty and agoraphobic life-worlds. *Sociology of Health & Illness, 22,* 640-681.

Dowling, M. (2007). From Husserl to van Manen. A review of different phenomenological approaches. *International Journal of Nursing Studies, 44,* 131–142.

De Wilde, J. P. (2019). *From islands to mountains: The experiences of final year STEMM doctoral students at a thesis writing retreat.* Master in Education dissertation, Imperial College London.

De Wilde J. P., & Cavalli G. (2021). Academic identity, the supervisor, and online communities of practice. In J. Sheldon & V. Sheppard (Eds.), *Online communities for doctoral researchers and their supervisors: Building engagement with social media. Taylor and Francis Group.

Foucault, M. (1984). *The Foucault reader*. Pantheon Books.

Forasacco, E. (2021). Flexible classroom design to facilitate learning, engagement and integration of knowledge and cultures. In K. Enomoto, R. Warner & C. Nygaard (Eds.), *Teaching and learning innovations in higher education*. Libri Publishing Ltd.

Gehlbach, H. (2004). A new perspective on perspective taking: a multidimensional approach to conceptualizing an aptitude. *Educational Psychology Review, 16*(3), 207-234.

Gleason, B. L., Peeters, M. J., Resman-Targoff, B. H., Karr, S., McBane, S., Kelley, K., & Denetclaw, T. H. (2011). An active-learning strategies primer for achieving ability-based educational outcomes. *American Journal of Pharmaceutical Education, 75*(9), 1-12.

Holley, L.C., & Steiner, S. (2005). Safe space: student perspectives on classroom environment. *Journal of Social Work Education, 41*(1), 49-64.

Illeris, K. (2014). Transformative learning and identity. *Journal of Transformative Education, 12*(2), 148-163.

Isomöttönen, V., Daniels, M., Cajander, Å., Pears, A., & Mcdermott, R. (2019). Searching for global employability: Can students capitalize on enabling learning environments? *ACM Transactions on Computing Education, 19*(2), 1–29.

Kermis, G., & Kermis, M. (2010). Professional presence and soft skills: A role for accounting education. *Journal of Instructional Pedagogies, 2*, 1-10.

Knowles, M. (1990). *The adult learner: A neglected species*. Gulf Publishing.

Kogan, M., & Laursen, S. L. (2014). Assessing long-term effects of inquiry-based learning: A case study from college mathematics. *Innovative Higher Education, 39*, 183-199.

Lu, V. N., Nghia, T. L. H., Bui, B. C., & Singh, J. K. N. (2022). Graduate employability agenda in global higher education: Are we moving in the same direction? In T.L.H. Nghia, B. C. Bui, J. K. N. Singh & V. N. Lu (Eds), *Graduate employability across contexts*. Springer.

Malik, S. A. (2017). Revisiting and re-representing scaffolding: The two gradient model. *Cogent Education, 4*(1), 1331533.

McGunagle, D., & Zizka, L. (2020). Employability skills for 21st-century STEM students: the employers' perspective. *Higher Education, Skills and Work-based Learning, 10*(3), 591-606.

Mercer, N., & Howe, C. (2012). Explaining the dialogic processes of teaching and learning: The value and potential of sociocultural theory. *Learning, Culture and Social Interaction, 1*(1), 12-21.

Merleau-Ponty, M. (2002). *Phenomenology of perception*. Routledge.
Moore, S. (2003) Writers' retreats for academics: Exploring and increasing the motivation to write. *Journal of Further and Higher Education, 27*(3), 333-342.
Newton, J., Williams, M. C., & Feeney, D. M. (2020). Implementing non-traditional assessment strategies in teacher preparation: Opportunities and challenges. *Journal of Culture and Values in Education, 3*(1), 39-51.
Nygaard, C. (2023). Enhancing student learning outcomes through contextualised learning activities. In K. Enomoto, R. Warner & C. Nygaard (Eds.), *Enhancing student learning outcomes in higher education*. Libri Publishing Ltd.
O'Donnell, A. M., & King, A. (Eds.). (2014). *Cognitive perspectives on peer learning*. Routledge.
Ozuah, P. O. (2005). First, there was pedagogy and then came andragogy. *Einstein Journal of Biology and Medicine, 21*, 83-87.
von Renesse, C., & Wegner, S.A. (2022). Two examples of ungrading in higher education United States and Germany. *ArXiv preprint*, arXiv:2209.14240.
Silcock, P. (2003). Accelerated learning: A revolution in teaching method?. *Education 3-13, 31*(1), 48-52.
Simpson, S. (2012). The problem of graduate-level writing support: Building a cross-campus graduate writing initiative. *WPA: Writing Program Administration, 36*(1), 95-118.
St. Aubyn, B., & Andrews, A. (2023). A pedagogical approach to enhance nursing students' written communication skills as learning outcomes. In K. Enomoto, R. Warner & C. Nygaard (Eds.), *Enhancing student learning outcomes in higher education*. Libri Publishing Ltd.
Starr, J. (2016). *The coaching manual*. 4th edition. Pearson.
Sutton, E. (2020). The increasing significance of impact within the Research Excellence Framework (REF). *Radiography, 26*, S17-S19.
Thorne, S. L., & Lantolf, J. P. (2007). A linguistics of communicative activity. *Disinventing and Reconstituting Languages, 62*, 170-195.
Van de Pol, J., & Elbers, E. (2013). Scaffolding student learning: A microanalysis of teacher–student interaction. *Learning, Culture and Social Interaction, 2*(1), 32-41.
Villarroel, V., Bloxham, S., Bruna, D., Bruna, C., & Herrera-Seda, C. (2018). Authentic assessment: creating a blueprint for course design. *Assessment and Evaluation in Higher Education, 43*(5), 840-854.
Vygotsky, L. S. (1978). Zone of proximal development: A new approach. In M. Cole, V. John-Steiner, S. Scribner, & E. Souberman (Eds. and trans.), *Mind in society: The development of higher psychological processes*. Harvard University Press.

Wegener, C., Meier, N., & Ingerslev, K. (2016). Borrowing brainpower–sharing insecurities. Lessons learned from a doctoral peer writing group. *Studies in Higher Education, 41*(6), 1092-1105.

Chapter 9
# Enhancing Learning Outcomes through a Student-Centred Learning-Teaching Process in a Master of Human Resource Management Program

Shelly Jose

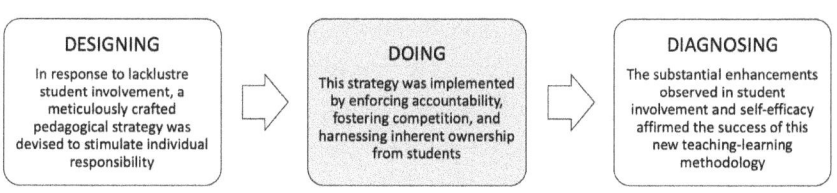

## Preamble

With his chapter, Shelly Jose contributes to this book, *Enhancing Student Learning Outcomes in Higher Education*, by showing how he enhanced students' learning outcomes through a student-centred learning-teaching process in a Master of Human Resource Management (HRM) Program. He relates to the three phases of the central ESLO model of the book in this way:

In the DESIGNING phase, the problem at hand is identified with a focus on fostering creativity, innovation, and analytical thinking amongst students. This design considers the necessity for a change management strategy targeted towards providing students with a safe psychological environment conducive to learning.

The DOING phase represents the practical application of the outlined design, employing social learning theories as the central intervention. This incorporates an innovative blend of personal accountability and collective cooperation, with a particular emphasis on amplifying student involvement as a key factor in enhancing their learning outcomes.

The DIAGNOSING phase relates to the evaluation and analysis of the intervention's success. Evident in the significant enhancement in student involvement, the efficacy of the implemented changes is assessed, highlighting the success of the outcomes. This suggests a continuous assessment loop, ensuring the effectiveness of the intervention and providing the flexibility for necessary improvements or adjustments.

## Introduction

The problem that led to my new pedagogical design, in brief, was a long-term lack of requisite student involvement and engagement in the learning-teaching process. In this chapter, I discuss a successful intervention which targeted the problem and triggered subsequent improvement in student engagement and student learning outcomes. Learning outcomes *"are designed to give a clear indication of the learning destiny that the learning opportunity provider intends the learner to reach"* (Scott, 2011:1). Drawing on this purpose, in the chapter, a learning outcome is defined as what the student has had augmented in terms of capability after successfully completing the course. It is worth noting that students acquire the necessary competencies not in isolation, but by immersing themselves in the communities and contexts in which they are learning (Kuhlthau et al., 2015). Thus, involving the immediate cohort community is a key element in the methodology used for a successful intervention.

The Master of HRM Program discussed in this chapter takes place in the context of the Indian higher education system, the evolution of which remains ongoing. Moreover, the system, largely designed by the erstwhile British administration, needs to circumvent, what could be termed 'the submissive mindset' even after 60-70 years of independence. It is alleged that much of what is ailing in the Indian higher education system could be attributable to the past (Pandya, 2014). That is, our higher education system demanded nothing more than obedient people with clerical minds who could handle the English language. Yet today, we require students who can contribute to society by original thinking.

In the Master of HRM Program under discussion here, much of the absence of student participation could be traced back to the fact that in the schooling sector, teachers likely expected their students to be passive and non-questioning. As Brinkmann (2015) notes, the majority of Indian classrooms are still characterised by rote learning techniques. As such, the primary contribution of this chapter is a demonstrated overcoming of these well-entrenched systemic deficiencies. In order to do this, Social Learning theory (Bandura, 1977) is utilised, in the context in which the progress takes place, more specifically the historical influences on the institutional psyche. The history of the British-administered past significantly influenced higher education in India (Pandya, 2014). The need to establish an education system, to produce administrators and clerks to serve the British India government, led to the establishment of universities and colleges in India. Yet, it is widely held that this education system was not intended to be of benefit in the more desired outcomes of creativity, innovation, analytic or original thinking (Basu, 1989; Khandwalla, 2014).

Business schools strive to balance academic and professional concerns because they deal with a professional pragmatic subject rather than hard science. Initially, business education generally relied on practitioners and business people for teaching (Bennis & O'Toole, 2005). However, scholars questioned the academic qualification of business education and preferred academically trained faculty members with doctoral degrees (Cheit, 1985) resulting in the proliferation of better researchers than better educators (Whetten, 2007). Of the four pillars of teaching, research, training and consultancy in the academic side of business management, teaching was the least prioritised.

Part of the reason for the criticism by executives and practitioners of the effectiveness of business education and research in the practical world (Clinebell & Clinebell, 2008; Pfeffer & Fong, 2002, 2004), is the insistence on the emphasis on scientific rigour, rather than practical relevance. Taking this insistence as their cue, the Association to Advance Collegiate Schools of Business (AACSB) revised accreditation standards in 2013 (AACSB International, 2013) in a call for moving toward professionalism. Under the themes of innovation, impact and engagement, respectively, AACSB expects business education to:

- Create value for employers and communities;
- Make a difference in business and society;

Chapter 9

- Make meaningful interactions with business professionals;
- Provide real-world learning experiences.

Being effective in the professional world has become a major element of AACSB's objective in its new standards, which requires special attention to developing various skills and the nature of learning and training processes to achieve them. Hard and soft skills have become the preference of the professional world from business graduates; hard skills include planning, organising, problem-solving, critical thinking and self-management, whereas soft skills include communication, teamwork, conflict resolution and interpersonal (Parente et al., 2012) skills.

This calls for a pedagogical shift from rote memorisation to active learning in the class. The academic community is expected to move from a teaching focus to a learning focus (Whetten, 2007). Moreover, embedding learning by doing in the learning process is also to be emphasised as the most effective path to achieving the professional acumen needed in business education (Armstrong & Mahmud, 2008). These aspirations are far removed from the contemporary reality described herein. On the one hand, the expectations are of a high order of progressive autonomy of the students, whereas the reality is one of being 'held captive' by the inhibitions of a bygone era. The primary contribution of this chapter is to demonstrate a successful transition in student learning methods (Biggs, 2011).

## *Overview of main sections and key takeaways*

Section 1 introduces the institutional background and the problem of unsuccessful student involvement in learning-teaching. Section 2 narrates the technique the faculty member used to overcome the deficiency in student involvement. Section 3 outlines the unfolding of the desired outcome and Section 4 gives a glimpse into the future course of maintaining and improving upon the success before I conclude this chapter.

Reading this chapter, you will gain the following three insights:
1. How Social Learning theory (Bandura, 1977) can be applied to mitigate the lasting impact of historical, educational contexts on current learning and teaching practices;

2. How Social Learning theory (Bandura, 1977) can inform and effect the preferred student-centred approach in higher education;

3. The importance of identifying root causes to design and implement effective solutions for improved student involvement using Social Learning theory (Bandura, 1977).

## Section 1: Background to my work with learning outcomes

With the emphasis on learning outcomes, especially in the higher education institution rankings, there was a need to shift to student-involved learning rather than teacher-centric instruction. The following explains the context in which the shift has taken place.

### *Institutional background and capability building*

The institute in question was established by the Catholic religious order Carmelites of Mary Immaculate in the southern Indian State of Kerala, dedicated to educational progress as its mission. Kerala was the first Indian state to have achieved nearly 100% literacy in the 1990s, and the institute was the first to start Social Work education in the southern region of India in the 1950s. By the turn of this century, the institute had branched off into Master of Business Administration, Master of Computer Applications, Masters in Human Resource Management and Post Graduate Diploma in Management, with a new campus, in 2001, located in the then developing outskirts of Kochi City in Kerala, India.

The institute is renowned for encouraging faculty members to improve their academic calibre. With a view to capacity building, the faculty members were exposed to the premier management institutes, such as the Indian Institutes of Management (IIMs), in a four-month faculty development program. During this program, methods including case teaching were demonstrated and encouraged as a teaching tool. The case method demands students to read cases and articles, usually running for several pages, before class discussion for active participation in the class. The case teaching method (Barnes, et al., 1994; Wassermann, 1994; Christensen & Carlile, 2009) is a major instructional method that, if handled well, can be a potent tool. Typically, students read and reflect on the case/article and often meet in small study groups before class and discuss with classmates. In class, under the probing and guidance of the faculty members, students delineate underlying issues, compare different alternatives, and finally, suggest courses of action bearing in mind the organisation's objectives or expose a concept to full dissection (Gupta, 2022).

However, this method was unsuccessful due to inadequate student preparation in the institute under discussion. As a faculty member, I would require readings to be done by the students before the class sessions. It was found that students were reluctant to read long papers running for more than about 3-4 pages. Besides the tedium of the long reading, a comprehending mode, rather than an analytic mode, was what they were used to in the earlier classes. On the other hand, for the faculty members, an interactive rather than a didactic mode (Kember & Leung, 2006) was prescribed. The students' reluctance would thwart the attempt at interaction in the class as planned by the faculty member. Precious time was lost in class, by the time the faculty member recognised that students have not read, or only a few have read and with insufficient analysis pertaining to what needs to be discussed. The students simply did not understand the method of preparing in advance and joining the process. The primary reason was that the institute attracted students from a different motivational category than the IIMs (Ray & Sinha, 2005). Usually, they must be taught the concepts before introducing the case. This is unlike the IIM students, who are expected to pick up concepts on their own or from the materials provided and apply them to more practical cases in class discussion. What is assumed as conceptual learning outside the classroom by the students, and using those concepts in the discussion as a method, became a non-starter.

In the institute, therefore, it became necessary to teach the concepts in classroom sessions, followed by cases once the concepts were clear. At the same time, student involvement in the learning-teaching process was a mandated requirement. This general requirement at higher educational levels would also be relevant for the various certifications, such as European Foundation for Management Development (EFMD) and the aforementioned AACSB, that the institution aspired towards. As a result, the faculty member faced the significant challenge in classroom sessions where the students were to be encouraged to be actively involved (Parsons & Taylor, 2011).

## Program learning outcomes

The Program Learning Outcomes of the Master of HRM Program are stated as follows:
- Our graduates will be able to generate multiple alternatives while resolving a problem or issue;
- Our graduates will be able to conceptualise the fundamentals of human behaviour.

Strategic HRM is a postgraduate course that students study in the last (fourth) semester of the Master of HRM Program (above), and its Course Learning Outcomes are as follows:
- Our graduates will be able to develop a value addition and sustenance rather than a mere transactional perspective of HR;
- Our graduates will be able to develop efficacy in analysing a strategy/strategic HRM-related article/case and appreciating its business implications;
- Our graduates will be able to analyse an organisation's Strategic HRM practices with an emphasis on suggesting improvements using the theoretical inputs gained during the course.

In addition to these stated program- and course-level learning outcomes, the context of the Strategic HRM course might be useful for the reader to understand the functional outcome of the Program. This postgraduate course started initially as a specialisation within the Personnel Management of the Master of Social Work (MSW) Program and was originally named MSW (Personnel Management) wherein the emphasis was heavily towards labour welfare, as most jobs were in the manufacturing sector. Later the course was developed independently of MSW into MA (Personnel Management & Industrial Relations) with more of a management orientation than social work orientation. In line with the nomenclature changes in the corporate world, the name was further changed to the present Master of HRM Program. Through all these name changes, the course plan and syllabus were also modified.

The students in this program are expected to study foundational courses in psychology, sociology, management and economics, in the first semester, prior to studying more specialised courses later within the Master of HRM Program such as research methods, global HRM, and strategic HRM. In addition, the program also includes field work in various organisations concurrent to their study. As part of the field work, each student spends a full day every week during the semester in the HRM departments of different organisations. The students are typically placed in entry-level human resource management jobs subsequent to their study.

## Faculty members: orientation types

I identified three different predominant faculty member orientations, in various combinations, in any particular faculty member. These orientations were emergent with the different talents and abilities of the individual and which I refer to as:

1. Student orientation;
2. Institution orientation; and
3. Subject orientation.

The student-oriented faculty members focused on student development inside and outside the classroom. They moved closely with the students in various management subject-related interactions and extracurricular activities. Those who were institution-oriented focused directly on institution building through various academic, semi-academic, industry interaction and extracurricular programs that gave visibility to the institute. The subject-oriented faculty members focused on developing knowledge, curriculum, and innovative delivery of various subjects. They attended extra training programs, both offline and online, that exposed them to other higher-standing institutes. Though the faculty members did not lose sight of all the above orientations, they did so with varying degrees of emphasis.

## The faculty member profile in the present case

In the present instance, I have ten years of industry exposure following my post-graduation. My innovations include introducing a viva-voce process for the written assignments to add accountability and to act as a check on real understanding. This was adopted by the institution more formally, as a collective effort for all subjects, with a lesser degree of effectiveness. When the viva was conducted as a mass exercise, it turned out to be more of a routine ritual than developmental tool. Indeed, the institutionalisation of a process is a poor substitute for individual attention to students which is the point of comparison. I also suggested bridging the academic-practitioner divide, for instance, through articles in *KERALA Personnel*, a publication of the professional body — National Institute of Personnel Management local chapter.

Hands-on training, such as a job evaluation assignment as part of the course on compensation management, was one of my other initiatives. The jobs at a small-scale printing press under the institute were chosen for this evaluation. I also volunteered to teach courses on business ethics and sustainable development- when it was mandated by the government that sustainability ought to be part of curricula at all levels of education in the country (Ministry of Human Resource Development, 2020). For this purpose, I attended workshops on curriculum design at the IIMs. Moreover, I had enriched my academic stock by attending various programs on strategic management, conducted by the Strategic Management Forum of India at IIM venues in different parts of the country. I also sought to operationalise the notion that knowledge needs to be constructed and not given (Bain, 2004), therefore seeking to bring about active learning (Freeman et al., 2014). Overall, I was given free rein to explore new subjects and experiment with new learning-teaching processes.

## Social Learning theory and methodology related to learning outcomes

It may be postulated that the very idea of classroom learning — as opposed to a virtual or distance mode of education (Bernard et al., 2004) — is premised on Social Learning theory (Bandura, 1977), which shifts attention to the external influences on responsiveness. The causes of behaviour in this vein are found not in the individual but in external environmental forces. Response patterns could be induced, eliminated, and reinstated by varying external sources of influence. Thus, there is an inducement by the faculty member to elicit appropriate responses from the student, reinforced by the exemplification by fellow students in the class. In the present instance, the faculty member made it a point to allocate the more conceptually complex papers to the more prepared students. Then, these more prepared students presented the allocated papers at the beginning of each module, thereby helping to stimulate the subsequent student presenters' motivation to fare even better. A similar approach to employing motivation is presented by Magitay-Becht and Herrera (2023 in this book).

Psychological functioning is best understood as a continuous reciprocal interaction between behaviour and its controlling conditions; there is a vicarious basis through observation of other people's behaviour (Bandura, 1977). When a faculty member conveys their belief that the student can accomplish self-study, analysis and presentation, this can enhance the student's confidence. Furthermore, the most accurate self-evaluations derive from comparisons with those similar in the ability or characteristic being evaluated. (Schunk, 2012). Thus, making presentations to the cohorts gives the students opportunities for comparisons and reality checks, allowing room for improvement.

## *The student feedback on teaching methodology*

The institute regularly surveyed student feedback to improve the learning-teaching process. We found that recycling any teaching and learning method all the time was less appreciated by students. For instance, too much of either lectures, presentations or cases was rated less desirable. The students seemed to prefer a balanced mix of all these methods, in line with insights on andragogy (Carney, 1986; van Rensburg, 2023 in this book). Indeed, the effective mix of active learning methods in higher education is well-established (Prince, 2004). The obvious imperative was to involve the student in the learning-teaching process, as the relation between student engagement and its relationship with various learning outcomes is well supported (Kuh, 2009).

It is also important to note that the students, especially the millennial and proximate categories, seem to prefer more by way of hands-on learning instead of lectures (Mohr & Mohr, 2017; Oblinger, 2003). The faculty members are cognisant that the lecture method retains class control (Fuller, 1969) in the hands of the faculty member. In contrast, methods — such as role play activities — hand over control entirely to the students, with other methods situated somewhere in between. The scenario that emerges is one of the various theories converging along with a new context characterised by the peculiarities of generational shifts, demanding new teaching methodologies to enhance learning outcomes in higher education settings (Ambrose et al., 2010).

## Section 2: The case of active learning

The higher education sector has been witnessing the change from the dominant teacher-centred approach to a student-centred approach. This change is exemplified, for instance, in the Europe based Tuning project (Wagenaar, 2014), following a shift from the instruction paradigm to the learning paradigm, among other changes. Some of the tenets of this paradigm change, are followed in the teaching method cited in this chapter. Such tenets include student-centred learning, rather than teacher-controlled learning, and are enacted in cooperative, collaborative and supportive learning environments, rather than competitive and individualistic notions of learning. In the new paradigm, teachers are no longer primary instructors but primary designers of learning methods and environments, especially in higher education, which requires collaborative work between faculty members and students in a spirit of teamwork; this aspect is subsequently addressed in Section 3.

### My practice towards enhancing student learning outcomes

Until 2005, the idea of learning outcomes was not given its due place in the institution. It was still teaching by instruction, rather than by student participative learning. As the institute commenced the process of opting for the various certifications, it became clearer that the pedagogy required had to change to accommodate the expectations and requirements of the educational community at large. In fact, I had experimented even earlier with the case method, having been exposed to the faculty development program at IIM Ahmedabad in 2002, wherein the inadequacies of the student preparation had caused considerable strain.

## An introduction to my practice – dilemma and solution

The dilemma was the students' reluctance to come to class having prepared by reading lengthy cases. Such reluctance resulted in the breakdown of the case method advocated by the IIMs in particular and higher education in general. The students would simply not come prepared with the readings, or even when a few had read them, they proved reluctant to speak up, because the remaining students might isolate them in a true collectivistic manner. Students made the assumption that even when they were unprepared, the faculty member would pardon them and move on with the usual lecture method- having no time to waste anyway. Because the instruction is a general one, that everyone ought to come prepared reading the articles/cases, it was not possible to adduce accountability for the lack of preparedness except in a general diffuse way.

Accountability had to be fixed individually, and thereby a sense of positive competition needed to be instilled. The inherent sense of ownership, that would be felt needed to be built into the process, as would the possibility of shame when unprepared or unable to demonstrate a certain amount of competency or even uphold the reputation of the class as a group. Avoidance of shame experiences is known to be more common and prominent in a collectivistic setting (Velayutham & Perera, 2004).

As explained earlier, part of the solution to the problem of inadequate reading was to assign different articles/cases to students for ownership, intense preparation and delivery, rather than all articles to all students. The Strategic HRM course was chosen for implementing the experiment. Part of the reason for choosing this course was that it was interdisciplinary as there were Strategy and HRM as two divisions within this course. The subject strategy needed to be introduced, whilst the HRM aspect also needed to be put forth in a different perspective through the strategy lens. The students studied the functional aspects of HRM in the first three semesters; then, the Strategic HRM course was offered to those students in the final semester of the Program. As a result of this Program structure, the Strategic HRM course brought about a positive impact on the immediate job placement of the students in the corporate organisations after their study. This positive impact is seen where one of the first implicit tasks of a new entrant would be to find their place in the direction in which the organisation is moving. At the functional level, the question that strategy is trying to answer is the alignment of the function with the organisation's overall objectives.

Though this is not necessarily the case, most discussions on strategy, even in textbooks, assumed a basic understanding of Strategy before venturing into the Master of HRM Program. However, treating the two divisions within the Strategic HRM course, namely Strategy and HRM, one after the other, would be inadequate without a proper transiting-in phase and one that integrates the two. So, this required special attention and skill on the part of the faculty member. The students had to be repeatedly instructed on the basic concepts that are unique and specific to strategy as a subject. Then, what students learned so far in the previous three semesters feeds effectively into the Strategic HRM course. This meant a focus on the theoretical discontinuities in (predominantly) Porter's (2008) environmental views of strategy and rebuilding thereof to a resource-based view (RBV) (Barney et al., 2001) of strategy. And finally, to bring in the practice of HRM with its consequents, such as organisational culture, as key intangibles acting as sources of sustained competitive advantage. The overall plan was to develop conceptual clarity of the subject strategy in the early part of the course and strategic HRM in the latter part.

## How my practice affects students' ways of learning

Articles from strategy literature and Strategic HRM were sequenced into a coherent story on strategy and Strategic HRM. The number of students in the class varied between 35 and 40. Each student could be expected to be assigned one or two related articles on a particular topic. The chosen articles were made available in a common folder for perusal and preparation by all students. The students were to prepare the specific article assigned to them and take the faculty member's guidance in one-to-one discussion before a class presentation. This way, a student 'owned and anchored' a particular paper, case or article. When presented in the class, the others benefited as if reading the article by themselves. This was followed by a class discussion. After the class, the presentation files were also made available to all in a shared folder. This way, the time that would have been wasted in searching for any reading material was at least partially offset for the students. However, the students were encouraged to search out more material on the subject to help further enrich their learning through post-class revisions. Four iterations of a topic were thus made possible. They were:

- Pre-class preparatory;
- Review of the preparation with a faculty member;
- Presentation and discussion in class;
- Own revision after class.

The students were thus automatically exposed to the article/s handled by the individual student, which required intensive reading and presentations and the remainder in extensive listening to fellow classmates' presentations. Students have benefitted from this method, as evidenced by the assessments (see Section 3). By way of criterion validation, faculty members, who evaluate the answer scripts, have commented on the consistently higher quality of the answers in this particular course on Strategic HRM over the years. Many students have also expressed, in addition to the usual evaluation, after a few years of completing the course, how they benefitted from the course in their actual job once placed in the organisations. One student also mentioned that he used some of the terms of strategy concerning HRM in a meeting, which caught the attention of the senior officers. This, in turn, contributed to the decision to give him independent charge of setting up a human resources (HR) department in an overseas site. Getting the attention of the 'higher-ups' and other functions is a challenge all HR staff face at the beginning of their careers. In terms of evaluation, this would mean that the method affected changes over and above immediate reaction, recall, behaviour and eventual results of the Kirkpatrick (2016) model. Such anecdotes go far beyond classroom learning into pragmatic results on the job arising from the competencies that the course developed.

## How I prepare and organise my pedagogy to enhance students' learning outcomes — the role of the faculty member

In their study on whether or not implementation intentions encourage changes in behaviour, when people possess powerful and somewhat hostile habits, Webb et al. (2009) found that an unstable environmental context was found to contribute to unwanted behaviour in the understanding of what brings in change in behaviour. Conversely, bringing in desirable behaviour is predicated on the frequency of the behaviour in a stable context. Following this precept, in terms of a higher education context, the task of the faculty member then is to provide the environment for the desired change in behaviour. In this method of the learning-teaching process under discussion, the role of the faculty member may be summarised as follows:

### Selecting the appropriate articles
This necessitates a survey of the latest literature on each topic, with the result that more articles are added yearly. For instance, most textbooks discuss the value chain, but this course goes beyond the chain metaphor with the shops and networks of Stabell and Fjeldstad (1998).

### Sequencing the articles
It is important to know what basic knowledge is required to comprehend a subsequent paper and sequence it in the most logical order.

### Coaching and mentoring the students one-to-one
Given the study habits of the students as one of reading and then merely reproducing in the examinations from memory, it is an uphill task for the faculty member to provide the students with skills of intensive reading with application in mind and extensive reading to complement already acquired knowledge.

### Facilitation of the transition from one article to the next
It is often unclear why one article is chosen or how one complements and extends a previous one. For instance, the article Structure is Not Organisation (Waterman et al., 1980) follows the Structuring of Organisations (Mintzberg, 1980) when it would appear more logical to have the sequencing order reversed.

**Summarising the main concepts in a seamless narrative periodically**
It is easy for the students to lose track of the articles and how one idea progresses to the next. The faculty member's role is to draw attention to the previous papers anaphorically and sometimes to read the articles to come cataphorically.

**Placing the paper within the overall topic, bridging article to article, idea to idea, and pointing out similar thoughts embedded in different articles**
Meanings are often embedded in different terminologies but essentially point to some common idea. Such terminological differences over conceptual commonalities need to be determined for increased insights into other authors' thought processes and terminologies with the result that ideas are cross-validated. For instance, 'strategic intent' (Hamel & Prahalad, 2010) translates to 'superordinate goals' in the 7s framework (Waterman et al., 1980), requiring classroom attention. Similar, is the case with 'ideology' in Mintzberg's (1980) model, which later papers drop in favour of the term 'culture' of the organisation.

**Helping the students develop presentation efficacy**
A student who 'knows but cannot present' is deficient in terms of holistic competency. Helping the students to improve their presentation skills would be imperative for their marketability.

In terms of value creation and delivery, the faculty member can also draw on the value shop metaphor (Stabell & Fjeldstad, 1998) applicable to educational institutions, the educational practice is mandated to schedule activities. The value shop metaphor applies resources in a fashion that is dimensioned and appropriate to the needs of the student's problem. In our case, this factor informed the method and the problem to be solved. That is, the lack of articulation on the part of the students, determined the choice and 'intensity' of the activities, discussion and guidance as sequenced above. Although the student and subject orientation was emphasised among the various faculty member orientations, it may be more specifically interpreted as 'institution building through student and subject orientation'. This is because, as a postgraduate professional institution, the methodology emphasises student involvement in the learning-teaching process, which is also a criterion that contributes to institution ranking exercises, as previously mentioned.

## Section 3: The change strategy that brought about the outcome

According to Nickols (2016), there are four change management strategies, and they are briefly discussed below:

- The 'Empirical: Rational' approach banks on the principle that people are rational and will follow their self-interest once revealed to them. Change is based on the communication of information and the proffering of incentives;

- The 'Normative: Re-educative' approach follows the principle that people are social beings and will adhere to cultural norms and values. Change is based on redefining and reinterpreting existing norms and values and developing commitments to new ones;

- The 'Power: Coercive' approach argues that people are basically compliant and will generally do what they are told or can be made to do. Change is based on the exercise of authority and the imposition of sanctions;

- The 'Environmental: Adaptive' approach insists that people oppose loss and disruption but adapt readily to new circumstances. Change is based on building a new environment or a climate and gradually transferring people from the old to the new one.

Generally speaking, there is no single change strategy. However, the foremost approach used in this instance may be said to be the environmental-adaptive strategy. This principle was used, however, not by a change of physical setting but by a change of the ambient process, which the faculty member guided. The scope and scale of this intervention were in terms of a 'tweaking' of systems within a unit, in this case, the classroom learning-teaching process. Regarding the degree of resistance, relatively strong resistance argues for coupling power-coercive and environmental-adaptive strategies. The faculty member's inherent privilege to apply soft persuasive power, also was used sometimes, by insisting on changes in content or delivery, or sometimes by insisting on further reading to effect the change in student behaviour. For instance, the students were encouraged to read Minzberg's (1980) original book on the 'Structuring of Organisations' rather than the summary version. Relatively longer time frames, in this case, argue for a mix of empirical-rational, normative-re-educative, and environmental-adaptive strategies. In terms of expertise, having available adequate expertise at making change argues for some mix of the strategies outlined above. Moreover, in terms of dependency, it may be argued that the student-teacher relationship by nature is one of progressive independence of the student by providing them with the ambience and guidance conducive for their development as outlined.

## Student perspective

The student feedback is taken twice a semester. It is mandatory, online and anonymous. In six months, the first feedback is taken around the first month into the classes and the second around the fourth month. Students evaluate the faculty member on qualitative as well as quantitative responses. Table 1 summarises quantitative responses (using the 6-point Likert scale) from the student evaluation conducted in January, 2019.

|   | QUESTION | AVERAGE SCORE | STANDARD DEVIATION |
|---|---|---|---|
| 1 | Always well prepared for the class | 5.16 | 0.81 |
| 2 | Could successfully relate the subject to real life | 5.23 | 0.66 |
| 3 | Encouraged me to think in depth about the subject | 5.23 | 0.75 |
| 4 | Encouraged class participation | 5.26 | 0.72 |
| 5 | Carried out continuous assessment | 5.19 | 0.74 |
| 6 | Gave enough assignments/cases | 5.26 | 0.72 |
| 7 | Provided timely feedback on assignments | 5.19 | 0.86 |
| 8 | Have good communication skills and explanation power | 5.29 | 0.73 |
| 9 | Could deliver lecture with confidence, poise and authority | 5.26 | 0.72 |
| 10 | Was available for discussion/ problem solving outside class room | 5.19 | 0.78 |

*Table 1: Quantitative evaluation by students (January, 2019).*

When the current course was first introduced, and before the methodology in discussion, the student feedback indicated that they would find the predominance of any one method tiring and not conducive to holding their attention. The student intake was also not from the same pool as the IIMs. However, it did not mean that the students were not capable. It was just that they were untrained in a system that required intense preparation prior to the class and live participation in the classroom.

Following the intervention, the students appreciated the involvement, which was not too taxing for them. Given the student profile, which was not entirely assumed to be an actively involved learning process, it was necessary to calibrate the student involvement so that it would not suddenly overburden them all. They were challenged to understand the papers all by themselves, but the faculty member was also available to fine-tune their understanding and presentation prior to the actual presentation. At the same time, the faculty member had not entirely given over the process to them. Suffice to recall that the lecture method retains the entire control in the hands of the faculty member. In contrast, the case study or article presentation method has the potential to be entirely driven by the student. In the present instance, it was a handholding by the faculty member towards student independence, akin to what Nygaard (2023 in this book) mentions as scaffolding students' development of the skills and competencies needed to thrive in the knowledge economy. They also felt the faculty member encouraged them in their development not just in the subject but also in facing an audience and communicating without hesitation and, in the process, personally becoming more competent. Indeed, the qualitative responses below clearly evidences the success of the intervention. These student comments were obtained from the same student evaluation administered in January, 2019:

- *"it is encouraging that he has been actively involved in a full-fledged teaching process and it is more resourceful as he has widened the horizon of understanding. it is good teaching"*
- *"Sir makes the topics very interesting. And uses a lot of examples to teach"*
- *"Related class with live examples"*
- *"Interactive sessions. Well prepared for the session"*

- *"Helps to do Higher order thinking"*
- *"Highly related classes with one another"*
- *"Sir thank u so much for bringing in a class with difference. And the case studies help us to relate better to the scenarios"*
- *"Sir was amazing in sem 4! We'll miss you Sir :)"*
- *"The lectures taken by sir is very good where he make [sic] us understand each and every topic"*
- *"Puts a lot of effort in getting class participation during classes"*
- *"Well prepared and able to connect the theory with practise through cases"*
- *"Sir's subject is full of us teaching the class"*

### *Teacher perspective – my reflections on learning outcomes*

The solution to most problems lies hidden in the problem itself (Prahlad & Hamel, 1990 as cited in Bhatt, 2002). In the present case, student participation was obviously a requisite, and the solution lay in trimming the subject into parts and addressing each in tranches. By assigning the students an article each, student ownership was ensured. A certain peer pressure to make the best of their ability and more tended to be created with the ownership. This way, knowledge, skill, attitude, and ownership aspects (Harden, 2002) were ensured. Those academically better were assigned the tougher papers, which would be a model for the latter ones who tended to watch and learn the content and presentation skills. The faculty member-student review interaction also augmented the skills before the presentation. It was premised on the observation that communication skills would be the vehicle for functional skills in Management (Hargie et al., 2004).

Positive behavioural engagement involving participation with enthusiasm, emotional engagement of being actively interested, and cognitive engagement of meeting or exceeding assignment requirements were, in a way, sought to be stimulated. In this way, the method supports the progressivism ideology in that the students are finally being prepared to be autonomous, and encompasses the enterprise ideology where students are given the skills to thrive in their careers and to contribute to the economy (Trowler, 2010).

## Section 4: Moving forward

Every academic year the papers are reviewed, and new ones are added. The challenge will be to keep up with the rapid changes that are happening in the subject due to the transformations happening in the HR profession. These transformations are attributable to factors such as pandemic-induced remote working, the emphasis on HR analytics and evidence-based HR. Student involvement in selecting topics and papers is another proposal whereby participation-induced involvement is expected to be enhanced even more. The student orientations down the generations must be carefully watched in a rapidly changing context. Already categories such as baby boomers, Gen X, Y and Z have been identified, spanning a period of roughly 70 years. Given the pace of changes, especially in educational media technology, the present method need not necessarily be appreciated by the coming generations.

In the spirit of moving away from traditionalism, student involvement needs to be closely matched with student orientation. Newer experiences, such as the forced online mode and the proliferation and acceptance of online courses otherwise, may present new challenges. The media/technology 'savvy' students may be more inclined towards using technology rather than teacher intervention, such as the one highlighted in this paper. Nevertheless, the teaching and learning process is said to be one of those jobs that is likely to survive the onslaught of technology-induced obsolescence.

## Conclusion

Identifying the hidden problem that does not present itself too easily and finding an appropriate, non-intrusive solution is important in human development. Creating a context of psychological safety in the process of change is also applicable in the case of student development. Some issues are not necessarily in the immediate vicinity but are historical. In the present instance, the educational system, based largely on obeying and obedience to the teachers in their earlier educational experiences, was identified as a probable reason for the students' inhibition in self-learning and speaking up. Having this clarity on the problem was important in order to work towards the solution. Students, especially in oriental cultures, may be reluctant to come out of their shells due to largely collectivistic tendencies. They can still be developed given the right kind of guidance and inputs, as evidenced in the program's success.

The technique provided the psychological safety, handholding, and progressive movement towards autonomy necessary for the students to take up jobs eventually, in the HRM profession. The root of behaviour is not within the individual but in external environmental factors. By altering stimulus and providing a new mode of interaction, new response patterns could be introduced, and old ones eliminated or desirable ones reinstated. The instructor's role becomes one of encouraging appropriate responses from the students, and Social Learning theory (Bandura, 1977) explains that these behaviours reinforce themselves through the exemplification provided by their peers. The interaction between behaviour and its controlling conditions is best understood as a continuous, reciprocal process that affects psychological functioning. Bandura (1977) argues that this is based on a vicarious process whereby people observe and learn from the behaviour of others.

The experience reiterates the importance and challenges of implementing the preferred student-centred approach in higher education. In combination with change management theories, Social Learning theory (Bandura, 1977) can be a powerful source of intervention even in times of rapid technological change with positive results in teaching and learning practices. It is also important to identify root causes beyond the immediately apparent ones to design and implement effective solutions for improved learning outcomes.

## About the Author

Shelly Jose, PhD, is Associate Professor in the Human Resource Management area at the Rajagiri College of Social Sciences, Kochi, Kerala, India. He can be contacted at this email: shellyjose@rajagiri.edu

## Bibliography

AACSB International (2013). *Eligibility procedures and accreditation standards for business accreditation.* Retrieved April 8, 2023, from http://www.aacsb.edu/-/media/aacsb/docs/accreditation/standards/businessstds_2013_update3oct_final.ashx?la=en

Ambrose, S. A., Bridges, M. W., DiPietro, M., Lovett, M. C., & Norman, M. K. (2010). *How learning works: Seven research-based principles for smart teaching.* John Wiley & Sons.

Armstrong, S. J., & Mahmud, A. (2008) Experiential learning and the acquisition of managerial tacit knowledge. *Academy of Management Learning & Education, 7*(2), 189-208.

Bain, K. (2004). *What the best college teachers do.* Harvard University Press.

Bandura, A. (1977). *Social learning theory.* Prentice Hall.

Barnes, L. B., Christensen, C. R., & Hansen, A. J. (1994). *Teaching and the case method: Text, cases, and readings.* Harvard Business Press.

Barney, J., Wright, M., & Ketchen Jr, D. J. (2001). The resource-based view of the firm: Ten years after 1991. *Journal of Management, 27*(6), 625-641.

Basu, A. (1989). Indian higher education: Colonialism and beyond. In PG Altbach & V. Selvaratnam (Eds.), *From dependence to autonomy: The development of Asian universities.* Springer Netherlands.

Bennis, W.G., & O'Toole, J. (2005). How business schools lost their way. *Harvard Business Review, 83*(5): 96-104.

Bernard, R. M., Abrami, P. C., Lou, Y., Borokhovski, E., Wade, A., Wozney, L., & Huang, B. (2004). How does distance education compare with classroom instruction? A meta-analysis of the empirical literature. *Review of Educational Research, 74*(3), 379-439.

Bhatt, G. D. (2002). Management strategies for individual knowledge and organizational knowledge. *Journal of Knowledge Management, 6*(1), 31-39.

Biggs, J. (2011). *Teaching for quality learning at university: What the student does.* McGraw-Hill Education.

Brinkmann, S. (2015). Learner-centred education reforms in India: The missing piece of teachers' beliefs. *Policy Futures in Education, 13*(3), 342-359.

Carney, T. (1986). Andragogy in action: Applying modern principles of adult learning. *Canadian Journal of Communication, 12*(1), 77–80.

Cheit E.F. (1985) Business schools and their critics. *California Management Review 27*(3), 43-62.

Christensen, C. M., & Carlile, P. R. (2009). Course research: Using the case method to build and teach management theory. *Academy of Management Learning & Education, 8*(2), 240-251.

Clinebell, S.K., & Clinebell, J.M. (2008). The tension in business education between academic rigor and real-world relevance: The role of executive professors. *Academy of Management Learning & Education, 7*(1): 99–107.

Freeman, S., Eddy, S. L., McDonough, M., Smith, M. K., Okoroafor, N., Jordt, H., & Wenderoth, M. P. (2014). Active learning increases student performance in science, engineering, and mathematics. *Proceedings of the National Academy of Sciences, 111*(23), 8410–8415.

Fuller, F. F. (1969). Concerns of teachers: A developmental conceptualization. *American Educational Research Journal, 6*(2), 207-226.

Gupta, R. (2022). Case method in teaching management – a critique. Retrieved July 2, 2023, from https://www.researchgate.net/publication/362834196_case_method_in_teaching_management-a_critique

Hamel, G., & Prahalad, C. K. (2010). *Strategic intent.* Harvard Business Review Press.

Harden, R. M. (2002). Learning outcomes and instructional objectives: Is there a difference? *Medical Teacher, 24*(2), 151-155.

Hargie, O., Dickson, D., Tourish, D., & Hargie, O. (2004). *Communication skills for effective management.* Palgrave Macmillan.

Kember, D., & Leung, D. Y. P. (2006). The influence of active learning experiences on the development of graduate capabilities. *Studies in Higher Education, 31*(2), 155-170.

Khandwalla, P. (2014). Designing a creative and innovative India. *The International Journal of Human Resource Management, 25*(10), 1417-1433.

Kirkpatrick, J. D., & Kirkpatrick, W. K. (2016). *Kirkpatrick's four levels of training evaluation.* Association for Talent Development Press.

Kuhlthau, C. C., Maniotes, L. K., & Caspari, A. K. (2015). *Guided inquiry: Learning in the 21st century.* Abc-Clio.

Kuh, G. D. (2009). What student affairs professionals need to know about student engagement. *Journal of College Student Development, 50*(6), 683-706.

Margitay-Becht, A., & Das, U. (2023). Enhancing student learning through hidden motivational learning outcomes. In K. Enomoto, R. Warner & C. Nygaard (Eds.), *Enhancing student learning outcomes in higher education.* Libri Publishing Ltd.

Mintzberg, H. (1980). Structure in 5's: A Synthesis of the Research on Organization Design. *Management Science, 26*(3), 322-341.

Mohr, K. A., & Mohr, E. S. (2017). Understanding Generation Z students to promote a contemporary learning environment. *Journal on Empowering Teaching Excellence, 1*(1), 9.

Nickols, F. (2016). Change management 101 – a primer. Retrieved August 16, 2023, from https://www.nickols.us/change.pdf

Nygaard, C. (2023). Enhancing student learning outcomes through contextualised learning activities. In K. Enomoto, R. Warner & C. Nygaard (Eds.), *Enhancing student learning outcomes in higher education*. Libri Publishing Ltd.

Oblinger, D. (2003). Boomers, Gen-Xers, and millennials: understanding the 'new students'. *Educause Review, 38*(4), 36-47.

Pandya, D. R. N. (2014). Indian education system–a historical journey. *Education, 3*(3), 46-49.

Parente, D. H., Stephan, J. D., & Brown, R. C. (2012). Facilitating the acquisition of strategic skills: the role of traditional and soft managerial skills. *Management Research* Review 35(11), 1004-1028.

Parsons, J., & Taylor, L. (2011). Improving student engagement. *Current Issues in Education, 14*(1), 1-32.

Pfeffer, J., & Fong, C. T. (2002). The end of business schools? Less success than meets the eye. *Academy of Management Learning & Education 1*(1), 78–95.

Pfeffer, J., & Fong, C. T. (2004). The business school "business": some lessons from the US experience. *Journal of Management Studies, 41*(8), 1501–1520.

Porter, M. E. (2008). The five competitive forces that shape strategy. *Harvard Business Review, 86*(1), 25-40.

Prince, M. (2004). Does active learning work? A review of the research. *Journal of Engineering Education, 93*(3), 223-231.

Ray, S., & Sinha, A. (2005). Management education: let a thousand flowers bloom amidst a hundred questions. *Decision, 32*(2), 4-17.

Schunk, D. H. (2012). *Learning theories: an educational perspective* (6th ed.). Pearson.

Scott, I. (2011). The learning outcome in higher education: time to think again? *Worcester Journal of Learning and Teaching*, (5), 1-9.

Stabell, C. B., & Fjeldstad, Ø. D. (1998). Configuring value for competitive advantage: on chains, shops, and networks. *Strategic Management Journal, 19*(5), 413-437.

Trowler, V. (2010). Student engagement literature review. *The Higher Education Academy, 11*(1), 1-15.

van Rensburg, H. (2023). Interactive practices in a library makerspace using technology to deliver positive student outcomes. In K. Enomoto, R. Warner

& C. Nygaard (Eds.), *Enhancing student learning outcomes in higher education*. Libri Publishing Ltd.

Velayutham, S., & Perera, M. H. B. (2004). The influence of emotions and culture on accountability and governance. *Corporate Governance: The International Journal of Business in Society, 4*(1), 52-64.

Wagenaar, R. (2014). Competences and learning outcomes: a panacea for understanding the (new) role of Higher Education? *Tuning Journal for Higher Education, 1*(2), 273-302.

Wassermann, S. (1994). *Introduction to case method teaching. A guide to the galaxy*. Teachers College Press, Teachers College, Columbia University.

Waterman Jr, R. H., Peters, T. J., & Phillips, J. R. (1980). Structure is not organization. *Business Horizons, 23*(3), 14-26.

Webb, T. L., Sheeran, P., & Luszczynska, A. (2009). Planning to break unwanted habits: Habit strength moderates implementation intention effects on behaviour change. *British Journal of Social Psychology, 48*(3), 507-523.

Whetten, D. A. (2007). Principles of effective course design: What I wish I had known about learning-centered teaching 30 years ago. *Journal of Management Education, 31*(3), 339-357.

Chapter 10
# The Use of Debate Cases for Enhancing Students' Reasoning Skills as Learning Outcomes

John D Branch and David Wernick

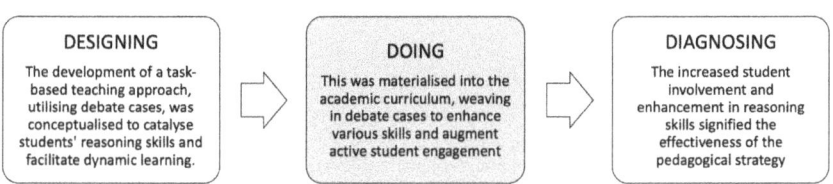

| DESIGNING | DOING | DIAGNOSING |
|---|---|---|
| The development of a task-based teaching approach, utilising debate cases, was conceptualised to catalyse students' reasoning skills and facilitate dynamic learning. | This was materialised into the academic curriculum, weaving in debate cases to enhance various skills and augment active student engagement | The increased student involvement and enhancement in reasoning skills signified the effectiveness of the pedagogical strategy |

## Preamble

With their chapter, John D Branch and David Wernick contribute to this book, *Enhancing Student Learning Outcomes in Higher Education*, by describing and discussing the use of debate cases for enhancing students' reasoning skills. They focus on the practical classroom use of debate cases, emphasising learning outcomes, especially from the student's perspective. They relate to the three phases of the central ESLO model of the book in this way:

In the DESIGNING phase, they discuss how to use debate cases to enhance students reasoning skills. They craft a creative learning framework where each debate case features a managerial dilemma with only two possible solutions. These solutions drive a debate aimed at stimulating students' reasoning skills. The authors show how their approach aims to move away from conventional teaching methods, and instead encourages active and student-centred learning, with an emphasis on experiential learning.

In the DOING phase, they explore the practicality of the designed framework by sharing personal experiences with incorporating debate case methodology into their teaching strategies. They use the argumentative structure of debate cases to exercise and enhance students' reasoning capacity, research skills, and project management skills. Additionally,

Chapter 10

debate cases encourage students to actively engage in their learning process, which ultimately leads to more effective learning.

In the DIAGNOSING phase, they reflect on the success of the debate case method from the students' point of view. The authors emphasise the importance of students' active engagement in the process, as it is a key factor in determining the effectiveness of the method. This reflection allows for a better understanding of how the students respond to the approach, and how adjustments can be made to better engage and support them in their learning.

## Introduction

Located in a leafy suburb of Peru's capital city Lima is ESAN, which is the country's leading business school, and one of the best business schools in Latin America. Twice per year (in January and June), professors from around the world descend on ESAN to teach intensive elective courses in its so-called *La Semana Internacional* (the international week). Joining students from ESAN's main campus are students from its satellites, which dot the country, students who follow its degree programmes online, and students from its exchange partner schools who are attending the electives week. The idea is simple: to globalize the curriculum of ESAN, by exposing students to different subjects, different cultures, and different pedagogical approaches.

It was at one of these *La Semana Internacional* weeks in the mid-2000s that we met…and immediately clicked. Indeed, sitting in the back of a mini-bus which was transporting us from our hotel in Lima to the ESAN campus, we bonded over 80s alternative rock, shared childhood memories of NHL legends, and most importantly, began our almost 20-year professional friendship which, for the past decade, has centred on writing and publishing debate cases.

In contrast to a traditional Harvard Business School case, whose open-ended managerial dilemma allows for seemingly limitless solutions, a debate case presents a situation in which the managerial dilemma has only two possible solutions — go or no-go — for instance, internationalise/do not internationalise, invest/do not invest. We contend that the ensuing debate about these two possible solutions is the power of a debate case for enhancing students' reasoning skills as their learning outcomes.

We define learning outcome broadly as a student's measurable achievement following a specific learning activity or an entire course of study. As suggested by the title, however, we key in on reasoning skills which, according to Kyllonen (2020), refer collectively to the *"power and effectiveness of the processes and strategies used in drawing inferences, reaching conclusions, arriving at solutions, and making decisions based on available evidence"*. Reasoning skills involve developing or evaluating claims vis-à-vis their supporting evidence and logic, which are necessary for assessing and managing situations.

## Chapter overview and key takeaways

The chapter has four main sections. In Section 1, we trace our personal histories of teaching with cases in general, and we overview the theory and practice of the case method. In Section 2, we introduce our specific uses of debate cases and detail a typical classroom debate. In Section 3, we detail the outcomes of using debate cases in the classroom. And in Section 4, we overview our plans to extend our use of debate cases in our professional practices before we conclude the chapter.

Reading the chapter, you will understand:
1. Our histories with the case method;
2. The evolution of the case method;
3. Various case formats;
4. Our specific uses of debate cases; and
5. The benefits of debates for enhancing students learning outcomes, especially their reasoning skills.

# Section I: Background to Our Work with Learning Outcomes

In this section, we trace our personal histories of teaching with cases in general, and we overview the theory and practice of the case method.

Chapter 10

*Why we started to work on enhancing students' learning outcomes*

**John**
As an engineering graduate, I began my MBA programme in 1991, being new to the case method. Unlike Ivey, IMD, or HBS, which are three of the leading 'case schools', the Faculty of Administration at the University of New Brunswick favoured more of a mixed-method pedagogy. But on reflection, the case method figured prominently in my MBA experience. For example, the mandatory strategic management course was taught entirely with cases… although that is not atypical for business schools.

During the summer of 1992, however, just before my internship at *Stomil-Olsztyn S.A. Tyre Factory* in Poland, I completed a one-week course on transitional economies at the Warsaw School of Economics. There was little by way of theory on the subject at that historic moment in time, and consequently, cases were the primary method for learning about transitional economies. In that week, I witnessed the power of the case method for enhancing student learning outcomes. Following my internship, I even wrote my own case, the subject of which was the tyre company and its transition from state ownership to a private entity.

After completing my MBA, I relocated to France to become a marketing lecturer at École Supérieure de Commerce de Rennes. I often joke that my title as lecturer was figurative, not only literal. Indeed, from the outset (despite my experience of the case method as an MBA student), my classroom was dominated by lecturing. It might have been arrogance, naïveté, or, more likely, a lack of confidence, but I considered myself the 'sage on the stage' — the walking Wikipedia in more modern parlance. I assumed my brilliance would magically or osmotically transfer to my students when I spoke. I remember spending hours scripting each 3-hour monologue with colour-coded highlights, which prompted me to change the slide, distribute a handout, or provide an example. I had learning objectives in mind, but I was oblivious to whether or not students actually achieved them.

Slowly, I began to adopt a more student-centric approach and ceded much educational responsibility to my students. I lectured less and relied more on experiential learning methods. The classroom became a kinetic space, with less of my voice dominating the 3-hour time block. I became the 'guide on the side', and the less I placed myself at the centre of attention, the more satisfied my students were… and the better they performed.

A limitation of the case method, however, emerged when I was living and working in Uzbekistan in the mid-1990s. The cases I had access to and used in my train-the-trainer sessions were about large North American multi-national companies, which typically faced North American commercial challenges, whose customers were North American. Not a single thing about these cases was familiar to my students. And not surprisingly, they had difficulty learning from the cases. In short, student learning objectives are hampered, not enhanced, when cases are not situated in contexts which are familiar to students. Consequently, I now almost always write my own cases… about companies which are known to my students, which face commercial challenges of their sort, and whose settings are culturally-proximate.

My most significant foray into case-based learning started just after joining the Ross School of Business in 2006. For two years, I served as the Director of Educational Outreach at the William Davidson Institute, a special unit of the University whose focus is the business of emerging economies. My mandate was to develop a teaching materials 'company' to rival those of Harvard Business School and the other major case producers, but with a narrower focus on international business, especially emerging markets. I hired and trained a staff of 4 case writers during my tenure there. I assembled a catalogue of more than 100 cases, notes, and other teaching materials. And I launched an e-commerce platform to distribute these materials.

**David**

My first introduction to the case method came well after I had completed my master's degree. And indeed, because my academic background was in the social sciences (political science and international affairs), cases were a novelty to me. Before formally beginning my PhD programme in 2004, I was offered a research associate position in the College of Business at Florida International University. Part of my charge was to work with the College's business instructors to help write cases. On the surface, case writing made sense, considering my experience in journalism.

Chapter 10

Nevertheless, to prepare for the position, I read numerous cases to learn their structure and format. I also attended case-writing seminars and workshops. And I began to think about using the case method to enhance student learning objectives.

Shortly after that, I was given the opportunity to co-author my own case with the dean of the College of Business. As a professor of information systems, the dean was interested in Publix Direct, the online home delivery grocery service which Publix Supermarkets launched in the late 1990s. The dean was particularly eager to document the technological aspects of the new service. We visited the Publix Direct headquarters near Atlanta for two days of meetings with the executive team, which included the company's CEO, director of finance, head of operations, and vice president of marketing. It was a fascinating experience, which gave me an insider's view of large companies' challenges when launching technology-based entrepreneurial ventures.

Although the technology aspects of Publix Direct were interesting, I found myself drawn to the strategic factors which motivated the company to make the $50 million investment. Indeed, both 'offensive' and 'defensive' factors seemed to be at play. For example, the company saw an opportunity to position itself as a leader in the emerging online grocery space. But it also wanted to protect itself from web-based grocers like Webvan, which had emerged during the dot-com era and attracted massive amounts of venture capital.

Publix Direct launched its service in South Florida in 1999, and its executive team hoped to expand quickly into central Florida and metropolitan Atlanta. Customer orders placed over the Web were fulfilled from a central distribution hub in Broward County, outfitted with the latest warehouse and communications technologies. The service seemed to strike a responsive chord among customers, who appreciated the convenience of not visiting a physical store for their weekly grocery orders. Right before the case was published in 2002, news broke that Publix Supermarkets were phasing out the venture. It was a complete surprise, and I never did discover the reasoning behind the decision. I suspect that the company decided that after the dot-com bubble burst in 2001, it no longer faced the threat of online competitors and could refocus its attention on its core, brick-and-mortar grocery business.

In any event, that first foray into case writing was an exciting experience which inspired me to want to write more cases, which I did in the years which followed. A key milestone occurred when I was asked to teach an introductory management course with an enrolment of nearly 300 students. Connecting with an audience of that size was a formidable challenge, so I embraced a student-centred 'active learning' pedagogy which included learning games, student debates, and cases, including some of my own. This seemingly novel approach resonated with the students, who appreciated my efforts to inject real-world examples and levity into what might otherwise have been a tedious, 3-hour lecture. I was convinced that I was enhancing student learning objectives. And I was rewarded with stellar evaluations and teaching awards. There was no turning back!

## Learning theory and methodology related to learning outcomes

Noted American educationalist and philosopher John Dewey popularised the concept of experiential learning in his 1938 classic *Experience and Education*. Frustrated by American public education, which he regarded as a disservice to children because of its focus on rote learning, Dewey advocated for an alternative which situated experience at the centre of education. Dewey defined learning as a mental process by which knowledge is constructed through the transformation of experience. Consequently, he believed that there is *"an intimate and necessary relation between the process of actual experience and education"* (Dewey, 1938:78).

It is the Chinese philosopher Confucius, however, who is usually credited with the invention of experiential learning. Indeed, the saying *"I hear and I forget. I see and I remember. I do and I understand"* is often quoted and, in most instances, attributed to him. But according to the website *English Language & Usage*, his compatriot, the Confucian philosopher Xunzi (340-245 BCE), ought to be dubbed the inventor of experiential learning. He wrote, "不闻不若闻之·闻之不若见之·见之不若知之·知之不若行之；学至于行之而止矣", which is translated loosely as: *"Not hearing is not as good as hearing, hearing is not as good as seeing, seeing is not as good as knowing, knowing is not as good as acting; true learning continues until it is put into action"* (Stack Exchange, 2019).

Xunzi's 20th-century equivalent is David Kolb, Professor of Management at Case Western Reserve University in Cleveland, who 'operationalised' experiential learning in his 1984 cyclical model (see Figure 1). According to Kolb (1984), people learn by progressing through an iterative cycle of four stages: 1) Concrete experience, 2) Reflective observation, 3) Abstract conceptualisation, and 4) Active experimentation (see also Bowd & Enomoto, 2023 in this book, which describes their Experiential Learning Curriculum Model, which draws on Kolb's model).

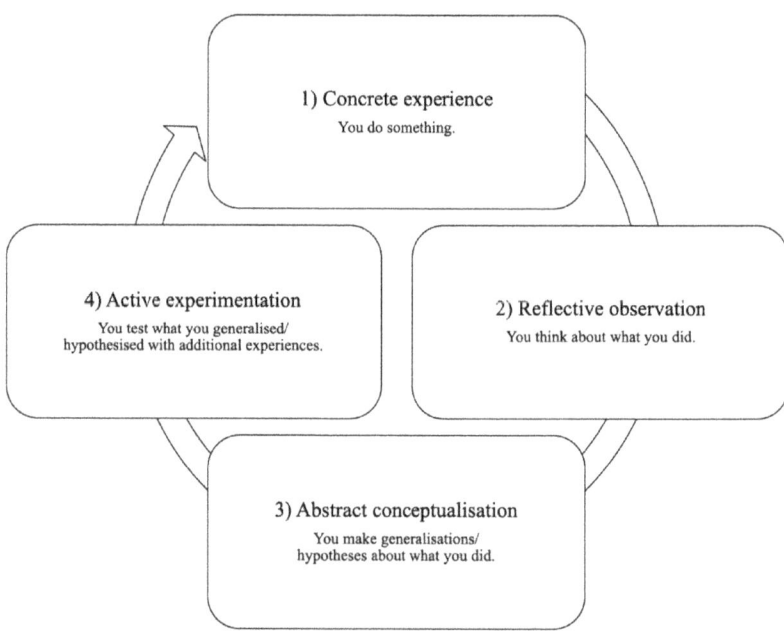

*Figure 1: The Experiential Learning Cycle (adapted from Kolb, 1984).*

We do not consider ourselves specifically as Deweyans, Confucians, Xunzians, or Kolbians (if such things exist). Nevertheless, experiential learning is the foundation of our pedagogical philosophies. Indeed, we both draw on the many pedagogical tools which leverage the power of experiential learning. These include simulations, videos, company visits, role-playing, and consulting projects. But our go-to pedagogical tool is definitely the case method.

In a nutshell, the case method provides students with simulations of real-life experiences. It pivots on Dewey's (1938) belief that there is an intimate and necessary relationship between experience and education. In the case method, students are presented with a 'story' of a critical point in the life of an organisation (the case). Students pretend that they are the protagonist in the story and must manage the critical point logically, objectively, and timely. The popular belief is that the case method originated in the late 1800s in the law school at Harvard University. Questioning the prevailing lecture method for legal instruction, its dean is said to have suggested that students might learn the law more effectively if given court proceedings to consider...if faced with real cases of jurisprudence to study and even try on their own.

Some years later, the medical school dean at Harvard University purportedly recognized his colleague's insight and adopted this idea of case-based learning. Indeed, rather than lecturing students on the ABCs of medicine — anatomy, bariatrics, and cardiology, for example — he invited instructors to provide students with the medical charts of real patients (the cases) whose illnesses they were required to diagnose and ultimately treat.

It was not until 1912, however, when the dean of Harvard Business School finally came to the idea that students could learn business and management principles from diagnosing and treating 'diseased' organisations. His challenge was that, unlike the legal and medical professions, which have systematically recorded court proceedings and patient charts, cases of these diseased organisations were not readily available. Consequently, he immediately dispatched his instructors to document these cases, a practice (case-writing) which continues today.

Whether or not this history is true, it certainly highlights the essence of the case method: a focus on organisational situations which require diagnosis and treatment. In summary, a case is a description of some organisational situation in which there is a disease. The disease can be a crisis, a problem, a challenge, an emergency, or a put-out-the-fire... although in some instances, it can also be a more positive opportunity. Either way, the case is experiential in nature, requiring the student to diagnose and treat the disease. Mirroring reality, a case is often messy and information-laden. And frequently, a case is time sensitive, with a 'call to action' which cannot be delayed by students with *"I need more information"*, *"I need more time"*, or *"Let's just wait and see"*.

Now, a traditional case (sometimes called a long case or Harvard case for obvious reasons) can reach 30 pages or even 40 pages in length. It requires significant class time to review and can be too expansive for teaching specific learning objectives. It is unsurprising, therefore, that alternatives to the traditional case have emerged throughout the last century. The mini case (or caselet), for example, is a 1-2 page narrower description of a situation which, by stripping away all the complexity of a traditional case, provides a more focused exercise for students. The incident process begins like a traditional case, highlighting a specific situation, but lacks sufficient information to make any progress, thereby prompting students to embark on research or other fact-finding missions. The action maze is a longitudinal case, which often unfolds step-by-step in an A+B+C sequence; students solve one case only to be confronted with the company's actual solution and another situation. As the name implies, a mousetrap is a case explicitly written to 'catch out' the students by revealing their faulty logic, preconceptions, or cultural biases. An illustrative case is written in a more journalistic style to illustrate some concept or theory. It requires little or no student action and might not even be considered a case in the true sense of the case method. Finally, as mentioned previously, a debate case presents a situation in which the managerial dilemma has only two possible solutions, the debate over which is the basis for classroom discussion.

## Section 2: Our practice towards enhancing students' learning outcomes

Truthfully, our entrée into the use of debate cases was not actually with debate cases. Indeed, initially, we used classic Harvard Business School cases, whose managerial dilemmas lent themselves to debates. We 'forced' two possible solutions from a case and then assigned teams of students to debate the solutions. But more recently, we have begun to author our own debate cases, with managerial dilemmas which have only two possible solutions. The following situations are the foundations of two of our latest debate cases.

On 7 September 2017, Amazon announced that it would build a second North American headquarters which was dubbed HQ2, and which, Amazon promised, would lead to a 5 billion USD investment and 50,000 high-pay, high-tech jobs (Amazon.com, 2017) The announcement also included an RFP (request for proposal) to cities around the United States and Canada. Amazon's wish list: a business-friendly environment, a highly-educated workforce, well-developed transportation options, a good quality of life, and a strong cultural fit (meaning a hip urban vibe seemingly necessary to attract 'Amazonians'). The RFP 'whipped government officials and development agents into a frenzy', who viewed it as a once-in-a-lifetime opportunity to make America's next great city. But the RFP process also created an interesting debate about the power of Amazon and other large organisations (professional sports teams, for example) to 'extract' publicly-funded concessions. Indeed, is it even appropriate for governments to subsidise private companies?

Hershey's is another large multi-national company and one of the world's leading chocolate manufacturers. Notwithstanding the company's much-touted commitment to purchase 100% certified and sustainable cocoa by 2020, and its extensive health and social welfare initiatives in cocoa-growing communities, Hershey's continues to receive 'flak'. This flak is for not doing more to curb child labour and modern slavery within its supply chain. In recent years, activists have organised and street protests against the company and launched online boycotts of its products. In a 2018 development, consumers filed a class-action lawsuit in the state of Massachusetts, claiming that the chocolate maker had violated the state's Consumer Protection Act- by not disclosing the use of children and slave labour to harvest cocoa (govinfo.gov, 2023). Hershey's claims that it has done nothing illegal and, indeed, that it is doing more than other companies in the industry. Do more or carry on? That is the debate.

Like any tool, however, a debate case can be used in various ways and for different educational purposes. The most obvious application of a debate case is for instruction— as the basis for an entire course session, with teams of students debating the two possible solutions. Perhaps less obviously, however, a debate case can also be used for assessment, as a final examination, for example, requiring students to 'take a stance' and argue one possible solution or even present their arguments for both possible solutions.

I (John) tend to use debate cases as part of a broader array of pedagogical tools. For example, I teach a course entitled BA500 Business Immersion for newly-matriculated students in a 1-year Master of Management programme. The students (about 120 in recent years) have no business or economics undergraduate training. Consequently, the course aims to help them learn a new language and culture by immersing them in business. Secondarily, but importantly, the course also aims to help the students enculturate into the business school regarding academic expectations, classroom norms, and so on. The course contains a mixture of lectures, exercises, projects, mini-cases and computer-based simulations, for instance. I use the Hershey's case in one of the first course sessions to: 1) introduce the students to the case method; 2) to establish the norms of classroom action and engagement; and 3) to reinforce the notion that, unlike in the physical sciences which rely on exactitude, there is often no correct answer in business school. I assign one team to each of the two possible solutions:

- Affirmative: Hershey's ought to stay the course with its present anti-poverty and sustainability initiatives in West Africa. It is doing its part to combat child labor; no further action is required.

- Negative: Hershey's ought to do more to combat the problem of child labor in West Africa. It is not meeting its obligations to its shareholders or stakeholders, and its practices are inviting reputational risk.

All teams have 60 minutes during the course session to prepare. Two randomly-selected teams (one affirmative and one negative) are then given 5 minutes each to present. Following the presentations, I open up the debate to other students.

I (David), on the contrary, generally use debate cases more systematically, often building a complete course with the debate format as the centrepiece. In my MBA-level international business course, for example, there is one debate in each course session, except the introduction and conclusion sessions. I mostly use debate cases which John and I have authored. A recent example is our case, *To Burn or Not to Burn: Louis Vuitton's Headstock Dilemma*. Although rarely discussed publicly, destroying unsold inventory — 'deadstock' in industry parlance — is a well-known practice among luxury goods makers. Indeed, industry titans such as LVMH, which owns Louis Vuitton, Dior, and Givenchy, go to great lengths to protect the exclusivity of their brands, by keeping their products out of the hands of those who obviously cannot afford them, and away from counterfeiters. For many luxury fashion houses, gathering surplus items and samples periodically and then carting them off to the incinerator is the most efficient way. Some governments even provide tax incentives for the practice. But the destruction of perfectly usable merchandise — particularly items of impeccable quality and craft — is ripe for debate. One team is assigned to each of the two possible solutions:

- Affirmative: Louis Vuitton ought to maintain its policy of destroying deadstock. The business risks of opting for a different course of action outweigh the potential rewards.
- Negative: Louis Vuitton ought to abandon its policy of destroying deadstock. The practice has become a liability in today's environment, and the company must change with the times.

The two teams have one week to prepare and are expected to conduct research outside the case. During the course session, each team presents arguments in an opening salvo. Time for rebuttal is then provided to the teams. The session ends with a Q&A.

In a few instances, the debate cases are more like the incident process case alternative described previously. I raise a specific situation, often 'ripped from the headlines', and the students have the week to research their possible solution. In one course session, for example, the debate centred on Apple's continued relationship with Taiwanese contract manufacturer Foxconn and its factories in China. The ongoing bluster of both the Chinese and American governments adds interesting context to the debate. And, of course, the lingering effects of the COVID-19 pandemic cannot be forgotten. One team is assigned to each of the two possible solutions:

- Affirmative: It makes business sense for Apple to move iPhone production out of China. While manufacturing in China made sense at one time, rising labor costs, growing trade tensions with the United States, and other issues have eroded China's appeal as a manufacturing hub. Apple ought to move on.
- Negative: It makes business sense for Apple to maintain iPhone production in China. No other country offers the same attractions, including an enormous labor force, high-quality manufacturing, and an ecosystem of suppliers. Apple ought to stay put.

Chapter 10

## How our practice affects students' way of studying

It ought to be obvious that debates are different from the traditional teaching mode, in which the instructor's role is 'sage on the stage', and students sit passively or, at best, transcribe lectures into their notebooks which they read later. Indeed, debates capture the spirit of so-called active learning, which has penetrated higher education in the last two decades, and which represents a profound shift from transmission-based teaching to student-centred learning.

First and perhaps most plainly is that debates are experiential in nature. They are simulated experiences but experiences nonetheless. Debates situate this experience at the centre of education, à la Dewey. Students must reckon with experience by pretending to be the protagonist in the debate case and, consequently, construct knowledge. Debates doubtless encapsulate the Deweyian idea that there is an intimate and necessary relation between the process of actual experience and education.

However, debates are also engaging, injecting elements of competition, emotion, and fun into the classroom. And debates can also be engaging for audience members, not only because of Q&A but by assigning them as judges or requiring them to provide feedback to the debating teams. The experiential nature of debates, therefore, is the power of debate cases to enhance students' learning outcomes… beyond simple note-taking and reading.

Key among the learning outcomes of debates is reasoning skills. In a debate, reasoning skills are the essence of the relation between the process of actual experience and education. Transmission-based teaching requires students to remember information— the lowest level of cognitive skill (*Remembering*) on Anderson and Krathwohl's (2001) taxonomy for learning, teaching, and assessing. But a debate hinges on creating arguments to defend one of the two possible solutions, thereby elevating students to the highest taxonomy level (*Creating*). Indeed, this creation of arguments requires such cognitive skills as generating, hypothesising, planning, designing, producing, and constructing.

Buttressing the *Creating* cognitive skills is evidence. The strength of an argument is dependent on both its logic and credibility. And credibility is buttressed with support by way of statistics, citations, and other types of information. With debates, students — many of whom might be called 'digital natives' — become more discerning information consumers, which is imperative when all human history is simply one click away. They improve their research skills.

Transmission-based teaching is often a lonely enterprise. Students might be seated together in a classroom, but interaction is limited. Post-classroom interaction is likewise limited... picture a student sitting alone in a library, reading notes or solving problem sets. It is ironic because real life is a 'team sport'. Debates demand interaction; students must work together, creating and presenting their arguments to defend one of the possible solutions. Teamwork is a staple of debates.

Teamwork requires project management — coordinating resources, including time, energy, people, information, and focus. This project management is needed in the debate preparation stage and during the debate itself. And, of course, debates allow students to practice their communication skills, both written and oral.

To summarise, using debate cases affects students' way of studying, according to what many in the debate world call the three Ms: matter, method, and manner (Youth Debating in Victoria, 2023). Matter is the content of the debate, the forcefulness of which depends on reasoning skills in combination with evidence. Method refers to the narrative of the debate stance. How was the stance structured? Did it flow? Was it logical? And manner alludes to presentation style: body language, tone, executive presence, and so on.

## How we prepare and organise our pedagogy to enhance students' learning outcomes

As mentioned previously, a debate case can be used in various ways and for different educational purposes. The following, however, provides details of the structure of a typical classroom debate, as per my (David) MBA-level international business course syllabus:

### Debate
Students will participate in one team debate during the course, which counts for 15% of their final grade (75 points). Debates are based on cases that the instructor assigns. During the first class session, students

will be informed of their team assignments, cases, and debate positions. On the day of their debate, two teams will square off against each other to persuade the professor and the class audience that their position is correct. The instructor will evaluate each team's performance and assign a grade. Grades will be based on the following criteria:

- Quality of arguments, both oral and written (60%)
- Preparation (15%)
- Communication (15%)
- Time management (10%)

The debates will begin with each team presenting a 3-minute opening statement. This statement should summarise the team's position on the case and provide compelling evidence to support their argument. It should demonstrate a thorough understanding of the nuances of the case but not recount the basic facts of the case. Participants are encouraged to do research outside the case and incorporate this information into their opening statement. Next, each team will offer a two-minute rebuttal. These rebuttals should highlight logical fallacies, errors, inconsistencies, and other weaknesses in their opponent's argument.

- A team's rebuttal is NOT a second opening statement and should be used to counter arguments made by their opponent in their opening statement, rather than to advance new ideas or repeat arguments made in the team's own opening statement.

Following the rebuttals, there will be a Q&A session wherein the instructor poses questions to each team and selects questions from the class audience. Finally, each team will deliver a three-minute closing statement in which they summarise the main arguments they have made during the debate. Following the closing statements, the audience will vote via secret ballot for the team they thought put forth the most persuasive arguments. Winning teams will be awarded bonus points.

Sequence for debates:
1. Opening statements (3 mins per team)
2. Rebuttals (2 mins per team)

3. Q&A (30-45 mins total)
4. Closing statements (3 mins per team)
5. Class votes for best presentation

Notes:
1. Each team should create a deck of PowerPoint slides to accompany their opening statement. Both the opening statement and the PPT slides MUST be emailed to the instructor via Canvas 36 hours prior to their debate (i.e., 11:59 pm on Tuesday). Failure to do so will result in a 10-point penalty.

2. An electronic copy of each debate team's opening statement must be uploaded to Canvas for the opposing team to view at least 36 hours prior to their debate (i.e., 11:59 pm on Tuesday). Failure to adhere to this rule will result in a 10-point penalty. The closing statement need not be posted in advance.

3. The opening statement delivered in class may not substantially differ from the one posted to Canvas prior to the debate.

4. Debaters should NOT read their opening and/or closing statements. These statements should be delivered extemporaneously or with the aid of note cards.

5. Each student on a team must have a speaking role in the debate, and oral contributions should be roughly proportional (i.e., no single student should dominate the debate).

6. ALL students, including those on teams not participating in a given debate, are expected to read and study the cases and come to class prepared to participate by asking thoughtful questions to the debaters.

**Peer evaluation**
Each student must complete a confidential peer evaluation to assess their teammates' contributions to the team project (evaluation form available in Canvas). Students will be asked to rate the performance of their teammates with respect to effort and initiative, dependability, and contribution

to research and writing. The instructor will use these evaluations to determine whether to penalise individual students for subpar performance. Peer evaluations are due on the day of the debate and should be handed to the instructor in a sealed envelope. Students failing to turn in a peer evaluation will receive a zero for the team project — with no exceptions.

**Debate evaluations**
For each of the four debates in which a student is a spectator, they must complete a debate evaluation form and submit it electronically by the end of class. The form asks students to evaluate the preparation and persuasiveness of each debate team and offer substantive feedback. Students failing to provide substantive commentary (as determined by the instructor) will NOT receive credit. A selection of these student comments may be shared with the debate teams when they receive their formal feedback and grade from the instructor.

## Section 3: The outcome

Although we have conducted no formal evaluation of a typical classroom debate, anecdotal evidence suggests that our use of debate cases is effective from a student perspective in a number of dimensions. The experiential nature of the classroom debates reinforces Dewey's central thesis — that knowledge is constructed through the transformation of experience. We often say that learning is an activity, not a passivity. And indeed, from our vantage point, you can 'see' the student learning manifesting itself in the kinetic action of the debate, from the opening salvos to the Q&A.

The debates are also highly engaging; consequently, the students appear to take more responsibility for their learning. I (John) even witnessed a group of students in the business school building one Friday night, opting to work on their debate rather than enjoying the normal festivities of an undergraduate weekend. The engagement is also extended to audience members, who are definitely more motivated to participate actively in the Q&A, and whose feedback to debate teams demonstrates that a debate has absorbed them. Incidentally, responses to the unstructured questions on end-of-semester course evaluations often include mention of the debates.

As mentioned previously, debates can inject elements of competition, emotion, and fun into the classroom. And we see that the inherent competition in a debate motivates students to perform. But there is also weekly competition, with each pair of debate teams trying to outdo the teams from previous iterations. The debates are certainly emotional activities, and are a very enjoyable deviation from the traditional (mundane) classroom. We sense that students' learning outcomes are enhanced as a result of these emotions, mirroring educational theory, which suggests that deeper learning occurs when students are affectively charged (see Science Daily, 2015, for example).

Concerning matter, method and manner (the 3 Ms), we are convinced that the debates enhance students' reasoning, narrative, and communication skills. More specifically, we see that students' arguments strengthen week by week. Indeed, their ability to articulate a logical and compelling stance improves with each debate. And this occurs not only as a result of the debates directly, but also because those students who are audience members are engaged in the Q&A, serve as judges, and/or provide feedback to the debating teams. Their reasoning skills are also enhanced because a debate forces students to consider the opposite stance, even if that is not their natural inclination. And a debate enhances students' reasoning skills as learning outcomes because it pushes students to create and consider alternative arguments supporting a stance, conjuring up the old saying that 'there are many ways to skin a cat'.

Similarly, students' ability to buttress their arguments with evidence raises with each debate. They become more discerning about which types of information lend more credibility to their arguments. They improve their research skills, and they progress in their ability to leverage the information to augment their arguments. Likewise, we see these improvements among all students, not just in the debaters. The following assessments in the peer feedback clearly evidence the enhancement of reasoning skills as learning outcomes:

- *"Team 1 Presented information from many different sources and supported all of their arguments with proper data. They did research outside the scope of the case study, which allowed them to give knowledgeable answers throughout the debate. They presented graphs and many visual aids during the opening statement, which kept me engaged."*

- "Team 2 verbally presented convincing data, with Matthew providing a detailed analysis regarding the business advantages of staying in China. Matthew's analysis of the 10k statement was crucial in quantifying the debate and provided real data towards the significance in China."

Switching to the method which we utilised, we also believe that the debates impact students' skills in structuring a stance. Indeed, the difference between the first and final debates is remarkable. The flow improves considerably, the narratives tighten, and the opening salvos and concluding statements become more forceful. As before, we see these improvements in all students, not only in the debaters alone. The following assessments in the peer feedback evidence the enhancement of skills in structuring a debate stance:

- "Team 2 did an amazing job. First, they knew how to respond to ethical questions. They were able to take the question and make the other team think twice about answering correctly. They we also able to stay true to their points and never deviated off topic. They had key points they wanted to present and got their point across."
- "Team 2's closing statement was also impactful and integral to the validity of their argument. By presenting firm facts and summarizing their most convincing points, Team 2 solidly closed their presentation."

In terms of manner, we are confident that students' communication skills are enhanced due to the debates. Any presentation (oral or written) is an opportunity for improvement. But the unique nature of a debate requires purposeful choices in tone, body language, word choice, for example. In our experience, it is the students who are audience members who often learn more than the debaters themselves, because the requirement to provide feedback elevates their sensitivity to the various aspects of manner. Debates also demand extemporaneous communication skills—the ability to 'think on your feet'. Indeed, addressing the opposing team's arguments, responding to rebuttals, and answering questions all require mental agility. The following assessments in the peer feedback evidence the enhancement of communication skills:

- "In terms of improvement, one of the speakers for Team 1 read off a sheet of paper, and that may have debilitated confidence that she was truly knowledgeable on the subject matter. Moreover, some of the speakers took defensive and antagonist tones at times. Perhaps, calm and collected attitudes may have been more conducive to the debate environment."

- "Team 2 also sped through their PowerPoint, making it difficult for the audience to retain the speaker's argument and the statistical data."

In addition to the 3 Ms, a typical classroom debate also enhances students' abilities to work in teams. Indeed, both the preparation and presentation of a stance are highly dependent on teamwork. And, of course, the persuasiveness of a stance, and consequently the outcome of a debate, reflect how students can work as a team to convince the judges. The following assessments in the peer feedback evidence the enhancement of students' teamwork abilities:

- "Team 2 demonstrated a lot of teamwork by supporting each other's arguments and complementing their ideas. They were very organized in the structure in which they were going to present, making the transitions very smooth between participants."

- "Conclusively, some of the members on Team 2 seemed to be better prepared to answer questions than others, perhaps in the future, they should distribute the workload a bit better."

## Teacher perspective – our reflections

The students of Gen Z are digital natives and, consequently, as the argument goes, have a limited attention span. According to research by Yahoo and OMD Worldwide (Lebow, 2022), people of this generation lose their active attention after 1.3 seconds. Our colleagues, therefore, often complain that teaching today is much more difficult – how do we keep our students engaged?

Our experience using debate cases, however, seemingly negates this conception of Gen Z students as the most difficult generation to teach. Indeed, we have witnessed extremely high engagement in the classroom debates, with both the debaters and the students who are in the audience. The question about engagement, therefore, might be less about the students and more about the choice of a pedagogical tool. It might suggest that action-based learning, which has taken off in many disciplines, might be even more important for enhancing GEN Z students' learning outcomes. For other examples of student engagement, see Sarccucci (2023 in this book) who describes his use of gamified low-stakes testing in a managerial accounting programme and van Rensburg (2023 in this book) who illustrates the use of her library makerspace in problem-centred projects.

That said, we have also recognised, through our widespread use of debate cases in recent years, that over-indexing on any single pedagogical tool can be dangerous. Debate cases are not a panacea. On the contrary, a mixed-method approach is almost always more appropriate because it acknowledges that different students have different learning styles, require different pacing, and are more or less comfortable in social situations. Taking a universal design mentality when designing courses (see Branch & Martina, 2013) can improve the probability that all students' learning outcomes will be enhanced.

## Section 4: Moving Forward

Our continued use of debate cases is a testament to our faith in their power to enhance students' reasoning (and other) skills as learning outcomes. However, we also recognise that other alternatives to debate cases would benefit students differently because their formats would enhance different learning outcomes. Consider the classic Harvard Business School case, for example, whose format triggered our use of debate cases. There is certainly educational value in the open-ended managerial dilemma of a classic Harvard Business School case. Indeed, seemingly limitless solutions to the dilemma would enhance students' ability to cope with the ambiguity of business.

Consequently, we have begun to author more traditional Harvard Business School cases. For example, I (David) spent my sabbatical at the University of Galway in Ireland. While there, I researched the Irish whiskey industry, which has seen a resurgence in recent years. In the early 20th century, Irish whiskey accounted for about 60% of global whiskey consumption. However, its market share plummeted to 3% following the Irish War of Independence and the prohibition of alcohol in the United States. The case which I have planned will detail the history of the Irish whiskey industry and then enumerate the various actions which individual distilleries, and the industry as a whole, have taken to rebound. The managerial dilemma will be forward-looking, focusing on what ought to be done now to continue the industry's growth.

I (John) am writing a traditional Harvard Business School case about Go Engineer, a reseller of CAD software, 3D printers, and associated wares. Go Engineer has grown in recent years due in part to the organic growth of computer-aided design and manufacturing and as a result of strategic acquisitions. But the company faces a managerial dilemma about its future. Although reselling has been its bread-and-butter, margins are thinning, and the company receives more and more calls for highly profitable technical advice and engineering services. Plus, there appear to be opportunities in the printing-on-demand industry, which is growing by leaps and bounds, as more and more companies engage in fast prototyping.

Our experiences living and working abroad have also led us to conclude that, despite its spread around the world, the case method continues to be contextually limited, which Nygaard (2023, in this book) also recognises as an issue in higher education more generally. Indeed, the experience I (John) had in the mid-1990s remains the same: most cases are often about large North American multi-national companies, which typically face North American commercial challenges, whose customers are, err, North American.

Consequently, we have begun developing a case-writing workshop to 'take on the road'. In the mid-2000s, I (John) developed and delivered a case-writing workshop for professors at Moscow State University. I also delivered the workshop to professors at various Filipino universities as part of a government-funded programme to enhance their pedagogical skills. It led to more than 100 cases about companies, entrepreneurs, and not-for-profit organisations in the Philippines. The idea here would be to partner with a regional business school, which can serve as both a recruiter of participants and a workshop host. We already have interest from ESCA, the leading business school in Morocco, and are exploring partnerships in Asia and South America.

## Conclusion

Reflecting on our chapter reminds us of Ralph Waldo Emerson's insight that life is a journey, not a destination. Indeed, our use of debate cases for enhancing students' reasoning skills — as learning outcomes — has evolved over many years, emerging from our personal histories of teaching with cases to become one of our go-to pedagogical tools. And our specific use of debate cases, in which two teams are pitted against each other to argue one of two possible solutions, remains in a permanent state of flux. Although we believe that the outcomes of using debate cases in the classroom are powerful, especially in contrast to more traditional instructor-centric pedagogical tools, we continue experimenting with variations on the central theme. And more recently, we have opened ourselves up to other alternative case formats, recognising their benefits for enhancing students' learning outcomes.

## About the Authors

John D Branch is Clinical Associate Professor of Business Administration at the Stephen M. Ross School of Business at the University of Michigan, USA. He can be contacted at this email: jdbranch@umich.edu

David Wernick is a Teaching Professor in the Department of International Business at the College of Business at Florida International University, USA. He can be contacted at this email: wernick@fiu.edu

## Bibliography

Amazon.com (2017). Amazon Opens Search for Amazon HQ2 – A Second Headquarters City in North America. Retrieved July 9, 2023, from https://press.aboutamazon.com/2017/9/amazon-opens-search-for-amazon-hq2-a-second-headquarters-city-in-north-america

Anderson, L., & D. Krathwohl (Eds.) (2001). *A taxonomy for learning, teaching, and Assessing: a revision of Bloom's taxonomy of educational objectives*. Allyn & Bacon.

Bowd, K., & Enomoto, K. (2023). Bringing employability to life: Developing employability skill sets and understandings as student learning outcomes. In K. Enomoto, R. Warner & C. Nygaard. (Eds.), *Enhancing student learning outcomes in higher education*. Libri Publishing Ltd.

Branch, J., & Martina, A. (2013). Universal design for learning in higher education. In C. Nygaard, J. Branch & C. Holtham (Eds.), *Learning in higher education – Contemporary standpoints*. Libri Publishing Ltd.

Dewey, J. (1938). *Experience & education*. Kappa Delta Pi.

Govinfo.gov (2023). *18-10360 – Tomasella v. The Hershey Company et al.* Retrieved July 9, 2023, from https://www.govinfo.gov/app/details/USCOURTS-mad-1_18-cv-10360/context

Kolb, D. (1984). *Experiential learning: experience as the source of learning and development*. Prentice-Hall.

Kyllonen, P. (2020). Reasoning skills. *Oxford Research Encyclopedias*. Oxford University Press.

Lebow, S. (2022). Gen Z has a 1-second attention span. That can work to marketers' advantage. *Insider Intelligence*, 15 December 2022. Retrieved July 9, 2023, from https://www.insiderintelligence.com/content/gen-z-has-1-second-attention-span-work-marketers-advantage/

Nygaard, C. (2023). Enhancing student learning outcomes through contextualised learning activities. In K. Enomoto, R. Warner & C. Nygaard (Eds.), *Enhancing student learning outcomes in higher education*. Libri Publishing Ltd.

Saccucci, F. (2023). How increased volume of low-stakes testing improved student engagement and performance without additional grading burden. In K. Enomoto, R. Warner & C. Nygaard (Eds.), *Enhancing student learning outcomes in higher education*. Libri Publishing Ltd.

Science Daily (2015). How emotions influence learning and memory processes in the brain. *Science Daily*. Retrieved July 9, 2023, from https://www.sciencedaily.com/releases/2015/08/150806091434.htm

Stack Exchange (2019). Origin of 'I hear, and I forget. I see and I remember. I do, and I understand.'? Retrieved July 9, 2023, from https://english.stackexchange.com/questions/226886/origin-of-i-hear-and-i-forget-i-see-and-i-remember-i-do-and-i-understand

van Rensburg, H. (2023). Interactive practices in a library makerspace using technology to deliver positive student outcomes. In K. Enomoto, R. Warner & C. Nygaard (Eds.), *Enhancing student learning outcomes in higher education*. Libri Publishing Ltd.

Youth Debating in Victoria (2023). The three M's. Retrieved July 9, 2023, from https://youthdebatinginvic.tripod.com/the three M's.htm

Chapter 11

# Bringing Employability to Life: Developing Employability Skill Sets and Understandings as Student Learning Outcomes

Kathryn Bowd and Kayoko Enomoto

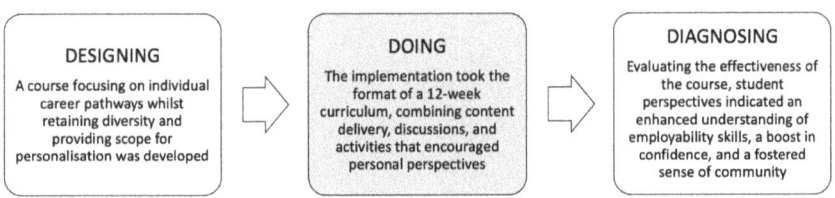

## Preamble

With their chapter, Kathryn Bowd and Kayoko Enomoto contribute to this book, *Enhancing Student Learning Outcomes in Higher Education*, by showing how they enhance student learning outcomes in a first-year undergraduate course that specifically focuses on unpacking the notion of employability. They relate to the three phases of the central ESLO model of the book in this way:

In the DESIGNING phase, they describe the curriculum design of a first-year course that aims to develop students' employability skill sets and understandings as learning outcomes, whilst raising their awareness of existing areas of strength, particularly in relation to transferable skills and personal attributes. The diversity of student interests is a significant consideration in the design phase, allowing for personalised learning experiences in the course.

In the DOING phase, they put the developed strategy into motion over a 12-week curriculum. Each week explores a different employability-related topic, offering a comprehensive blend of delivered content, activities, and discussions. Students are encouraged to express their perspectives, while the assessments linked to the course learning outcomes further allow for personalisation.

In the DIAGNOSING phase, they evaluate the course's effectiveness in enhancing students' understandings of employability. The evaluation demonstrates the benefits of their Experiential Learning Curriculum Model implemented in the course to build students' employability skill sets and facilitate their understanding of employability. The feedback shows promising signs of improved student confidence and increased employability awareness, as well as fostering a sense of community among the first-year students, indicating the success of the curriculum design.

## Introduction

In our chapter, we focus on a first-year undergraduate course called *ARTSEXP 1001 — Crafting Careers* (hereafter *ARTSEXP 1001*) which is taught at the University of Adelaide, Australia. The course addresses a common knowledge limitation among early-year undergraduate students. It teaches them how to engage with employability-focused understandings, tools and skill sets, which help them position themselves for entry into their chosen professional fields. To improve students' employability (Yorke, 2006; Knight & Yorke, 2004), we embedded the development of various tools and skills in the curriculum design of *ARTSEXP 1001*. Our definition of employability is multifaceted, comprising a range of transferable skills and personal attributes, which we refer to as employability skill sets (as shown in Figure 1). *ARTSEXP 1001* has specific learning outcomes that align with this notion of employability. In this chapter, we demonstrate how we enhance each of these employability-related learning outcomes using a theory-informed Experiential Learning Curriculum Model.

As educators in higher education, we often encounter the reality that, for many students beginning an undergraduate degree, their understanding of employability extends only as far as tools such as resumes and portfolios, and to a fairly broad understanding of the value of a high Grade Point Average and good communication skills. Indeed, students' understanding of employability is often limited to tangible tools, and many are less aware of the importance of non-tangible employability skill sets (Figure 1) and how these can significantly strengthen their employability.

Furthermore, first-year students tend to demonstrate limited awareness of, and even underestimate the value of, the skills and attributes they already possess through existing paid work and voluntary and community activities. This lack of a broader understanding, on the part of the students, of what employability involves motivated us to contemplate:

1) how we can effectively raise their awareness of employability skill sets; and

2) what they can do to start developing these skill sets from the beginning of their undergraduate studies.

Set against this backdrop, we implemented the Experiential Learning Curriculum Model in *ARTSEXP 1001*, designed primarily for students enrolled in Arts-based degree programs. Such programs are not directly linked to specific career pathways, unlike degrees in Dentistry, Nursing, Law, Accounting, and Engineering, for instance. Considering this Arts-specific situation, the first-year *ARTSEXP 1001* course curriculum and assessment tasks were designed to enable a total of six course learning outcomes at the end of a 12-week semester.

## Chapter overview and key takeaways

Section 1 provides a brief overview of experiential learning and explains how our pedagogical approach adopted in *ARTSEXP 1001* is underpinned by experiential learning theory (Kolb, 1984). Then, in Section 2, we describe our theory-informed Experiential Learning Curriculum Model. We detail how our Model is implemented through a 12-week semester, and how each element contributes to specific student learning outcomes. This is followed by Section 3, in which we explore student responses to this Experiential Learning Curriculum Model. Finally, in Section 4, we consider how this Model might be extended to other disciplinary areas and higher education institutions before concluding our chapter.

Reading our chapter, you will gain the following three insights:
1. How students can begin developing employability skill sets and understandings related to individual employability and career pathways from the beginning of their degree;

2. How our Experiential Learning Curriculum Model can be used to build students' employability skill sets and facilitate their understanding of employability;

3. How a first-year, cohort-based and scaffolded Experiential Learning Curriculum Model can help individualise and support students' aspirations towards their career goals.

## Section 1: The background to our work with learning outcomes

Learning and teaching at the University of Adelaide are underpinned by a series of strategic priorities under the banner of a strategic plan titled: *Future Making*. As part of this, and in accordance with Australian Federal Government priorities, employability-based learning has become a more explicit focus of learning and teaching activity, alongside discipline knowledge-based learning. For example, one of the five pillars in the Strategic Plan, "*A 21$^{st}$-century education for a growing community of learners*" (University of Adelaide, 2021a:11), identifies the improvement of graduate employability as a priority, and an aim of including work-integrated learning opportunities in all programs across the university.

Thus, there has been an increasing strategic push towards employability-based learning outcomes at the university. However, whilst the links between discipline learning and employability outcomes are relatively clear in some areas, in others, such as Arts-based disciplines, the links are less prominent and not immediately evident, largely because employment opportunities are significantly more diverse. This means that a 'one-size-fits-all' approach to fostering employability is unlikely to be effective. A more individualised approach may be more appropriate, reflecting the diversity of opportunities and learning outcomes of Bachelor-level study in Arts disciplines. Supporting students to develop their understanding of 'connections' between learning outcomes and employability, and how they can build their employability both during and alongside university learning activities, provides a way to reflect this diversity and position students as lifelong learners.

Furthermore, lifelong learning is integral to the University of Adelaide Graduate Attributes. The university website articulates that these attributes are not just curriculum-based but are *"also developed within the total university experience, as they encourage students to reflect on the broader purpose of their university education"* (University of Adelaide, 2022). The University Graduate Attributes are as follows:

1. Deep discipline knowledge and intellectual breadth;
2. Creative and critical thinking and problem-solving;
3. Teamwork and communication skills;
4. Professionalism and leadership readiness;
5. Intercultural and ethical competency;
6. Australian Aboriginal cultural competency;
7. Digital capabilities;
8. Self-awareness and emotional intelligence (University of Adelaide, 2022).

Most of these attributes can be directly or indirectly linked to employability in a graduate's chosen field. However, the fact that only one graduate attribute explicitly references discipline knowledge strongly indicates the perceived importance and value of broader skills and understandings. This can be seen, for example, in the Adelaide Digital Capabilities Framework, which consists of six areas of proficiency — including digital learning, information and media literacies, and digital identity (University of Adelaide, 2021b). These capabilities can be applied to a wide range of professional fields. In other words, these Graduate Attributes statements clearly point to the importance of building student employability skill sets by facilitating an individualised understanding of the connection between learning outcomes and employability, and a sense of the career possibilities associated with their degree. As a result, these Graduate Attributes provide a useful, well-defined framework for course/program and student employability development. The University Graduate Employability Framework (University of Adelaide, 2021a:3; also discussed in Enomoto & Warner, 2023 in this book) defines employability *"as the achievement of a set of understandings, skilful practices, and personal attributes, that make it more likely for a graduate to successfully transition to employment and to contribute in ways that benefit themselves, the*

Chapter 11

*workforce, the community, and the economy*" (Advance HE, 2015; Bennett, 2020; Yorke, 2006 in University of Adelaide, 2021a).

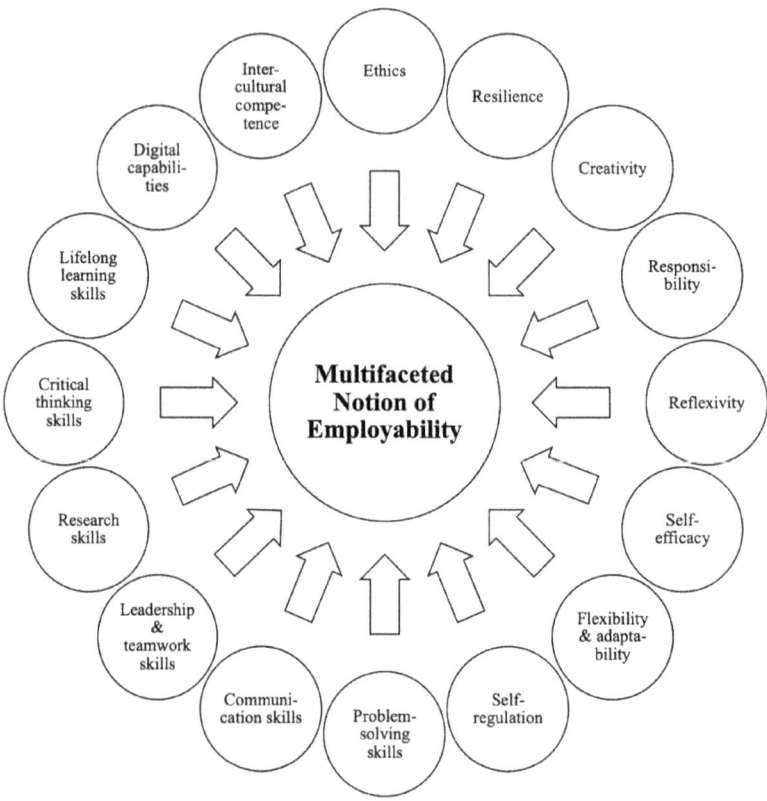

*Figure 1: Multifaceted notion of employability, comprising a range of transferable skills and personal attributes as employability skill sets.*

Informed by both the Graduate Attributes and the Graduate Employability Framework, we have jointly developed and depicted the notion of employability as multifaceted, consisting of a wide range of transferable skill sets and personal attributes (Figure 1). This depiction was conceived by drawing upon our combined knowledge and decades of university teaching experiences in our own disciplines (Author 1 in the discipline of Media; Author 2 in the discipline of Japanese). We used this multifaceted notion as our motivational foundation for this chapter on student learning outcomes. Thus, to bolster a first-year student's employability in the *ARTSEXP 1001* course, many of these facets needed to be purposefully included and meaningfully acquired as learning outcomes at the end of the course.

## The Experiential Learning Curriculum Model

Learning by doing is central to the approach taken in developing the *ARTSEXP 1001* course curriculum. Knowledge application and experiential learning provide students with opportunities to put their learning into practice. To realise this, we adopted an experiential learning approach that encourages them to experience, reflect, conceptualise and experiment to build professional skills and enhance their knowledge and confidence. In this regard, our Experiential Learning Curriculum Model draws heavily on Kolb's experiential learning cycle (1984), which locates experience as foundational to learning (Konak et al., 2014) and deploys the concepts of the Zone of Proximal Development and scaffolding (Vygotsky, 1978) to ensure students are well supported and prepared to engage in and learn from their systematically staged learning experiences. The concept of experiential learning takes a constructivist approach to pedagogy, significantly influenced by Dewey's work on pedagogy (1938). Dewey (1938) views learning as social, interactive processes embedded in the curriculum that students participate in through their lived experiences. Thus, our Experiential Learning Curriculum Model is nested within Dewey's view of learning.

Kolb's experiential learning cycle (Kolb, 1984; Kolb & Kolb, 2005) consists of four stages: 1) concrete experience, 2) reflective observation, 3) abstract conceptualisation, and 4) active experimentation. Figure 2 shows how this experiential learning cycle is embedded within our Experiential Learning Curriculum Model and what students do in each of the four stages. As Figure 2 depicts, in *ARTSEXP 1001*, the Model systematically provides students with staged and scaffolded opportunities to experience, reflect, (re)conceptualise and experiment (Kolb, 1984) through both classroom learning activities/discussions and Assignments 1-4 (see Section 2). To effectively support students in achieving their learning outcomes towards their career goals, the Model is underpinned by the principle of constructive alignment (Biggs & Tang, 2011), where learning activities and assessment tasks are aligned with learning outcomes.

In addition, core to the implementation of the Experiential Learning Curriculum Model is the provision of meaningful opportunities for students to experiment, explore ideas, and share their experiences with their peers through classroom activities and small-group discussions, typically involving three to four people. As a result, the Experiential Learning Curriculum Model can facilitate peer learning, which is valuable in improving employability, owing to its emphasis on the development of personal skills such as teamwork and conflict resolution (Donald & Ford, 2023).

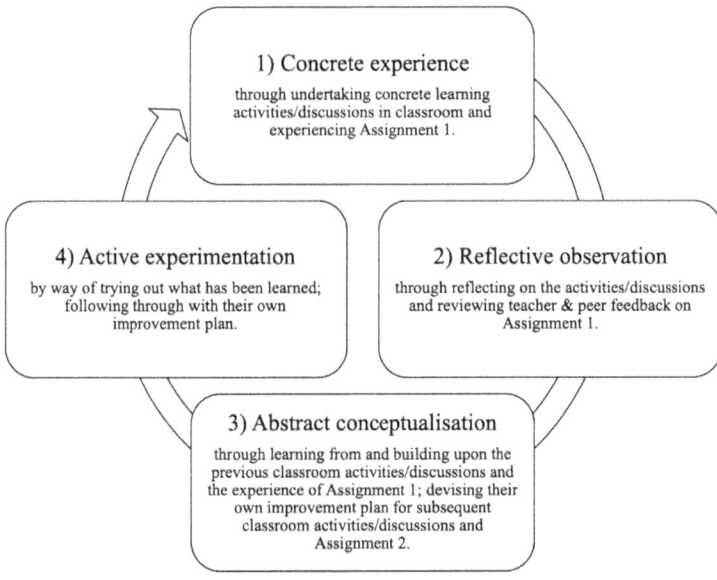

*Figure 2: The experiential learning cycle embedded within the Experiential Learning Curriculum Model (Adapted from Warner & Enomoto, 2015:28).*

Adopting a scaffolded approach, the Model enables students to adapt the pace and style of learning to reflect their individual styles and to gain insight into their identities as emerging professionals. For example, critical reflection can be seen as essential to effective applied learning (Ash & Clayton, 2009), and students are encouraged to actively use organisational tools, such as STAR-L/P (Situation, Task, Action, Result/

Reflect-Learning/Planning) and 4Rs (Reporting/Responding, Relating, Reasoning, Reconstructing), to meaningfully engage with their learning experiences through the experiential learning cycle, involving deep reflection. Indeed, Gibbs (1998) argues that having an experience is not in itself sufficient for learning, as, without reflection, the experience may be forgotten or its potential for learning lost. Moreover, goal-setting is integral to building employability within the context of study and as a means of establishing a goal-oriented professional practice. The value of goal-setting can be reinforced within a course through the linking of course activities to clearly articulated course learning outcomes, which provide students with an understanding of what is expected of them and what they can expect to gain by undertaking the course (Harden, 2002; Spady, 1994). Bates et al. (2019) report that students who commit to career-related goals during their university study are well-placed to develop career behaviours that enhance post-graduation employability. Similarly, Zimmerman's study (2002) on self-regulated learning and motivation highlights the importance of goal-setting in students' learning process.

While some degree programs embed employability skill sets and understandings from the beginning, for others, a focus on employability really only occurs in the final year, as students undertake internships or placements and engage in university-supported networking activities. In broader Arts-related (e.g. Humanities and Social Sciences) degrees not targeted at specific career outcomes, employability is a problematic concept to unpack and embed because of its complexity. What constitutes employability for a student majoring in History might look very different from what constitutes employability for a student majoring in Linguistics. Career identity varies from student to student. In addition, Bates et al. (2019:9) suggest that a sense of "Professional Purpose" grounded in individual values, aspirations and societal outlook can drive the pursuit of career-related goals. Such a mindset can motivate individuals to pursue professional goals and aspirations (Bates et al., 2019), but without necessarily focusing on developing specific transferable skills and personal attributes.

Chapter 11

## Work-integrated learning (WIL) as an enabler for employability-related learning outcomes

Before we describe our practice towards enhancing students' learning outcomes in Section 2, it is necessary to discuss the concept of work-integrated learning (WIL) as an enabler for student employability-related learning outcomes. WIL is *"an umbrella term for a range of approaches and strategies that integrate theory with the practice of work within a purposefully designed curriculum"* (Patrick et al., 2008 in University of Adelaide, 2021a). Milliken et al. (2021:52) state that research has shown the *"importance of scaffolding WIL across a degree, from the first year, to engage students in a variety of placement and non-placement WIL activities"*. Drawing on Kift (2004), they point out that students in their first year have specific needs that reflect their transition towards becoming self-managing or self-directed learners (Milliken et al., 2021:53). Embedding WIL and employability-focused activities in the first year of a degree can help to scaffold this element of students' progression. Milliken et al. (2021) also note that various scaffolded WIL experiences across a degree program can effectively support students in building career readiness. A partnership approach to WIL is identified as one that emphasises learning, adopts a long-term view and aims to benefit all parties (Orrell, 2004). The perspectives provided by WIL experiences can support the development of critical and adaptive practice (Billett, 2009), which can have ongoing benefits. Likewise, Zegwaard and Coll (2011) argue that WIL can provide students with more effective career clarification than is possible through career support activities such as career counselling.

The issue is not that universities do not offer employability-related activities and opportunities. Indeed, these are widely available, but many of them are co- or extra-curricular in nature. Therefore, unless students know their value and importance, such activities and opportunities might not be taken to develop their employability skill sets. Oftentimes, understandings of the concepts of WIL, internships and placements are conflated (Milliken et al., 2021). Conflated understandings can lead to academic focus being directed more towards internships and placements as a primary means of offering WIL opportunities to students through courses. Such focus occurs potentially at the expense of the fact that other types of WIL activities can be effectively embedded and equally experienced by students within a course curriculum. Therefore, in our particular context, we consider *ARTSEXP 1001* as representing one type of WIL (Figure 3) through which first-year students can develop their employability skill sets (Figure 1) as learning outcomes.

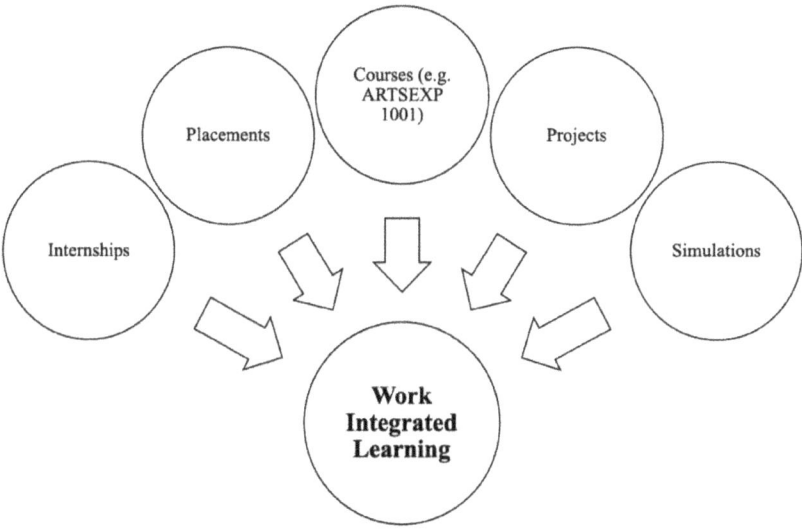

*Figure 3: Types of WIL.*

Significantly, student access to work-based WIL — such as internships and placements (Figure 3) — can be limited, particularly for those students in equity groups. In our Australian higher education context, such groups include students from Indigenous, low socio-economic, regional/remote, and/or non-English speaking backgrounds, and/or with a disability (Department of Education, Australian Government, 2020). This is despite WIL being found as a powerful enabler for developing all students' employability-related outcomes (Australian Collaborative Education Network, 2022). Thus, this is where course-based WIL — such as *ARTSEXP 1001* — can help bridge the gap to provide greater access across these equity groups. However, to do this effectively, course-based WIL activities must be carefully designed and embedded within a course curriculum.

Furthermore, WIL tends to be concentrated towards the end of a degree as part of the process of transition from higher education to professional practice (Milliken et al., 2021). However, Milliken et al.'s study (2021:60) found that *"due to the significance and impact of the first year, it is essential that students are provided with WIL opportunities to look forward and visualise their long term, professional orientation and career possibilities"*. Further, Dean et al. (2021) suggest that scaffolding WIL across a degree provides opportunities for students to practise and learn more independently.

## Section 2: Our practice towards enhancing students' learning outcomes

Enhancing student learning outcomes through early engagement with employability was identified as an opportunity that had been somewhat limited across the suite of Arts-based undergraduate degrees offered by the University of Adelaide. The chance to introduce a course specifically focused on enhancing employability-related skills and understandings arose as part of a broader shift in Faculty-based courses offered by the (then) Faculty of Arts (now Faculty of Arts, Business, Law and Economics). A compulsory first-year course aimed at introducing students to university study was replaced by a series of 'core competency' options, giving students the choice between an employability-focused course, an introduction to a European or Asian language, or an introductory STEM course.

In this chapter, the term 'Arts' encompasses various degrees housed in the Schools of Humanities, Education, Social Sciences and Music. For many Arts students, employability-focused understandings, tools and skill sets do not become prominent drivers of engagement and activities until their final year. This occurs either as part of their studies or with the realisation that they will need to find their way into their chosen career post-university. Limited student engagement with employability-focused understandings, tools and knowledge can hamper the transition from university to professional practice. Therefore, the Experiential Learning Curriculum Model is designed to provide opportunities for Arts students to develop their awareness of and engagement with these from the beginning of their degree.

In developing the *ARTSEXP 1001* course, six learning outcomes were identified, informed by the Graduate Attributes and the Graduate

Employability Framework (outlined in Section 1):
1) Demonstrate understanding of potential career directions and settings;
2) Articulate short and medium-term career goals and strategies to work towards these;
3) Demonstrate understanding of one or more industries or industry sectors relevant to career interests;
4) Demonstrate understanding and application of key employability skills;
5) Produce a professionally focused resume and portfolio;
6) Communicate effectively with peers (University of Adelaide Course Outlines, 2023).

These Course Learning Outcomes were used as parameters for designing the course content, activities and assessments, with all weekly topics, class learning activities, and assessment tasks aligned with elements of these outcomes. In so doing, we followed the principle of constructive alignment (Biggs & Tang, 2011) to ensure that all learning activities and assessment tasks were aligned with the intended course learning outcomes. In addition, it was also essential for us to design and carefully scaffold the first-year course curriculum and assessment tasks, through which students effectively learn how to capitalise on the skill sets they have already developed in building their professional employability, and to establish goals to further this skill set. To realise these learning outcomes, students undertake the process of:

a) identifying what they have already experienced or can experience to develop their employability skill sets in and outside the university (e.g. student club activities, group projects, study abroad, volunteering, part-time work), and

b) labelling what skill sets they already have and will be able to gain by linking their personal experiences and attributes to specific types of transferable skills and attributes depicted in Figure 1.

This approach aims to engage students directly with their learning by positioning them as active participants in acquiring knowledge and skills and applying them to real-world problem-solving. Students are encouraged to learn for themselves and are equipped with the skills to do so through class activities that support individual knowledge and skills acquisition. This is done by providing opportunities for students to apply their course learning to their career goals and pathways and through problem-solving-based activities, such as role play, to explore questions that might be asked in a job interview in their chosen industry/sector. At the same time, we ensure that class activities are contextualised as much as possible, because some students might view such activities as being too generic to be relevant to their individual career goals and pathways. Indeed, the study by Jorre de St Jorre and Oliver (2018) points to the significance of contextualising learning outcomes when assessing for employability, reporting that students tend to engage more with learning outcomes when they are contextualised (See Nygaard, 2023 in this book for further discussion). Empowering students to learn through a contextualised, experiential learning approach builds confidence and knowledge. For our students to begin the initial stage of the experiential learning cycle, we needed to ensure that everyone understood that the classroom was a 'safe space' for students to experiment with ideas and skills without worrying about being judged by peers and teachers.

The development of the course was also informed by student feedback. Both authors, in their roles within the (former) Faculty of Arts as Director of Work Integrated Learning (Author 1) and Director of Student Experience (Author 2), regularly canvass students about elements of their learning experience, and this helped to inform the development of *ARTSEXP 1001*. In addition, in the initial offering of the course, in the first half of 2022, students raised several issues related to course delivery and activities through formal and informal feedback. The teaching pattern of a 3-hour seminar per week for 12 weeks was noted by some students as the preferred mode, as it mixes content delivery, activities and discussion, but by others as less than ideal – some considered three hours too long, while others suggested a more traditional 1-hour lecture plus 2-hour workshop each week. The 3-hour classes have been retained for now, but the option of switching to a 2-hour weekly workshop, complemented by online activities, is being explored. Another issue was that the second step of the career readiness plan assignment – which requires students to identify advertised job opportunities – does not fit all career areas. For example, not all teaching jobs are advertised externally, while some jobs in policing and government are primarily advertised internally. As a result of these voices and feedback, we saw it as vital to ensure that all classroom activities/discussions and assessment tasks are inclusive, regardless of career areas.

## *Teaching employability skill sets through engaging first-year students in understanding employability*

*ARTSEXP 1001* is part of a list of 'core competency' courses offered to students in the first year of an Arts-based degree at the University of Adelaide. Students must undertake one core competency course during the first year of their degree. They choose from the list that, as well as *ARTSEXP 1001*, includes introductory courses in language and literacy areas and introductory STEM courses. They can do their 'core competency' course in the first or second semester of their degree, and it complements a first-year program that includes core courses in their chosen area of study, and, in most cases, one or more elective courses aimed at broadening their undergraduate experience.

*ARTSEXP 1001* was introduced at the beginning of 2022, with its first offering in Semester 1 of that year (reflecting the Southern Hemisphere academic year start of February). The course attracts a relatively small cohort of around 30 students each semester. Because these students choose to enrol in this course, rather than a language or STEM course, most demonstrate a high level of engagement with the course content and activities. The official course description for *ARTSEXP 1001* outlines the course as follows:

> "*This WIL course will introduce students to key concepts around professional identity and development, and will encourage them to start positioning themselves as emerging professionals from the first year of their studies. It will provide a valuable link between higher education and professional practice by embedding understandings of career directions and goals, professional identity and career strategies, and providing students with the tools to manage and develop these*" (University of Adelaide, 2023).

The notion of embedding understandings of professional identity and professional development was central to the development of the course. It was made particularly challenging by the range of students choosing to undertake it. While the course is aimed at students in Arts-based degrees, these degrees include a wide variety of specialisations, from Media to History to Teaching to Criminology. The diversity of student interests is further extended by the fact the course attracts a small number of students from discipline areas outside the Faculty of Arts, Business, Law and Economics – for example, from Health and Medical Sciences. This diversity of cohort means that while there is a common core to the course, to gain maximum benefit from the course, students need to be able to individualise both the knowledge they develop and the focus of their assessment tasks. This helps ensure that the course's content and learning are relevant to each student's interests and encourages them to build confidence and take ownership of their learning and professional development.

Course content is built around a 12-week curriculum of weekly 3-hour seminars. Each seminar focuses on a topic related to employability. Some highlight tools, skills and knowledge that students can begin developing now – tools such as resumes and portfolios; skills such as networking and communication; and knowledge such as the range of curricular, co-curricular and extra-curricular opportunities that can help to enhance their employability. Others are more forward-looking, such as workplace cultures, professionalism, social media, and career pathways. Overall, the aim is to both build students' knowledge and equip them with skills and understandings that will support them to navigate their own way through university and into professional practice.

The weekly seminars include a mix of content delivery, activities and discussion. The services of Career Educators from the University's Careers Service are also utilised. For the first semester of 2023, a Career Educator delivered an hour-long workshop on face-to-face networking and another on establishing and developing a LinkedIn profile. Additional perspectives were also introduced through a series of short employability-focused videos developed in 2022, featuring University of Adelaide graduates discussing topics including internships, resumes and other employability-related areas. Each of the videos runs for just a few minutes, but they are embedded in course content to provide a clear sense of the links between course content and the professional experiences of recent graduates. The content presented and discussed in class is the same for the whole cohort. Still, students are encouraged to bring their individual lens to engaging with the topics and activities – for example, in considering how important or otherwise portfolios are to their likely career options, and what this means for them.

| Week | Topic |
| --- | --- |
| 1 | Course Introduction – the 'SMART' (Specific, Measurable, Attainable, Relevant, Time-based) formula |
| 2 | Professional Communication |
| 3 | Researching Careers and Career Pathways |
| 4 | Developing a Professional Resume |
| 5 | Starting a Professional Portfolio; Reflective Writing |
| 6 | Networking and Personal Branding |
| 7 | Writing Cover Letters and Preparing for Job Interviews |
| 8 | The Value of Soft (Transferable) Skills |
| 9 | Professionalism and Social Media |
| 10 | Curricular, Co-Curricular and Extra-Curricular Opportunities |
| 11 | Understanding Workplace Cultures |
| 12 | Looking Ahead |

*Table 1: ARTSEXP 1001 weekly topics.*

However, it is in the assessment where the greatest opportunities for individualisation of the course lie. Four assessment tasks (Assignments 1-4) are each linked to several of the Course Learning Outcomes identified in Section 1. A summary of these can be seen below:

Chapter 11

| Assessment task | Activity | Weighting | Week due | Course learning outcomes* |
|---|---|---|---|---|
| Assignment 1 | Presentation | 20% | In class from week 4 | 1, 2, 3, 4, 6 |
| Assignment 2 | Career readiness plan | 30% | Mid-point of semester | 1, 2, 3, 4 |
| Assignment 3 | Resume and portfolio | 30% | Week 12 (final week of teaching) | 3, 4, 5 |
| Assignment 4 | Reflection | 20% | Week 13 (first non-teaching week) | 1, 2, 3, 4 |

*Table 2: ARTSEXP 1001 course assessment summary.*

\* Course learning outcomes
1. Demonstrate understanding of potential career directions and settings;
2. Articulate short and medium-term career goals and strategies to work towards these;
3. Demonstrate understanding of one or more industries or industry sectors relevant to career interests;
4. Demonstrate understanding and application of key employability skills;
5. Produce a professionally focused resume and portfolio;
6. Communicate effectively with peers.

**Assignment 1 – Career focus presentation**
The first of the assignments, the career focus presentation, connects to Course Learning Outcomes 1, 2, 3, 4 and 6. Collectively, these outcomes indicate assessment activity demonstrating an understanding of potential career directions and industry settings, employability skills, goals, and strategies to work towards these. It also provides an opportunity for the students to develop and demonstrate the capacity to communicate

effectively with peers through the presentation and the follow-up Q&A session.

In their individual presentation to the class, each student discusses their chosen industry sector and the career opportunities and challenges it presents. While at this stage of their degree, many students have only a very broad idea of their likely direction, they are asked to consider a career possibility (with the guidance that researching this possibility might shift their thinking towards or away from this path and that either is a valid outcome). This assignment allows students to explore a potential career pathway – recognising that many students begin a university degree with only a broad idea of where this degree might take them. It also opens up opportunities for peer learning – even with a typical class of 25-30 students, there tends to be little duplication of content as, within degrees and specialisations, students engage with a broad range of career pathways. For example, students in the Bachelor of Criminology interested in policing have focused on topics including state-based policing, federal policing and detective work. This diversity of topics provides opportunities for students to learn from their peers – those in the same or similar degrees learn about congruent fields that might be relevant to them in the future, while those in different degrees are made aware of potential career pathways they might not have considered.

In the presentation, they are asked to contextualise their chosen sector within the broader industry (Jorre de St Jorre & Oliver, 2018), talk about their goals and interests, and research elements of the sector such as demographics, work patterns, work and education requirements, and opportunities both at the graduate level and for experienced practitioners. This can help them identify pathways and longer-term – as well as short-term – outcomes for their study and career progression. It can also introduce them to aspects of the career they might not have been aware of – such as gender balance, remuneration and possibilities for progression. At the end of the presentation, questions from the class are encouraged to enhance the peer learning aspect. This direct interaction is not just a learning opportunity but also a chance for students to build a sense of cohort by engaging directly with their peers' interests and professional development. To provide a light moment in the presentation, students are rewarded in grading for including a 'fun fact' about their industry sector in their presentation ('two points for a good Fun

Fact'). This encourages them to find a quirky or interesting piece of information to share with their peers. They are also encouraged to include a photo of their pet (or a friend's pet, their indoor plant, or something else personal but shareable) as their final slide. This serves the purpose of encouraging cohort-building by providing an easy and 'safe' item for post-presentation chat (there are usually plenty of questions about the pet's name, age, habits and so on) – something valuable in a class where few students know each other at the start of the semester and where the range of degree and professional interests spans a broad spectrum.

**Assignment 2 – Career readiness plan**

The career readiness plan builds on the groundwork laid in the presentation and links to Course Learning Outcomes 1, 2, 3 and 4 (see Table 2). It allows students to demonstrate an understanding of industries and industry sectors, career directions, employability skills, and short- and medium-term goals. While it starts from a similar point to the presentation, it requires significantly greater depth and a focus on future planning through setting goals and establishing strategies to achieve or work towards them.

The career readiness plan is a complex work requiring sustained engagement from students – it cannot be effectively produced at the last minute – and necessitates some intensive thinking. Of the four assessment items in this course, it is the most substantial in terms of both workload and thought. Still, it produces outcomes useful to students throughout the rest of the course (with a broader goal of being useful on an ongoing basis – students are encouraged to see it as a continuing work-in-progress, even after assessment). Informal feedback indicates they find it challenging but rewarding by the end of the process.

The career readiness plan is worth 30% of the overall course grade and is completed around the semester's mid-point. It asks students to consider their current strengths, areas for development, and future plans. It incorporates a number of steps which students need to undertake to develop the final document and achieve the associated Learning Outcomes. Each step builds on the previous one, producing an outcome that is multi-layered and which supports the goals of professional and personal development and early-stage career planning.

*Step 1:* The first step is for students to identify their existing areas of strength, particularly in relation to soft (transferable) skills. This helps build their self-awareness and provides a sense of their starting point for future development. The assignment guidelines suggest that as well as relying on their own knowledge, they ask friends and/or family for their views and, as an additional source of information, undertake an online employability survey provided through the University's Careers Service. This survey can provide a broad guide to areas of strength and areas for future development, and it can be re-taken multiple times during a student's degree.

*Step 2:* The next step is for them to explore job advertisement websites to identify roles relevant to their area of professional interest. They are asked to identify three advertised roles – one they could (hypothetically) apply for upon completion of their degree, one they could apply for with two or three years of professional experience, and a more aspirational role they could potentially apply for after five or six years of professional practice. For each role, they are asked to identify the job criteria and map them against the strengths identified in Step 1 and potential areas for development. Some of these areas for development might involve technical skills (such as detailed knowledge of specific software platforms), while others might be more generic and transferable (such as leadership skills). The reasons for this step are two-fold: one is to alert them to the kinds of roles that might be available to them post-graduation; the other is to help them develop a sense of how prepared they need to be on graduation and of how they might need to develop their skills and knowledge in subsequent years to progress in their careers. This awareness provides a foundation for Step 3.

*Step 3:* This step asks students to identify four generic and transferable skills/attributes they believe they need to develop to succeed in their chosen industry. The options are left open-ended, but commonly identified skills/attributes include time management and networking. Once they have identified their four areas, they are asked to outline a strategy and timeframe for developing each of these areas. Responses to this are varied – some students take a broad approach, such as:

- *"I will work on developing my time-management skills in my uni work next semester",*

while others provide specific detail and timelines, such as:
- *"I will buy a monthly planner and note down all my assignment deadlines and other activities, and I will pin this to my bedroom wall so it is a constant reminder".*

This type of discrepancy in detail highlights one of the challenges of this assignment – some students' reluctance/inability to go beyond broad-brush strokes in their thinking and planning. Even though the importance of detail is noted in the assignment guidelines and discussed in class before the due date, it is not always reflected in the finished work.

*Steps 4 & 5:* Building on this, Steps 4 and 5 require students to establish a timeline of activities that includes elements of professional development, career planning and non-career plans. This aims to establish a framework for achieving the goals – or steps towards these – identified in the preceding three steps. By establishing a framework, students can gain a stronger sense of how, when and if these goals might be achievable and the steps they might need to take along the way for this to happen. It also identifies non-career activities — such as extended travel or aspirations for home ownership — that might need to be considered in planning. Students are asked to set out a timeline that reflects each year of their time at university, the year following completion of their degree, and several two-year intervals after that. For a student starting a three-year degree in 2023, the timeline years would be 2023, 2024, 2025, 2026, 2028, 2030, and 2032. They then map against this timeline relevant curricular, co-curricular and extra-curricular activities, study-related goals, and external activities contributing to their professional development, career progression, and life events/activities. Typically, the first few years of the timeline are the most specific and detailed, with later years broader and relatively speculative. The timeline is positioned as a framework that can be adapted and changed in response to changing ideas, goals, and activities rather than a static piece of work. There is no specific required format for the timeline, but students are encouraged to make it visually engaging and easily readable, as well as specific as possible, with the idea that this will help to establish it as a working document – something that has a life beyond assessment. For example, a typical timeline element for a student's second year of university might look something like Table 3.

| January | Semester 1 | Mid-year break | Semester 2 | End of year break |
|---|---|---|---|---|
| Begin looking for voluntary opportunities in social media marketing | Start planning for student exchange to Canada in first half of next year | Short course in search engine optimisation | Finalise planning for exchange | Start looking for internship opportunities for next year |
| Continue casual work at supermarket | Apply for student mentor role | Update resume and portfolio | Networking event at uni in September | Update resume and portfolio |
| | Sister's wedding in mid-April | Work on building skills in Photoshop – produce 2 items for portfolio | Apply for summer jobs in social media marketing | Travel to Japan for two weeks |

*Table 3: A typical timeline element for a second-year student.*

*Steps 6 & 7*: Once they have established their timeline, they move on to Step 6, which is a short reflection on the process of developing their plan. This provides an opportunity for students to consider the thinking that went into the plan, and to reflect on not only the outcomes but also the factors that impacted their decision-making, the choices they made, and whether their goals and aspirations were realistic. The final step, Step 7, collates all the resources used in putting together the plan.

The career readiness plan is a complex assessment that presents several challenges for students. One is the complexity and the need to work through it step by step, as each step builds on the previous one. Another is the necessity of making decisions – even hypothetical ones – at this early stage in their degree. For those students just starting to learn about their chosen field, thinking ahead to the extent of looking at potential jobs several years after the completion of their studies can take them well out of their comfort zone. The step-by-step nature of the assignment is aimed partly at reducing the impact of this cognitive dissonance by providing a 'road map' for completion. Nonetheless, despite – or perhaps because of – the challenges, students frequently identify the career readiness plan as one of the most useful aspects of the course, as it requires them to think about their futures in a structured and detailed way and to identify opportunities that can help them work towards their goals.

**Assignment 3 – Resume and portfolio**

The third piece of assessment is a resume and portfolio (see Table 2). This reflects Course Learning Outcomes 3, 4 and 5 by supporting further development of understandings related to career pathways, central to the employability skill sets needed for these pathways, and producing a professionally focused resume and portfolio – a key element of the student's employability toolkit.

The resume and portfolio assignment develops and builds on content and activities undertaken in weekly seminars. One weekly topic focuses on resumes and another on portfolios, while broader topics such as professional identity are covered in other weeks. While a more straightforward exercise than the career readiness plan, developing a professionally focused resume and portfolio while in the early stages of a degree program can be a daunting undertaking for students who are just starting to understand where their degree might be able to take them, and how they can begin to establish their professional identity and overall employability.

While most students already have a resume, these are generally aligned with the types of work typically undertaken by students – particularly retail and hospitality. The resume activities in this course focus on shifting the narrative from student to emerging professional. Content delivered and discussed in classes highlights the importance of foregrounding activities, skills and knowledge relevant to their intended professional field. This is done with the aim of producing a document that is valuable during the remainder of their studies if and when they choose to undertake an internship or seek casual work in a field related to their studies, as well as laying the foundations for post-university employment. Class content and discussion emphasise the value of highlighting professionally focused activities – for example, by prioritising experience relevant to their career direction, whether paid or unpaid, over paid retail or hospitality work. This prioritisation helps to begin building their professional identity and to demonstrate awareness of the importance of relevant experience. The value of tailoring the resume for specific roles is also discussed in class. This learning is then used as the foundation for the resume element of the assignment, which asks students to submit a one- to two-page professionally focused resume that could be used to apply for an internship or casual role in their chosen field.

The development of a professional portfolio is also covered in class prior to its introduction as an assessment item. The broad career interests of the student cohort present challenges in working through this course element. Some fields, such as music and media, rely heavily on portfolio/show reel content to demonstrate skills and experience; others, such as teaching or criminology, tend to be less oriented towards using a portfolio. Class discussion emphasises the broad value of a portfolio as a means of showcasing skills, knowledge and experience, while acknowledging how understandings and uses of portfolios can differ.

There tends to be one common thread in students' responses to the idea of developing a portfolio – most have few artefacts to include. There are exceptions – some music students, for example, have extensive audio and video of their performances – but for most, the idea of producing a portfolio containing five or six items showcasing their skills, knowledge and experience – as required for assessment – initially presents obstacles. A common concern expressed early in the semester is that individuals have 'nothing' to include in their portfolios. With this in mind, class content and discussion focus on how students can best develop effective portfolio items. One pathway is to treat the portfolio as a skills-development experience that leads to outputs – for example, taking the opportunity to learn a new software platform such as Adobe Photoshop and including the finished photographic work in the portfolio. Another is to find ways to showcase skills they already possess and attributes they can already demonstrate, capitalising on ideas of transferable skills. We work through examples of this in class. For example, we discuss the skills and attributes associated with a community/sporting role, such as being captain of a soccer (football) team. This role allows individuals to demonstrate leadership, teamwork, communication, time management and other transferable skills. It is not, however, a role that produces tangible outputs. So, in class, we consider how a student might articulate the associated learnings and attributes – for example, they might use a team photo as a visual device to anchor a brief discussion of their role as captain and how this both demonstrates and contributes to a range of transferable skills that may be relevant in a professional setting. They can also articulate their experience of learning a new skill to produce outputs for their portfolio – for example, in learning to use Photoshop to produce portfolio items, what transferable skills were needed, and how were these developed?

Utilising these strategies helps to ensure every student has the required number of portfolio items for assessment. It broadens their thinking about how a portfolio can most effectively be developed to suit their current and future needs. It is intended as a starting point – the version produced by the end of the semester is assessable, but it is also positioned as the first draft of a portfolio to which they can continue to add. They are encouraged to present the portfolio online – using a template-driven website building site, such as WordPress or Wix – but this is not an assessed element.

**Assignment 4 – Reflection**

The final assignment for the course is a reflection on their experiences and learning from the course (see Table 2). It relates to Course Learning Outcomes 1, 2, 3 and 4 by providing an opportunity for students to reflect on their learning in the course throughout the semester and their developed understanding of employability skill sets, knowledge and understandings, as well as goal-setting and strategies to work towards goals. Students are asked to refer to goals they set at the start of the semester and to consider their progress towards these or whether their goals have changed over the 12 weeks. The reflection is relatively short – 800 words – and the assignment criteria note that it should:

> 'capture the goals, attributes and activities you have explored during the semester, and should consider what you have learned from these and how they might influence your actions over the next few years'.

It also identifies reflection as a valuable skill not just at university, but also during their careers, to extract the maximum value from any learning experience. For most students, it is likely to be the first reflection they write during their time at university, so it is a valuable opportunity to explore reflective writing and what they can learn by doing it (see also Enomoto & Warner, 2013). The assignment is supported by in-class content and activities to build students' confidence and understanding of this form of writing.

Overall, the assessment workload for the course is relatively substantial for a first-year course. While the word count is within university policy guidelines, the assessment tasks require students to undertake a considerable amount of employability-focused thinking and planning at a time when they are still finding their way in university study. However, engaging in this area at such an early stage positions them to maximise the opportunities provided through their degree, through co-curricular and extra-curricular activities, and through detailed knowledge and understanding of what is needed to develop their own pathway through their undergraduate studies to what lies beyond. The Course Learning Outcomes, which are embedded in the assessment items as well as in-class content and activities, provide a framework for this.

## Section 3: The outcome

In this section, we look at the outcomes of our work with the Model. We start by focusing on student perspectives before we share our own reflections as teachers.

### Student perspective

Understanding of student responses to the course has been obtained in two key ways: first, through the official post-course student survey conducted online and made available to all enrolled students. The Student Experience of Learning and Teaching (SELT) survey for the first two iterations of the course yielded valuable feedback on the course, assessment and content. Although not intended as a student survey, the Reflection assignment also provided useful feedback on aspects of the course. The student comments obtained from these sources highlighted several key themes. The qualitative nature of the comments means that only broad emerging themes and trends can be identified. Still, these are useful in understanding how students responded to the course in its first two iterations in 2022. A total of six main themes emerged.

### Theme 1 – The importance of goal-setting

Goal-setting was identified in student reflections as a valuable aspect of the course. Each semester's first seminar focuses on setting goals using the 'SMART' (Specific, Measurable, Attainable, Relevant, Time-based) formula. The importance of goals, and strategies towards these, is reinforced in classes and assessment items. Some students noted that they had not initially thought about setting goals for their time at university, but had since realised the value of goals and strategies to achieve them. Among the most widely identified were networking, time management, and confidence-related goals, such as public speaking. Some also mentioned an initial lack of confidence in setting goals, but this changed over the semester. It was gratifying to discover the extent to which the idea of goal-setting resonated with students – the fact that it was so widely highlighted in the reflections shows it was an idea that stayed with them throughout the semester.

### Theme 2 – Learning to identify, link and label relevant skills

Students identified the skills gained in the course as something they would use 'in real life', and that the scaffolded activities had helped to provide a starting point for future development. The course was described as providing a head-start on career planning, and as setting them up with skills that will be useful throughout their time at university and as they move into professional practice. Central to the aims of the Experiential Learning Curriculum Model was supporting students to learn how to identify, link and label relevant skills and to consider how these can be put into practice – in the process, boosting their confidence. The student responses suggest the Model supports them in achieving this aim.

### Theme 3 – Planning

The assessments, while challenging, were identified by students as helping them to develop a better understanding of their potential career pathways post-university, with one student in the SELT survey nominating the opportunity to 'jump-start' their career through their career readiness plan as particularly helpful. Several students mentioned in class that they were not 'planners', instead preferring to respond to opportunities and events as they happened – for them, the career readiness plan was particularly challenging – while others welcomed the opportunity to engage with their goals and passions critically. Some underestimated the time it would take to complete the plan. The centrality of planning in the course content and approach helped to support students in developing their skills in this area – whether or not they were 'natural' planners – fulfilling several of the Course Learning Outcomes.

**Theme 4 – Building a sense of community**
The peer interaction elements of the course were noted as valuable by some. This reflects the fact that almost all students who have completed the course so far have been in their first semester or two of university study, and they welcome the opportunity to meet and interact with like-minded individuals, particularly those studying the same degree as them. Several noted they had made new friends; in one case, the classes were described as 'feeling like a family'. The opportunity to learn more about different degree areas – and possible career pathways – from peers was also identified as useful. While bringing together a diverse cohort of students from across a wide-ranging faculty runs the risk of creating 'silos' within the class, the presentation assignments, in particular, help to build a sense of cohort through interaction. This is supported and extended by class activities – many of which are small-group exercises.

**Theme 5 – Boosting confidence**
A number of students reflected that the course had made them more aware of their pre-existing skills and capacities and of the value of these in relation to employability. This provided additional elements for their resume (and, in some cases, their portfolios) and helped boost their confidence about their capabilities now and in the future. This discovery or enhanced awareness of their capacities extended in some cases more broadly, prompting greater self-awareness in relation to decision-making.

**Theme 6 – Raising awareness**
Students identified a number of opportunities to develop their employability of which they were either previously unaware or had little previous knowledge. These included volunteer work, internships and student exchanges – suggesting that the awareness-raising element of the course has helped build students' knowledge of possibilities.

In summary, it appears evident that many students found the course challenging – particularly concerning the research and planning needed to complete the assessment tasks successfully. Yet, there was a widely held view that it was valuable and that it helped to achieve its stated aims of building awareness of employability skills, knowledge and understanding, and of enhancing their employability from the start of their degree. It is noteworthy that, particularly in the reflection, students' responses about the impact of the course included adjectives such as 'fully', 'really' and 'truly' – suggesting they found it of significant value rather than just broadly useful. The goal-setting elements of the course appeared to particularly resonate, with students noting an appreciation of the planning that needs to go into success and the importance of being proactive. Furthermore, the evidence from student responses suggests that the course is achieving its stated aims. The Experiential Learning Curriculum Model effectively supports students to navigate understandings of employability and leads to the development of an employability skill set. Fostering an understanding of how they can develop their skill sets – as well as what they already have working for them – helps to address the issue of lack of awareness identified at the start of this chapter.

## Teacher perspective – our reflections

The idea of instilling understandings of employability in first-year students is not new (Gedye et al., 2018; Cotronei-Baird, 2020), but equally, it is not a common part of degrees in broad-based areas such as Arts. Consequently, *ARTSEXP 1001* presented challenges in adapting employability learning to students at the beginning of their degree program and across a wide range of professional areas. Jointly developing the multifaceted notion of employability (Figure 1), used as our motivational foundation for this chapter on student learning outcomes, brought together two authors from non-cognate disciplines, in a way that not only highlights the transferability of employability skill sets, but also showcases the diversity and richness of perspectives that can help to bring understandings of employability to life.

One of the most gratifying elements of teaching the course so far has been the experience of watching students discover their potential direction and goals. As the comments above suggest, many begin the course as uncertain university newcomers in the first – or in some cases — second semester of their degree. As they grow to understand employability and their potential career direction, they develop a stronger sense of focus, learning how to set goals and work towards them. Particularly through their assessment items, they explore how to set both larger life goals and smaller-scale objectives and how to progress towards these by establishing steps along the way. This helps to bolster their confidence, particularly once they realise they already have attributes, skills and capacities of value in enhancing employability and that they can build on these.

The 'light bulb' moment of awareness that accompanies the realisation of existing skills and capacities can also be seen in some students' 'discovery' of opportunities that they either did not know existed or had not anticipated might be accessible to them. For example, while students are usually broadly aware of the existence of international student exchanges, they are often unaware of short-term study tours or the funding support that might be available to them to study internationally. This information can be the difference between something unattainable – for financial, family, or work responsibility or other reasons – and something that can become a reality with organisation and planning. Linking such activities to enhanced employability can be a further motivation to set a goal and work towards it. In each semester the course has been taught so far, several students have made a firm plan to undertake an international study experience due to the information made available and discussed in class.

An unexpected benefit has emerged from the enrolment of a few mature-age students in the course – they have provided the perspectives of someone with significant work experience to enhance class discussion. They often provide examples from their own lived experience to illustrate the relevance of concepts introduced in class. In turn, their confidence is boosted by a sense of being able to make a contribution as a mature-age student.

The use of video feedback has been a notable element of the course. Video – rather than written – feedback is used for the career readiness and resume/portfolio assignments. A rubric is also utilised to ensure standardisation and replicability in grading, but all other feedback for these two assignments is delivered by recorded video. These recordings – generally four to eight minutes long – are purposely casual in tone and presentation and are not edited before being uploaded to the Canvas learning management system. This positions them as the recorded equivalent of a conversation – albeit one-way – about the assignment and reflects the personal nature of the assessment items by providing feedback that has a personal feel to it. The structure and format are relaxed, with a summary comment followed by a step-by-step 'walk-through' of the assignment. Both positive and constructive feedback are provided, and the individualised nature of the assignments is recognised (e.g. *"resumes typically include XX, but I can see how including YY might work better for you"*). From the perspective of a marker, this feedback allows for each student's work to be considered individually as well as against a standard set of grading criteria, but it also provides opportunities to boost the confidence of students who might be struggling and to provide suggestions about next steps for students who are doing well. Being able to directly engage with what students have done well and how they might develop going forward has been rewarding and effective. While the content of each video requires a small amount of pre-recording preparation, the process is slightly less time-consuming overall than text-based feedback.

Overall, though, the most rewarding aspect of teaching the course so far has been seeing the sense of empowerment that most students take away from it. They do so by learning about goal-setting and attainment and considering their career direction and aims in depth. By putting in place a plan to help them reach their goals, they become more confident learners and more ready to make the most of their time at university, taking charge of their future and seizing opportunities, while not being locked into a set path.

## Section 4: Moving forward

It is evident from student responses to class activities and assessment tasks, SELT feedback, and their work that the Experiential Learning Curriculum Model can effectively enable students to achieve the six employability-related learning outcomes stipulated for the course (outlined above). However, we expect to continue refining the Model and adjusting the assessment to reflect the rapidly changing educational and professional environment, particularly due to the continuing growth of tools such as artificial intelligence. We also plan to reassess the Course Learning Outcomes to meet the changing demands of the wide range of industries that attract graduates from Arts-based degrees.

Meanwhile, several elements of the curriculum model would benefit from additional refinement. One relates to the scalability of the course. So far, enrolments each semester have totalled around 30 students, allowing for a personal approach to classroom teaching and feedback. It is evident from anecdotal and formal feedback that students value the personal interactions embedded in course activities and discussions. Many more students would benefit from undertaking the course, particularly those from equity groups: Indigenous, low socio-economic, regional/remote, and/or non-English speaking backgrounds, and/or with a disability (Department of Education, Australian Government, 2020). This could be addressed by targeted academic advice. However, this has implications for funding and staffing and for finding a balance between increasing enrolments and retaining the elements of personal interaction.

Another issue is that the course is aimed at students in Arts-based degrees, and it is evident from student feedback that the small number of students from other areas of the university have found it less relevant to their interests. This suggests that these students need to be discouraged from enrolling or the course needs to be broadened to accommodate them more effectively. However, broadening the course content would risk diluting the value of at least some of it.

Many of the weekly topics noted in Table 1 could be adapted to suit different academic disciplines and potential career pathways for students. The overall framework of the topics and assessment tasks utilised in our Model is broadly transferable to disciplinary areas other than Arts. However, such an adaptation of the course might need to incorporate specialised content – for example, for STEM students. The course structure and assessment tasks also have scope to be applied to similar courses in Arts-based degrees in other higher education environments.

## Conclusion

In this chapter, we have presented the theory-informed Experiential Learning Curriculum Model, which enhances first-year students' learning outcomes. The Model enables students' Course Learning Outcomes through a range of weekly course delivery and classroom engagement elements, as each of the six learning outcomes has been directly linked to each element of the Experiential Learning Curriculum Model. This is reinforced and developed through the four assessment items, each of which is also explicitly linked to elements of the Course Learning Outcomes.

The Model, which draws heavily on Kolb's (1984) experiential learning cycle, uses the elements of experience, reflection, (re)conceptualisation and experimentation to scaffold and support students' learning within the framework of the Zone of Proximal Development and scaffolding (Vygotsky, 1978). The theory-underpinned Curriculum Model also aligns learning activities and assessment tasks with learning outcomes to produce more effective teaching and learning environments following the principle of constructive alignment (Biggs & Tang, 2011). As evidenced in Section 3, this Model can facilitate first-year students to develop facets of employability, as depicted in Figure 1. Indeed, 21st-century skills such as critical thinking, problem-solving, teamwork and adaptability have become increasingly essential for graduate success (Trilling & Fadel, 2009).

*ARTSEXP 1001 – Crafting Careers* allows students to individualise and take charge of their own learning within a cohort-based and structured WIL course (see Figure 3). This means that while all students work towards the formal Course Learning Outcomes, each student does so in a way that reflects their individual goals, aspirations and directions. In effect, the overall learning outcomes are individualised and contextualised for each student but within a coherent and scaffolded framework, the Experiential Learning Curriculum Model.

While students clearly find aspects of the course challenging, particularly some of the deep thinking that is required at an early stage of their degree, formal and informal feedback indicates that they also find it valuable. The opportunities to identify, label and link attributes and employability-related skills they already possess provide a strong foundation for future employability development and help to build students' confidence about their goals and capacities to achieve these. In addition, planning to broaden and strengthen their employability skill sets provides a way forward, not just during the rest of their degree but also in the years that follow. The course addresses a common gap in understanding and awareness among first-year students, particularly in Arts-related fields, through unpacking the multifaceted notion of employability. This is crucial to enhancing student learning outcomes, particularly in first-year undergraduate courses.

## About the Authors

Kathryn Bowd is a Senior Lecturer and Associate Dean, Work Integrated Learning, in the Faculty of Arts, Business, Law and Economics at the University of Adelaide, Australia. She can be contacted at this email: kathryn.bowd@adelaide.edu.au

Kayoko Enomoto is an Associate Professor, Head of the Department of Asian Studies and Associate Dean, Student Experience, in the Faculty of Arts, Business, Law and Economics at the University of Adelaide, Australia. She can be contacted at this email: kayoko.enomoto@adelaide.edu.au

## Bibliography

AdvanceHE (2015). *Embedding employability in higher education*. AdvanceHE.

Ash, S. L., & Clayton, P. H. (2009). Generating, deepening, and documenting learning: The power of critical reflection in applied learning. *Journal of Applied Learning in Higher Education*, 1(Fall), 25-48.

Australian Collaborative Education Network (2022). Retrieved August 11, 2023, from https://acen.edu.au/wil-in-gos/

Bates, G. W., Rixon, A., Carbone, A., & Pilgrim, C. (2019). Beyond employability skills: Developing professional purpose. *Journal of Teaching and Learning for Graduate Employability*, 10(1), 7-26.

Bennett, D. (2020). *Embedding employABILITY thinking across Australian higher education*. Department of Education, Skills and Employment, Australia.

Biggs, J., & Tang, C. (2011). *Teaching for quality learning at university: What the student does* (4th ed.). McGraw-Hill Education.

Billett, S. (2009). Realising the educational worth of integrating work experiences in higher education. *Studies in Higher Education*, 34(7), 827-843.

Cotronei-Baird, V. S. (2020). Academic hindrances in the integration of employability skills development in teaching and assessment practice. *Higher Education*, 79(2), 203-223.

Dean, B., Yanamandram, V., Eady, M. J., Moroney, T., O'Donnell, N., & Glover-Chambers, T. (2020). An institutional framework for scaffolding work-integrated learning across a degree. *Journal of University Teaching & Learning Practice, 17*(4), 1-16.

Department of Education, Australian Government (2020). Retrieved August 11, 2023, from https://www.education.gov.au/higher-education-statistics/resources/2020-section-11-equity-groups

Dewey, J. (1938). *Experience and education.* Kappa Delta Pi.

Donald, W. E., & Ford, N. (2023). Fostering social mobility and employability: The case for peer learning. *Teaching in Higher Education, 28*(3), 672-678.

Enomoto, K., & Warner, R. (2013). Building student capacity for reflective learning. In C. Nygaard, J. Branch & C. Holtham (Eds.), *Learning in higher education – contemporary standpoints.* Libri Publishing Ltd.

Enomoto, K., & Warner, R. (2023). Enablers of student learning outcomes based on eight cases of second language learning and teaching in higher education. In K. Enomoto, R. Warner & C. Nygaard (Eds.), *Enhancing student learning outcomes in higher education.* Libri Publishing Ltd.

Gedye, S., & Beaumont, E. (2018). "The ability to get a job": Student understandings and definitions of employability. *Education + Training, 60*(5), 406-420.

Gibbs, G. (1998). *Learning by doing: A guide to teaching and learning methods.* Oxford Centre for Staff and Learning Development, Oxford Brookes University.

Harden, R. M. (2002). Developments in outcome-based education. *Medical Teacher, 24*(2), 117-120.

Jorre de St Jorre, T., & Oliver, B. (2018). Want students to engage? Contextualise graduate learning outcomes and assess for employability. *Higher Education Research & Development, 37*(1), pp. 44-57.

Kift, S. M. (2004). *Organising first year engagement around learning: Formal and informal curriculum intervention.* Paper presented at the 8th Pacific Rim First Year in Higher Education Conference – Dealing with Diversity. Melbourne, Australia.

Knight, P., & Yorke, M. (2004). *Learning, curriculum and employability in higher education.* Psychology Press.

Kolb, D. A. (1984). *Experiential learning: Experience as the source of learning and development.* Prentice Hall.

Kolb, A. Y., & Kolb, D. A. (2005). Learning styles and learning spaces: Enhancing experiential learning in higher education. *Academy of Management Learning and Education, 4*(2), 193-212.

Konak, A., Clark, T. K., & Nasereddin, M. (2014). Using Kolb's Experiential Learning Cycle to improve student learning in virtual computer laboratories. *Computers & Education, 72*, 11-22.

Milliken, H., Dean, B. A., & Eady, M. J. (2021). The value of embedding work-integrated learning and other transitionary supports into the first year curriculum: Perspectives of first year subject coordinators. *Journal of Teaching and Learning for Graduate Employability, 12*(2), 51-64.

Nygaard, C. (2023). Enhancing student learning outcomes through contextualised learning activities. In K. Enomoto, R. Warner & C. Nygaard (Eds.), *Enhancing student learning outcomes in higher education*. Libri Publishing Ltd.

Orrell, J. (2004). Work-integrated learning programmes: Management and educational quality. *Proceedings of the Australian Universities Quality Forum*, 176-181.

Patrick, C-J., Peach, D., Pocknee, C., Webb, F., Fletcher, M., & Pretto, G. (2008). *The WIL (Work Integrated Learning) report: A national scoping study* [final report]. Queensland University of Technology.

Spady, W. G. (1994). *Outcome-based education: Critical issues and answers*. American Association of School Administrators.

Trilling, B., & Fadel, C. (2009). *21st-century skills: Learning for life in our times*. John Wiley & Sons.

University of Adelaide (2021a). *Future Making: Strategic Plan update 2022-2023*. University of Adelaide. Retrieved April 11, 2023, from https://www.adelaide.edu.au/vco/strategic-plan

University of Adelaide (2021b). *Digital capabilities*. University of Adelaide. Retrieved June 9, 2023, from https://www.adelaide.edu.au/learning-enhancement-innovation/projects-and-initiatives/digital-capabilities#the-six-digital-capabilities

University of Adelaide (2022). *Graduate Attributes*. University of Adelaide. Retrieved April 11, 2023, from https://www.adelaide.edu.au/learning/resources-for-educators/graduate-attributes

University of Adelaide (2023). *ARTSEXP 1001 – Crafting Careers. University Course Outlines*. University of Adelaide. Retrieved April 21, 2023, from https://www.adelaide.edu.au/course-outlines/110961/1/sem-1/

Vygotsky, L. S. (1978). Interaction between learning and development. *Readings on the development of children, 23*(3), 34-41.

Warner, R., & Enomoto, K. (2015). Embedding research skills in the curriculum design of a pathway programme for international students. In C. Guerin, P. Bartholomew & C. Nygaard (Eds.), *Learning to research – researching to learn*. Libri Publishing Ltd.

Yorke, M. (2006). *Employability in higher education: what it is – what it is not* (Vol. 1). Higher Education Academy.

Zegwaard, K. E., & Coll, R. K. (2011). Using cooperative education and work-integrated education to provide career clarification. *Science Education International, 22*(4), 282-291.

Zimmerman, B. J. (2002). Becoming a self-regulated learner: An overview. *Theory Into Practice, 41*(2), 64-70.

Chapter 12
# A Pedagogical Approach to Enhance Nursing Students' Written Communication Skills as Learning Outcomes

Bernie St. Aubyn and Amanda Andrews

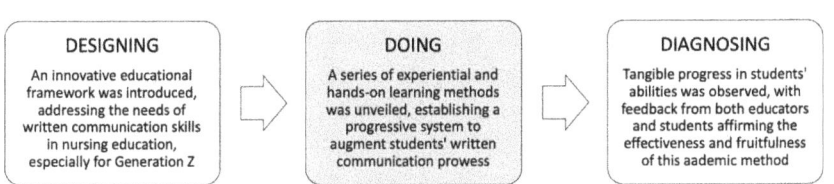

| DESIGNING | DOING | DIAGNOSING |
|---|---|---|
| An innovative educational framework was introduced, addressing the needs of written communication skills in nursing education, especially for Generation Z | A series of experiential and hands-on learning methods was unveiled, establishing a progressive system to augment students' written communication prowess | Tangible progress in students' abilities was observed, with feedback from both educators and students affirming the effectiveness and fruitfulness of this aademic method |

## Preamble

With their chapter, Bernie St. Aubyn and Amanda Andrews contribute to this book, *Enhancing Student Learning Outcomes in Higher Education*, by showing how they have used a pedagogical approach that enhances undergraduate nursing students' written communication skills and brings them from novice to advanced beginners. They relate to the three phases of the central ESLO model of the book in this way:

In the DESIGNING phase, they identify the requirements for written communication skills in nursing education in the U.K., as expressed by different influencers on nurse education, including institutional organisations, prospective employers, and society. They describe a novel pedagogical approach — *The Training Trilogy* — which they have designed to teach the required written communication skills to nursing students, particularly Generation Z.

In the DOING phase, they describe how they use three activities from their pedagogical approach to enhance students' written communication skills. They show their *Training Trilogy* in action and present the various experiential and practical learning methods they employ in a scaffolded approach with three parts.

In the DIAGNOSING phase, they document and reflect on the possible success of their pedagogical approach as they represent evaluations from both students and educators. The outcome of the pedagogical approach is accounted for, and this feedback is used to evaluate views on the effectiveness of executing the design and to assess any areas to be improved.

## Introduction

In this chapter, we present a novel pedagogical approach, the *Training Trilogy*, which we have developed for a professional training course in nursing at Birmingham City University in the U.K. Our pedagogical approach is developed to enhance nursing students' written communication skills as learning outcomes. We enable students' written communication skills by way of developing them from novices to advanced beginners within the framework of Benner's (1984) 'Novice to Expert' theory (to be detailed in Section 1). We are now recruiting the next generation of nursing students, Generation Z. This digital-native generation of students pose unique challenges to nurse educators (Chicca & Shellenbarger, 2018), including their preference for digital technology, shorter attention spans, and immediate feedback (Seemiller & Grace, 2016). Whilst we will give a detailed description of our *Training Trilogy* in Section 1, the three parts are:

1) The Principles: a two-hour classroom-based teaching session;

2) The Hearing: a low-fidelity simulation of a substantive hearing; and

3) The Locked Box: a game designed for the students to solve puzzles relating to a clinical scenario.

Working to enhance students' written communication skills in nursing is not an arbitrary choice made by our university. We have come to focus on this issue, because it has been argued that such skills are of great importance by many influencers on Nurse Education in the U.K., including institutional organisations, prospective employers and society. In practical settings, working as a nurse, it is important that one can compose professional written communication in a person-centred, safe, and compassionate manner. That itself is an integral aspect of becoming a qualified reflective practitioner. Written communication also forms the evidence that a practitioner relies on if any issue arises and they need to defend their practice, such as a complaint, professional hearing or court case.

It is, therefore, an essential nursing skill to be mastered (Andrews & St. Aubyn, 2017). The skills involved in written communication are not only required for competent dealings with the public, patients and colleagues but also must be discharged within a legal framework and comply with the law. O'Daniel, and Rosenstein (2008) identified the consequences of poorly written communication, including miscommunications between healthcare professionals, an increased risk of medication errors, and decreased patient satisfaction. Written communication is an essential nursing skill that underpins all care aspects, including assessment, planning, implementation and evaluation. Therefore, written communication skills are dynamic and need to be developed throughout the training course, in line with the nursing course requirements and have both an evidence-based and practical application.

Our work with enhancing nursing students' communication skills is also a consequence of the competitive climate within our locality, in the middle of England, where at least five other Higher Education Institutions (HEIs) offer the same training course for students. We must adapt to stay competitive and remain the university of choice within the locality. Our HEI needs to create the optimum learning environment, embracing the preferred educational needs of the students, if this success is to be maintained.

## Chapter overview and key takeaways

The chapter is divided into four sections. In Section 1, we provide the background to the enhanced learning outcome by scoping in detail the impact of the influencers on undergraduate nurse education in the U.K. In Section 2, we showcase how we enable the learning outcomes over the three parts of the course. In Sections 3 and 4, we share and reflect upon the evaluations from the students and our own experience, and discuss how these evaluations will be factored into the future development of the enhanced learning outcomes for our undergraduate nursing students.

Chapter 12

Reading this chapter, you will gain an understanding of:

1. The impact of different influencers on the development of an enhanced learning outcome within an undergraduate BSc nursing course;

2. An engaging pedagogical approach to adopt and successfully engage with Generation Z students;

3. A range of effective methods that can be used to teach written communication skills in an undergraduate BSc nursing course.

## Section 1: Background to our work with learning outcomes

The idea for the enhancement of our chosen learning outcome initially came from the fact that many different influencers are transforming Higher Education (HE). Such transformation is particularly pertinent to the arena of nurse education where, instead of being paid to train, student nurses must now pay university fees for their training in the same manner as other undergraduates. There is now more focus on the learning outcomes because they become the measure by which the education delivered can be quantified and the fees justified.

Moreover, whereas the educational institutes traditionally determined the content of the course, the emphasis is now on producing a graduate nurse fit for practice as determined by the prospective employers. Prospective employers cannot employ a person as a qualified nurse unless they have checked that they are registered with the Nursing and Midwifery Council. When developing the undergraduate curriculum to produce nurses fit for practice, society's expectations are also impactive. There is an expectation that all qualified nurses will practice in a way that upholds public trust and confidence, and this needs to be recognised. The governance of nursing practice is carried out by the Professional Regulatory Statutory Body (PRSB), which for nursing is the Nursing and Midwifery Council (NMC). The PRSB also states that the nurse educators must be NMC registrants.

In conjunction with the competitive market, the need to meet the employers' requirements led us to enhance the University's course learning outcome relating to written communication (below). These learning outcomes are established when the HEI and PRSB officially approves a course. Our challenge, therefore, was to enhance the existing, validated learning outcome described in the BSc Nursing Course Handbook (Birmingham City University, 2019) — that students will be able to identify, explain and critically evaluate:

- the provision of person-centred, safe and compassionate care; and
- the importance of communication skills and the ability to reflect upon their own accountability.

Moreover, in nursing courses, the course learning outcomes must be written to comply with the NMC future nurse proficiencies (NMC, 2018a) (below). HEIs must structure their education courses to comply with NMC education standards and design their curricula around the published proficiencies for a particular course. Students are assessed against these proficiencies to ensure they can provide safe and effective care. Proficiencies are the knowledge, skills and behaviours that nurses and midwives need to practice (NMC, 2018b). NMC Future Nurse Proficiencies are *"Underpinning communication skills for assessing, planning, providing and managing best practice, evidence-based nursing care"*. This involves the provision of *"...clear verbal, digital or written information and instructions when delegating or handing over responsibility for care"*; and the use of *"...clear language and appropriate written materials, making reasonable adjustments where appropriate to optimise people's understanding of what has caused their health condition and the implications of their care and treatment"* (NMC, 2018a:28).

Another influencer on course learning outcomes is the prospective employer, who is obligated to employ registered nurses, and the nurses must adhere to the NMC code (2018). The Code (NMC, 2018c) stipulates the professional standards that registered nurses must uphold. Student nurses will be required to be registered with the NMC once they have successfully completed their training. The NMC code is central for the revalidation process and professional reflection. Recognising the significance of the Code's impact on practice and employment, it is a criminal offence for anyone to falsely represent themselves as being on the NMC register. The statements below identify the behaviours required by the Code in relation to our chosen learning outcome – written communication. In enhancing our learning outcome, we considered the NMC Code specifically in Part 2 of our training trilogy. The NMC Code (2018:13) states that all registrants must *"keep clear and accurate records relevant to your practice. This applies to the records that are relevant to your scope of practice. It includes but is not limited to patient records"*. To attain this, our students must:

- *"complete records at the time or as soon as possible after an event, recording if the notes are written sometime after the event;*
- *identify any risks or problems that have arisen, and the steps taken to deal with them, so that colleagues who use the records have all the information they need;*
- *complete records accurately and without any falsification, taking immediate and appropriate action if you become aware that someone has not kept to these requirements;*
- *attribute any entries you make in any paper or electronic records to yourself, making sure they are clearly written, dated and timed, and do not include unnecessary abbreviations, jargon or speculation;*
- *take all steps to make sure that records are kept securely;*
- *collect, treat and store all data and research findings appropriately"* (The NMC Code, 2018:13).

Society is the final influencer on nurse education in the U.K. that we considered in relation to our enhanced learning outcome of written communication. The successful education of nurses not only requires that the students acquire knowledge and skills, but it also involves the process of developing nurses to become part of a professional healthcare community (Torbjornsen et al., 2021) within society. The Mid Staffordshire NHS Foundation Trust Public Inquiry Report (Francis, 2013) was written following a Public Enquiry into the serious failings within an NHS Foundation Trust in the U.K. The 'fall-out' from the findings led to the development of the 6Cs (as listed above) by the Chief Nursing Officer. The purpose of the 6Cs is *"to ensure people are looked after with* care *and compassion by professionals who are* competent, communicate *well, have the* courage *to make changes that improve care and can deliver the best, and* commit *to delivering this all day, every day"* (NHS England, 2012:5).

The following statements focus on the communication element of the 6Cs, in line with the learning outcome for our training trilogy. Within the 6Cs, communication is *"central to successful caring relationships and to effective team working. Listening is as important as what we say. It is essential for 'No decision without me'. Communication is the key to a good workplace with benefits for those in our care and staff alike"* (NHS England, 2012:5). Indeed, research has shown that patients' main worry when they are unwell is whether they are in 'safe hands' (Mako et al., 2016) and have some autonomy over their care. Using the 6Cs (especially communication) will assist nurses in their engagement with patients, helping to develop the culture of considerate care now required by society in the U.K.

## The pedagogy

HE is moving towards a more demand-driven focus, and this is clearly evidenced in undergraduate nursing education, ensuring that the educators are preparing 'nurses fit for purpose' and fit for the future. A demand-driven organisation, therefore, must consider the pedagogical approach it adopts. HEIs who offer undergraduate training courses have always favoured the behaviourist approach, as it enables academics to educate students in larger groups and disseminate information in a dictatorial, almost conditioned manner (Thompson, 2019). The behaviourist approach adapts learning outcomes to assess the students' learning.

Yet, HE worldwide is moving towards operating in an increasingly competitive environment and delivering a 'measurable product' represented by courses' learning outcomes. There must therefore be a corresponding shift in the pedagogical approach used, which could be part of each institution's unique selling point when recruiting students. The prevailing cohort of students entering HE today are categorised as Generation Z, who are technologically focused and adaptive to self-directed learning methods and styles (Shatto & Erwin, 2016, Ziatdinov & Cilliers, 2021). HEIs need to recognise the characteristics of this generation to enhance course learning outcomes, as Generation Z students have their own unique and individual attitudes, beliefs, social norms and behaviours, which all impact engagement and motivation in the learning arena. It is thus a requisite that nurse educators ensure learning outcomes are in tune with the students' preferred learning styles.

The pedagogical approach of constructive alignment considers the notion that the students learn in three ways. They ingest the learning and then construct and transform the knowledge for themselves (Macintosh-Franklin, 2016). This constructivist approach moves away from the behaviourist approach and towards a more student-focused pedagogy that reflects Generation Z learning behaviours. The use of this approach, therefore, aligns with Generation Z students, as it allows for knowledge transfer to be constructed over time. Thus, students have time to interact with the learning and apply it to their own social constructs, which also involves them learning by observation and practice (Shatto & Erwin 2016). For the HEI, the learning outcomes are the measures by which we assess that the knowledge is acquired at the correct academic level (Certificate level, diploma level and degree level). HEIs must not lose sight of the need to deliver a contemporary, 'measurable product' in line with a competitive marketplace. Therefore, our chosen learning outcome of written communication has implications for institutional organisations, prospective employers and society. These 'influencers' must all have to be considered if we are to produce a nurse 'fit for purpose' in the 21$^{st}$ century, which is a significant challenge for nurse educators.

A useful concept considered when developing the teaching resources required for the achievement of learning outcomes is the 'Novice to Expert' theory (Benner, 1984). This theory presents a systematic way of assessing how students develop proficiencies over a given learning period. It is widely used by nurse educators when constructing learning outcomes as it shows progression over time which fits in with nursing education ethos as the students' progress from Novice to Advanced beginner by successfully completing their nurse training (Table 1).

| Stage | Definition | Potential strategies for skills and knowledge acquisition | Example of writing tasks |
| --- | --- | --- | --- |
| Novice | The learner has had no previous experience making them struggle to decide which tasks are most relevant to accomplish | Teach simple, objective concepts/attributes that are easily identified | Correct structure for date and time on records. Correctly recording patient observations in the clinical setting |
| Advanced beginner | The learner has enough real-world situations that the recurrent component is easily identified when it is related to rules and guidelines | Increase assistance and support in setting priorities to clients' needs by providing guidelines for recognizing patterns | Accurately record factual patient details in records. Construct a comprehensive plan of care for a patient in pain |
| Competent | The learner has been on the job for two or three years and is able to see actions in terms of goals or plans and works in an efficient and organized manner | Offer in-service education or opportunities | |
| Proficient | The learner performs by using pieces of evidence (i.e., maxims) that provide directions to see a situation as a whole | Use case studies to stimulate critical thinking, especially in situations with principles or rules that are contradictory | |
| Expert | The learner grasps the situation and understands what needs to be accomplished beyond rules, guidelines, and maxims | Provide opportunities for experts to share their skills and knowledge and also their analytical abilities to solve new situations | |

*Table 1: Benner's (1984) novice to advanced beginner stages used for constructing undergraduate nurse education learning outcomes.*

The influencers identified, including Generation Z, and the underpinning pedagogical approach shown above, were considered equally when we enhanced the course learning outcome relating to written communication. A training trilogy: three-way written communication, will be outlined in the following sections, to share with our readers how we developed our students from Novice to Advanced beginner over the three years of their nurse training.

## Section 2: Our practice towards enhancing students' learning outcomes

When considering undergraduate nurse education learning outcomes over the three-year course, we aim for the student to achieve the 'advanced beginner' stage, as we have identified in line with Benner's (1984) Novice to Expert theory. Nurse education courses in the U.K. must include both theory and placement opportunities. This prerequisite enables the student nurses to 'apply' knowledge to theory in real-world situations.

### *Introduction to our trilogy of training*

The enhancement of our identified learning outcome — written communication — must reflect the preferred learning styles of the student cohort, Generation Z. Chicca and Shellengarger (2018) found that this generation mostly interacts with people online or digitally, and this type of interaction can limit their development of social and relationship skills. This resonates with our experiences of this generation of students.

Indeed, Part 1 of our training trilogy involves the students being brought together into a classroom for a teaching session, face to face. This is scaffolded with an online review and refresh test hosted on an interactive virtual learning platform. This method of delivery not also helps develop their in-person social and relationship skills but also enables their preferred learning style to be facilitated, thereby maximising student engagement. This teaching method resonates with part one of the constructionist alignment pedagogy, namely the ingestion of learning.

We embedded a simulation session in Part 2 of our training trilogy to enhance the written communication learning outcome. Simulated learning provides a real-life interactive experience-miming reality (Moyer,

2016). This experience allows students to construct knowledge and develop critical thinking within a safe learning environment. Indeed, critical thinking for nurses is essential, especially when dealing with an unexpected or specific event Brookfield (2012). This teaching method resonates with Part 2 of the constructionist alignment pedagogy, whereby students construct knowledge, and skills begin to develop.

In Part 3 of our training trilogy, games and puzzles were used with an element of competition to open a locked box. Generation Z, the digital nursing student, needs engagement and stimulation, realism and entertainment, as opposed to more reading and PowerPoint presentations, to support their learning (Davis, 2021). Generation Z has been identified as lacking the use of critical thinking in their studies (Shatto & Erwin, 2016), yet gamification has been proven to promote learner engagement, critical thinking and enjoyment (Garrison et al., 2021). This teaching method resonates with the third part of constructionist alignment as students transform the knowledge for themselves.

## The preparation of our training trilogy

An intense period of preparation was requisite to deliver our training trilogy, given that we needed to have a complete 360° overview of all three parts of the trilogy to ensure we 'kept on track' with the students' learning journey. Therefore, we revisited all our influencers' learning outcomes and mapped the completion of our training trilogy across the three parts of the course. The next stage for us, as educators, was to prepare the resources to be available 'off the shelf' for use as required. Our nursing course has two intakes per year, so the teaching for the different cohorts overlaps, and we often found ourselves teaching different parts of the training trilogy to different cohorts in the same week. Significant preparation time was needed to develop the training trilogy, but it was worthwhile to enhance our learning outcome for students from Generation Z.

# Part I: The Principles

Part 1 of the training trilogy was a 2-hour classroom-based teaching session. As in many aspects of nursing practice, written communication is underpinned by a set of principles framed by the requirements of both the NMC and the law. When applied in practice, these principles are generic, enabling the nurse to use higher-order thinking and write accurate records across all clinical settings. The teaching session was taught using the following:

- A PowerPoint® presentation outlining the Principles of Written Communication;

- Storytelling; we used examples from our own clinical experiences, observations from professional and legal hearings (NMC Tribunals and Coroner's Court) and from other practitioners' experiences of using their written records to defend their practice;

- Mentimeter® discussions were embedded into the PowerPoint® presentation, encouraging active participation by the students.

## Part 2: The Hearing

Part 2 of the training trilogy was a low-fidelity simulation of an NMC Fitness to Practise Committee Substantive Hearing. The NMC publishes all hearing information in the public domain. We found a case where poorly written records formed a pivotal part of the charges. To use this in the simulation, we reviewed the case and edited the content for teaching purposes, which included the defendant's statement of facts taken from the case notes. This statement was available for the students to review online before the simulation session.

They were instructed to review the statement considering the principles of record keeping, previously taught in Part 1 in forum groups on the virtual learning platform. Students were randomly selected to stand up, introduce themselves to the facilitator undertaking the role of an NMC representative and be prepared to answer questions relating to the statement of fact they have already reviewed. The rest of the students in the session are asked to observe their colleague in the witness box and give constructive feedback about the witness' demeanour and ability to defend their record. The facilitator remained in the role and modified their approach and questions concerning the student's ability and/or answers. This session is timetabled after the students gained clinical experience so they can also reflect on documentation they will have seen

in practice settings. The teaching session was taught using the following:
- A classroom to emulate a NMC hearing room;
- The case notes and statement;
- A copy of the NMC Code (2018) and suggested questions for the hearing.

## Part 3: The Locked Box

Part 3 of the training trilogy used a classroom based locked box game. The students were divided into groups of eight and given a brief about the game. The aim of the session was for the students to solve puzzles relating to a clinical scenario. To complete the locked box, the students needed to reflect on the learning from Part 1 and Part 2 of the course and apply this knowledge to the practical task. The locked box had five educational puzzles about the principles of written communication (see Table 2 below for an example puzzle).

---

Question 2

Fact and Opinion should not be mixed up in nurse documentation. You should always write factual and not include any irrelevant speculation or your opinion.

Which of the following statements are facts?

HINT: There are FOUR correct statements to generate the four-digit Code needed to unlock the box!

1. The patient was slurring her words and was obviously drunk
2. The patient looked unwell
3. The patient had a temperature of 36° as recorded on their observation chart
4. The patient was found on the floor
5. Dave said, 'I have a lot of pain today.'
6. Mr Jones looked like he was uncomfortable in the chair
7. The doctor has instructed the nursing team to record Mr Smith's blood pressure every 2 hours for 8 hours following his operation
8. The patient had not drunk much today because his jug was full.

*Table 2: Example locked box 'puzzle'.*

Once the students had solved each puzzle, they received a numerical code allowing them to open a box with an answer to a clinical scenario question. When all the puzzles were solved, the students could complete the locked box. The teams were competing against the clock and each other to finish first. Finally, there was a debriefing session where the students were encouraged to reflect on their engagement, communication and team-working skills in the activity (See Branch, 2023 in this book, on the importance of reflecting on experience as a mechanism for improving professional practice). Our particular teaching session was taught using the following:

- A classroom;
- Boxes with 4-digit numerical locks;
- Clinically based puzzles and scenarios;
- A clock;
- Instructions and debrief notes.

In this way, the training trilogy is delivered over 6 hours with an expected 4 further hours of online learning.

## Section 3: The outcome of the training trilogy

The enhancement of our chosen learning outcome (written communication) has developed over time. The consideration of our three influencers (the university, prospective employees and society) has enabled us to reflect on the importance of written communication, not only for undergraduate education but also for the ongoing professionalism of our students as qualified nurses.

We needed to ensure the tripartite approach of our training trilogy was both phased and developmental, in line with the proficiencies across the rest of the nursing course. We achieved this phased and developmental approach by teaching written communication principles in the first part of the course. Then, as students developed more clinically in Part 2, their knowledge of written communication was constructed using simulation. Finally, as students approach qualification in Part 3, the locked box enabled them to transform and apply their knowledge, resonating with the needs of a newly qualified nurse (NQN). As we have stated, Generation Z students are digital natives, born at the time the world wide web became publicly available. However, the imperative to facilitate their digital learning needs must not override the necessity for them to develop into a social being, fit for working in the 'real world' of clinical practice.

The training trilogy has enhanced the course learning outcome by blending different teaching styles. Thus, we propose the points for consideration below:

- Never underestimate the time required to do the initial preparation for each part of the trilogy and the time to 'reset' the resources after each training session;

- Afford the students time to embed the acquired knowledge using the mode that suits their individual learning needs best, e.g., online forums, WhatsApp® groups, Jam-boards or Padlet®;

- Debriefing is highly valued across Generation Z students, so facilitate time for this and factor- in that different students develop at different times by providing your contact details;

- Remind students that the usual confidentiality rules apply and that they are learning within a safe environment.

## Student perspective

The adoption of a tripartite approach has been successful on many levels for our students. Our evaluations were collated using a three-phase approach for the three parts of the course (Figure 1).

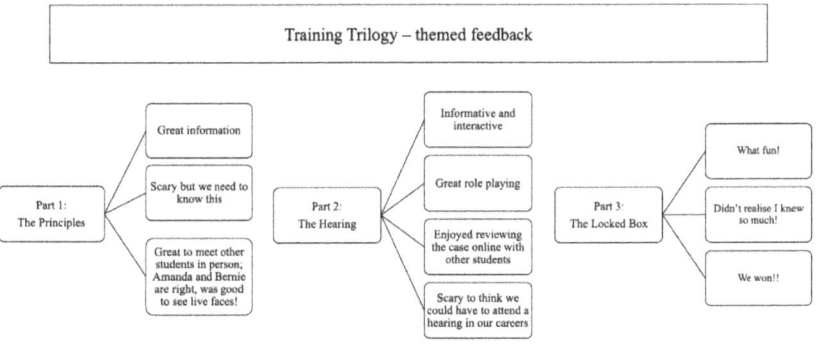

*Figure 1: Training trilogy themed feedback.*

As Table 3 shows, debriefing occurs during and after each session. The students are given time to share experiences from their own clinical practice and time for questions. Facilitating a safe learning environment helps the students share their experiences more openly with one another and with us as educators.

Training Trilogy – Part 3, The Locked Box.
Debrief
Congratulations!
We hope you enjoyed the experience.
All Teams' roles are valuable and important to make the team work well.
- How did it feel?
- Good / Bad feelings
- What could you have done differently to complete the tasks?
- What did you learn about your ability to work in a team?
- What did you learn about your communication skills?
- Did you:
    o Introduce yourselves
    o Did you take charge, or were you happier to be instructed
    o Were you an 'ideas person' or a 'completer finisher'?
    o What personality traits did you recognise in yourself?

*Table 3: Locked Box debrief.*

## Educators' perspective

The development of our training trilogy was not without its challenges. Working in a busy educational environment means it is easier to use existing teaching resources and deliver them in a time–honoured fashion. Trying to find the time to develop new and innovative teaching resources was also hindered by the fact that we have different roles within the organisation.

Our motivation to keep developing resources to enhance our chosen learning outcome (written communication) can also be linked to previously identified over-arching influencers. From a university perspective, we must be mindful of recruitment and retention, and we also need to uphold and enhance the organisation's reputation, especially in the competitive economy in which we operate. Prospective employers need to know that we are producing a potential workforce of practitioners that are 'fit for practice'. This is quality assured by our own NMC registration, which ensures that we teach using the NMC Code (2018) and that our end 'product' can uphold public trust and confidence within society.

To reflect on our training trilogy, as Figure 2 shows, we adopted the 'Stop, Start, Continue Method' of evaluation (Cunningham & White, 2022). This structured qualitative feedback method is commonly used for nursing student feedback in higher education.

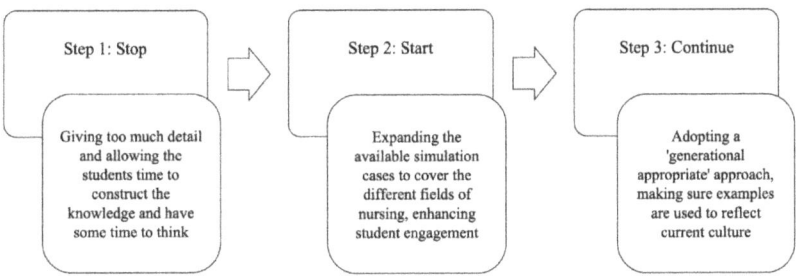

*Figure 2: 'Stop, Start, Continue Method' of evaluation (adapted from Cunningham & White, 2022).*

## Section 4: Moving forward – the next step

Our next steps in further enhancing our chosen learning outcome (written communication skills) are to develop larger-scale interactive resources. The first is a formative online resource whereby the students can consolidate their existing knowledge relating to the topic. The student is then able to generate a certificate of completion to contribute towards their professional revalidation.

Our next project will then be to develop an in-person interactive resource based upon the concept of an 'an escape room'. Students will be given a clinical scenario based upon record keeping and using their knowledge of good record keeping principles they will be tasked to solve skills and puzzles which will lead to an 'escape' from the 'room'. This resource will form part of the students' 'nearly qualified day' at the end of their nurse training degree and provide them with a memorable and impactful experience relating to good record keeping.

As technology advances, we also need to consider using Virtual Reality (VR) in conjunction with this method of gamification to continue engaging the new generations of students by facilitating their preferred learning styles. An embryonic idea is the use of VR to reproduce a 'court room' setting and let students fully engage with and appreciate the experience of giving evidence in a witness box with only their records for reference to the care they provided.

Another point for us to consider will be that Generation Z will soon be followed by Generation Alpha, known as the 'wired generation' because of their clear connection to technology and technological innovation (Ziatdinov & Cilliers, 2021). As such, we will need to take into consideration all future technological advances, so as to ensure that learning outcomes are achievable for the generations yet to come.

## Conclusion

This chapter has considered the impact of different influencers on the development of an enhanced learning outcome within an undergraduate BSc nursing course and considered a suitable pedagogical approach to adopt and successfully engage with Generation Z students. A variety of methods of teaching written communication skills were discussed to showcase the enhancement of our course learning outcomes pertinent to written communication skills development. This chapter aimed to convey an understanding of the thinking behind the enhancement of our chosen learning outcomes — written communication skills — across three key areas; the impact of our influencers, the pedagogy that needs to be adopted for Generation Z students and the variety of teaching methods we employed within our training trilogy.

The highly competitive HEI environment in which we find ourselves is always at the forefront of our minds as we endeavour to provide the students with a bespoke and engaging learning experience that caters to their specific digital needs. From a university perspective, the competitive environment has driven the provision of more resources being made available for the development of a generation-appropriate learning environment.

## About the Authors

Amanda Andrews is a Senior Lecturer in the College of Nursing and Midwifery at Birmingham City University. She can be contacted at this email: Amanda.andrews@bcu.ac.uk

Bernie St. Aubyn is a Senior Lecturer in the College of Nursing and Midwifery at Birmingham City University. She can be contacted at this email: Bernie.st.aubyn@bcu.ac.uk

## Bibliography

Andrews, A., & St. Aubyn, B. (2017). Court-proofing professional records – An innovative simulation teaching resource in A. Hørsted, P. Bartholomew, J. Branch, & C. Nygaard (Eds.) (2017). *New innovations in teaching and learning in higher education.* Libri Publishing Ltd.

Benner, P. (1984). *From novice to expert, excellence and power in clinical nursing practice.* Menlo Park Publishers.

Birmingham City University (2019). *BSc Nursing Course Handbook.* Birmingham City University.

Branch, J. D. (2023). Physician, heal thyself: Enhancing student learning outcomes through reflective practice. In K. Enomoto, R. Warner & C. Nygaard (Eds.), *Enhancing student learning outcomes in higher education.* Libri Publishing Ltd.

Brookfield, S. D. (2012). *Teaching for critical thinking: tool and techniques to help students question their assumptions.* Jossey-Bass.

Chicca, J., & Shellenbarger, T. (2018). Connecting with Generation Z: Approaches in Nursing Education. *Teaching and Learning in Nursing, 13*(3), 180-184.

Cunningham, C. M., & White, T. L. (2022). What are they trying to tell me? Large-scale viability of the Start, Stop, Continue teaching evaluation method. *Innovations in Education and Teaching International, 59*(1), 60-69.

Davis, C. (2021) Gamification brings effective learning, along with a bit of fun, to nurse education. *Healthcare Leadership Review, 40*(5), 1-4.

Francis R. (2013). *Report of the Mid Staffordshire NHS Foundation Trust Public Inquiry: Executive summary (HC 947)*, The Stationery Office.

Garrison, E., Colin, S., Lemberger, O., & Lugod, M. (2021). Interactive learning for nurses through gamification. *The Journal of Nursing Administration*, 51(2), 95–100.

Mackintosh-Franklin, C. (2016). Pedagogical principles underpinning undergraduate nurse education in the U.K.: A review. *Nurse Education Today*, 40(1), 118-122.

Mako,T., Svanang, P., & Bjersa, K. (2016). Patients' perceptions of the meaning of good care in surgical care: A grounded theory study. *BMC Nursing*, 15(47), 1-9.

Moyer, S.M. (2016). Large group simulation: Using combined teaching strategies to connect classroom and critical learning. *Teaching and Learning in Nursing*, 11(2), 67-73.

NHS England (2012). *Compassion in Practice strategy and the 6Cs values*. Retrieved April 24, 2023, from https://www.england.nhs.uk/6cs/wp-content/uploads/sites/25/2015/03/cip-6cs.pdf

Nursing and Midwifery Council (2018a). *Standards of proficiency for registered nurses*. Retrieved April 24, 2023, from https://www.nmc.org.uk/standards/standards-for-nurses/standards-of-proficiency-for-registered-nurses/

Nursing and Midwifery Council (2018b). *Standards framework for nursing and midwifery education*. Retrieved April 24, 2023, from https://www.nmc.org.uk/standards/standards-for-nurses/standards-for-pre-registration-nursing-programmes/

Nursing and Midwifery Council (2018c). *The Code*, Retrieved April 24, 2023, from https://www.nmc.org.uk/standards/code/

O'Daniel, M., & Rosenstein, A. H. (2008). Professional communication and team collaboration. In R. G. Hughes (Ed.), *Patient safety and quality: An evidence-based handbook for nurses*. Agency for Healthcare Research and Quality.

Seemiller, C., & Grace, M. (2016). *Generation Z goes to college*. Jossey-Bass.

Shatto, B., & Erwin, K. (2016). Moving on from Millennials: Preparing for Generation Z. *The Journal of Continuing Education in Nursing*, 47(6), 253–254.

Thompson, P. (2019) *Foundations of educational technology*. Oklahoma State University Libraries. USA.

Torbjornsen, A., Hessevaagbakke, E., Grov, E. K., & Bjornnes, A. K. (2021). Enhancing student learning experiences in nursing programmes: An integrated review. *Nurse Education in Practice*, 52(1), 1-7.

Ziatdinov, R. & Cilliers, J. (2021). Generation Alpha: Understanding the next cohort of university students. *European Journal of Contemporary Education 10*(3), 783-789.

Chapter 13
# How Increased Volume of Low-Stakes Testing Improved Student Engagement and Performance without Additional Grading Burden

Franco (Frank) Saccucci

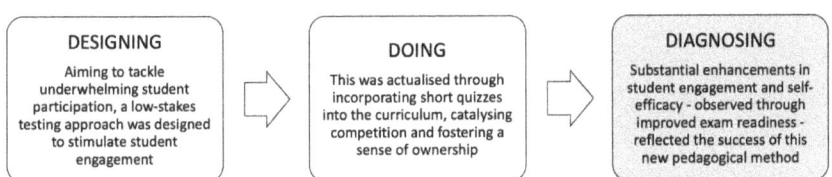

| DESIGNING | DOING | DIAGNOSING |
|---|---|---|
| Aiming to tackle underwhelming student participation, a low-stakes testing approach was designed to stimulate student engagement | This was actualised through incorporating short quizzes into the curriculum, catalysing competition and fostering a sense of ownership | Substantial enhancements in student engagement and self-efficacy - observed through improved exam readiness - reflected the success of this new pedagogical method |

## Preamble

In his chapter, Franco (Frank) Saccucci contributes to this book, *Enhancing Student Learning Outcomes in Higher Education*, by illustrating how an increased volume of low-stakes testing in the classroom improved student engagement and performance without causing additional educator fatigue to either the marking efforts or budget. He relates to the three phases of the central ESLO model of the book in this way:

In the DESIGNING phase, he explains why and how he developed the approach incorporating regular low-stakes testing into his teaching approach. He demonstrates how quizzes are carefully planned to strengthen students' memory and practical use of formulas, while a peer-marking system is introduced to reduce the teacher fatigue from grading.

In the DOING phase, he describes how he implements low-stakes testing in the classroom setting. Short quizzes are seamlessly integrated into class sessions, and the peer-marking system actively engages students in a less conventional aspect of the learning process. The approach fosters a 'gamified' atmosphere that further motivates student engagement and participation while ensuring consistent oversight of the effectiveness of the process across different institutions.

In the DIAGNOSING phase, the author evaluated the effectiveness of this teaching approach through student surveys and direct observations of student performance. The survey feedback indicated an increased preference for this testing method and improved readiness for major exams. The observations supported enhanced student engagement, demonstrating the success of the intervention in improving learning and performance. An unexpected outcome was the gamification of the learning process, which further enhanced student motivation.

## Introduction

To tackle an underwhelming level of student participation, I introduced a low-stakes testing approach. Here, low-stakes testing is identified as continuous assessment tasks with a low weighting (1% per assessment) towards the overall final grade. The classroom experiment was conducted in courses where the learning outcomes required students to recall and properly use formulae. Students' confidence in exercising such cognitive skills was found to be enhanced with repetition, which was facilitated with higher volume, low-impact testing. In this experiment, I did not tire myself with the additional volume of testing, rather I found the logistics of the increased testing to be a refreshing change of pace, and therefore a small break from traditional classroom delivery.

The course used for this experiment is *Introduction to Managerial Accounting* — a compulsory course for obtaining a bachelor's degree in business. Achievement of the course learning outcomes requires cognitive skills, such as calculating break-even analysis, product cost, and variances analysis. This subject area of managerial accounting may not feed into every student's desired career path though. Thus, developing a teaching approach which effectively contributes to their motivation, engagement, and attentiveness will help students achieve the necessary cognitive skills needed to reach the learning outcomes.

The chapter profiles an experiment of an educator's increased frequency of in-classroom low-stakes testing while maintaining student engagement. This student engagement was partly due to the gamification process that 'accidentally' followed the in-class testing. The occurrence of gamification in the experiment occurred by chance, but was agreeably noticed and welcomed at the end of each test. The gamification happened when the students compared who achieved the full grade on the five-minute quiz. This appeared to be a friendly competition which gave the students the drive and desire to do well on the five-minute quiz. To do well, the students remained sufficiently attentive to develop the cognitive skills needed to complete the formulas correctly; such formulas were part of the learning outcomes.

The students wanted to do well in the announced in-class pop quiz, which was their immediate short-term goal. According to the theory of goal-setting, immediate, specific, and moderately challenging goals are more motivating than long-term, vague, and too easy or difficult goals (Loke et al., 1981, as cited by Bai et al., 2020). In this experiment, the students' short-term goal was to do well in today's class, where the quiz was announced. The experiment was conducted at two separate universities. At one university, it was conducted in a typical undergraduate program; at the other university, it was conducted in the *Management Development Program*, which caters specifically to working adults wanting a certificate in management.

This chapter is influenced by an earlier definition of innovative teaching and an aligned set of principles. This earlier definition was an extension of some of the first thoughts from innovative teaching from the 1980s, as defined by Lunde & Wilhite (1996:156) who stated that "*...innovative teachers more properly include those who are alert to new ideas, forge them into something uniquely their own, test them, and persist until their students are engaged, and their teaching is transformed*". This definition relates well to the experiment detailed in this chapter. The chapter explores the idea of decreasing the grade weight and increasing the frequency of testing — while maintaining the student acceptance of these — and without placing any significant burden on the educator's marking efforts/budget. A student survey was explicitly circulated for this experiment; survey responses to one question indicated that over 94% would want to continue with the above testing logistics in other classes. Moreover, in another survey question, over 90% noted that such testing logistics kept them more engaged and attentive than on a day where no in-class quiz occurred. Hence, an observation made in this experiment, was that more engaged and attentive students had a higher probability of acquiring the cognitive skills needed to achieve the learning outcomes of this managerial accounting class.

The second influence on this chapter is from the American Association for Higher Education (AAHE) which *"conducted a series of conferences… and identified seven key principles which characterised the practices of educationally successful undergraduate institutions"* (Page, 2000:547). The chapter will focus on three of the seven principles to determine if the increased volume of low-stakes testing increased student engagement and performance. These three principles are: 1) giving timely, as well as appropriate feedback, 2) appropriate time for tasks leads to better learning, and 3) active learning techniques. These principles, that partially guided this research design and logistics, will be discussed in greater detail in the following sections.

## Chapter overview and key takeaways

Section 1 provides background on the impetus for the experiment detailed in this chapter. The section also demonstrates how the experiment's higher volume of low-stakes testing method contributes to the research area of student motivation. Section 2 details the pedagogy employed in the experiment conducted at two separate universities. Section 3 highlights similar findings between two groups of students at different universities with varied motivations. Section 4 suggests how the practice/experiment logistics can also be transferred to other disciplines in higher education.

Throughout the sections of this chapter, the following insights will be gained:

1. How an earlier definition of innovative teaching and three basic principles of successful education contribute to innovation in today's classroom;

2. The logistics of increasing the test frequency and not creating teacher fatigue, while maintaining student acceptance and increasing student engagement and performance;

3. The increased testing and peer-graded quizzes added a sense of gamification in the classroom, which unexpectedly increased the students' enjoyment of the course.

## Section 1: Background to my work with learning outcomes

The need to make a change came to me when, halfway through one class, I noticed at least a third of the students secretly trying to be on their phones, sending, receiving, or downloading. In the back of my mind, I thought about what would motivate them to be more attentive, because I, just before the class, had reinforced how important the class topic would be, especially in the first few years of their career. As the class concluded, I remembered how motivated they were in the review class before the midterm. Then, a phrase came to me: 'We are all motivated by how we are evaluated'. Then, I thought: 'Was I to give more midterms/tests to motivate? Who would have the time or a budget to do extra grading?' Since my university is a teaching university, innovative teaching practices are paramount; the university policy allows the educator to create a grade weighting that falls within the approved ranges of the Master Course Syllabus for that specific course. For example, the assignment dealing with creating a master budget had a grade weight between 10%-20%; therefore, the same course taught by two different faculty could have one course with a budget assignment of 10% while the other course had it at 20%.

In addition, there is also no shortage of literature highlighting the weaknesses of motivating students through grade-focussed teaching. As Swartz (2011:NP) states:

> "There is no question that we can use grades to get students to change their behaviour, but are we getting them to learn more? One danger is that grade-focused teaching corrodes the very meaning of learning. The purpose of learning becomes merely the achievement of grades. Not the mastery of the material."

Indeed, who among us would not love for our students to be only inspired by the subject area we teach? Thus, to challenge this, this chapter demonstrates a teaching approach that can be considered as part of the 'basket of motivators', as grades are not the sole motivator (to be discussed further in Section 3). I will describe how students can be motivated through low-stakes testing involving a touch of gamification-stimulated engagement.

Combining speaking with doing improves retention to 90% (Arthurs, 2007). In the experiment profiled here, the students could do low-stakes testing following my classroom content delivery. This allowed the students to do a low-stakes quiz following my class discussion. The wide range of learning styles represented in a large group of students makes a single type of instruction ineffective for some in the course (Arthurs, 2007). In concord with Arthurs, the low-impact testing allowed students a hands-on approach without too much stress. Plus, from the survey results specific to this experiment, it appeared most students, regardless of learning style, wanted to continue with the higher volume lower stakes testing.

There were two questions which the experiment needed to address. The first question was would the student want to continue with higher volume lower stakes testing. The second question was if doing this allows the student to be more prepared for the mid-term and final exam. A student survey was (deemed to be) the best methodology to acquire the necessary data to address the questions. A future experiment might utilise statistical analysis to compare two groups of students, with one group having high-volume, low-stakes testing and one group without such testing.

The challenge was how to use testing to motivate engagement and improve student performance. Continuously studying, or taking a multiple-choice test soon after learning, improved final recall relative to no activity, but taking an initial short answer test improved final recall the most (Butler & Roediger, 2007). In my experiment, students echoed Butler's and Roediger's (2007) findings by indicating they felt more prepared for the mid-term and final exam. An additional benefit, of having the low-stakes quizzes marked by their student peers, was that it did not create any additional marking fatigue for the educator. Student engagement in higher education is critical as numerous studies have reported a positive relationship between student engagement and student learning outcomes, including academic performance and self-reported gains (Astin, 1993; Pascarella & Terenzini, 2005; Pike & Kuh, 2005; Zhao & Kuh 2004: Ko et al., 2015).

During the experiment, I was pleasantly surprised that gamification became the 'icing on the cake' of all this. Indeed, Buckley & Doyle (2016:1162) found that gamified learning environments positively impact student learning: *"Results show that while generally positive, the impact of gamified interventions on student participation varies depending on if motivated intrinsically or extrinsically"*. It is important to note that it was not the original intention to gamify this experiment with the frequency of low-stakes testing. However, a game-like atmosphere occurred when students exchanged their peer-evaluated quizzes. Here they enthusiastically compared and discussed their answers with each other as the educator waited to gain their attention.

In 2006, Robinson, in a study on learning games incorporating the use of clickers, showed that *"...Games can also motivate many students, even those who do not normally study for class"* (Robinson, 2006:27). Again, it is essential to note in my own study that it was not intended initially to gamify this in-class quiz logistics- it just simply happened. The logistics of having it marked by a fellow student and then returning it provided immediate feedback, followed by a sense of gamification with students comparing each other's answers to see who answered correctly. This immediate feedback is one of the earlier principles identified in this chapter by AAHE (Chickering & Gamson, 1987) which characterised the practices of educationally successful undergraduate institutions. Another principle the AAHE discussed is the need for active learning. For example, Arnold (2014:37) states: *"In a game-like or competitive, peer-focused setting, feedback is almost always immediate, targeted and designed to enable the player to alter their approach for better, more desirable results"*. Therefore, taking a short, frequent, low-stakes test allows students to do something different from continuous sitting and listening.

## Section 2: The experiment of active learning that enhances learning outcomes in higher education

As educators, we strive for student engagement and attentiveness with the hopes of contributing to a desired student performance. Many educators have delivered class content while noticing that a percentage of the students do not seem to be attentive and engaged. This lack of attentiveness may seem more evident for some of us who teach a mandatory course in any program. A student in this experiment may simply want to pass the course to meet a graduation requirement.

Chapter 13

The experiment attempted to introduce additional and incremental testing into the classroom to maximise engagement without creating marking fatigue for the educator and student resistance. We all appreciate how we do our best to consistently mark from one student to the next; however, as we mark in greater volume, this becomes more of a challenge. For example, a study by Klein and El (2003:379) on a 7$^{th}$ grade class found that, of the 31 papers which were submitted, *"…the first grades assigned by the teacher were lower on average than a designated specialist's assigned grade"*. However, *"as the teacher worked their way through the marking, the grades gradually increased and eventually exceeded the grades assigned by the specialist doing the same marking"*. In contrast, in my experiment, the increased volume did not lead to the inconsistency found in Klein and El's study above (2003). This is because fellow student peers mark the additional low-stakes tests, therefore, not creating any marking fatigue on the part of the educator. The experiment continued with the following two themes/questions:

1. Did students perceive themselves to be engaged knowing an in-class quiz was to be given while in the class?

2. Did this perceived engagement give them a sense of preparedness for the midterm and final exam within the course?

Ten quizzes were given in a 12- or 13-week semester, and one accelerated six-week semester. The experiment involved two post-secondary institutions in Edmonton, Alberta, Canada. One institution was MacEwan University, while the other was the University of Alberta. MacEwan University is a public undergraduate university with slightly over 12,000 full-time equivalent students, ten baccalaureate degrees, one applied degree and 43 diploma & certificate programs. At MacEwan University, the experiment was done within the Bachelor of Commerce program. The University of Alberta has slightly over 40,000 full-time equivalent students, 18 faculties, 200 undergraduate and 500 graduate programs. At the University of Alberta, the experiment was done within the Faculty of Extension, which is now called Online and Continuing Education.

In the experiment, I was the educator for both the MacEwan University and the University of Alberta students. Therefore, the teaching approach and philosophy were similar for both groups. I wanted to determine if the higher volume of lower-stakes testing had similar effects on the two groups. The convenience of access to these two groups also drove the rationale behind selecting the two groups. The experiment with the University of Alberta involved 30 students within the Management Development Certificate program. This program targets working adults with evening and weekend programming. The second group of students involved MacEwan University's Bachelor of Commerce students, typically full-day students. At MacEwan University, 172 students were tested. The number of students tested at one institution compared to another was due to the availability of accessing the students' feedback.

The experiment was tested in a mandatory managerial accounting class at both institutions. Both institutions originally had a scheduled midterm exam, a final exam, an assignment and one online 15% quiz. This experiment introduced an additional ten quizzes, each five minutes long. The quiz question pertained to some concepts discussed in the current class. At the University of Alberta, the grade weight of 5% for these in-class quizzes was reallocated from a budget assignment's grade weight of 15%; therefore, under the revised grading, the budget assignment was now worth 5% less. At MacEwan University, the grade weight of 5% for the top five in-class quizzes was reallocated from an online quiz weighted initially at 15%; therefore, under the revised grading here, the online quiz weighted 10%.

At MacEwan University, the incremental quizzes were given to two mandatory accounting courses in each winter and fall 13-week semester and in one accelerated summer semester, for a total of five courses. At the University of Alberta, the additional incremental quizzes were given in a 12-week semester where the mandatory course was required for the Management Development Certificate. The MacEwan fall and winter courses have 26 classes in any one course within a semester, each 90 minutes long. Only 10 of the 26 classes had the surprise/pop quiz. There were two evening classes per week at the MacEwan six-week summer course, each three hours; therefore, out of the 12 evening classes, 10 had the quiz. At the University of Alberta program, there were 12 weekly evenings; therefore, 10 of the 12 had the quiz.

The five-minute quiz was announced at the beginning of the class and given ten minutes prior to class ending. The students were only told at the beginning of any specific class if a quiz would occur in the last part of the class. A pop quiz strategy was also used with the intention of having higher-class attendance throughout the semester. The students were allowed access to textbooks or e-books during the quiz. Once the allotment of 5 minutes was over, students were asked to pass their quiz answers to another student. The educator discussed the solutions to the quiz question. Each student then marked another student's answer and returned the quiz to the original student.

I noticed that when students exchanged their quizzes with each other, there was a great deal of discussion, joyful conversation, comparison of answers, and a slight tone of fun competitiveness. It almost appeared game-like; this gamification element contributed to the student's acceptance and, perhaps, even enjoyment of the in-class quizzes. As a reminder to the reader, the quiz only pertained to the content in that specific class. Each student quiz was initialled and signed by the student marker before passing it back to the student who wrote it. The student was responsible for filing and keeping their quizzes. Crucially, such logistics of having students peer mark and keep their filing system for the in-class quizzes created no additional marking stress for the instructor. At the end of the semester, the students could submit their top five quizzes for 5% of their marks. As the chapter unfolds, I discuss the pros and cons of paper-based quizzes (such as those above) versus computer-based (online) quizzes.

## How my practice affects students

The experiment in the University of Alberta course was one of eight courses needed to complete the Management Development Program. Most students are working adults, ranging from engineers/technicians/production supervisors who want some business acumen to students who are younger adults in entry-level positions with a non-business diploma/degree or some post-secondary students looking to progress in their company. There are no admission criteria to this Management Development program. Here the experiment was done in a 12-week evening program. The students usually seem motivated because being here is their time and money. The students welcomed the in-class quizzes in part because they gave them a sense of preparation for the mid-term and final exam. The students appeared attentive when the educator indicated that this topic would be on the low-stakes five-minute quiz. Attention is thought to be the gateway between information and learning (Keller et al., 2020).

At MacEwan University, normally, a third of the students were attentive and motivated to be prepared for their future Chartered Professional Accountant's exam. Other remaining students were motivated by achieving a high-grade point average or simply wanting to pass a required course in the program. The students at the University of Alberta were motivated to be attentive by either wanting to know the subject matter for work-related purposes or simply to pass the course to achieve the Certificate in Management Development.

When the University of Alberta evening class was surveyed, one of the questions was: 'Did having the 5% in-class quizzes help you better prepare for the midterm?' Of the 30 students surveyed, 25 responded 'yes'. An earlier study by Elbarrad & Saccucci (2016) found that evening students surveyed, in a mandatory managerial accounting class within the Management Development Program at the University of Alberta's Faculty of Extension, seemed to enjoy any form of gamification or non-traditional assessment. This result was partly due to the students who typically worked all day did not want to simply sit and listen for a three-hour evening class. (Elbarrad & Saccucci, 2016:842).

At MacEwan University, the experiment occurred in a mandatory introductory managerial accounting course for the Bachelor of Commerce degree. There is an admission criterion to be accepted. Most students are full-time and attend classes during the day. In an informal survey at the beginning of the semester, approximately 33% of the students indicated they aspired to become Chartered Professional Accountants. This 33% of students naturally seemed attentive in class because of such aspirations. This course is not considered an 'easy' course- the curriculum is demanding, but a student can do well in the course if they do the necessary work. When these students were surveyed, one of the questions was" 'Did knowing there was going to be an in-class quiz help you to be more attentive in the class?'; 161 out of 172 responded 'yes' to this question.

## How I prepare and organise my pedagogy

I would take five to ten minutes to prepare a simple five-minute question and print sufficient copies for each student. Once the question was prepared, it would be saved to my desktop for use in another section. The question should have some challenge but be very attainable if a student was being attentive. Bearing in mind that another student will be grading the question within one or two minutes, it is, therefore, best to avoid questions where a longer narrative requires some interpretation. From my experience, student peer grading works best with short answers, such as answers to numeric or multiple-choice questions.

At the beginning of the class, I announced that there would be an in-class quiz in the last ten minutes; therefore, students would not know if an in-class quiz would occur until the beginning of the respective class. I gave it ten minutes: five minutes to answer the question and the remaining five minutes to peer mark, student marker initials and return the quiz to the original student. I reminded the students to keep their marked quizzes and to submit their top five out of ten quizzes on the last day of the semester. I circulated a control sheet to the students in the last week of the semester. On the control sheet, the student places their name and student ID as well as completing a table/chart. This table has two columns and six rows. In the first column, they identify the quiz number; in the second column, they provide the mark out of one. The student does this for their top five quizzes; in the sixth row, they provide the total out of five. They then submit the control tally sheet and the top five student-marked quizzes. I simply then take the mark out of five and place it in their grade book. The question that may come to mind is why paper-based when technology is so readily available. The rationale for such will be discussed below.

The requirements are simple, one piece of paper is all that is needed. Once I prepare my questions, I can easily reuse them in the following semester. One thought that may come to the reader is why bother with a manual process. I attempted to try an online automated quiz approach in one class outside of this experiment. In this separate smaller experiment, the online pre-scheduled quizzes were done outside the classroom and automatically marked through a learning platform called Moodle.

It was convenient and quick, but there was no sense of classroom gamification and/or fun peer-to-peer competition. I also noticed a decreased level of classroom engagement or attentiveness. In part because it was outside of the regular classroom time. In this smaller experiment, the quizzes were fewer but weighed more on the grade. When it is student peer marked, the student learns twice, once when answering the question and again when marking some other student's answer. In the next section,

I demonstrate how my practice/experiment increased student motivation and attentiveness through a higher volume of low-stakes testing.

## Section 3: The outcome

### Student Perspective

In my methodology of using a survey, there were two straightforward questions. These survey questions were carefully formulated to generate the necessary data to assess the effectiveness of this experiment:

- Q1: Would you want to continue with the small five-minute open book in-class quiz?
- Q2: Did having the 5% in-class quizzes help you better prepare for the midterm or final exam?

I circulated the paper-based survey during the second last week of the semester. While the students were completing the survey, I stepped out of the classroom and asked them to insert their completed survey into the envelope situated at the front of the class. The last student to complete the survey would then let me know while I was waiting in the hallway. The additional student comments in the margin occurred by one student asking permission to do so — then permission was granted to all students taking the survey. In hindsight, the survey could have had an open-ended question slot for student comments to make it complete.

The responses to the two questions and student comments are included in this section. The rationale behind circulating the survey was simply to get student feedback on this new approach to testing. The responses to each question are separately identified in Tables 1 and 2.

|  | MacEwan University (Daytime) | University of Alberta (Evening) |
|---|---|---|
| Yes | 161 (94%) | 28 (93%) |
| No | 11 (6%) | 2 (7%) |
| TOTAL | 172 | 30 |

*Table 1: Responses to the first question.*

Table 1 shows that most responses from both daytime and evening classes indicated yes.

From my observation, students had a sense of pride when doing well on the in-class quiz. Doing well also gave the student confidence, while not doing as well provided an incentive to do better on the next quiz. Being that it is the best five quizzes out of ten and that each quiz could be completed as an open book gave the students little or no stress. To increase the incentive, I would indicate that one of the first five quiz questions would be on the midterm in an expanded version, while one quiz question from the second half of the quizzes would also be on the final exam in an expanded version. Knowing that at least one quiz question would be on the midterm and one on the final gave the student some practice for both exams. Table 2 also shows that most responses from both daytime and evening classes indicated yes.

|       | MacEwan University (Day Time) | University of Alberta (Evening) |
|-------|-------------------------------|---------------------------------|
| Yes   | 142 (83%)                     | 25 (84%)                        |
| No    | 30 (17%)                      | 5 (16%)                         |
| TOTAL | 172                           | 30                              |

*Table 2: Responses to the second question.*

The survey had simple 'Yes or No' type questions with no space allocated for narrative responses. However, as outlined above, students were invited to write comments in the margins of the survey, indicating their improved course engagement and performance. For example:

- "The in-class quizzes were helpful and gave me an idea of what the test may contain."
- "I think the in-class quizzes are a great way to pick up on mistakes to avoid for the future."
- "Keeps students on track."
- "I feel the quizzes could have been a little bit more challenging."

- "I thought the quizzes were very fair and helped my learning by pushing me to review the material before coming to class."
- "I would suggest having more in-class quizzes, however, keeping the same 5% weight."
- "I would make them worth 10% and have the final decrease by 5%."

One key takeaway from these comments is that the students felt more prepared for the mid-term and final. This sense of confidence was boosted because the student had a series of low-stakes test-taking opportunities to continuously practice and rehearse answering questions. Given the learning outcomes in these courses called for students' cognitive skills development involving calculations, such practising and rehearsing helped develop those cognitive skills under a test-taking environment. This brings about a 'win-win' situation for both students and educators, because the educator has no to little marking burden. Interestingly, although the experiment was with two separate student groups at different universities with widely differing student motivations, the results were remarkably similar. This would suggest the value of the higher volume low-stakes quizzes and their transferability.

## Teacher Perspective

The comments in the previous subsection allowed me to reflect on my own innovative practice. I found that in the five minutes allowed to write the one-question quiz, most students finished within that time frame while a few were still working on it. Given one of the principles identified in the introduction of this chapter from the AAHE, "*allocating realistic amounts of time* [on tasks] *means effective learning*" (Chickering & Gamson, 1987:4). I am convinced that the five minutes was sufficient and that the few students who could not complete it in five minutes were either an unusual exception or were not attentive enough during class. I will monitor this for the next round of surveys and will also reinforce in class that only one question from the quizzes in expanded form will be on the mid-term and final exam. In the future, if I notice that five minutes is insufficient time, then I will consider increasing the time limit.

As mentioned earlier, we have all read numerous articles on how grades are not the sole motivator. No one thing is everything; this includes testing and grades. However, innovative and proper testing can be part of the 'basket of motivators' contributing to improving student engagement and performance. A parallel to saying grades are not an effective motivator is to say money is not the only motivator in our employment. Most of us can agree that money is not the only motivator, but it is simply one of them, albeit an important one.

When I announce at the beginning of the class that there will be an open book in-class quiz at the end of today's class, I do it with an enthusiastic voice, a smile and encouraging body language. I say things along the line of, 'What a great opportunity to do some practice before the big game (meaning mid-term or final)'. I also say things along the line of, 'Enjoy this low-stress, low-stakes, open-book challenge. Please start and have fun'. I walk around the class, and occasionally a student wants some clarification on some part of the question. This walking around provides an agreeable break from the lecturing I have just completed. Moreover, I found that questions with humour brought a more relaxed demeanour to the classroom when writing the five-minute quiz. For example, a question would be along these lines,

> 'Franco (which is me, the chapter author) runs a small custom design furniture business. His mother-in-law is looking for a custom design tulip wood dining room table. His wife is happy that he is doing this for her mother, but he is trying to explain to his wife that the full cost, including overhead, and labor is much greater than his mother-in-law is willing to pay. He realises that this is a no-win situation with his mother-in-law on one end and his spouse on the other. For a moment he recalls when he had a more carefree life of an undergraduate student with no mother-in-law product pricing challenge. With the data provided below, calculate the direct cost and the full cost of the custom design dining room table.'

The point here is to have some fun with the question. All the questions do not have to be humorous all the time. I would not recommend this. Try to mix it up if possible with some humour and some practical real-life style questions that may be applicable to their future entry-level positions. As Pedersen et al. (2017:622) states, *"teachers sharing stories from their own clinical experiences stimulates both engagement and excitement but may also provoke unintended stigma & influence"*. This extends the theory of didactic learning, by using a practical application theory. It is important to avoid your own biases in any of your real-life industry-related practical questions, as the wrong tone may unintentionally surface in the question.

To continue with innovative testing methods, I am considering enabling students to personalise the module learning outcomes to their specific interests (see Swann, 2023 in this book). Here in this instance, for one of the ten in-class questions, the student can opt out of doing the in-class question and create an industry-related question from the topic discussed in the current class. In this instance, I will grade it out of one mark at the end of the class and return it to the student.

As described earlier, I noticed the sense of gamification and fun peer-to-peer competition that occurred when the students exchanged quizzes. The noise level of conversation and laughter increased as they exchanged and compared their answer. It seemed like a fun competition for them. I would give them a minute to settle down; allowing this minute for them if it occurred in the class as it is great to see them get excited. I would remind them to keep their quiz and only submit the top five at the last class with the control lead sheet at the end of the semester. In terms of what went well in the innovative practice, in a survey circulated at the end of the semester, most students' response to one specific question indicated they would want this repeated in their future courses (see Table 1 and also the student comments above). In a follow-up experiment survey, I will have a section for the students to respond to the following additional questions, for example:

- What did you like and what did you dislike about the additional in-class quizzes?

- What would you like to see change next semester with this practice?

In the future, I would firstly make sure that the question could be completed in five minutes appropriate for an attentive student. Secondly, I would take one in-class question verbatim, and insert and build a slightly larger mid-term and final exam question from it. Out of the ten, five in-class questions are completed before the first mid-term and the remaining five are completed before the final exam. I was surprised how I enjoyed the change of pace for the last minutes of a class when an in-class quiz was given. The change of pace was like a small break, and I did not feel as tired at the end of the class.

## Section 4: Moving forward

I see myself using this practice in other courses I teach. This was tested in an analytic course called Managerial Accounting. As discussed earlier, Question 2 was, 'Did having the 5% in-class quizzes help you better prepare for the midterm and final?' The responses from both daytime and evening classes indicated a majority responded that having the in-class quizzes helped them better prepare for the midterm and final. Open-ended questions will be considered for any future surveys.

The learning outcomes had an underlying premise to develop cognitive skills in recalling and properly using formulas. The survey findings demonstrated that the students felt more prepared for the mid-term and final because both would have questions pertaining to the formulae and their proper use. The survey results demonstrate that students feel better prepared for mid-term and final — thus with possible positive impacts on their course learning outcomes. The survey results also demonstrate students' desire to have this continued. Therefore, the future version of the course will continue with the high-volume low-impact testing.

A reader of this chapter may wonder why I use a paper-based system when in-class technology is so available. The response to this was partially discussed earlier in the chapter. To continue with that line of thought, the answer is, I found that in an informal experiment, the online outside-the-classroom quiz created no sense of classroom gamification and no friendly student peer-to-peer marking and fun competition. There was also no increase in class attentiveness/engagement because the online quiz was outside the classroom. The sample size of the small informal experiment with the online quizzes through our online learning platform Moodle was just too small to draw any significant conclusions. Going forward, I will keep considering if I use paper alone or a combination of paper or online.

Going forward into the following semesters, I will continue with small frequent in-classroom quizzes with an overall grade impact of less than 10%. These smaller quizzes will not have an additional marking burden because they will be either student peer marked or marked from an online e-learning portal. Regardless of small frequent quiz logistics, they will continue to be in the classroom near the end of the class and relate to some content discussed in that current class. Each educator has their own constraints when it comes to marking. My university has no funding for markers, and our individual classes have a maximum of 40 students. Some educators may have markers, and some may not; therefore, each educator can find the appropriate balance. The 'secret ingredient' here is trying to make it fun, low impact, with friendly competitiveness.

I plan to take this one step further and introduce this in professional industry seminars. Every year, I have the opportunity to deliver a few seminars to the industry. These are non-credit one or two-day seminars that are topic specific. The logistics I am considering are as follows, as I am about to deliver one of several modules in the day, I will mention that there will be a fun question at the end of the module. The first one who answers it correctly will receive a point. The point will be placed on a flip chart next to the person's name. This will give some recognition to the individual. The one who has the most points will be rewarded with a prize (which could simply be a new campus logo water jug/bottle or equivalent). I will then survey the participants to determine if this fun, competitive no grade competition helps them to be more attentive during the day.

## Section 5: Conclusion

This chapter has shed some light on how increased low-stakes testing can contribute to greater student attentiveness and engagement. Announcing at the being of the class that there was going to be an in-class question five-minute quiz question encouraged the students to be more attentive and engaged. This increased attentiveness, in turn, contributes to the student developing their cognitive skills in answering the analytical question in the managerial accounting quiz. Consequently, these increased cognitive skills assist the student in reaching the course's learning outcomes. I usually mention before class starts how the upcoming lecture topic connects to a learning outcome. In a class session with an in-class quiz, I plan to extend this now to illustrate how the short in-class quiz question links to one of the learning outcomes. Educators often witness a lack of students' awareness and understanding of learning outcomes and how they are embedded (Enomoto & Warner, 2023 in this book).

Increased testing does not have to be accompanied by educator fatigue. Simple logistical adjustments of paper-based or online can avoid such marking fatigue. I was pleasantly surprised by the students' small level of competitiveness when exchanging the peer-marked quizzes and how this added a small component of gamification, contributing to the student's enjoyment of the testing. I know through my years as an educator that combining the thoughts of increased testing, student acceptance, lower marking fatigue, and student enjoyment rarely, if ever, go together, but here in this experiment, there is some evidence of such a combination. Every educator can decide for their own classroom between online, paper-based, or some combination. If an educator had it online, then they may consider having the answer reviewed in the classroom when the time limit for the quiz is over. I welcome your thoughts and feedback.

## About the author

Franco (Frank) Saccucci is an Associate Professor at MacEwan University in Edmonton, Alberta, Canada. He can be contacted at this email: saccuccif@macewan.ca

## Bibliography

Arnold, B. (2014). Gamification in education. *American Society of Business and Behavioural Sciences, 21*(4), 32-39.

Arthurs, J. (2007, January). A juggling act in the classroom, managing different learning styles. *Teaching & Learning in Nursing, 2*(1), 2-7.

Astin, A. W. (1993). *What matters in college? Four critical years revisited.* Jossey Bass.

Bai, S., Hew, F., & Huang, B. (2020). Does gamification improve student learning outcome? Evidence from a meta-analysis and synthesis of qualitative data in educational contexts. *Educational Research Review, 30*(2), 1-20.

Buckley, P., & Doyle, E. (2016). Gamification and student motivation. *Interactive Learning Environment, 24*(6), 1162-1175.

Butler, A., & Roediger, H. (2007, July). Testing improves long-term retention in a simulated classroom setting. *European Journal of Cognitive Psychology, 19*(4-5), 513-527.

Chickering, A. W., & Gamson, Z. F. (1987). Seven principles for good practice in undergraduate education. *AAHE bulletin, 3*(7), 2-6.

Elbarrad, S., & Saccucci, F. (2016). The effectiveness of using educational tools to enhance undergraduate students' learning experience to cost accounting principles: An applied study. *Turkish Online Journal of Education and Technology*, 842-849.

Enomoto, K., & Warner, R. (2023). Enablers of student learning outcomes based on eight cases of second language learning and teaching in higher education. In K. Enomoto, R. Warner & C. Nygaard (Eds.), *Enhancing student learning outcomes in higher education*. Libri Publishing Ltd.

Keller, A., Davidesco, I., & Tanner, K. (2020). How orchestrating attention may relate to classroom learning. *Life Science Education, 19*(3), 1-3.

Klein, J., & El, L. P. (2003). Impairment of teacher efficiency during extended sessions of test correlation. *European Journal of Teacher Education, 26*(3), 379-393.

Ko, J., Park, S., Yu, H.S., Kim, S.J., & Kim, D.M. (2015) The structural relationship between student engagement and learning outcomes in Korea. *Asia-Pacific Education Researcher, 25*(1), 147-157.

Lunde, J., & Wilhite, M. (1996) Innovative teaching and teaching improvement. *To Improve the Academy, 15*, 155-167.

Page, D. (2000). Improving undergraduate student involvement in management science and business writing courses using seven principles in action. *Education, 120*(3), 547-557.

Pascarella, E. T., & Terenzini, P. T. (2005). *How college affects students: A third decade of research. Volume 2.* Jossey-Bass.

Pedersen, K., Moeller, M., Paltved, C., Mors, O., Ringsted, C., & Morcke, A. (2017). Students learning experiences from didactic teaching sessions including patient case examples as either text or video. *Academic Psychiatry, 41*, 622-629.

Pike, G. R., & Kuh, G. D. (2005). First-and second-generation college students: A comparison of their engagement and intellectual development. *The Journal of Higher Education, 76*(3), 276-300.

Robinson, S. (2006). Using games and clickers to encourage students to study and participate. Allied academics international conference. *Academy of Educational Leadership*. Proceedings, 11(2), 25-29.

Swann, S. (2023). Student-centric pedagogy: What happens when learning outcomes are customised to students' own interests. In K. Enomoto, R. Warner & C. Nygaard (Eds.), *Enhancing student learning outcomes in higher education*. Libri Publishing Ltd.

Swartz, B. (2011). Do grades as incentives work? Why "smart" incentives can never be smart enough. *Psychology Today*. Retrieved July 9, 2023, from https://www.psychologytoday.com/au/blog/practical-wisdom/201101/do-grades-as-incentives-work

Zhao, C. M., & Kuh, G. D. (2004). Adding value: Learning communities and student engagement. *Research in Higher Education, 45,* 115-138.

# Chapter 14
# Partnering with Clinical Provider Organisations to Enhance Learning Outcomes for Healthcare Practitioners

Amanda Andrews and Bernie St. Aubyn

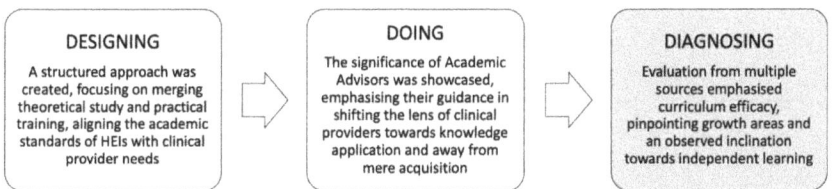

DESIGNING — A structured approach was created, focusing on merging theoretical study and practical training, aligning the academic standards of HEIs with clinical provider needs

DOING — The significance of Academic Advisors was showcased, emphasising their guidance in shifting the lens of clinical providers towards knowledge application and away from mere acquisition

DIAGNOSING — Evaluation from multiple sources emphasised curriculum efficacy, pinpointing growth areas and an observed inclination towards independent learning

## Preamble

With their chapter, Amanda Andrews and Bernie St. Aubyn contribute to this book, *Enhancing Student Learning Outcomes in Higher Education*, by showing how a higher education institution (HEI) can work together with clinical provider organisations to enhance learning outcomes for healthcare professionals. In so doing, they ensure that the education courses they provide to clinical provider organisations are recognised and validated appropriately within an academic system, whilst meeting the requirements of clinical practice. They relate to the three phases of the central ESLO model of the book in this way:

In the DESIGNING phase, their main focus is developing a cohesive approach to teaching healthcare that combines theoretical and practical elements. This is accomplished by aligning the academic requirements of HEIs with the practical needs of the clinical provider, resulting in a well-rounded student learning experience.

In the DOING phase, they show how Academic Advisors play a vital role in guiding clinical provider organisations to shift their focus towards 'applying' knowledge, instead of just acquiring it. This approach, which aligns with Bloom's (1956) Taxonomy of Learning, ultimately leads to a more meaningful and enriched learning experience for students. The critical role of Academic Advisors is evident, as they guide clinical providers in their transition from 'clinical currency' to 'academic currency', thereby enriching the students' learning environment.

In the DIAGNOSING phase, the authors evaluate the curriculum's success, informed by feedback from clinical providers, students, and academic advisors. This phase identifies the effectiveness of the curriculum, areas needing improvement, and a noted shift towards self-directed learning, thus underlining the pedagogical model's effectiveness.

## Introduction

Continued Professional Development (CPD) accredited courses are becoming an increasingly popular way for healthcare practitioners to gain academic credit for their professional development within the workplace which can be used towards formal academic awards/qualifications. A range of clinical provider organisations in the corporate, public, or voluntary sectors, can be supported by HEIs in providing their employees with CPD opportunities in a variety of subjects. Thus, in this chapter, we showcase how our university — Birmingham City University in the U.K. — through such CPD opportunities, establishes and maintains collaborative partnerships with clinical providers to advance mutual interests in clinical healthcare practice and nursing education and research.

The academic requirements of the clinical providers vary, ranging from one course for accreditation all the way to a full academic award. Whatever the requirement, all clinical providers are provided with an Academic Advisor (AA) — the role we undertake as academics from their HEI partner. Such collaborative partnerships, involving a designated AA, ensures that effective communication is maintained and thus, the partnership continues to generate income. The clinical provider organisation can be confident that their AA is up to date with the partner HEI's academic policies and procedures. This means that the clinical provider can effectively focus on their clinical content. As an HEI, our university however, needs to appreciate that the existing 'off the shelf' courses may not necessarily meet the needs of a particular potential clinical providers.

In nursing education, collaborative partnerships between clinical provider organisations and HEIs have become increasingly important to meet the changing needs of healthcare practitioners. Collaborative partnerships, in order to be effective, must help reduce the theory-practice gap by way of increasing healthcare practitioners' opportunities to develop their skills, confidence, critical thinking and decision-making. As university nursing educators, we see that advancement in clinical practice in healthcare settings is fast-paced. Thus, it is crucial for us as nursing educators to effectively design our delivery to meet the changing needs of the healthcare practitioners (hereafter, students) working on the ground at the appropriate level.

In this specific context, we developed a course design by which nursing students' learning outcomes can be enhanced through collaborative partnerships. In HEIs, their program/course learning outcomes are the core, and guiding element of curriculum design and educational quality management (Prøitz et al., 2017; Sweetman, 2017). In addition, in nursing education, if the learning outcomes of nursing programs/courses are inappropriate and not measurable, such programs/courses cannot be accredited; therefore the students cannot be qualified as healthcare practitioners upon graduation. Thus, our learning outcomes must meet the needs of clinical practice in addition to quality assurance requirements (Kubiak, 2020). Learning outcomes, therefore, need to incorporate both 'theory' (academic knowledge) and 'practice' components, which must be clearly communicated to our clinical provider organisations as the purpose of our course. Such a communication process must clearly unpack how we ensure that the clinical objectives of the clinical providers are fitted into our academic framework of learning outcomes — for accreditation and quality assurance — helping to bridge the well-documented 'theory-practice gap' seen in our sector (Rolf, 1996; Landers, 2000).

## Chapter overview and key takeaways

The chapter is divided into four Sections. In Section 1, we provide the background to the enhanced learning outcome by discussing the challenges faced by clinical providers and HEIs and how and why their collaborative partnerships have been developed. In Section 2, we showcase the structure and process needed to establish and maintain effective communication in these partnerships in relation to enhancing students' learning outcomes. In Sections 3 and 4, we share and reflect upon the evaluations from our clinical providers, participating students, and our own experience, before we discuss how these evaluations will be factored into the future development of our course structure and delivery.

Reading this chapter, you will gain an understanding of:
1. The challenges faced by clinical providers when attempting to combine the clinical currency from practice and the academic currency from the HEI;

2. The pedagogy which facilitates our university's collaborative partnership with clinical providers to enhance their students' learning outcomes;

3. The structure and processes involved in effective collaboration between clinical providers and HEIs in producing a validated HEI course.

## Section 1: Background to our work with learning outcomes

One of the key healthcare providers with whom we work collaboratively is the National Health Service (NHS). In the United Kingdom, working as part of the NHS is challenging on many levels, and when considering CPD for staff, senior managers need to consider several relevant key factors. Those key factors which impinge on CPD for clinical staff within the NHS include:

- Financial constraints;
- Maintaining safe staffing levels;
- Shift patterns;
- The value based upon the training delivered, e.g., academic currency (Degree level training);
- Understanding of how the university 'style' of learning outcomes (academic currency) links to what is needed in practice to enhance care (clinical currency).

All NHS nested organisations must consider their education commissioning across the whole of their particular organisation in line with the available finances. The education structure must ensure that a safe level of staff remain in the clinical area while also ensuring that staff are released for CPD and remain updated with new innovations and developments. In more recent years, work patterns have changed, and nursing staff now work longer shifts (12 hours), with no overlap between an early and late shift, where traditionally, nurses were released to attend CPD sessions.

Nursing became an all-graduate profession in 2009, whereby students must attend universities to gain their degree-level academic qualification to enable them to register with the Nursing and Midwifery Council (NMC). However, this switch of itself was not without some controversy, with a critical discourse analysis (Gillett, 2012:297) of the national press coverage (and its sizeable impact upon public perceptions) lauding: *"…a traditional and stereotypical construct of nurse identity and suggest[ing] that increasing nurse education produces nurses who are 'too clever to care'"*, and the *"…dominant nostalgic discourse constructs a golden era of nurse education [which]…potentially acts as a barrier to creating an effective nurse education system for the 21$^{st}$ century"* (Gillett 2014: 2495). As well as these seemingly skewed perceptions of the graduate nurse, the 21$^{st}$ century has brought with it ever greater demands — technical, clinical, academic and workplace — upon nurses, clearly exemplified by the work pattern changes (as mentioned above), with their impact on when already qualified nurses can now attend CPD sessions.

Moreover, this change in student nurse education has impacted upon the 'currency' of the courses such existing qualified staff were undertaking. It is no longer sufficient for training courses to be vocational or specialised with 'clinical' currency (a certificate of attendance). The courses now must shift to awarding the nurses undertaking them 'academic' currency (university credits). The awarding of university-level credits thus facilitates the qualified nurses to build their 'academic' currency in line with newly qualified nurses who have already achieved bachelor's degrees (with their associated academic currency credits). The learning outcomes of training courses now must be written to fall in line with university policies to ensure they are fit for accreditation whilst also reflecting clinical competency requirements.

Our university, Birmingham City University, has a department that supports this 'currency' shift by enabling healthcare organisations to keep their own intellectual property for learning but offers a collaboration to develop university-accredited courses. There is a cost for this provision, with the clinical providers organisation receiving academic support to construct and accredit the courses and ongoing support with assessment and final ratification of results, for the student's academic assessments, through the university award boards process. We further discuss how this relationship is integral to enhancing the course learning outcomes in Section 2.

## The Pedagogy

The pedagogical approach of constructive alignment considers the notion that the students learn in three ways. Biggs' constructive alignment model triangulates learning outcomes, teaching and learning activities and assessment to create an academic environment for higher-level learning (Biggs, 1999, as cited in Gallagher, 2017). They ingest the learning and then construct and transform the knowledge for themselves (Macintosh-Franklin, 2016). Applying this pedagogical approach to collaborative partnerships allows for qualified healthcare professionals to learn and combine their knowledge and clinical skills into the academic arena and then transfer this higher learning back to their clinical settings. In support of constructive alignment (Biggs & Tang, 2011), Bloom's Taxonomy (Bloom, 1956) is a well-established pedagogy with which most clinicians will be familiar. This familiarity with an educational tool also helps form the clinical lead's relationship with their AA. Healthcare professionals (clinical lead) who train others, with the support of their AA, can use Bloom's taxonomy to write learning objectives that describe the skills and abilities they desire their learners to acquire and demonstrate (Adams, 2015).

Bloom's taxonomy contains six cognitive skills categories ranging from lower-order to higher-order skills. Subsequently, Anderson and Krathwohl (2001) revised the original taxonomy from 1956 to replace the original nouns with action verbs, further enhancing the useability of the taxonomy within education and clinical partnerships (See Figure

1). These categories require different degrees of learning and cognitive processing. In our HEI, the words within the taxonomy are used to indicate the academic level of assessment within each course. This will be further explored in Section 2.

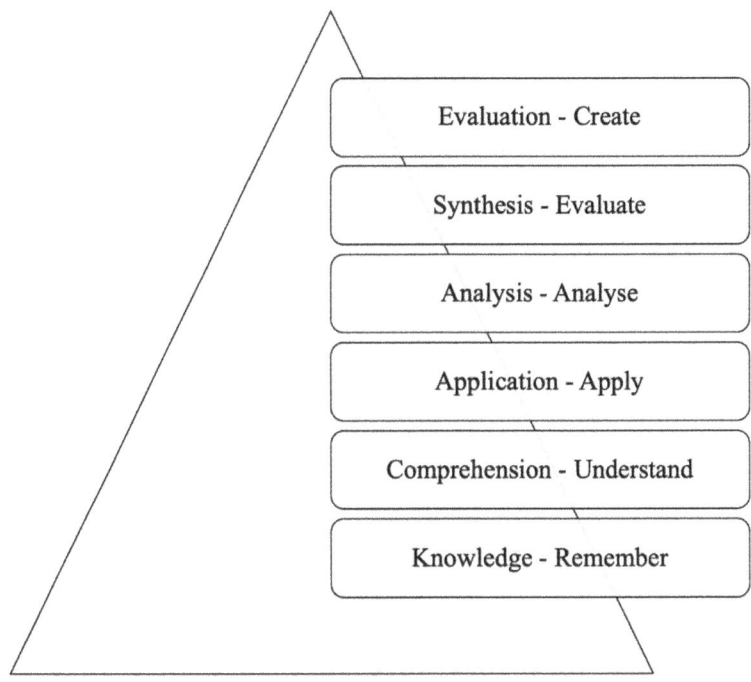

*Figure 1: Bloom's Taxonomy original nouns revised with action verbs (adapted from Bloom, 1956; Anderson & Krathwohl, 2001).*

The challenges of collaborating with healthcare professionals and the underpinning pedagogical approach shown above are considered equally. Both these elements are required to enable a successful validation of learning resources when we work with our clinical providers to enhance the 'clinical currency' of their learning outcomes in line with our HEI 'academic currency'.

## Section 2: Structure and processes needed to ensure effective collaborative 'currency' development

The role of the HEI in this collaboration is to award academic accreditation to the clinical provider's learning courses. The main aim of accreditation is to enhance the clinical learning outcomes, by ensuring the content is not only based on educational theory but also promotes consistency of learning across groups of learners. The collaborative approach, adopted by our HEI, enables the intellectual property to remain with the clinical provider, who also delivers the teaching and assesses the students' work.

As Academic Advisors to the clinical provider organisation, our role is to support them in embedding educational theory within the clinical content. The choice of AA is not undertaken lightly by our organisation, as this relationship is the foundation of the success of the collaboration. Our HEI aims to professionally 'match' the AA to the clinical provider; by this, we mean that the AA will have either the same or similar clinical background in healthcare to that of the clinical provider and their course requirements. The clinical background of the AA, coupled with their academic skills, is key in building a trusting and respected relationship with a new clinical provider. The process begins with the clinical provider outlining what they want the students to achieve from the course. The learning outcomes come into play at this point, and the clinical skills are embedded into theory. The clinical provider is encouraged to think about the learning to be achieved by completing the following phrase: 'By the end of this course/, the student will be able to…'. This generates a series of statements from the clinical provider organisation that are either clinically focused or knowledge-based. For example:

- Write a care plan for a patient in pain;
- Describe how the gastrointestinal tract functions when thinking about constipation management.

To enhance the learning outcomes to the required educational level (UK Government, 2023) for assessment, we then start to work with the clinical provider organisation to build the 'clinical' outcomes into the educational taxonomy. As previously mentioned, Bloom's Taxonomy (Figure 1) is a well-established pedagogy with which most clinicians will be familiar.

This familiarity makes the coming together of clinical and educational 'currencies' much easier for both parties. As Figure 1 shows, Bloom's Taxonomy differentiates between cognitive skill levels (Adams, 2015) and provides 'action verbs' for use in creating academic 'currency' learning objectives at the required academic level for assessment. This can result in a deeper learning experience for students and a transfer of knowledge and skills to a greater variety of clinical tasks. Thus, Table 1 (below) demonstrates how we worked with a clinical provider to add academic 'currency' to their clinical, collaborative learning outcomes nested within Bloom's Taxonomy.

| Clinical learning outcome | Required educational level | Bloom's Taxonomy | Final collaborative learning outcome |
|---|---|---|---|
| Write a care plan for a patient in pain | Level 6 Bachelor's degrees | APPLY Execute, implement, solve, use, demonstrate, interpret, operate, schedule, sketch | Demonstrate, using evidence-based care, the ability to manage a patient in pain |
| Describe how the gastrointestinal tract functions when thinking about constipation management | Level 7 Master's degrees, postgraduate certificates and postgraduate diplomas | ANALYSE Differentiate, organise, relate, compare, contrast, distinguish, examine, experiment, question, test | Examine how the gastrointestinal tract functions when defining constipation management |

*Table 1: Bloom's Taxonomy and the creation of collaborative learning outcomes.*

In accordance with HEI requirements, we then work with the clinical provider to complete the course specification document and course handbook. These documents are mandatory for the HEI but also help the clinical provider to structure their teaching across the required number of hours for the course. At our HEI, the required number of hours for a 20-credit course (Between 7 -10 'European Credit Transfer' equivalent) is 200 hours. The course specification document enables the clinical provider to write an overview for the course, identify indicative content, structure the teaching methods with a student-centred learning focus in line with our pedagogy, and identify the type of assessment to be undertaken. The course specification document also requires the development of a reading list which helps the clinical provider to focus on the educational content resources for the course.

For accreditation to be awarded, the course documentation must meet the university's quality standards. The production of detailed and accurate high-quality course documentation enhances the learning outcomes and helps ensure a seamless approval process. The HEI also requires the clinical provider to complete documentation for an institutional review and an approval event. An institutional review aims to ensure the students recruited to the clinical provider's approved course can access learning resources and facilities on par with what the HEI provides. Although the clinical provider recruits the students, they are also enrolled with our HEI, and it is essential for the students' experience and the HEI's reputation that resources are available to the students. The AA completes the institutional review at the location the clinical provider organisation is planning to deliver the training and includes reviewing:

- The teaching environment;
    - Health & Safety requirements
    - Heating, lighting, space, and comfort areas
    - Disability facilities
- The availability of visual aids and internet access;
- The availability of learning resources and materials;
- The provision of any specific facilities required for the course such as facilities for practical work.

The approval event is unique to the requirements of the partnership, and the AAs are involved in all stages, supporting the clinical provider organisation to final approval. The AA needs to maintain effective communication to ensure the partnership organisations are informed of the stages of the process, timelines for completion and the dates of attendance for all required meetings. Many clinical provider organisations have their own start date in mind for their course, and AAs work with them to develop a realistic timeline to achieve their preferred commencement date. There are two important timelines: the documentation timeline and the approval process timeline. The documentation timeline needs to consider the following:

- The setting up of a shared file 'repository' (OneDrive™);
- The sharing of course templates;
- The review of draft documentation;
- An internal review of the documentation by HEI quality assurance academics.

The paperwork then goes into the approval process timeline. This timeline includes the following:

- Panel review of due diligence documentation;
- HEI financial and legal due diligence completion;
- Panel review of the course documentation and feedback to the clinical provider;
- An institutional visit;
- An approval meeting.

Following approval of the course, our role as AAs changes to one of ongoing academic support and guidance. We have subject matter knowledge and experience, which enriches the partnership on both an academic and clinical basis. It is also imperative that this relationship is nurtured to ensure continued engagement and collaboration between the HEI and clinical provider organisation. Our ongoing role as AAs involves the following:

- The delivery of induction training sessions for all clinical provider teams;
    - Marking workshops
    - Virtual learning environment training
    - HEI policy and procedures

- The delivery of an 'introduction to our HEI session to confirm that the students are part of the HEI's educational community;
  - Library services
  - Academic development department services
  - Student services
  - Campus facilities
- The provision of academic support for students as required, e.g., referencing advice;
  - Creation of an Academic Resources virtual learning platform (Moodle)
- Internal moderation of assessed work and liaison with the external examiner;
- Supporting the clinical provider through the examination process and formal award boards;
- Quality assurance and evaluation support.

Working with clinical providers is very rewarding for us as AAs. An in-depth knowledge of Bloom's taxonomy and its use in the creation of collaborative learning outcomes is an essential requirement of the AA. This knowledge ensures that the required educational level (UK Government, 2023) is applied to the clinical providers' clinical learning outcomes to produce the final collaborative learning outcome (Table 1). It is also imperative that managers within our organisation are aware of the commitment required for the role within our workload allocation. Bringing together all the structures and processes required for a collaborative partnership needs time and commitment, not only from us as AAs but also from managers within our organisation.

## Section 3: Evaluation of our collaborations

The collaborative approach used within our university for validated provision has been in operation for several years. Recently, we have seen that the funds available for CPD within healthcare have become limited, therefore this collaboration model is becoming increasingly popular, as it is a more cost-efficient and effective training delivery method.

## Clinical providers' perspectives

The writing of learning outcomes is familiar to many of our clinical providers. In a small-scale survey, we recently circulated, 75% of the clinical providers surveyed stated that they had written clinical learning outcomes on previous occasions for an education course taught in the clinical setting. One clinical provider had an existing course in use, but it was not a university-validated course leading to an accredited award. Free text comments from the partners revealed some of the challenges our clinical partners faced when working with an HEI to enhance their clinical learning outcomes for validation:

- *"The academic language required often seemed to overcomplicate what the learning outcome required."*
- *"You ended up shoehorning the expected language into the learning outcome."*
- *"Trying to be concise yet give sufficient detail in order for the learner to understand."*
- *"Actually generating a learning outcome from a clinical requirement and then converting it into academic language at the right level that the programme (course) is at, in order that the student can demonstrate they have met that outcome."* (Partner Organisations 2023).

The survey highlighted the most common challenge our partners expressed regarding the use of different metalanguages. They found it challenging to coherently translate clinical needs (clinical currency) into the academic language of learning outcomes (academic currency). The role of the AA is essential to help overcome this key challenge, as the learning outcomes need to be established early in the accreditation process. This helps to ensure a timely conversion of the partners' clinical requirements ready for accredited academic delivery. The nurturing of the partnership by the AA is dependent on the AA possessing some key skills. These skills have been identified in feedback by some of our partners as being clinically competent, effective communication and professionalism. The comments obtained from the 2023 formal Partners Evaluations clearly exemplify such nurturing of the partnership:

- *"You are approachable, kind and respectful, always acting with dignity to uphold the professional standards of both your own organisation and our profession, and whilst you may demonstrate flexibility, those standards are never compromised."*

- *"I find you to be an excellent communicator, always willing to share your own experience, skills and knowledge whilst respecting that in others. You very naturally work in a collaborative manner, always with integrity and never shying from giving difficult messages. You maintain clear professional boundaries whilst acting as a critical friend with objectivity and thought."*

- *"Your knowledge of both the subject area and, of course, of the workings of XXX (our HEI) and the XXX (partnership) process is invaluable, and you have made my job so much easier over the years we have worked together. You have enabled me to develop the course we offer, making it more attractive to students and ensuring that the students get the most from it that they can, helping to enhance their expertise in their chosen specialism."*

Furthermore, these evaluation comments also demonstrate that the relationship established with the AA is critical to the success of the partnership.

## Students' perspectives

Anecdotal feedback, from some of the students of our partners, has provided the following insights. The students reported that the allocation of academic credits to the course (academic currency) ensured that they employed critical thinking skills to achieve a good pass mark. The feedback from their marked assignment included advice on improving their academic writing skills and critical analysis, which they also found beneficial for their future academic endeavours. The fact that the courses are accredited (academic currency) and not simply taught (clinical currency) means that successful completion of the courses often results in career development and clinical competency. The idea that enhanced learning outcomes can change lives and help students to understand their employability and career pathways resonates with the works of Magitay-Becht & Das (2023 in this book) and Bowd & Enomoto (2023 in this book). This is an important consideration for completing the course from the students' and employers' perspectives. The reward of academic credits on successful completion of the course can encourage commitment to the course. The students also report valuing the academic support from the AAs, especially when returning to study after a while and often at a higher academic level:

- *".. she was incredibly supportive in the run-up to submitting the first assignment, no question too daft; nothing too much trouble – it makes a massive difference to have this support when returning to study for the first time in a good while."* (Student evaluations 2023).

This quote further indicates the effectiveness of the relationship between the partner organisation and the HEI institution.

## AA perspectives

Points for consideration:

- The quality of the established collaboration depends on the relationship forged between the AA and the partnership organisation. It is, therefore, paramount to identify the correctly qualified AA with the required skill;
- The ongoing synergy between the AA and the partnership organisation impacts on the continuation of the partnership and HEI income generation;
- Taking time to have all the necessary structures and processes in place before the commencement of the partnership is important because this ensures that the HEI presents a professional outward-facing service to prospective partners.

The opportunity to influence clinical practice is one of the key reasons for HEI staff agreeing to undertake the role of the AA. All AAs hold a clinical qualification, and this role allows for a direct conduit to clinical practice through collaboration with clinicians. All healthcare professionals must revalidate their professional registration frequently; the role of the AA ensures the HEI staff have clinical currency through direct contact with practice partners, which is essential for revalidation purposes.

## Section 4: Moving forward

Our next step in further enhancing the collaborative partnership and enhancing learning outcomes is to develop our structures and processes for validated provision. There are potential challenges that remain nested within the existing structures. The approval process includes the completion of due diligence with the clinical provider. If the clinical provider's organisation falls short of the HEI's operating standards and this could impact negatively on the HEI's reputation, then the partnership would not be approved. A conflict of interest could arise if the clinical provider required a course that was already validated by the HEI. The HEI would not validate this course as it could impact on the HEI's own validated courses and reduce potential income and student numbers.

Further challenges may arise if the finances or the educational drivers of potential clinical providers alter, and they no longer require academic accreditation for their courses. Our experiences as AAs have taught us that the following two aspects need to be considered to enhance the job satisfaction for the AA and clinical providers:

- The induction training sessions could be attended or facilitated by the AA which would ensure the partnership develops right from its beginning.
- The AA network at the HEI could be enhanced to provide peer support and ensure that there is parity of support and input from the AAs across all partnerships.

Finally, to cement our ongoing relationships with clinical provider partners, opportunities for joint publications and conferences could be explored to showcase this unique and bespoke service provision.

## Conclusion

Within our chapter, we aimed to provide an understanding of how our HEI works collaboratively with healthcare clinical provider organisations on the validated provision of courses. As AAs within this process, we hope that we have outlined how this role is integral to the success of this provision and collaboration. The challenges stakeholders face when attempting to combine the clinical currency from practice and the academic currency for a validated course have been considered, along with the student-centred pedagogy, which facilitates a collaborative approach to enhancing learning outcomes. Strengthening the structure and processes involved in effective collaboration between stakeholders and HEIs in producing a validated course will help to plug the theory-practice gap by combining education and clinical currency, ensuring better patient care.

Our experiences have shown us that clinical providers value the exposure to the HEI environment and are overwhelmed by the amount of work and time it takes to combine the clinical currency from practice and the academic currency from the HEI to enhance learning outcomes for healthcare practitioners. The clinical providers appreciate the fact that all AAs are, indeed, registered nurses who understand and empathise with the challenges and tensions of the clinical provider organisations.

## About the Authors

Amanda Andrews is a Senior Lecturer in the College of Nursing and Midwifery at Birmingham City University. She can be contacted at this email: amanda.andrews@bcu.ac.uk

Bernie St Aubyn is a Senior Lecturer in the College of Nursing and Midwifery at Birmingham City University. She can be contacted at this email: bernie.st.aubyn@bcu.ac.uk

## Bibliography

Adams, N. E. (2015). Bloom's Taxonomy of learning objectives. *Journal of the Medical Library Association, 103*(3), 152-153.

Anderson, L. W., Krathwohl, D. R., & Bloom, B. S. (2001). *A taxonomy for learning, teaching, and assessing: a revision of Bloom's Taxonomy of educational objectives*. Pearson.

Biggs, J., & Tang, C. (2011). *Teaching for quality learning at university*. Open University Press.

Bloom, B. S. (1956). *Taxonomy of educational objectives: the classification of educational goals. Handbook 1, cognitive domain*. Longman Group Ltd.

Bowd, K., & Enomoto, K. (2023). Bringing employability to life: Developing employability skill sets and understandings as student learning outcomes. In K. Enomoto, R. Warner & C. Nygaard. (Eds.), *Enhancing student learning outcomes in higher education*. Libri Publishing Ltd.

Gallagher, G. (2017). Aligning for learning: including feedback in the constructive alignment model. *All Ireland Journal of Teaching and Learning in Higher Education, 9*(1), 1-12.

Gillett, K. (2012). A critical discourse analysis of British national newspaper representations of the academic level of nurse education: too clever for our own good?. *Nursing Inquiry, 19*(4), 297-307.

Gillett, K. (2014). Nostalgic constructions of nurse education in British national newspapers. *Journal of Advanced Nursing, 70*(11), 2495-2505.

Kubiak, C., Walker, S., Draper, J., Clark, E., Acton, F., Rogers, J. & Dearnley, C. (2020). 'They come with their own ideas of what they want': Healthcare educator, advanced practice student and manager perspectives on learning outcomes. *Journal of Education and Work, 33*(4), 312-325.

Landers, M. G. (2000). The theory-practice gap in nursing: the role of the nurse teacher. *Journal of Advanced Nursing, 32*(6), 1550–1556.

Mackintosh-Franklin, C. (2016). Pedagogical principles underpinning undergraduate Nurse Education in the U.K.: A review. *Nurse Education Today, 40*, 118-122.

Margitay-Becht, A., & Das, U. (2023). Enhancing student learning through hidden motivational learning outcomes. In K. Enomoto, R. Warner & C. Nygaard (Eds.), *Enhancing student learning outcomes in higher education*. Libri Publishing Ltd.

Prøitz, Tine S., Havnes, A., Briggs, M., & Scott, I. (2017). Learning outcomes in professional contexts in higher education. *European Journal of Education, 52*(1), 31–43.

Rolfe, G. (1996). *Closing the theory practice gap: a new paradigm for nursing*. Butterworth-Heinemann.

Sweetman, R. (2017). HELOs and student centred learning – where's the link? *European Journal of Education, 52*(1), 44–55.

UK Government (2023). *What qualification levels mean*. Retrieved April 11, 2023, from https://www.gov.uk/what-different-qualification-levels-mean/list-of-qualification-levels

Chapter 15

# Student-Centric Pedagogy: What Happens When Learning Outcomes Are Customised to Students' Own Interests

Sarah Swann

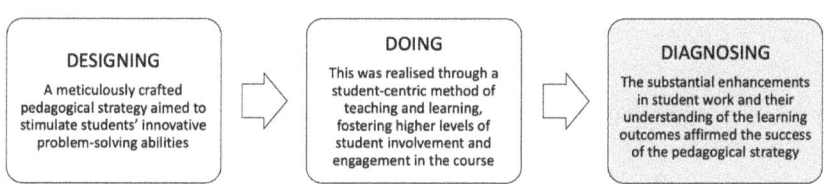

## Preamble

With her chapter, Sarah Swann contributes to this book, *Enhancing Student Learning Outcomes in Higher Education,* by showcasing how students customise and, in some cases, personalise learning outcomes to their own interests. She relates to the three phases of the central ESLO model of the book in this way:

The DESIGNING phase centres around creating an integrated pedagogical model bridging the theoretical and practical elements of two academic subject areas: Childhood Studies and Education Studies. This is achieved by aligning the academic prerequisites of higher education institutions with students' own practical action and agency, thereby ensuring a comprehensive learning trajectory.

The DOING phase involves the tangible implementation of the curriculum using tools such as constructive alignment and Bloom's Taxonomy. The critical role of the teacher is evident as she guides students in their transition from 'disenfranchised learner' to a position of 'control and ownership', thereby enriching the students' learning environment.

The DIAGNOSING phase involves a meticulous evaluation of the curriculum's success, informed by feedback from the assessment as a final written product. This phase identifies the effectiveness of the curriculum, areas needing improvement, and a noted shift towards self-directed learning, thus underlining the effectiveness of the pedagogical model.

## Introduction

This chapter is about making assessment engaging and worthwhile for all students. By placing the student at the centre of their learning experience, I aimed to foster both an inclusive and challenging learning situation. It would inspire students to use their agency and freedom to achieve their learning outcomes, whilst trusting they would get it right. However, interpretations of how assessors interpret the fulfilment of learning outcomes in analytical writing are curiously absent. Thus, this chapter also presents how I went about assessing this work, since assessment is never a neutral endeavour. That is, assessment is not neutral on the side of the student who arrives to assessment with particular funds of knowledges (Kiyama & Rios-Aguilar, 2017) and skills which are either partially or fully compatible with the assessment task, or they are not. Neither is assessment neutral on the side of *"the teacher-judge"* (Foucault, 1995:304) who acts as a gatekeeper of quality-assurance within a tightly-regulated system of knowledge and power.

I begin by moving back a few steps to my early career as a secondary school educator to describe one critical incident (Tripp, 1993). This incident lays bare the tensions between responding authentically to student need in the moment, while being called to ransom for deviating from the planned learning outcomes by agents of the 'Wellington boot factory'. The 'Wellington boot factory' refers to a top-down management system, functioning as a Taylorist metaphor for mass, institutionalised compulsory education, capturing the rhythm and supposed efficiency of everyday teaching and learning in schools. I then elaborate and discuss the potential of students to customise and personalise flexible ways of meeting universal learning outcomes assessment. This potential is exemplified by the third-year undergraduate elective module, *Children, Crime and Social Justice*, at Leeds Beckett University, UK. To illustrate how the students achieve the module's intended learning results, I primarily utilise data from two students' coursework pieces. In so doing, I show how they fulfil the learning outcomes by constructing diverse and multi-layered knowledge. I weave relevant data from my lecture notes, notes from student tutorials, and my grading rationalisations into my interpretation.

*Chapter overview and key takeaways*

In Section 1, I describe my background in working with student learning outcomes to ensure quality and standards are upheld. I then describe the nature of my current work role in the context of UK Quality Assurance frameworks, giving a brief methodological description of how modules are designed for learning. This serves to position a module's learning outcomes within the wider UK infrastructure of quality assurance and standards in higher education (HE). In Section 2, I describe what kinds of knowledge were possible for students via customising formal learning outcomes, and what 'counts' as legitimate scholarship. Section 3, then exemplifies what this looks like in practice via two case studies. In Section 4, I highlight possibilities for moving forward, before presenting a reflective conclusion.

Reading the chapter, you will gain the following insights into how 'permitting' students to customise learning outcomes can:

1. Form a basic, universal gateway into working with students' interests coherently and convincingly;

2. Create space and value for personal voice and the sharing of personal perspectives in academic writing;

3. Remove the veil that obscures how educators interpret and assess students 'performances' of learning outcomes.

# Section 1: Background to my work with learning outcomes

The design of any module is inextricably entangled with the epistemological position by which it is underpinned. Therefore, it is vital to explicitly unpack the underlying dynamics at play, since the routes I took for teaching and learning in this module originate from my own theories of what it means to teach and learn, think, know and understand. My knowledge derives from formal training as a secondary school educator.

Chapter 15

I qualified in 2003, when a neoliberal approach to education trained me in a particular input-output model of working. As a concrete artefact of the educational aspirations of the time, Blair's (2001) famous *Education, Education, Education* speech set the goal of 50% of young people progressing to HE by 2010. Upon Blair's election, policymakers began calculating how to translate the rhetoric of *"investing in human capital"* and unlocking *"the potential of every young person"* (DfEE, 1997:3) into reality. The reality became increased managerialism, regulation and surveillance; the resulting by-products were the *"paradox and fabrication"* of *"good school/bad school"* (Ball, 1997), and reconstructed schools and reconstructed educators throughout the education system (Pierlejewski, 2020; Woods et al., 1997). The trickle-down effect of emphasising quality and standards was that the looming, omniscient threat of performativity always lurked in the background (Ball, 2003).

As a then-recent graduate of English whose 'eyes had been opened' to the systems, I learned to work within via the likes of *Keep the Aspidistra Flying* (Orwell, 1936). Becoming professional at this time involved both calculating and trying to resolve the philosophical tensions between the reality of working in the 'Wellington boot factory', and my naturally progressive inclinations. As I wrote:

> *"Education provides a sequence of academic production – the Department for Education sets outcomes for each stage of education for the learning, development, and care of children from birth to 18. Vast quantities of numerical data are collected, recorded, and analysed in schools… to determine which pupils are making 'progress' against these set outcomes and which pupils are not"* (Swann, 2019).

Learning 'outcomes' are now the dominant standard discourse for products of learning. Still, I was working directly with its predecessor, the learning 'target', emphasising the educator's skill, knowledge, and capacity to progress children's learning. Formative learning, or the Assessment for Learning (AfL) strategy, sought to raise standards, and was later described as:

> *"a powerful way of raising pupils' achievement… based on the principle that pupils will improve most if they understand the aim of their learning, where they are in relation to this aim and how they can achieve the aim*

*(or close the gap in their knowledge). It is not an add-on or a project; it is central to effective teaching and learning"* (Department for Children, Schools and Families, 2008:5).

Thus, a learning 'objective' aligned to clear learning 'outcomes' is central to teaching and learning. It is easy to see why this remains popular: it provides certainty and structure through tangible quantitative 'outcomes', which, when transferred onto data sheets, makes for easy identification of which children are or are not 'on target'. However, this reduction of knowledge and skills to calculated targets constitutes not a level playing field but another form of disciplinary power resting on a new form of *"correct training"* (Foucault & Rabinow, 1984:325). The extent to which education had become depersonalised was exemplified thus: learning outcomes were about taking 'aim', and data sheets fired out individual 'targets'. Middle and senior leaders 'drilled down' into the data to identify school-wide patterns and trends of underperformance so they could take strategic action.

Emphasis on meeting national targets in compulsory also established what might be interpreted as a rational mass-organised reaction to — what Black and Wiliam (1998) called *"the black box"* of teaching, learning and assessment. At the educator level, lessons followed a standardised four-point structure: 1) the engaging starter activity; 2) the setting of a learning objective and learning outcomes; 3) the main learning activities; and 4) the plenary. That teaching could be delivered via this step-by-step process is logical when it originates in a concept of learning as linear and incremental progression. It encourages efficiency, maintains quality, and so might be seen as at least a partial solution to the issue of how best to reduce educational inequalities. Yet the intense drive towards quality can sacrifice equity; a child who is not progressing typically is easily left behind within such a system.

Various systems were developed to assess pupils regularly and track their progress. At any point in the year, pupils needed to know at what level they were currently working, what their aspirational target was, and know exactly what they needed to do to improve. With the onset of PowerPoint, delivery rapidly became more standardised, via the pre-packaged four-point lesson, a rather corporate input-output model of education dictating what the educator and learner should do.

That learning outcomes could both inhibit and constrict the teaching and learning process became evident for me. This occurred during a formal mock-Ofsted (British Office for Standards in Education, Children's Services and Skills) lesson observation, where I had deviated from the over-planned lesson plan I had submitted to the observer. I was required to condense the interpretation of poetry with neatness and precision down into something measurable; henceforth I introduce the learning 'objective' and differentiated learning 'outcomes'. This makes for an interesting comparison with Nygaard's (2023 in this book) encounter with the 'one size fits all' ideology of an undifferentiated classroom at the start of his own career.

This was a low-ability Year 9 (aged 13-14) class where approximately one third of the pupils had a reading age of six years old. To manage this, I integrated poetry and music, as it made language rhythms explicit. In this lesson, I selected The Beatles' (1967) *Lucy in the Sky with Diamonds* to develop retrieval and inference skills. Both skills involve close reading- the former a lower-level thinking skill, and the latter a higher-level thinking skill- and decoding and analysis methods at word, sentence, and text level. We shall allude to these skills as they are enacted in Higher Education in Section 3, with our final year university students who, with a mode-average age of 21, were eight years ahead of this class.

The beauty and challenge of using this song for analysis was that it had no ultimate meaning. I had crafted a learning objective that read something like *Unlock the mysteries of this magical psychedelic wonderland using language for clues*. The song can be read as an adult fairy tale, for it presents the world as a fantasy. It contains strings of vivid, dreamlike and surreal imagery: *Picture yourself in a boat in a river, with tangerine trees and marmalade skies; cellophane flowers; newspaper taxis; rocking-horse people; looking glass ties*. My starter activity was to ask pupils to listen to the song and draw a picture of the line which stood out to them on a whiteboard. This helped me to see — this class's starting points via their drawings which revealed each child's immediate conceptions. I would then begin the lesson by critically unpacking their drawings.

Three learning outcomes for this lesson were differentiated into red, amber, and green categories which both connected to the retrieval and inference skills on the National Curriculum and correlated to pupils' individual attainment targets. While the three targets collectively represented incremental mastery of retrieval and inference skills, at the heart of each lay Vygotsky's (1978) Zone of Proximal Development (ZPD). Other authors in the Learning in Higher Education series, have used aspects of this concept to interpret something of the mental life of learning in HE (for example, see Dobozy & Nygaard, 2021; Perry & Edwards, 2021), and while secondary schooling is at the previous stage, the basic principles remain the same. The red target denoted the knowledge and skill that 'all' pupils would be able to demonstrate by the end of the lesson. The amber target was the middle ground that 'most' pupils would reach and was, therefore, the ZPD (Vygotsky, 1978) where most questions should be aimed (see De Wilde and Forasacco, 2023 in this book for further discussion of ZPD). The green target was the aspirational target which only 'some' pupils would demonstrate. I always asked the children to decide for themselves which outcome they were aiming to meet that lesson, and, on this occasion, I had asked a 'red' boy what his target was, and he chose 'amber'.

In the early days, as a young educator keen to 'get it right' feeling the weight of responsibility upon me, my lesson plans were always over-planned, overly detailed, and overly precise. Skills and knowledge differentiated the questions I had crafted in the lesson plan. I had thought carefully about this, using Bloom's Taxonomy (Bloom et al., 1956; Krathwohl, 2002). I went on to unravel the workings of teacher questioning in more detail in another publication (Swann, 2023). The planned movement of skill always proceeded from knowledge towards evaluation.

Using the rough sketches, the class had produced, I started my targeted questioning, and meaning unfolded organically as pupils engaged with them. I could not locate my original formal lesson plan; however, I can draw on the notes from my teaching planner. To our "red" boy who had drawn strange, swirling eyes, I asked a string of questions which focused on the meaning of the mystery 'girl with kaleidoscope eyes'; the whole interaction taking no more than three minutes. Yet, according to the inspector, it was here I went wrong. For a while, I had conceptualised one boy's red target correctly in my lesson plan. My chain of planned questioning in practice veered into 'amber' and then 'green' terrain. In other words, I had over-stretched a 'red' child, though this was not how I saw it. I viewed the 'red' questions, I had planned, as not fitting where this 'red' child was working at.

I surrendered by 'sucking up' this feedback on this lesson observation and submitting basic lesson plans without any planned questions. The questions I just kept to myself on notes made in my planner. This was an example of me learning the art of *"performativity"*, defined as *"individual practitioners"* having *"to organise themselves as a response to targets, indicators and evaluations"* (Ball, 2003:215).

Yet, learning outcomes in all their efficiencies of breaking learning down into predictable stages with end outcomes can be a *"false god, to whom too much attention is paid and probably by the wrong people"* (Scott, 2011:1). The issue was that this child's 'output' level was pre-ordained. At age 13, but with a below-average reading age, his academic destiny had largely been categorised via the data spreadsheet of 'targets' or *"data doppelgängers, ghostly apparitions which emulate the actual embodied child"* (Pierlejewski, 2020:253). Pierlejewski's work explores the power of data to alter the subjectivities of both the child-learner and the adult-educator and I saw the effects of this first-hand as a teacher.

As a novice teacher though, I was not swayed by data. I just adjusted my questioning, believing it was intuitively obvious why I did so. It was because I did not see our 'red' boy as being any different to any other 13-year-old boy. He had a reading age of six, but it did not mean he was cognitively bereft. It made no sense to me why interpretation skills correlated to reading age, since he could respond critically and creatively to inference questions. My understanding of interpretation was grounded in reader-response theories, which for me did not mean that our 'red' boy should be stuck with all the lower-cognitive skill factual knowledge and understanding questions, like *'what is a metaphor?'*. Learning is complex, chaotic, uncertain, and unpredictable; thus, any form of teaching should value the craft knowledge and skill of reacting adaptively to learners' responses. Later, I was inspired by Shirley Brice Heath (1983), consolidating my understanding of the diverse ways we are each socialised into different literacy practices, only some of which are valued by education.

This was one critical incident (Tripp, 1993) which convinced me that stringent learning outcomes and targets will only ever suit training rather than a liberal, open-ended concept of education anyway, and this is reassuring. It would not be acceptable for a nurse to take an interpretive approach to the number of units of insulin she 'thinks' she administered to her unconscious patient. There is a definite place for hard fact and hard knowledge. Indeed, we see in St. Aubyn and Andrews' (2023 in this book) discussion of the importance of written communication in nursing and the consequences of not adhering to training knowledge.

Having outlined something of the epistemological conundrum of evaluating educational quality via learning 'outcomes' in compulsory schooling, the following section explores the learning theory and methodology related to learning outcomes in relation to my current institutional role within HE.

## Learning theory and methodology related to learning outcomes

Metrics may well have intensified the creeping quality-assurance tendrils of the secondary school 'Wellington boot factory' into Higher Education- through various systematic and bureaucratic systems. Fortunately, we have not yet reached a point where we are using pre-determined categories to differentiate our students formally into 'red', 'amber', and 'green' categories.

In my position as Course Director at a teaching-intensive University in the UK, I have overall responsibility for managing and performing the courses to which I am assigned. My role involves ensuring *"an excellent education and experience for students"* (Leeds Beckett University, 2018:1). Hence, the bulk of my work is student-focused. I keep an observant eye on student development and progression. Across different course teams, I have led pedagogical developments, ensuring that course delivery is compliant with the University's quality assurance and enhancement framework. I also have responsibility for reporting and responding to the University's Academic Quality and Standards Committee in accordance with that framework and the annual quality governance cycle. My role involves coordinating monitoring and enhancement using key processes, informed by performance metrics, to drive engagement and change when required. All courses are subject to annual monitoring and review. We use a range of metrics, which have evolved in line with the Office for Students (OfS) (2023) B3 baselines for student outcomes and the Teaching Excellence Framework's (TEF) benchmarks. These can be summed up as performance against hard, measurable student continuation and completion outcomes, degree outcomes, and graduate employment.

That academic quality is assessed via hard, measurable outcomes does reflect the instrumentalism of HE. However, quality assurance can only give us a certain truth about education. Quality assurance does not pay attention to the 'what' and 'how' students are learning. In terms of quality *"enhancement"*, Biggs (2013:ix) reminded us of *"…improving quality, not controlling quality"*. Attention to improvement, rather than control of quality, gives us a different truth: authenticity, flexibility, and sensitivity to students' starting points. Other researchers have since done a sound job of unpacking the meaning of 'quality assurance' as applied and practised in HE (see Nygaard et al., 2013; Tight, 2020), so I will not rehearse those debates here. Rather, I focus on one small aspect: how 'quality' is assured through students' (and educators') adherence to learning outcomes at the module level.

A module's learning outcomes follow from course aims; forming the basic building blocks of module design. A module is a self-contained unit of learning, and the learning outcomes define what students should know and understand (the knowledge) and be able to do (the skill and competency) upon completion of the module. In this sense, learning outcomes demystify assessment and can also provide a structure for students to organise their own learning materials and set concrete tasks to manage their time. From this perspective, learning outcomes are student-centred. What students *can* do to fulfil the learning outcomes tell us about what it means to 'know' and 'do' in the context of a module, to which we now turn.

## Section 2: My practice towards enhancing students learning outcomes

*Children, Crime and Social Justice* is a final-year undergraduate module in which students, that do not study Criminology for their undergraduate degree, can acquire knowledge of criminological perspectives, the workings of the youth justice system and the relationships between inequality, crime, childhood, and social justice. Students choosing this elective module come from two distinct degree courses: BA (Hons) Childhood Studies and the BA (Hons) Teaching and Learning degree.

The module explores the way that the youth justice system is structured and responds to situations where children and young people break the law. Topics focus on youth crime, policing, youth offending teams and custody. It asks which children and young people can rightfully be punished and so engages with issues of the age of criminal responsibility. The taught curriculum draws on theory and research from Criminology, Education, History, Psychology, Sociology, Philosophy and Childhood Studies to consider different explanations for offending. Such explanations include the impact of inequalities related to social class, gender, and ethnicity; and different forms of social and state intervention in the lives of children and young people. The module also explores children's and young people's perspectives on these matters.

Collectively, the learning outcomes identify the learning to be reached, attained, or achieved by the typical undergraduate student learner after progressing through the three distinct years ('levels') of their degree. This module's learning outcomes connect to the course-level learning outcomes for the two degrees to which this cohort of students 'belong'. Written in the context of the national subject benchmark statements produced by the Quality Assurance Agency (QAA, 2023), each level of study is reflected in the frameworks for higher education qualifications (QAA, 2014). The tasks and assessments students complete for the modules at each level increase in complexity.

Although earlier, I selected the term, adherence, to denote the structure and rigidity of quality assurance, improving quality for me means working 'with' students and learning outcomes. This is to form both a gateway and a structure for working with students' interests in a coherent and convincing way. My work can also be seen as part of a long line of academics who have sought to position students as co-creators to increase responsibility (Maensivu et al., 2013). This module is assessed via the four learning outcomes displayed in Table 1.

| | |
|---|---|
| Learning outcome 1 | Critically explored and evaluated key criminological perspectives related to crime, children and young people |
| Learning outcome 2 | Critically explored and evaluated research related to different approaches within the youth justice system |
| Learning outcome 3 | Applied this learning to explore the relationship between inequality, crime, childhood and social justice |
| Learning outcome 4 | Developed a well-constructed argument, showing engagement with a range of perspectives |

*Table 1: Learning outcomes for L6 module, Children, Crime and Social Justice (Leeds Beckett University, 2022a:2).*

Since I picked up this module for the first time, the learning outcomes helped me structure the content and material, the teaching strategies, and design the final assessment. The traditional *"Explore and Evaluate…"* essay question had gone before with a choice of thoughtfully selected but rather broad topics (Table 2, Leeds Beckett University, 2021:2). This had been assessed through the same learning outcomes (Table 1) and marking descriptors (Leeds Beckett, 2022b) I went on to use with this cohort of students.

- Discuss and critically evaluate debates about child welfare and justice in relation to youth justice strategies.
- Discuss and critically evaluate debates about prevention and punishment in relation to youth justice strategies.
- Discuss and critically evaluate the evidence for young people's routes into and out of offending.
- Discuss and critically evaluate the debate that early interventions may create a group of permanent child suspects.
- Discuss and critically evaluate the evidence that young people's experiences of crime and youth justice are racialised.
- Discuss and critically evaluate the evidence regarding social class, crime, and youth justice.
- Discuss and critically evaluate the evidence regarding gender differences in the experience of crime and youth justice.

*Table 2: Traditional essay titles.*

Yet, the problem with traditional essays, with predefined titles, is that they tend to predefine the knowledge required, and the temptation is for the educator to take a monologic *sage on the stage or bore at the board* (Kramer, 2017) approach to the lectures. Knowledge must be discovered and then known rather than constructed and applied. This creates the tendency for students to simply reproduce knowledge they have learned from other people, resulting in dry, bland essays that lack passion, interest, and intent. The overly broad essay titles also raised critical questions on how comprehensive a 4,000-word essay assignment could ever claim to be in its coverage of *"gender differences"* in relation to *"the experience of crime and youth justice"*, for instance. Reusing essay titles or setting questions where the material is readily accessible online is also an invitation to plagiarise. With the advent of essay mills and Artificial Intelligence, ensuring academic integrity by designing out plagiarism was another factor (Eaton 2021; Lancaster 2020). The External Examiner had also commented that she examines mainly essay-based assignments and had advised for more creative assignment tasks, which partially influenced the way I developed this module when taking it over. At the student engagement level, I feel that the traditional essay task does not consistently capture students' skills and knowledge potential. Not only are students not always fully engaged or invested in writing essays (Sharp et al., 2020), but so too are the markers who are induced by boredom by marking them (Erturk et al., 2022). My selfish desire to read interesting work was another factor in me changing the assessment task.

*How my practice affects students' way of studying*

My priority was to design an authentic assessment. Having reviewed the content of the previous essays, I decided to create a task which would allow students to integrate their knowledge into a problem-solving solution, so I rewrote the assessment task to: 'Design a youth justice intervention or a crime prevention strategy for a crime of your choosing'. This required students to submit a 4,000-word essay assignment, although they could include illustrative diagrams, images, and maps as they saw fit, which I encouraged. I provide a summary for each to help the reader understand how I directed students to meet each learning outcome.

# Approaches to learning outcome 1

The starting point for this assessment was for students to identify a crime problem or scenario of their choosing. This then enabled students to develop a hypothesis which answered basic questions like: 'why did this crime happen?', 'why did this child break the law?' This required students to identify and dissect the risk factors at the heart of their chosen crime. The skill here was students selecting a manageable topic, neither too broad, nor too narrow. It would not be possible to cover the involvement of children in the 2011 English riots, for instance. Instead, students would need to focus on one aspect of riot-related offences in detail — for instance, how a crime was incited and organised through social media.

The *"key criminological perspectives"* (Leeds Beckett 2022a:2) were the tools that students used to make sense of children's relationship to crime. The perspectives students drew upon should enable students to show the complex nature of their chosen crime topic but should be written in such a way as to provide debate and discussion. Rather than seeing perspectives as true or false, I tried to encourage students to view them as useful or not useful concerning understanding and dissecting their chosen crime topic. *"Perspectives"* (Leeds Beckett 2022a:2) were, first, only as credible as the relevancy of materials selected, and second, only as effective as the way these came to be articulated, framed and *"critically evaluated"* (Leeds Beckett 2022a:2) in each student's analysis. Credible perspectives could take any number of forms: raw facts, legal definitions and legislation, policy documents, witness testimonials, crime documentaries, an established tool such as the Index of Multiple Deprivation (IMD), media discourse from the British newspaper archive, a theoretical perspective, and so on. It was what students did with the perspectives that mattered.

Some students authentically justified their choice of topic using quantitative data from reliable sources such as the Ministry of Justice, National Statistics, or the British Crime Survey. Critical exploration and evaluation meant students used this information to explain why their crime happened. The quality of criticality occurred through progressively more complex interactions with the perspectives. For the most part, students demonstrated their learning by moving back and forth between different perspectives.

The assignment, of course, could not be based on opinion- every point needed to be justified. I explained to students that the easiest way of putting this is to see the crime-committing child as a site of intervention or prevention. Still, they needed to use academic research to unpick exactly which factors they would later be attempting to intervene upon or prevent. This helped simplify what was a sophisticated expectation of exploring often particularly difficult categories of young offenders.

## Approaches to learning outcome 2

For the second learning outcome, students had to compile and synthesise findings from high-quality theoretical and empirical *"research"* (Leeds Beckett 2022a:2). This would form the backbone of their assignment. To support this outcome, they were required to read independently. Peer-reviewed journal articles and books, as well as reports by reputable organisations, of course, gave credibility and reliability than did non-expert sources.

At a very general level, the second learning outcome offered a base from which to pursue complex questions of *doli incapax* and the age of criminal responsibility, and conceptual tensions between structure and agency central to understanding the relationship between children, crime, and youth justice. At a more specialist level, students were expected to *"explore and evaluate"* (Leeds Beckett, 2022a:2) related research, for example the scuttling gangs (Davies, 2008, 1998) of Victorian England or a contemporary issue such as knife crime.

Deep reading of the research enabled students to explore some of the contradictions and puzzles of modern youth justice at a deeper level. They could answer questions like 'why' and 'how' we should differentiate between punishments given to children and adults. I stressed that as exploration and evaluation of their chosen topic were grounded in theoretical argument and empirical research, well-chosen academic quotations needed to be engaged with rather than just left hanging. In a writing workshop, we explored different models of how we might achieve this.

## Approaches to learning outcome 3

For learning outcome 3, students were assessed on their ability to solve an intellectual problem: a solution to a crime problem of their own choosing via either a crime intervention or a crime prevention strategy. They needed to apply their knowledge to create a solution. As I explained to students, this was the 'now what?' question to solving crime involving problem-oriented thinking. This required them to convert information, interpretation, and reflection from their engagement with learning outcomes 1 and 2 into action to facilitate change.

Focusing on the crime intervention first, the basic question posed to students was, 'How do we punish children who commit crime?' Students needed first to explore how the punishment of crime has a number of aims (i.e., retribution, rehabilitation, deterrence as well as protecting the public). They then needed to assess different points of view on the different ways to punish (i.e., a custodial sentence vs a rehabilitation order) and articulate their understandings of what works and what does not. This was a reactive, response-led approach to social justice. Students had the opportunity to explore diverse crime interventions used on children from the prison hulks of the 1700s (Campbell, 1994), which Pip described in *Great Expectations* as something of a *"wicked Noah's ark"* (Dickens, 1860-1/1994:34) to modern failures like Rainsbrook Secure Training Centre (Ofsted, 2021).

Designing a crime prevention strategy was the second angle students could take, and most chose this option. The basic question students posed was, 'How do we prevent children committing this crime again?' Their design would focus on alleviating or at least reducing the potential for crimes associated with and committed by children and young people. In contrast to the crime intervention, this was a proactive, intelligence-led approach to crime. It might be viewed as a sort of 'pre-crime' prevention program, which targets children and young people at risk of crime. To be effective, fulfilment of this learning outcome required a thorough understanding of the risk factors of those children and young people on the cusp of entering the Criminal Justice System: where, when and what types of crime occur; which children are committing it, for which reasons; and who is affected by it.

## Approaches to learning outcome 4

Learning outcome 4 assesses each assignment as a two-dimensional, constructed written artefact of the knowledge and skills each student had been able to demonstrate in this module. We know that writing is a powerful learning method, and writing style matters since a *"well-constructed argument"* (Leeds Beckett University, 2022a:2) connects to clarity and readability. In higher education, a *"well-constructed argument"* (Leeds Beckett University, 2022a:2) is also a socially situated discourse that privileges certain academically sanctioned criteria in the ways *"critical"*

(Leeds Beckett University, 2022a:2) exploration and evaluation are done. In the case studies which follow, the extracts I have selected from the work of two students' deliberately places emphasis on *"the conflicting and contested nature"* (Lea & Street, 2006:157) of students' writing practices.

## How I prepared and organised my pedagogy to enhance student learning outcomes

I asked all the students to complete a pre-teaching questionnaire to help me both understand their intuitive interests in this module and help me to start building relationships. Some responses are captured in Table 3 and display mixed motivations:

| Question | Student response |
|---|---|
| Why did you choose the Children, Crime and Social Justice module? | • Have an interest in crime documentaries and wanted to learn more about children and crimes.<br>• I have an interest in law and did it at A Level.<br>• Insight into something new – I enjoy new things.<br>• I want to become a child psychologist and wanted to see …how they get into it etc.<br>• This was the module which stood out to me and I am intrigued by it.<br>• Interested why children commit crime and how schools can help prevent it.<br>• It is very relevant to what I do with one of my companies. Reducing serious organised crimes using the power of music.<br>• I enjoyed last year's Social Justice module and thought I could link it with my dissertation. |

| Question | Student response |
|---|---|
| How do you think completing this module might develop you academically, personally, or professionally? | • Give a broader understanding of what leads children to commit crimes and if the system truly supports them.<br>• ... interested in historical aspects of this.<br>• ... not 100% sure on future career so it is interesting to see if it could be something I do.<br>• Academically it will help me become a more reflective thinker and seeing the wider contextual picture in life. Personally it will help me understand how context can effect behaviour in children. Professionally it will enable me to understand the profession of CAMHS/ mental health more.<br>• Greater insight ... Allows us to empathise with children.<br>• I feel it is a more mature module that requires a level of sensitivity and will open my eyes further to the injustice faced by children from our society.<br>• It will help me understand the children I work with better and also with grant applications etc..<br>• As I want to progress into the legal field I am hoping to gain some context.<br>• ... help me develop, progress as an educator. |

*Table 3: Pre-teaching questionnaire. Students' responses.*

I addressed student diversity by including a variety of learning activities, so students could choose those activities that were most relevant, useful or interesting to their topic of inquiry. The weekly schedule provided a summary of the learning activities for this module in advance of teaching. Students had two pre-recorded lectures each week; a weekly in-person seminar to stimulate reflections and questions; peer review of academic writing (the good and not-so-good), a writing workshop; and individual and small group tutorials to work through possible plans for their assignments. Engaging with all of these helped students begin to articulate and carry out a solid plan for their reading, writing and assignment completion.

Despite our best efforts and the hours they take to prepare, traditional lectures, whilst offering a straightforward linear transmission of knowledge, do not always capture students' attention, especially when they are PowerPoint-driven and text-heavy. The purpose of my lectures was not to give students all the information they needed relating to their specific crime topic, which would have been impossible. The lectures served as starting points for each student's own study and served the following purposes:

- to give an overview of a crime-related topic;
- to discuss empirical research and findings;
- to cover historical and legal perspectives;
- to cover theoretical perspectives; and
- give one or two applications of these in relation to children, crime, and youth justice.

I began each lecture with 1-3 broad learning objectives linked to the module learning outcomes, distilling them to crisp, tangible and 'doable' outcomes in much the same way as I did as a secondary school educator. For example, in lecture three, conceptualisations of crime, there were two learning objectives: 1) To identify and understand risk and protective factors at the individual, family and environmental level, and 2) To identify and critically appraise different routes out of crime.

The skill for students is to follow and pull together connecting strands of information from the lectures, from their independent reading, and their experience and assimilate them into a cohesive whole. Unsurprisingly, independent, self-directed study was a huge factor in students achieving success in their assignments. The expectation was for them to complete 100 hours of this throughout the 12-week module. Digital resources here were particularly important as they offered both choice and flexibility. As students expressed topics of interest, I set up "Special Interest Folders", which allowed them to dip in and out of crimes of different categories as interest or necessity dictated. These folders helped students to develop their knowledge and understanding of specific crime topics such as children involved in anti-social behaviour, football hooliganism, assault, theft, break-in, burglary, knife crime; riots and looting; county-lines and organised illegal drug-dealing networks, murder.

Due to the spectrum of crimes potentially under study, I maintained some 'broad-brush stroke' points over the 12-week teaching program. First, in relation to criminal law, the child's position in relation to crime is ambiguous. Tension exists with the notion of the child as an innocent in need of protection, versus the concept of them as a wrong-doer, a hardened offender, or even an evil doer. Second, many young offenders are also victims with complex needs, leading to a balanced approach of welfare and justice models. The paradox of the individual child offender who embodies both characteristics simultaneously was revealed in close-up studies of children such as Mary Bell (Sereny, 1998, 2013).

There are no absolute answers and no absolute rule for how students must meet the knowledge requirements for each learning outcome. This is owing to the knowledge being dependent on the quality of students' own investment and engagement with the research; the ideas and theories covered within the lectures and seminars; as well as students' own personal construction system. In this sense, assignments were inquiry-based; students were positioned as being fully responsible for topic choice and meeting the learning outcomes. Although students actively choose the topic, content and resources, and in that sense, led their own learning process, as the weeks progressed and students began to firm up their topics, I provided ideas, hints, tips and resources as a 'guide on the side'. In this sense, the assessment allowed students (and me, the educator) to engage in a constructivist-oriented approach to learning.

To authentically meet the learning outcomes, the topic needed to be well-focused to allow each student to develop a clear line of argument and justification for their design. In the second lecture, I took students through some example assignment titles to show them explicitly what was needed and the range of topics they might choose. While there was flexibility in the choice of topic, I did make it clear that students were responsible for ensuring their work did meet each learning outcome, as these were what their work was assessed against.

## Section 3: The outcome

Regarding hard outcomes, marks ranged from 52%-82% across this student cohort. Student evaluations were positive, via the informal feedback they provided along the way, but hard to prove since only two filled out the official module evaluation form in an anonymised format (both students expressed that they were happy).

However, I can say with certainty that the assessment was authentic in that every student identified a topic of interest. All students seemed enthusiastic about their chosen topics and found their work interesting and useful. As a collective whole, the assignments reflected an interest in a range of crime types and engaged in debate and dilemmas about how and at what age to punish or rehabilitate 'dangerous' or 'disadvantaged' young offenders, and how society might create the conditions to stop crime. I met with most students for 1-1 tutorials to explore which crime topic they each deemed significant, worthwhile, and meaningful to study. This particularly rewarding form of dialogic teaching and learning allowed me to get to know students individually and gave me insights into their motivations.

Students covered crime topics inspired typically by a case we had covered in the lectures or seminars or a topic of interest in the news, but sometimes by a career interest or personal experience. Most students crafted titles which functioned well as a statement of their intentions in writing this essay. Some were concise, while others chose attention-grabbing titles. Examples include:

- *Designing a crime prevention strategy targeting 'at risk' boys between the ages of 10 and 12 who are in care;*
- *UK Drill's 'folk devils': developing a crime prevention strategy for knife crime in London – a theoretical perspective;*
- *Knife crime prevention and intervention in Nottingham through improved youth facilities and better-quality school support;*
- *Designing the perfect museum on (sic.) youth crime;*
- *Exploring the role of* [names a local neighbourhood program] *in Children's Crime Trajectories;*
- *Using Bronfenbrenner's Social Ecological Model to analyse the Bulger case with sporting prevention to prevent the murder of Jamie Bulger;*
- *The influence of schizophrenia on the 'Slenderman' case;*
- *Mary Bell: psychopathic child murderer or disadvantaged 11 Year Old that was failed by the justice system?;*

- The impacts that poverty has across county lines on children who are being led into gang crimes;
- A recognition of children and young people's involvement in county lines drug dealing;
- Prevention of crime through psychological and physical changes in children, underpinned with gestation and early stages of child development;
- Youth crime prevention strategy for the Asian Muslim community in Bradford.

## Student Perspective

As the titles unfolded into the content to be assessed via the four learning outcomes, two short case studies show how the assignment task allowed students to meet the learning outcomes meaningfully. The case studies document students' fulfilment of the learning outcomes concerning their interests and share some of my observations as I assessed their work. This helps to remove the veil that obscures how educators interpret and assess students' performances of learning outcomes. To unpack learning outcome fulfilment, I refer to the wording of the Level 6 marking descriptors, found in the student's module handbook (Leeds Beckett, 2022b).

**Case study 1: Jack**

Most assignments did use the 'here's the crime problem and here's the solution' approach described in Section 2. However, where there might be alignment between the module and the student's future career destination, I encouraged it. For instance, Jack (a pseudonym) had a love for and respect for history. In the pre-teaching questionnaire, he had stated, *"I want to pursue museum work as I'm really interested in them and how they operate (and) present history"*. For his assignment, he quickly decided to design *"the perfect museum on [sic.] youth crime"*, and overall, he made an *"accomplished"* (Leeds Beckett, 2022b:14) job of what was an innovative idea. Although Jack had expressed an interest in museum work, he had not stipulated a particular role. Still, as his assignment progressed, the analytical focus of his written work tended towards curatorship with a touch of the tour guide. Through careful research of museums in the UK, Jack identified a niche in the market:

> "...there is no specific museum dedicated to youth crime in the UK. The closest example of a museum on youth crime comes from the National Justice Museum in Nottingham (2022), which focuses on crime and social justice in general" (Jack's assignment, 2022:1).

For the first learning outcome, Jack had to consider the story of children, crime, and social justice he would tell and how he would tell it. He thus had to think through curatorial decisions, such as the exhibits he would include and exclude, and how any choice would inevitably result in bias and potential distortion. The relationship of children and youth to crime has a fascinating, turbulent, often upsetting and sometimes tragic history. While it might be tempting for Jack to cover topics such as children who kill (Smith, 2011; Sereny, 1972/2013), the difficulty lay in presenting such complex, difficult and confronting topics to an audience.

Jack's (2022:3) contribution towards the first outcome, therefore, begins by sketching out what he calls the *"romanticisation"* of crime by the media, which he argues *"display a life of crime as something to marvel at and perhaps even pursue"*. Charting the influence of wider popular culture, Jack was able to point out the ethical issues of dramatising and even glorifying gruesome details for entertainment in examples such as the Netflix true crime drama series, 'Dahmer-Monster: The Jeffrey Dahmer Story' (Murphy & Brennan, 2022). From this, he moves analysis into The True Crime Museum in Hastings, which in its *"glamourising [of] serial killers in their exhibitions"*, makes *"the culture of gangsters, such as the Krays, seem like something that should be admired"*. This helps him to set out a core purpose, almost a mission statement for his own design:

> "The youth crime museum being constructed throughout this essay will go about projecting youth crime and the routes into it as not something to strive for...by focussing on the grim reality of crime, rather than the stereotypical media representation and romanticisation" (Jack's assignment, 2022:3).

## Chapter 15

To meet the third learning outcome, Jack began to explore the purpose and potential of his design of a museum experience as *"a worthwhile educational outcome"*, which, for learning outcome three, would enable visitors to *"...explore the relationship between inequality, crime, childhood and social justice"* (Leeds Beckett University, 2022a:2). This focus necessitated operating across different historical periods, balancing breadth with a depth of coverage for learning outcomes 1 and 2. Using the *"visitor experience"* as a perspective helped him to achieve this, as it enabled him to think about the potential of his museum to move away from the traditional *"austere glass-case museum"* model (Greenhill, 1992:1) and instead connect with human perception, imagination, and particularly in the case of victims or perpetrators of crime, memory as well.

There was, however, a tendency to make rather glib comments which, while referenced, were thin on knowledge and sometimes grammatically unsound. One example is: *"A museum that gives an interactive experience to its visitors through its collection will likely give those that visit the museum that is remembered fondly for a long time (Black, 2012)"* (Jack's assignment, 2022:1). Jack's overall use sources was deemed *"accomplished"* rather than *"compelling"* (Leeds Beckett, 2022b:14) owing to frequent lapses into superficial reference to research rather than detailed discussion. This superficiality is exemplified by the above sentence where, we can see how the reference to Black's (2012) work is just attached at the end to support what is a vague point. No development follows on for how Black's (2012) practical guide on how museums can engage visitors might be applied or even refined to meet Jack's argument that museums can be a powerful tool for audiences to *"explore the relationship between inequality, crime, childhood and social justice"* (Leeds Beckett University, 2022a:2).

Jack was interested in the potential for interactivity and the opportunity for visitors to get their hands-on physical artefacts. He referred to the National Justice Museum, devising his own ideas for historically authentic exhibits to include. This required evaluating which objects have played a unique and significant role in the relationship between children, crime, and social justice. If cost, availability, and sheer scale were not considered, he discussed the possibility of developing a prison hulk *"into a floating museum"* (Jack's assignment, 2022:2). It is scarcely believable to a modern audience that over two hundred children aged 10-15 would ever be imprisoned on a prison hulk, sharing the same space as adult convicts.

Hence, this certainly offered potential as an innovative educational experience. That Jack explains his plan for enabling visitors to engage with and understand the past is meaningful and relevant for learning outcome 3:

> *"Renovating this ship so that it can be made available for public access and accurately depict the conditions that young convicts faced during the time of their usage would provide an interactive, engaging museum experience to visitors of the museum"* (Jack's assignment, 2022:2).

Jack (2022:2) suggested *"integrating the senses into the museum"* to *"accurately depict conditions...such as the smell of the sea"*. While this was a good and memorable start, my criticism was that Jack was presenting a tame and overly sanitised experience for visitors, which did not match the *"floating dungeon"* (Vaux, 1819:109) experience described by one convict confined on a prison hulk.

To achieve *"exemplary"* or *"extensive"* (Vaux, 1819:109) fulfilment of the learning outcomes in this example, Jack needed to invest his exhibition with historical authenticity- excavating specific facts and findings from the research. Jack's domain-specific knowledge, whilst *"widespread"* (Leeds Beckett, 2022b:14), often lacked depth. More detailed knowledge would enable him to consider how his exhibit might capture the unbearable living conditions of a prison hulk: filth, vermin, overcrowding, and proximity to disease and death. Addressing the experiences and living conditions of those living on prison hulks which would have allowed him to pull out atmospheric details like the *"barred potholes"*; the *"bunks which allowed less than 50cm width for each man"* (McKay, 2022:27), the *"coarse slop clothing"* (Vaux, 1819:109) and the guards, *"devoid of all feelings... brutal by nature, and rendered tyrannical and cruel by the consciousness of the power they possess"* (Vaux, 1819:10). Moreover, applying details from Vaux's (1819) autobiography would have allowed Jack to describe replicating the prison hulk routine and help visitors learn and understand this part of history in a truly *"interactive and engaging way"*. Peeling back the layers of details would have brought to life an authentic museum experience where visitors are made to think and feel *"different approaches within the youth justice system"* (Leeds Beckett, 2022a:2) for themselves.

Described as *"Schools of Vice"* (McKay, 2022:27), prison hulks were mastless ships anchored down; isolated from the rest of society. Thus, as a heritage site for meaning-making, how children experienced these prison hulks importantly also offered visitors an opportunity to experience the disparate meanings attached to *"social justice"* (McKay, 2022:27) for learning outcome 3. To achieve *"originality"* (Leeds Beckett, 2022b:14), Jack might have drawn links to social justice between the past, present, and maybe even future. The prison hulk exhibit potentially provides a warning for our own turbulent times where the British Home Office plans to house 500 asylum seekers on an offshore barge for eighteen months, for instance.

There was, however, evidence of *"theoretical concepts and principles"* being *"applied in new contexts with originality"* (Leeds Beckett, 2022b:14). This was apparent in Jack's (2022:4) creative description of a 3-D space for his museum, to serve as a physical metaphor for visualising routes into and out of crime:

> *"The plan of the museum is to create a design that shows how there are multiple pathways into crime, including the route of family, schools and the general community. The museum will do this by making different sections accessible based on these factors that can lead a young person towards committing criminal acts and leading the visitor down these different routes after coming to a sort of crossroads in a typical young person's life".*

This was an *"impressive"* (Leeds Beckett University, 2022b:14) interpretative angle to take, given it covered the spatial character of his museum as a medium for advancing knowledge. However, it was not *"exceptional"* (Leeds Beckett University, 2022b:15) as this was not explained systematically through an abstract concept; so analysis and evaluation again lacked depth. What does, however, follow is a bold statement of the civic role of his museum, which begins to engage with the third learning outcome creatively:

> *"The museum will also…give a soft warning to visitors on the risk of youth crime occurring. Everyone should be aware of these risks and do what they can to ensure that the young people in their lives are diverted away from crime as much as possible. The museum will also ensure that support is available to any person that needs it"* (Jack's assignment, 2022:4).

Jack's limited background reading of formal research limited the fulfilment of learning outcome 2. However, his thinking through the role, functions and practices of museum education and its fulfilment of social outcomes like equal access, fairness and social justice raised Jack's overall performance.

**Case study 2: Amelia**
The second case study considers how learning outcomes can create space and value for personal voice and sharing personal perspectives in academic writing. For Amelia (a pseudonym), meeting the learning outcomes for this assignment held *"relevance"* to her personal history, as they created a structure to tap into and make sense of how her older brother had been led into drug addiction. This unique and highly personal assignment used storying to render the divergent experiences of two siblings visible, explaining their later divergent pathway *into* or *away from* drug use.

Amelia was not a dispassionate observer of her chosen crime topic, she had grown up in dire poverty with her mother and siblings, witnessing alcoholism, drug abuse and domestic violence. One brother had been sectioned and diagnosed with both extreme post-traumatic stress disorder and borderline personality disorder. At the time of writing her assignment, Amelia was a mother, following in the path of some academics she had cited by trying to forge a better life for her and her daughter through HE (see, for instance, Hudson, 2019). Under these conditions, fulfilment of the learning outcomes necessitated a *"pedagogy of disclosure"* (Bleich, 1995). Through the materiality of extracts taken from Amelia's assignment, I show how it is possible for assessment to recognise different genres of writing and language use. I also include some conceptual illustrations Amelia built into her final assignment, which I assessed as artefacts of knowledge and skill for learning outcomes 1 and 2.

Beginning with learning outcome 3, Amelia focused on how one local neighbourhood program functioned as a crime prevention strategy. This was a program, which Amelia had attended herself as a child, and to which she credited as a deterrent serving to shift her away from the abuse of both drugs and alcohol. However, while it worked for her, her older brother, who had also been on the program, was a victim of such abuse from the age of 12. leading to a permanent Class A drugs addiction.

To meet learning outcomes 1 and 2 in-depth, Amelia harnessed together a variety of perspectives on the influence of the individual, family, and neighbourhood through her comparison of Male 1 and Female 1. That Amelia chose to refer to herself and her brother in depersonalised language as *"two siblings", "Male 1"*, and *"Female 1"* is pertinent to learning outcome 4. Whilst pointing to an understanding of the conventions of a more dispassionate but conventional academic writing style, this also allowed Amelia to subjugate her personal experiences to reasoned analysis:

> *"Male 1 did not receive any support from outside influences, such as school. Although they were both poor attenders at school, the Education Welfare Officer (EWO) acted as a mentor to Female 1 during high school, while Male 1 did not receive support…Both were 'Chavs', but Female 1 didn't want to be…As soon as she could get a job (at 15), she started trying to dress in a way that would stop her being associated with Chavs and tried to stop acting in the way she had been (speaking in a Chavvy way etc.), for Male 1 it had become ingrained in who he was (and still is), and the media that was aimed (mainly) at lower class males did not help"* (Amelia's assignment, 2022:15).

Deploying personal experiences helped Amelia to develop an authentic and often nuanced perspective on crime for learning outcome 1. For instance, Amelia's lived perspective addresses the institutional response of the police to vulnerability:

> *"The first time the Mum found out Male 1 had been smoking weed was in 2003 when he came in (at age 12) throwing a whitey* [a drug slang term for feeling nauseous]. *The next morning, she took him down to the police station, she explained that he had been smoking cannabis and that she'd taken him down so that they could frighten him into not doing it again. They told her that there was nothing they could do about it"* (Amelia's assignment, 2022:15).

The challenge for Amelia in meeting the first two learning outcomes was how to create a balance between her personal voice and formal scholarship: which aspects of her background she should bring into this assignment, and how to entwine these with research and the scholarly literature. Various constructivist approaches allowed Amelia to extend what she already knew and strengthen the quality of overall critical evaluation and her academic 'stance' (Hyland, 2005; Hyland & Feng, 2018). First, she reassembled her lived experiences into a theoretical argument which involved jig sawing. She carved up her own experiences (Figure 1) and those of her brother (Figure 2) using Bronfenbrenner's (2005; 2006) bioecological theory of human development. This helped her learn, understand, and deconstruct Bronfenbrenner's key concepts authentically and integrate them. It also allowed her to organise her thinking in a logical way for learning outcome 4.

Analysis, overall evaluation and interpretation was to a *"compelling degree"* (Leeds Beckett, 2022b:14) because the interrelation between these nested layers of influence allowed Amelia to move beyond simple description of her own personal experience, to a deep exploration of how patterns of interaction within each layer influenced each other and affected the ways she and her brother developed over time. Amelia can also express the value of using the theory clearly, *"while the abuse of drugs is an individual act, it is embedded within many social structures: family, friends, community and society"* (Amelia's assignment, 2022:19).

Knowledge and content had a well-defined focus. Amelia selectively focuses on social class to meet learning outcomes 1 and 2. Following on from a lecture that I gave on *"folk devils and moral panics"* (Cohen 1972/2002), Amelia had talked about this in relation to the marginalised 'chav' identity she had inhabited. She had spoken in the tutorials about being a chav and the inevitability of becoming a teenage mother. I encouraged Amelia to write it how it was in her assignment which she consistently did in clear and expressive language to meet learning outcome 4:

> *"… in this area, being a chav was a status symbol to be proud of, anyone with authority was the enemy and other subcultures such as 'sweaties' or goths, couldn't step foot into* [names neighbourhood] *without being intimidated or worse. Being a chav here meant many things, you were part of a community, you meant something to someone, but this came with the pressure to conform, to speak and dress in a certain way, to like certain music and Lambrini and Richmond ciggies and never be a grass"* (Amelia's assignment, 2022:7).

Chapter 15

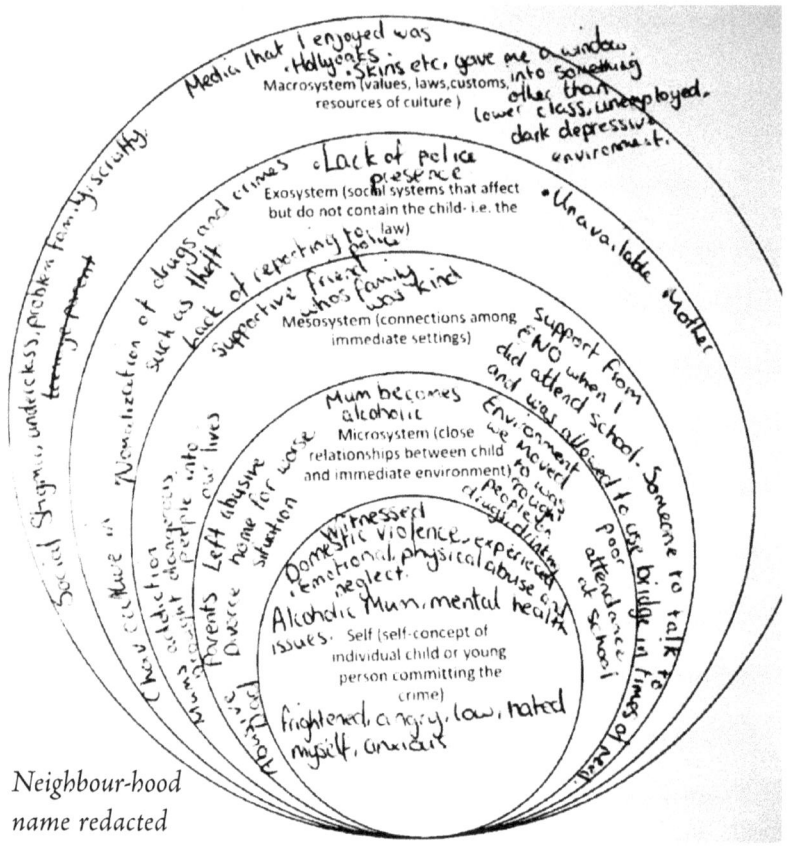

*Figure 1: Amelia's application of Bronfenbrenner's bioecological theory to Female 1.*

The striking hostility of the language used to describe marginalised white-working class identities in the UK was something we had discussed in seminars and tutorials: 'scrubbers', 'scroatbags', 'toerags', 'chavs', 'scum' and *'scumbags'*. In relation to drugs, we also have the stereotype of the *'thieving crackhead'*.

These conversations were important as I could then make bespoke recommendations for readings. I recommended the work of specific female academics (see, for instance, Hanley, 2012; Hudson, 2019; Nayak 2006; Tyler 2013, 2008) which would show how this disparaging language, connected to alienated social class identities, is created out of moralising discourse and middle-class contempt. The influence of class-consciousness, the 'psychic economy' (Reay, 2005) and even the claustrophobia of social class which comes from those woman-centred personal narratives is reflected in extracts from Amelia's own writing. Social class has for Amelia, "…*left open wounds that when prodded ooze with harsh memories of despair and regret that stain the life Female 1 is trying to carve out of the brick walls presented to a working class person*" (Amelia's assignment, 2022:7). Shortly afterwards, in her discussion of the exosystem, Amelia argues in a similar vein that:

> "*This community and its symptoms would be the proletariat that initially put drugs in Male 1's hands, that he would then use to soothe and mask his wounds and scars, eventually leading to him 'living' a life plagued by addiction*" (Amelia's assignment, 2022:8).

*Figure 2: Amelia's application of Bronfenbrenner's bioecological theory to Male 1.*

Chapter 15

On p.11 these words, contrast with the perspectives of illicit drug-taking offered by the popular films and programs and Amelia mentions, for example, *Pure* (Girotti, 2017-19), *Trainspotting* (Boyle, 1996) and *Shameless* (Walsh, 2004-2013). The importance of this specialist reading also resulted in Amelia making critical evaluative points such as *"Chav became something of an abusive slur to describe Britain's poor"* (2022:7). That chav is a uniquely British term is then supported through quotations from published research which results in meaningful explanations:

> *"Imogen Tyler writes that Chav became "Widely understood to be an acronym for 'Council Housed and Violent' or 'Council-Housed-Associated-Vermin', chav was the popular (con)figuration of that imagined 'underclass of people cut off from society's mainstream, without any shared sense of purpose', that Blair had first bodied forth in his maiden speech (Blair 1997:162-3)"* (Amelia's assignment, 2022:7).

I selected this extract though as there are also performance weaknesses against learning outcome 4 here. The ways in which Tyler (the primary source) is managed against Blair (the secondary source) makes it unclear whose voice we hear. However, this had to be weighed against Amelia's overall voice's clarity, conviction and fluency and the complexity of the evaluation Amelia was collectively creating.

Plotting Adverse Childhood Experiences (ACE) onto Bronfenbrenner's bioecological theory fulfilled the marking descriptor, *"theoretical concepts and principles"* being *"applied in new contexts with originality"* (Leeds Beckett University 2022b:14). Enduring patterns of *"proximal processes"* (Bronfenbrenner, 2005:180) can be found on the spidergram Amelia included in her analysis (Figure 3) to depict something of the lived reality and the workings of *"her"* microsystem in her childhood home. Although she acknowledges her spidergram produces *"...only snapshots of memories due to it being difficult to recall that period of time"*; it nonetheless showcases understandings of *"proximal processes"* (Bronfenbrenner, 2005:180) as the *"primary engines of human development"* (Bronfenbrenner, 2005:6). The originality originated, not only from the layered conceptual model Amelia created, but in her focus on adverse childhood experiences. Her originality also came from the way the content of her work challenged Bronfenbrenner's very framing of the nature of proximal processes. In this sense, the assignment's fulfilment of the learning outcomes exceeded what I had explicitly taught.

A detailed evaluation of the exosystem came next (see Figure 4). The setting for the crime was her local home community, a downtrodden estate in a former pit village. She focuses on this as a geographic hot spot where crime took place but also pays attention to the identities of those who live there. In doing so, her assignment comes to paint an ambiguous picture of neighbourhood effects.

On one hand, Amelia concurs with the research literature. She emphasised the isolation of her community from the rest of society, and in her own words, argues that it was this physical and psychic *"division"* which *"leads to behaviours that should probably be at least queried… to go unchecked and become the norm"*. This was a place where children typically threw stones and even bowling balls at cars, lorries, and buses; they smashed wing mirrors off cars; rode pit bikes on pavements; pulled up bollards; and ran backwards and forwards across the road in moving traffic. It was a neighbourhood where there was drinking on the streets and drug use and drug dealing were common. On the other hand, this was simultaneously the geographical space where Amelia said she *"belonged"*. As Amelia (2022:7) elaborates,

> *"…although…a bad environment and the situations were dangerous, I felt accepted and a sense of comfort and belonging…that I didn't experience often in the family home which made it easier for us to become exposed to the situations we experienced."*

Chapter 15

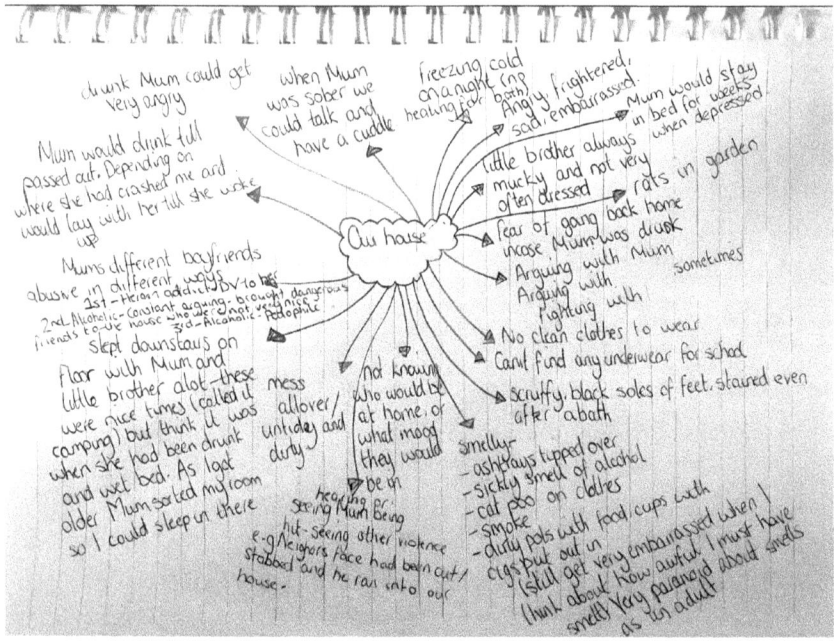

*Figure 3: Amelia's application of Bronfenbrenner's exosystem to "My House".*

Figure 4 captures a curious mix of moments of comfort outside her home, *"In Winter some peoples [sic.] houses smelt like they were cooking stew or something tasty- was nice to walk past"*, Amelia (2022:7). with scenes of trouble, disturbance, and disorder. The reason why Amelia's analysis, evaluation and interpretation fell short of *"authoritative"* and *"conclusive"* (Leeds Beckett, 2022b:15), which were the markers of the next marking descriptor, was to do with the level of mastery expressed. Amelia needed to explicitly connect the relationship of children and crime in the context of poverty with the concept of social justice. For instance, while Amelia references the seven domains of deprivation (UK Government, 2019:3), she was not able to define why one local neighbourhood program 'worked' on her as a crime prevention strategy, but had no impact on her brother, and what this means in terms of making changes to the program to secure social justice for future generations of children in the area. It was in Amelia's assignment where the greatest authenticity might be found

Student-Centric Pedagogy

for it was in this kind of multi-level thinking that I wanted to bring to this module.

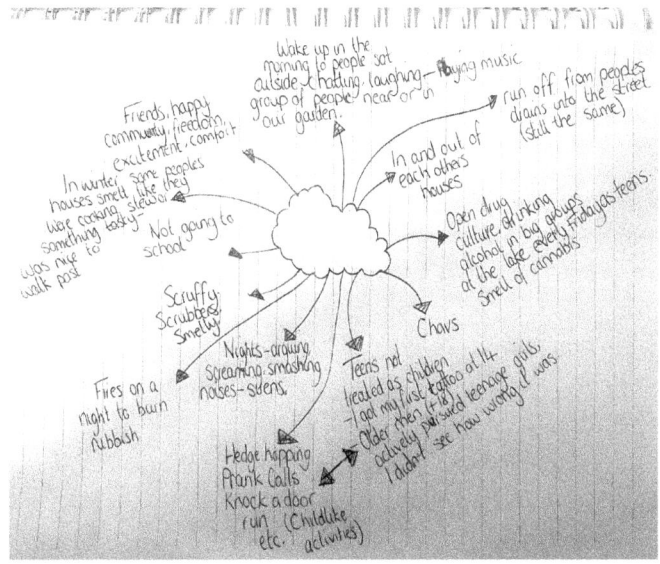

*Figure 4: Amelia's application of Bronfenbrenner's exosystem to [named neighbourhood].*

To end this section, it is worth passing a brief note on the methodological lacunae of these case studies since they are a small unrepresentative sample of the assignments submitted by the whole student cohort. These assignments were selected because I believed them to be good illustrations of how students customised the learning outcomes to suit their interests. Case studies of assignments that had secured informed consent might have been made. Having developed two short case studies of students' understandings, I now turn to my educator's broader perspective.

## Educator perspective – my reflections

This was the first time I had taught the *Children, Crime and Social Justice* module. So, I perhaps arrived with clearer, more open eyes and without preconceived notions of what students should cover in terms of content or how teaching and learning of this content "should" be done. I was given six weeks and ten official hours on my deployment to prepare for it, so time pressure to plan and write the lectures and seminars was another factor. Although I wrote the lectures and prepared the seminars, I turned the detailed and focused work over to the students, who set their own agenda, and figured out the path they wanted to take through the module and the assignment. This also made for a clearer, more open exchange with students since I had to admit and accept that I did not always have the answers or knowledge base to answer their questions. When I did not know the answer, I worked with the students to find it which explains the constructivist approach I took. This resulted in a dialogic approach.

Practical considerations aided this work. Importantly, this small group enabled me to take a bespoke approach to the learning outcomes. My experience of picking up modules at short notice had made me relatively unintimidated by teaching new content. It helped that while I was not a criminologist by training, my background in sociology, and teaching on psychology modules, had helped me build up a bank of relevant theoretical knowledge which might be applied to the topic of children, crime, and social justice. I brought some practical experience working with young offenders, was fully versed in academic skill development, and experienced working with diverse student groups. Though, if success is gauged via quantitative data, I did not manage to raise any student's mark to 100%. As with the previous assessment, this assignment generated a spread of marks. If we assume marking between both years was consistent, I am not sure I can claim the module precipitated academic advancement for the students. As a closing remark to this section, the External Examiner commented:

> *"There is a strong element of feeding forward in a supportive and constructive way".* The *"standard of work is high and even the weaker students have made a good attempt to address the question and it is more their academic skills that have resulted in a lower mark than their engagement with the subject matter"* (Leeds Beckett, 2023:2).

I must note that being an educator is one of the most rewarding parts of my job, and I felt privileged to be able to support students with their individual topics. It was impossible to assess whether completing this assignment this way led to transformational learning. However, as artifacts of undergraduate students' identities as developing learners, the resulting assignments serve as a reminder of the diverse experiences, skills, expertise and funds of knowledges (Kiyama & Rios-Aguilar, 2017) students potentially bring to bear on any assignment.

## Section 4: Moving forward

This chapter has provided two illustrations of how 'permitting' students to customise and tailor assignments to their own interests on one undergraduate module can support the fulfilment of learning outcomes in diverse ways. As a Course Director now overseeing a suite of postgraduate distance-learning courses through a period of 'streamlining', I will review how students are assessed across different modules and degrees. I will first look at how module learning outcomes relate horizontally and vertically for overall cohesion. I can potentially create scale by integrating the potential for customisation across both modules and postgraduate courses. To support the continued enhancement of teaching and learning to support student success, I list the straightforward, pragmatic changes I will make as a module leader:

### Structuring seminars to include more metacognitive work

More metacognitive work is needed to increase students' acquisition, mastery and application of knowledge and critical thinking. To make learning more explicit against the learning outcomes, I will create four sets of metacognitive question cards. Students will use these in an academic speed dating activity. The metacognitive strategy will loosely follow these stages of the writing process: planning and pre-writing; drafting; revising, and editing. As well as helping students to reflect on their own thinking, this activity will help me better understand how learning outcomes are organised and negotiated in the student's mind.

Chapter 15

### *Library engagement: A 'Children, Crime and Social Justice' event*

Research should be used to give direction to the assignment and allow differentiation between perspectives. I had overestimated all students' in-depth research skills, and critical and analytical skills did need upskilling overall. To improve this, I would work with librarians to transform the library into an 'interactive mystery tour' where students are asked to collect and decipher evidence from research studies.

### *Understanding the way students assess problem-solving tasks*

Overall performance was weak on learning outcome 3, the higher-order creative problem-solving task. To understand how students assess problem-solving tasks, in one seminar I will unpack an imaginary crime-prevention scenario from science fiction. Philip K. Dick's (1956/2002) short story, *Minority Report* imagines an agency of precrime which imprisons people for crimes they would have committed had they not been prevented. As a crime-prevention solution, this will hopefully lead to an engaging discussion of the potential, the possibilities, and the problems of 'predicting' youth crime, as well as authentic application of concepts such as risk, power, and surveillance, dataveillance and predictive policing (Gaub & Koen, 2021).

### *Work experiences to enrich knowledge and skills*

Finally, work placement and work experience are built into both degrees; I have written about what some of this work practically entailed elsewhere (Swann, 2021; Swann, 2022). Practical work experiences would be a good way for students to be exposed to a more nuanced understanding of the complex relationship between children, crime, and social justice. The Appropriate Adult is an important procedural safeguard for young and vulnerable people. The real-world experience of this role could enable students to meaningfully examine the position of a young suspect at the centre of a complex web of relationships between the police, the appropriate adult and the legal adviser.

## Conclusion

What emerges from this case study of students customising the module's universal learning outcomes to their own interests is a hopeful exploration of the potentiality of assessment. In the face of Artificial Intelligence, the ability of the human brain to think, to reflect, to imagine and to use these to problem-solve might be the factors which distinguish us from the robots. I have only scratched the surface of the rationale, possibilities, and potential for personalising learning outcomes. Yet, I hope I have touched on some relevant topics to all educators. I would like to end this chapter by thanking the students who graciously allowed me to use their work and words and, in doing so, help broaden our understanding of how students construct meaning from learning outcomes.

## About the author

Dr. Sarah Swann is Course Director in the Carnegie School of Education at Leeds Beckett University, UK. She can be contacted at this email: S.Swann@leedsbeckett.ac.uk.

## Bibliography

Abbott, P. (Executive Producer). (2004-2013). *Shameless* [TV series]. Channel 4; UK.

Ball, S. J. (1997). Good school/ bad school: paradox and fabrication. *British Journal of Sociology of Education.* 18(3), 317-336.

Ball, S. J. (2003). The teacher's soul and the terrors of performativity. *Journal of Education Policy*, 18(2), 215-228.

Biggs, J. (2013). Foreword. *Quality enhancement of university teaching and learning.* (pp. vii-ix). Libri Publishing Ltd.

Black, G. (2012). *The engaging museum: Developing museums for visitor involvement.* Taylor and Francis.

Black, P., & Wiliam, D. (1998). *Inside the black box: Raising standards through classroom assessment.* Kings College London, School of Education.

Blair, Tony (2001). Full text of Tony Blair's speech on education, Speech by Rt Hon Tony Blair, The prime minister launching Labour's education manifesto at the University of Southampton.

Bleich, D. (1995). Collaboration and the pedagogy of disclosure. *College English*, 57(1), 43–61.

Bloom, B., Engelhart, M., Furst, E., Hill, W. & D. Krathwohl. (1956/2020). *Taxonomy of educational objectives: The classification of educational goals. Book 1, Cognitive domain.* Longman.

Boyle, D. (Director). (1996). *Trainspotting.* United Kingdom: PolyGram Filmed Entertainment.

Bronfenbrenner, U. (2005). *Making human beings human: Bioecological perspectives on human development.* Sage.

Bronfenbrenner, U., & Morris, P.: A. (2006). The bioecological model of human development. In R. M. Lerner & W. E. Damon (Eds.), *Handbook of child psychology: Volume 1, theoretical models of human development.* John Wiley & Sons.

Campbell, C. (1994). *The intolerable hulks: British shipboard confinement, 1776–1857.* Heritage Books.

Cohen, S. (1972/2002). *Folk devils and moral panics.* Routledge.

Davies, A. (1998). Youth gangs, masculinity and violence in late Victorian Manchester and Salford. *Journal of Social History*, 32(2), 349–369.

Davies, A. (2008). *The gangs of Manchester: The story of the scuttlers, Britain's first youth cult.* Milo.

Department for Children, Schools, and Families (2008). *The assessment for learning strategy.* DCSF.

De Wilde, J., & Forasacco, E. (2023). Developing STEM doctoral students' collaboration skills as learning outcomes. In K. Enomoto, R. Warner & C. Nygaard (Eds.), *Enhancing student learning outcomes in higher education.* Libri Publishing Ltd.

DfEE (1997). *Excellence in schools. Cm 3681.* The Stationery Office.

Dick, P. K., (1956/ 2002). Minority report. In Dick, P. K. (Ed.) *Minority report.* Gollancz.

Dickens, C. (1860-61/1994). *Great expectations.* J. M. Dent.

Dobozy, E., & Nygaard, C. (2021). A learning-centred, five-tier model of innovation in higher education. In Enomoto, K. & Nygaard, C. (Eds.), *Teaching and learning innovations in higher education.* Libri Publishing Ltd.

Eaton, S. E. (2021). *Plagiarism in higher education: Tackling tough topics in academic integrity.* Libraries Unlimited.

Erturk, S., van Tilburg, W.A.P. & Igou, E.R. (2022). Off the mark: Repetitive marking undermines essay evaluations due to boredom. *Motivation and Emotion 46*, 264–275.

Foucault, M. (1995). *Discipline and punish: The birth of prison.* Vintage.

Foucault, M., & Rabinow, P. (1984). The means of correct training. In P. Bean (Ed.) (2003), *Crime critical concepts in sociology*. Psychology Press.

Gaub, J. E., & Koen, M. C. (2021). Cameras and Police Dataveillance: A new era in policing. In Arrigo, B. A & Sellers, B. G. (Eds.), *The pre-crime society: Crime, culture and control in the ultramodern age*. Policy Press Scholarship.

Girotti, K. (Director) (2017-19). *Pure*. CBC Television; Canada.

Greenhill, E. (1991). *Museums and the shaping of knowledge*. Routledge.

Hanley, L. (2012). *Estates: An intimate history*. Granta.

Heath, S.B. (1983). *Ways with words: Language, life, and work in communities and classrooms*. Cambridge University Press.

Hudson, K. (2019). *Lowborn: Growing up, getting away and returning to Britain's poorest towns*. Chatto and Windrush.

Hyland K. (2005). Stance and engagement: A model of interaction in academic discourse. *Discourse Studies, 7*(2), 173–192.

Hyland, K., & Feng, J. (2018). 'We believe that…': Changes in an academic stance marker, *Australian Journal of Linguistics, 38* (2), 139- 161.

Kiyama, J.M., & Rios-Aguilar, C. (Eds.). (2017). *Funds of knowledge in higher education: Honoring students' cultural experiences and resources as strengths* (1st ed.). Routledge.

Kramer, M. W. (2017). Sage on the stage or bore at the board?, *Communication Education, 66* (2), 245-247.

Krathwohl, D. (2002). A revision of Bloom's taxonomy: An overview. *Theory into Practice, 41*(4), 212-218.

Lancaster, T. (2020). Academic discipline integration by contract cheating cervices and essay mills. *Journal of Academic Ethics, 18*, 115–127.

Lea, M. R., & Street, B. V. (1998) Student writing in higher education: An academic literacies approach, *Studies in Higher Education, 23*(2), 157-172.

Leeds Beckett University (2018). *Course director job description*. School of Education and Childhood. Leeds Beckett University.

Leeds Beckett University (2021). *Student module handbook: L6 children, crime and social justice*. Leeds Beckett University.

Leeds Beckett University (2022a). *Module learning outcomes. Student module handbook: L6 children, crime and social justice*. (p. 2). Leeds Beckett University.

Leeds Beckett University (2022b). *Marking descriptors. Student module handbook: L6 children, crime and social justice*. (pp. 14-17). Leeds Beckett University.

Leeds Beckett University (2023). External examiner module report for children, crime and social justice 2022-23. Leeds Beckett University.

Maensivu, M., Nikkola, T., & Moilanen, P. (2013). Students constructing the curriculum- An experiment to increase responsibility. In C. Nygaard,

N. Courtney & P. Bartholomew (Eds.), *Quality Enhancement of University Teaching and Learning*. Libri Publishing Ltd.

McKay, A. (2022). Floating hell: the brutal history of prison hulks, *BBC History Magazine*, October, pp. 27-31.

Murphy, R., & Brennan, I. (Producers). (2022). *Dahmer-Monster: The Jeffrey Dahmer Story*. [TV series]. Netflix. Retrieved August 7, 2023, from https://www.netflix.com/gb/

Nayak, A. (2006). Displaced masculinities: Chavs, youth and class in the post-industrial city. *Sociology, 40*(5), 813-831.

Nygaard, C. (2023). Enhancing student learning outcomes through contextualised learning activities. In K. Enomoto, R. Warner & C. Nygaard (Eds.), *Enhancing student learning outcomes in higher education*. Libri Publishing Ltd.

Nygaard, C., Courtney, N., & Bartholemew (2013). Theoretical and empirical perspectives on quality enhancement in higher education. In C. Nygaard, N. Courtney & P. Bartholomew (Eds.) *Quality enhancement of university teaching and learning*. Libri Publishing Ltd.

Office for Students (2023). Condition B3: baselines for student outcomes indicators. Retrieved 7 August, 2023, from https://www.officeforstudents.org.uk/media/490d884f-03aa-49cf-907d-011149309983/condition_b3_baselines.pdf

Ofsted (2021). Rainsbrook secure training centre: Annual inspection. Retrieved 7 August, 2023 from https://files.Ofsted.gov.uk/v1/file/50170043

Orwell, G. (1936). *Keep the aspidistra flying*. Victor Gollancz.

Perry, B., & Edwards, M. (2021). Using arts-based instructional strategies in e-learning to increase students' social-emotional learning outcomes. In K. Enomoto; R. Warner & C. Nygaard, (Eds.), *Teaching and learning innovations in higher education*. Libri Publishing Ltd.

Pierlejewski, M. (2020). Constructing deficit data doppelgängers: The impact of datafication on children with English as an additional language. *Contemporary Issues in Early Childhood, 21*(3), 253–265.

Quality Assurance Agency (QAA) (2023). Subject benchmark statements. Retrieved 7 August, 2023, from https://www.qaa.ac.uk/quality-code/subject-benchmark-statements

Quality Assurance Agency (2014). The frameworks for higher education qualifications of UK degree-awarding bodies. Retrieved 7 August, 2023, from https://www.qaa.ac.uk/docs/qaa/quality-code/qualifications-frameworks.pdf?sfvrsn=170af781_18

Reay, D. (2005). Beyond consciousness? The psychic landscape of social class. *Sociology. 39* (5), 911-928.

Scott, I. (2011) The learning outcome in higher education: Time to think again?. *Worcester Journal of Learning and Teaching*, 5, 1-8.

Sereny, G. (1972/2013). *The case of Mary Bell: A portrait of a child who murdered.* Random House.

Sereny, G. (1998). *Cries unheard: The story of Mary Bell.* Macmillan.

Sharp, J.G., Sharp, J. C., & Young, E. (2020) Academic boredom, engagement and the achievement of undergraduate students at university: a review and synthesis of relevant literature, *Research Papers in Education*, 35(2), 144-184.

Smith, D. (2011). *The sleep of reason: The James Bulger case.* 2nd ed. Faber & Faber.

St. Aubyn, B., & Andrews, A. (2023). A pedagogical approach to enhance nursing students' written communication skills as learning outcomes. In K. Enomoto, R. Warner & C. Nygaard (Eds.), *Enhancing student learning outcomes in higher education.* Libri Publishing Ltd.

Swann, S. (2019). Data for decanting and the hatching of life trajectories. *BERA blog.* Retrieved August 7, 2023 from https://www.bera.ac.uk/blog/data-for-decanting-and-the-hatching-of-life-trajectories

Swann, S. (2021). Building employability skills through collaborative group work. In K. Enomoto; R. Warner & C. Nygaard, (Eds.), *Teaching and learning innovations in higher education.* Libri Publishing Ltd.

Swann, S. (2022). Constructing the employable graduate through active learning projects. In K. Enomoto; R. Warner & C. Nygaard, (Eds.), *Active learning in higher education- Student engagement and deeper learning outcomes.* Libri Publishing Ltd.

Swann, S. (2023). A lesson in Shakesperean insults: Artful questioning to unlock the language and meaning of conflict in Romeo and Juliet. In C. Tsolakis; M. Mamoura & E. Frydaki, (Eds.) *New Approaches to the Investigation of Language Teaching and Literature.* IGI Global.

The Beatles (1967). Lucy in the Sky with Diamonds [Song]. On *Sgt. Pepper's Lonely Heart Club Band.* EMI Studios.

Tight, M. (2020). Research into quality assurance and quality management in higher education. In J. Huisman, & M. Tight, (Eds.) *Theory and method in higher education research.* Emerald Publishing Limited.

Tripp, D. (1993). *Critical incidents in teaching: Developing professional judgment.* Routledge.

Tyler, I. (2008). "Chav mum chav scum", *Feminist Media Studies*, 8(1), 17-34.

Tyler, I. (2013). *Revolting Subjects: Social abjection in neoliberal Britain.* Zed Books.

United Kingdom Government (2019). English indices of deprivation 2019. https://www.gov.uk/government/statistics/english-indices-of-deprivation-2019

Vaux, J. H. (1919). *Memoirs of James Hardy Vaux: Written by himself in two volumes. Volumes 1-2*. W. Clowes.

Vygotsky, L. S. (1978). *Mind in society: The development of higher psychological processes*. Harvard University Press.

Woods, P., Jeffrey, B., Troman, G., & Boyle M. (1997). *Restructuring schools, reconstructing teachers*. Open University Press.

www.ingramcontent.com/pod-product-compliance
Lightning Source LLC
LaVergne TN
LVHW051058100526
838202LV00086BA/6888